KU-346-966

PENGUIN HANDBOOK

PH72

RETIRE AND ENJOY IT

CECIL CHISHOLM

Cecil Chisholm was educated at George Watson's College, Edinburgh. He was taught languages so well there and at the city's University that he had no difficulty in following the professors at Gottingen, Germany, where he studied economics. He spent his first ten active years as a newspaperman, eventually reaching London via Bournemouth and Manchester, but soon came to agree with the American view that daily newspapers are a young man's job. Entering industrial journalism, he became chairman and editorial director of a well-known industrial publishing house for twenty years. He wrote two other books, as a result of experience and research concerning retirement, *The £ s. d. of Retirement* and *Retire into the Sun*. At one time he directed a theatre and in 1932 published *Repertory*, a standard reference book on the subject. Cecil Chisholm died in 1961.

Cover design by Bruce Robertson

CECIL CHISHOLM

RETIRE AND ENJOY IT

WITH MAPS AND LINE DRAWINGS

═══════

Ah, make the most of what we may yet spend . . .
Rubaiyat of Omar Khayyam

═══════

PENGUIN BOOKS

Penguin Books Ltd, Harmondsworth, Middlesex, England
Penguin Books Inc., 3300 Clipper Mill Road, Baltimore 11, Md, U.S.A.
Penguin Books Pty Ltd, Ringwood, Victoria, Australia.

—

First published by Phoenix House 1954
Published, in a revised edition, by
Penguin Books 1961

—

Reprinted 1962, 1964

—

—

Made and printed in Great Britain
by Cox and Wyman Ltd, London, Reading, and Fakenham.
Set in Monotype Baskerville

TO
EVERY WIFE
WHO IS HELPING
TO MAKE IT
A SUCCESS

CONTENTS

In the seven years since I wrote this book much has happened, most of it good for the retiree. The Welfare State has got fully into its stride. The many problems of retirement are more widely realized. Industry is at last alerted to its own responsibilities. A few sociologists are collecting useful data. Best of all, the diseases and discomforts of ageing are being vigorously and often ingeniously tackled by one of the newer branches of medicine – geriatrics. All this has been heartening to see, all on the credit side.

There is still a debit side. Too many old age pensioners are still going woefully short. Accommodation for the retiree with a small income above his national pension is simply impossible to find in many areas. The problem of the lonely and the isolated remains virtually untouched.

For three of these years the British citizen enjoyed an exceptional piece of luck. I refer to the 'price plateau'. By a series of happy accidents, including some fascinating flukes, our economy remained free of inflation for upwards of three years. (This despite eleven changes in Bank Rate in the four relevant years!) From January 1958 until September 1960 the cost of living never varied by more than $1\frac{1}{2}$ per cent. Save for one solitary month it ran steadily between 109 and 110.5. Yet this consumer's paradise Britain, and Britain alone, enjoyed. What happier economic climate could be imagined for the retiree on a fixed income? In the previous six years (1952–7) cost of living had risen by 3.6 per cent per year, 21.6 per cent in all, which meant roughly 4s. 4d. in the £.

Of course the price plateau was too good to last. In the event Chancellor Heathcote-Amory cut it abruptly short by cheapening credit too fast around the autumn election of 1959. In 1961 we are still paying for his tempting but disastrous error of judgement. And we shall continue to pay. The times are already less comfortably easy. When the throttling down of credit has had its effect, a modest dose of inflation will again be essential to allow us to recover our industrial pace.

So every word I wrote about the dangers of inflation stands.

Fortunately for us our inflation is merely of the creeping variety. Perhaps that is why people take it so calmly. Perhaps that is why successive Chancellors have risked playing so perilously with it. As a result we nearly had a runaway one in the first half of 1956. As a journalist I saw two such and hope never to see another. In May 1923, standing before a greengrocer's shop in Münster, I saw the owner change the price of potatoes on the blackboard provided for the purpose above his little window. It was just after three. 'When was the last rise?' I asked him. 'Just before I closed at mid-day.' The new rise made several plump *Hausfraus* burst into tears: they would have to go home for more paper marks.

Very gradually the public attitude to old people is softening and the climate of opinion is warming up. This is merely a return to the old attitude bred by religion and schooling. If it lacks the authority of a religious discipline it does suggest a certain opening of eyes to special difficulties and often handicaps of the ageing man or woman.

At the end of these seven years there are signs that the difficulties of the elderly retiree are beginning to be studied by many of the great industrial firms. Unilever have run a pilot course on Planning for Retirement. The Industrial Welfare Society has an occasional conference on the subject. The complexity of the retiree's problems is coming to be understood a little. One or two firms like Rubery Owen not only run regular courses but provide a special shop with a slower tempo for some elderly workers. But we are far from the happy situation in the United States where the unions share the interest of employers in the dilemma of the elderly worker who wants to keep at it.

This change in the social climate has been fostered largely by the doctors. Even seven years ago geriatrics was about as popular with the ambitious young doctor as the Poor Person's Defence with the lively young barrister. But the shortage of consultant posts, especially in general medicine and other hospital fields has lured many able young men into the field of geriatrics. Indeed it is in process of becoming one of the more fashionable fields for the up-and-coming young medico. So young specialists are now available to staff the geriatric units, slowly but steadily replacing the old chronic sick wards in our hospitals. How pleased the pioneers like Lord Amulree and Dr Trevor Howell must be at the change. For results have been quick to follow. Those achieved by the pioneer Dr Lionel Cosin at the Oxford Geriatric Unit are widely known. In the Oxford area the length of an elderly patient's stay in hospital has been reduced from 286 days in 1947 to 32 days in 1957. Using similar methods Dr R. E. Irvine of the Hastings Geriatric Unit has now only 3 per cent of his patients staying a year or more, 8 per cent for over three months. Yet the average age of the patients occupying his 230 beds in this residential area is 80!

These new methods allow the relatives of the elderly retiree to have intervals of rest. They give the hospital staff a chance to help the patient with all the skills of modern medicine, nursing, physiotherapy, occupational therapy, and social work. The aim is to share the burden of the old person's care between the hospital and the home. Effective treatment by modern methods when an old person is ill soon allows him to regain his place in the community. Already in 1957 97 per cent of all old people were living outside institutions. And the number must be growing steadily.

The problem of the lonely retiree however persists. This sense of loneliness seems to be a personal reaction to a given situation, say the loss of a life-long companion. It steals indifferently over widow and widower, over recluse and 'hearty'. But almost always it passes with the years. Either through the building up of a new social group or through the growing indifference of age to other people. Peter Townsend's inquiry in East London, *The Family Life of Old People*, is a feather in the cap of English sociology. It deals unusually well with the plight of the lonely, its causes and remedies. Elsewhere we still stumble awkwardly in the trail of American and Scandinavian research.

Inevitably in a book so packed with facts, changes

have been endless. The financial chapter has been largely rewritten. A crowd of fascinating new hobbies have grown up, from tropical fish to Hi-Fi. These clamoured for space – and got it. Ingenious people have discovered new ways of earning money in their spare time. As a result of all this, the Penguin edition of this book is considerably longer than the original one.

The book is still a chocolate with a soft surround encasing a hard centre based on three years' research, so any definite conclusions are based on a reasonable number of facts. A steady flow of letters from readers of this book and *£ s. d. of Retirement* over seven years has compelled me to add, to subtract, to modify at many points where wider data had been provided.

Let me hear from you if, and please only if, you detect any error or have any additional facts or experience to contribute. As I am often away, address me C/o Phoenix House, Bedford Street, London wc1, who will see that your letter reaches me.

Fairlight
Sussex
August 1961

FOREWORD

WHEN I first retired a few years ago I came up against a surprising number of new problems. Naturally I looked round for a handbook on the subject. To my surprise there was none of any sort. I had to bark my shins against all the snags in the path. Gradually I found myself producing my own handbook on retirement. It has many faults but it is based on first-hand post-war experience, either my own or that of others.

The subject is obviously a ticklish one. It tempts to preaching and the platitudes with which some American books on the subject overflow. One is apt to accept the easy generalization where only specifics can help. On closer examination the cases of no two retirees are ever precisely alike. To report one's own small experiences is no answer to the problems of the other fellow. I was therefore compelled reluctantly to inquire into the whole complex of major retirement problems and to analyse and record as many of the helpful answers as I could find.

This has turned a lightly approached retirement hobby into a collar job. It has meant the issuing of countless questionnaires, the interviewing of a large number of specialists, and the bombardment of many overworked officials. In the end it has proved impossible to finish the work of inquiry on budgets and on earning in time for this volume. Here there were no experts to consult. I had to provide all my figures from research into hundreds of individual cases. The complete reports on these two subjects I left therefore for a later volume, £ *s. d. of Retirement* (1957).

Many experts in specialized fields have helped me generously. In particular I am indebted to Mr E. S. Baynes, who cares for retirement problems for the Incorporated Sales Managers' Association; to Mr Walter Herriot, the pensions authority; to Dr Trevor H. Howell, senior physician, Queen's Hospital, Croydon, on geriatrics; and a host of other good friends. An expert woman retiree, Mrs A. C. Smart, has helped me with an exceptional set of figures and the wisdom drawn from a wealth of experience.

Into a book on so tricky a subject errors must have crept. For corrections of fact, for expert advice, I shall be most grateful. And in putting any question of your own, you will remember that I am neither an employment exchange nor a Universal Aunt.

Fairlight, Sussex
January 1954

PREPARE FOR SOME NASTY SHOCKS

'PLEASE excuse my bad handwriting,' writes my just pensioned bank manager, as I pass the page for press, 'this retiring business has a terribly upsetting and un-settling effect. One is shaken out of all one's habits. One has to leave all one's friends. Inflation has halved the value of my pension: it will now provide only the bare necessities and none of the comforts we're used to at home. "What next? What next?" I ask myself.'

Probably a majority of those about to retire in these days see it like that. Inflation has played havoc with most retirement plans. The pension that still spelt easy comfort in 1938 may mean something like penury now.

How different it was in the old days! Then most of us were eager to pack up the job. That eagerness, as a nostalgic retiree observes, seems to have disappeared. And how vivid it used to be amongst those approaching their personal date-line! They had everything worked out – their tickets bought, the chicken farm in Sussex leased, the trout rods ready, the rose catalogue read and re-read, the removal firm engaged. Retirement for them couldn't come too soon. But now, to many, it seems something to try to postpone.

To others it is the break with the work itself or the loss of status that hurts. Every job makes its owner into somebody: to retire is to become anonymous, a nobody. With the end of the job something is apt to die in the man of exceptional energy.

The more absorbing the work the more serious the blow. What more fascinating form of skill, what more exciting gamble than to pit your brain against the hazards of wind and weather by insuring ships and their cargoes at sea? Here is a man-sized job and an exacting one. Perhaps wisely Lloyd's insist that their members retire at sixty. For many years statistics showed that three years was the average expectancy of life for retired Lloyd's brokers.

This book is written to help you make a success of your own retirement. Today the task may not be easy. There may be a host of obstacles to be overcome. But success is important for your future. For in old age enjoyment of life best fortifies the will to live.

It is never too early to plan for one's retirement. The mere act of retiring has so many unexpected results that the thing is apt to start off with a series of unnerving jolts. Impressed with this the Americans are already setting about revolutionizing all the conditions and practices of retirement in the United States. Preparation courses for retirement are already in full swing in some cities. Clinics are being opened to condition people of middle age for the later years of life. The problems of retirement are being studied and their genuine difficulties tackled with admirable energy, skill and even zest. In this country little has as yet been thought or planned on the subject. I hope this little book may help to increase interest.

The people who get most out of retirement and old age are first, the artists, next civil servants, after them, salesmen, doctors, lawyers, and journalists. Most of these people have certain advantages in facing up to the revolution in living conditions and habits that is retirement. The artist, painter, musician can never really stop working at his vocation. He simply slackens pace. In peace time most civil servants and bankers have three advantages over the rest of us. The civil servant is sheltered from the ups and downs of business, from fear of the future or dread of dismissal. His hours of duty are regular. His work usually combines routine with interesting variations. His hours of work allow for a full-scale cultivation of interests, hobbies, and games. Salesmen, doctors, and journalists enjoy retirement because they make friends easily and like people. Most of them are cheerful extroverts who can easily work up an interest in local sport, local movements and social doings, and occupy their time profitably.

I began to plan my own retirement seriously before I was twenty-seven. Too early? Not if you want to enjoy it. What about Max Beerbohm's witty defence of the idea? Having published his *Works* (one slim volume of essays) in 1896, he not merely planned but announced his imminent retirement from the more arduous struggles of life at the ripe age of twenty-three. 'And I who crave no knighthood, shall write no more,' said Max. 'I shall write no more. Already I feel myself to be a trifle outmoded. I belong to the Beardsley period. Younger men, with months of activity before them, with fresher schemes and notions, with newer enthusiasms, have pressed forward since then. *Cedo junioribus.*'

Has Max ever regretted this graceful withdrawal from the arena of affairs? More important, did he need much money to achieve it? Very modest resources have sufficed to provide the leisure for Max to cultivate his talents to such perfection on the Bay of Rapallo.

The average man must save for thirty or forty years to make his time his own. So why not make sure that the work and the savings of a lifetime can be enjoyed by reasonable planning and a little active preparation? In real life there is no other way to ensure happiness in retirement: the unplanned happy accident is a mere fluke.

Almost any amount of trouble will repay you. After all your retirement is as important as your marriage or your choice of career. It means as drastic a break in your life as leaving school, or emigrating, or beginning a new career. There is no continuation of the old life in retirement, as many people suppose. Retirement means as complete a break with all the old habits as arrival in Rijeka or Helsinki. You are in a country entirely new and unknown to you from the moment that you take your hat off the office peg for the last time. And it is country for which you have neither map nor chart. You have to find out the way for yourself. There are no R.A.C. scouts on duty on these roads.

The unforeseeable is always happening to the retiree. (An odious word, but no one has found a better!) So the imaginary Mr Baldwin, in R. C. Sherriff's *Greengates*, found on the very day of retirement, as his suburban train took him home from the office, complete with his presentation clock. 'He watched the familiar electric signs pass by for his last inspection,' says Sherriff (himself a retired banker), 'and began to realize how little he had prepared himself for what had happened this afternoon. Freedom – leisure: they were words for inspiration, and he was like an old canary with its cage door open, crouching on the furthest end of its perch. He had made no plans. If he had thought of it at all he had rarely planned anything beyond an extra half-hour in bed and a morning in the garden, but mostly he had put the matter uneasily from his mind. Retirement, he told himself, could take care of itself when it came. And now he began to think as a marooned man might think as he calculates the time his food will last.'

A fair picture of some of the shocks awaiting the man who retires without a plan. Unplanned retirement can be a frightening business. Witness the endless paragraphs in the newspapers headed 'Tragedy of Retirement' and winding up invariably with the coroner's verdict 'suicide while of unsound mind'.

These are the men and women who have failed at the new task of retirement. Usually they have no one to blame but themselves. While few of us can altogether control our business or our family lives, we *can* control more or less completely that part of life that follows retirement. The retiree is his own master. He has neither a difficult director nor a young family to consider at every step. At last he can plan freely within the limits of his income and his commitments.

In my experience the best of all plans is to *taper off gradually*. Many of the happiest old people I know credit their success to this technique. Admittedly it is not always easy to slow down gradually, particularly in the Civil Service and in the larger institutions. But it is becoming easier since the whole attitude to retirement is changing rapidly. While the doctors ridicule the folly of retirement at a stroke of the clock, the scientists are proving that ability to work is a function of biological not of chronological age. A man is as old as his arteries, his heart, his glands, his lungs, his kidneys, *et cetera*. He never ages uniformly overall, but always piecemeal. Therefore to name a certain age as ending *ipso facto* his ability to do useful work is sheer nonsense. Further, men now remain fit much later in life than they did. We are living longer too. The expectancy of life has increased comfortingly during the last half-century. In 1841 average expectation in this country was forty years. The census of 1931 showed a rise to fifty-nine years for men and sixty-three years for women. Today the figure has risen to sixty-eight years for men and seventy-one years for women.

The Registrar-General's actuaries put the expectation of life between 45 and 80 as follows:

Age	Men	Women
45	72	77
55	$73\frac{1}{2}$	78
65	77	80
75	82	84
80	85	86

These figures are a little lower than those you see quoted usually; they refer to the entire population; those of the insurance actuaries refer only to people who have taken out assurance policies.

These figures make cheerful reading. With every year medical science and hygiene add a few months to the average citizen's expectation of life. Consoling though this lengthening of the span of life may be, it has another side. There is a grim finality about these same figures. The figures mean the man compulsorily retired at sixty-five can look forward normally to

around another twelve years. However twelve years
gives 4,380 days to use and enjoy, no mean allowance,
but a limited one. Well may we consider the Chinese
sage's warning: enjoy yourself, it is later than you think.

Successful retirement is almost always due to previous
planning. I have tried it both ways, the first time
without a plan, the second with one. The first effort
was due to rather sudden illness and was a failure: I
was back in harness within eight months. The second
was carefully planned over roughly nine years and it
has been a success.

In each instance I started the process by tapering off
gradually. In the first case I knocked one day off my
working week for a couple of years, then a second and
then was compelled to retire almost completely. That
was in 1938, at the age of fifty. On the second occasion,
at the age of sixty, I knocked off first one day, then two,
now three. Even now I am still tapering off and soon I
shall only leave my local station for London once a week,
eventually once a fortnight. Now I go up on a breakfast
train one day and come back on a tea train on the
following day, using my club as a *pied-à-terre* in town.
How few people realize what inexpensive city accommodation a modest club affords the country
cousin.

By tapering off one avoids the shock, and the feeling
of loneliness and even of humiliation, which the sudden
uprooting from all one's old ways of life means. One
has time to train oneself into the new routines and
duties while still enjoying the old. The transition from
a round of duties and responsibilities to freedom of
action is gradual and easy. The tension of responsibility

is imperceptibly relaxed; the old ties are gently loosened; transition from pressing and urgent tasks to leisure and freedom can be almost imperceptible. To work two or three days a week, or several half-days, is to savour the contrast between effort and relaxation, between tension and calm, possibly between town and country. This is surely to have the best of both worlds, the world of action and the world of leisure. Contrast gives spice to life.

On a winter evening, looking over the copse to a wild sea only a mile away, I could draw up to the fire, take up my book, and thank heaven that there was no 8.15 to be caught tomorrow morning. Or if the weather were merely dull and heavy, I could look forward to my two active days in town next week. By the time I had enjoyed these two days of pleasant meetings and hard work, the idea of sitting back quietly tomorrow and watching the sun on the sea was again tempting. At sixty-seven two days of Fleet Street were enough. One came back to the cottage in a mood to enjoy every moment of its country quiet.

In some sections of business and professional life it is still almost impossible to taper off. The Civil Service, banks, insurance companies, large industrial concerns and commercial houses are amongst the most rigid in this matter. Their absurd convention of complete retirement at a fixed age is long since out of date. That absorbing new branch of medicine, geriatrics (the care of the old), has proved its absurdity long since. But action in such matters may be delayed for twenty years if neither necessity nor propaganda come to the support of the reformers. Luckily the harsh necessities of a manpower shortage are fast knocking down the barriers to this reform. The demand for workers, particularly for skilled executives, is so pressing that later retirement and every possible type of part-time work will rapidly have to be accepted as normal by the Government, the professions, and industry alike. With well-known firms driven to open special factories in order to secure even disabled men, miners with silicosis, even paralysis sufferers tied to invalid chairs, to get the work done, the barriers against part-time work by older people must soon come crashing down. In the end the Government itself will have to bring about the change.

Nevertheless many people tend to postpone retirement until they are no longer able to enjoy it vigorously. The delay is often caused by a fear of being perpetually hard up on the limited income that will be available. This is often a mistaken fear. There are probably more dangers in retiring on a large income than on a smaller one. A majority of the bored and unhappy retirees are well off. They have no need to worry about supplementing their retiring income. They have no spur to achievement, no real difficulties to overcome, no positive source of worry. For the average man and woman that is an unhealthy situation.

The human machine is marvellously constructed, but it is built to work under tension. Too much tension may lead to a duodenal, cardiac disease, thrombosis: too little may lead to depression, apathy, decay of the faculties, and a series of nervous disorders. Whether we like it or not, we must continue to react to moderate tensions if we are to keep fit and sane. Complete relaxation for even one year is as dangerous to a human being as it is to a piece of delicate machinery. Therefore the retiree, man or woman, who has to earn another few hundred a year to enjoy some modest comforts, is far more likely to live long and to enjoy good health than his more affluent colleague. A little work that you fancy (not too much) is what does you good.

The idea that one is indispensable is largely a childish form of egoism expressed in wishful thinking. I have replaced at least a score of self-styled indispensables (including myself) in my time without any extraordinary effort. Too many men (and women too), like Ibsen's Master Builder, Solness, are afraid to let in 'the younger generation that has come knocking at the door'.

This particular technique, the art of educating and guiding younger understudies into biggish jobs, is far better understood in the United States than here. However there are a few Englishmen who know how to do it. My friend A started life in the office of a provincial weekly newspaper, got promotion to the reporters' room of another and ended up at fifty as managing director of a third. His first two newspapers had been located in pleasant places, one a seaside resort, the other an old university city. The third was situated in a typical Lancashire industrial town. He retired at fifty to get away from the smoke and gradually interested himself in a series of quite small concerns mostly run by ambitious and able young men. Today he merely requires to come up from the coast once or twice a week to take a hand in the paper mill, the printing machinery business, the permanent wave makers, the book publishing businesses in which he is interested. There is always some problem or other which his wealth of experience can help to solve. His investments are not large but they bring him in relatively high dividends and some directors' fees and expenses. Also his eggs, once all in one basket, are now nicely distributed. His active brain need never be idle, yet he is still able to golf, walk, meet friends on five days of the week.

This is an example of a completely reorganized business and social life started at fifty. A not merely sold the bulk of his shares in the Lancashire company concerned and resigned his managing directorship: he left Lancashire and came down to the south coast. This involved leaving the town council and the Bench. Such a retirement has to be planned far ahead and carried out carefully step by step to a timetable. It doesn't just happen. To sever so many roots, to leave the familiar scene, to make so many readjustments, requires courage and firmness as well as judgement. The planning of the post-retirement programme can be great fun: it is considered overleaf.

2

HAVE A PLAN OF SOME SORT

EVERY retiree should have at least some sort of programme and work to it. The time to make such a programme is now if you are over thirty. For your dreamed-of retirement may well call for much more money than you are saving now. Always it requires a number of new arrangements and special efforts which only appear necessary when you begin to consider the problems of your later years realistically and in detail.

Here are some points that such a programme may usefully cover:

1. Settle a date for your retirement, allowing a reasonable time-lag for delays and difficulties, e.g. 1970–2. Regard the later date as rigid.

2. Take steps to explore the possibility of tapering off gradually.

3. Make a list of the things you want to do first in retirement. Have at least one ambitious project.

4. Decide on the work you would like to do to earn a little extra, or the business you would like to start or take over.

5. Decide on all the steps in the way of special training, available capital, equipment, and sales outlets you need before you can hope to succeed in this new interest.

6. If possible do some work of this sort in your spare time to try out your ability, your equipment, the cost, the available market.

7. Decide where you want to live in retirement, if you are going to move.

8. Discuss the subject in all its aspects with your family and friends. They know your capacity – and your limitations – more clearly than you do, because they are outsiders. They may have some useful ideas.

9. Make a list of your probable weekly and annual expenditure in retirement. Allow for more travel, more meals at home, for extra expense on garden, hobbies, games. Have you allowed big enough margins for these?

10. Make a list of your present hobbies, cultural interests, social service work, political work, sports. Assess how much of your average week they will fill.

11. Draw up a specimen week's time-table for retirement. But make it flexible. Try to remember the activities and amusements that delighted you most as a child: you probably have special aptitudes for these interests and can take them up afresh fairly easily.

12. See that one at least of your interests means helping others: a common danger of retirement is self-absorption. It is vital to interest yourself in others, if only to avoid the dangerous disease of old age.

Why settle a date for my retirement so far ahead, you may ask? The answer is that most unsuccessful retirements are unplanned and they appear to be unsuccessful because they are haphazard. Your work may stop but your life goes on, and twelve months spent on the golf-course and in the car, or on the bowling-green and the river, end by boring the keenest pleasure seeker to tears. You must have some active and more serious interest if you are not to find your mind rusting. The one way to make sure of enjoying any project or interest in retirement is to plan for it, to prepare yourself for it and to look forward to it.

Annoying as it may be to those of us who like to stay put, it is often better to move away from your old home when you retire if you conveniently can. Many cannot. Family, business or public work tie them to the old home. For them retirement is always a good deal more difficult. Where a move is impossible, more brief holidays, more outings are one remedy. A car is another.

The need for a change of scene and of environment on *first* retiring seems harsh and illogical. Yet a strong case has been made for it in at least one American research. A family house is seldom a very cheerful place without the family: it is not the ideal setting for elderly people in retirement. Most of our impressions, the visual stimulus of life, come to us through our eyes. When you have seen a place a hundred times you cease to see it: your eye merely relies on the film of memory to produce the picture. So the scene entirely loses its impact, its bite.

A new scene sets the eye working, stimulates the mind and the imagination with fresh, brightly etched pictures. How fresh are some of your memories of beautiful places seen only once on holiday: live with one of them and the picture would dim, the whole setting would lose its colour. Again to live long in a house is to fill it with memories: not all memories are happy. A house known for thirty years is apt to house ghosts as well as people. Finally, to live long in the same place is not merely to make friends, but to lose them: it is hard for elderly people to replace the friends they lose with new ones in a place where they once knew everybody by sight.

'I have lived here so long that now nobody knows me,' was the cry of an exceptionally charming old friend of mine in her eighties. Yet all her life she had been an adored friend and neighbour in a charming circle. In a new place one is plunged, willy-nilly, into a new social group: the newer the village or suburb, the more easy it is to get into the swim.

But this change of scene cannot be left too late. *For many there must nowadays be a second retirement around 75 to 80*. By that time the one desire is usually 'to stay put'. On this necessity for a second retirement for the long-lived I reported in some detail in £ s. d. *of Retirement* (1957).

While planning out an easy and flexible programme for your week, remember your wife's part in it. She is not retiring. On the contrary, in most cases she will have you at home 'under her feet' for seven days a week instead of two. She will have ten or a dozen more meals to cook every week, many more fires to provide in the winter months, probably more entertaining to do. All this means more work and less fun. The simplest form of entertainment, tea, may involve a morning's baking of scones and/or biscuits and cakes. It all means work. It all takes time. It all costs money.

The mere proximity of a husband in the house is a trial to a woman. He and she will quickly come to the end of their conversational gambits. No longer can he come back every evening laden with news of the great outer world, bursting with tit-bits of gossip about the little world of the office. This will cramp his conversational style.

All of which stresses the virtue of tapering off

gradually into semi-retirement. A husband who is still away from home two days a week does give a woman time to turn round once a week. There is a breathing space in each week in which to get the washing and some cooking done, time to see her own particular friends. Women enjoy a hen party. They enjoy their own jokes and they may tell yours. There is often more laughter at madam's tea-table than at your own cocktail party. What *do* they find to laugh about so hilariously?

Some men spend their lives in jobs that bore them for three hundred odd days in every year. Often such men can turn to the work they like in retirement. To some of these the last years are the happy ones. My friend B is such a one. On his sixty-fifth birthday he left a well-paid business job on a famous London newspaper, with a pension. Next day he took over the chairmanship of an industrial concern whose directors he had helped by sage advice for more than twenty years. His new job entails the running of a factory as well as the selling of its products. His whole range of abilities from producing to financing has full play. These are his fullest and most rewarding days, as his beaming smile shows. Yet he manages to spend half of his week on the coast with his invalid wife.

There are far more opportunities of this sort for lively minds than people realize. If you are still young-ish and a little bored, keep your eyes open to the difficulties of your friends and help them when you can without asking for definite remuneration. In precisely this quiet way many of the most glittering opportunities are created.

On the whole we in England take altogether too dim a view of the possibilities of retirement in the way of developing entirely new interests, apart from earning money. At sixty-five Alfred Emery Perkins left his sales managership with the Crucible Steel Co. of America and took ship for England the same week. An expert metallurgist with two university degrees, he wanted to study at Oxford, preferably literature, to freshen his mind by meeting new ideas (however odd), by meeting new people. Eventually he hopes to write, chiefly about his own experiences and the curious people he has met, 'all in a friendly and good-humoured vein'. Here is a retiree who is starting a new life with a vengeance! But isn't he right?

'I don't have many years left,' he says. 'Too many people back home sit around and mope when they retire. They die on the vine!'

Nothing is so stimulating as change. My friend C spent most of his active business life managing a shipping business in Hong Kong. When the Chinese made things too difficult, he realized all his available assets and came home. But not to slump into an easy-chair. First he invested his cash very carefully, then he dug round among the companies he had known in China until he found an opening for himself. Just a small, part-time, poorly paid opening that would give him some additional income while he looked about for what he *really* wanted. Having spent most of his life perspiring in hot office buildings in the Far East, he wanted a life in the open air, with a business under his own control. A fruit farm seemed to be the ideal answer. There was none available in the south (he needed a warm climate);

so he bought a largish house which had a few acres of reasonably good soil surrounding it, hired a skilled fruit-farm worker, gave him a commission on results and set to work to learn the ropes. This involved reading closely good text-books, studying and acting upon the advice of the two technical papers on fruit growing. Some of the crops he tried lost him money, some failed completely, but others paid. To these he now confines his attention, growing chiefly juicy melons grown individually, early strawberries, large peaches and early peas, asparagus, and chrysanthemums for the Christmas market.

Even the successful barrister wants a little extra money and an active mental interest when he leaves the bustle of the courts. Archibald Crawford Q.C., an eminent Scottish advocate, was kept busy for many years in teaching classes of business men how to talk to groups of business executives, to trade union officials, to foremen. Surely a happy thought.

When he returned from an exciting time in the Second World War, one younger man, D, felt that he could no longer live the City man's life. He bought quite a few acres in a very inexpensive county, grows *only* Cox's Orange Pippins and a particularly luscious greengage. This farm enables him to indulge his second hobby, travelling. He is able to spend January and February somewhere in the sun, before the spring spraying starts in early March. (These fruit-trees have to be sprayed seven times a year!) These are some of the more energetic recipes for retirement.

Most of us, however, prefer something less ambitious, something that will allow us to enjoy the real privileges of retirement – spare time, leisurely hobbies, more social life. (This side of earning in retirement is dealt with fully in Chapter 9.)

Some men are so versatile that they are able to acquire an entirely new art, like painting, or a craft like pottery, or even a profession, like teaching, after retirement. Sometimes more than one!

One of the most astonishing switches of this sort was accomplished by the Victorian novelist, William de Morgan. For forty-five years de Morgan was an unsuccessful painter, and a little more successful tile-maker. At sixty-one he was compelled to close down his business. Six years later he produced his first novel, *Joseph Vance*, which was an immediate best-seller, and later a novel, *Alice – for Short*, a sensitive study of a child's reactions to slum conditions which may easily become a classic.

Within eight years de Morgan had reached the top of his new profession of popular novelist. In 1914 when the First World War broke out, he made a fourth *volte-face*, becoming a designer of aircraft and anti-submarine devices. Apparently he was able to switch from the technics of novel writing to those of engineering as easily as he had passed from Pre-Raphaelite painting to tile making.

However well off you may be now, it is well to start serious work on a money-earning job or hobby some years before retirement. These are difficult times. The value of the pound is apt to fall. You may eventually *need* a little extra money. Or you may want to preserve your independence in retirement. When the retiree is living with son or daughter, this can be a matter of vital importance. The feeling of dependence on others is dangerous not merely to the spirit but to health itself. An untold number of retired men and women feel humiliated in even having to accept house room from their children. In very many cases this affects the older retiree's health. As medical research has too painfully proved, the family is the unit of health. The climate of his home often affects the elderly retiree's health for the worse.

The independent elder's fear of being a trouble to others can be very real. It was touchingly expressed by my old friend, Sidney Dark, a versatile journalist, equally happy as the theatre or gossip columnist of the *Daily Express* or as editor of the *Church Times*.

'Whether one is young or old, to do anything is to find something else to do. Doing nothing is to enlist in the Satanic army of nuisances. That is the dread that is apt to haunt the man well stricken in years . . . the dread of becoming unable to fend for oneself and so to be dependent on others . . . for a man like myself . . . with a consuming hatred of exploiting affection, it is a nightmare.'

The way to avoid that nightmare is to have one's profitable side-line as an anchor to windward in every financial blizzard.

Before studying means of increasing one's income it may be wise to consider where one can get the most value for every penny spent when one does retire. To save a pound is often as useful as to earn one. Some ways of living cheaply in retirement are outlined in detail in Chapter 6.

3

WHERE SHALL I GO?*

HAVING once decided to retire, the first problem that raises its ugly head is, where? About this matter of location one cannot start thinking too soon. Nothing is more important to one's comfort and content. The wrong choice of home and neighbourhood may spoil the whole enterprise.

Our own first choice was a blunder of this sort. My wife and I hit on an East Dorset village which we had known and adored separately in early youth. That village seemed to have everything. Lying on a lovely bay within sight of the sea, it was yet sufficiently far away to save one from having to live with its often dreary winter face. And, a peculiarly Dorset charm, green woods and golden moorland ran right down to the edge of the water. The village was within easy distance of a pleasant town in which I had worked as a young journalist and still had a few old friends. It was also expertly reported as being a cheap place to live. What more could one ask?

When we ran down to look at it after thirty years, the village seemed to be untouched. There was the same vista of blue waters glittering in the autumn sun, with purple heathland rolling north. The little white house with its neglected garden offered infinite opportunity for gardening in the days of leisure ahead. Yet within six months we were fleeing the spot. Why? Because we

* See maps on pages 44–9

had not studied the neighbourhood closely enough. We had been content to go down for single days when we ought to have spent several weeks living on the spot. Superficially the same, the village had been in fact transformed completely from a rustic retreat into an industrialized suburb of a nearby town.

The quiet of the village had been destroyed by a mighty stream of east to west traffic. Garages and a petrol pump had taken the place of the old village smithy. Near the village several factories were at work (day and night, as it happened). The old village pub had become a neon-lighted roadhouse. What still looked like a stretch of sunny blue water just beyond the heath was really a couple of miles of marsh. One now had to drive seven miles round by road before it was possible to put a toe in the water. To shop in the pleasant seaside town nearby meant a car-park fee of sixpence to a shilling every time you stopped. Shops, cinemas, and pubs were all charging 'high season' prices with gusto. In fact this was the last place in Britain to retire to. Even the old community spirit had gone with the influx of new people from all parts of the kingdom. Which shows the danger of trusting to youthful memories in choosing a place of retirement. Nothing ever remains quite the same for thirty years, least of all oneself.

The more accurately you check up on every detail affecting your new home, the fewer headaches it will cause you. This does entail a lot of hard work. How different it all was fifty years ago! When that ambitious but unsuccessful man of letters, Henry Ryecroft, suddenly found himself the possessor of an annuity of three hundred a year, everything his heart could desire was at his feet. 'Having only himself to support,' says Gissing, 'Ryecroft saw in this income something more than a competency. In a few weeks he quitted the London suburb where of late he had been living, and, turning to the part of England which he loved best, he presently established himself in a cottage near Exeter, where, with a rustic housekeeper to look after him, he was soon thoroughly at home.'

How far would £5 15s. 4¾d. a week go today? Think of his perfect housekeeper '. . . a low-voiced, light-footed woman of discreet age, strong and deft enough to render me all the service I require, and not afraid of solitude'. She would demand just a little more than the entire annuity in board and wages.

How could he have afforded to rent that plain little villa of his? 'My house is perfect,' he says. 'Just large enough to allow the grace of order in domestic circumstance; just that superfluity of intramural space, to lack which is to be less than at one's ease. The fabric is sound; the work in wood and plaster tells of a more leisurely and a more honest age than ours. The stairs do not creak under my weight; I am waylaid by no unkindly draught; I can open or close a window without muscle-ache.'

No housing difficulties for the lean annuitant in these happy days! Gissing was writing in the last year of the Victorian era. What he was able to rent for say £1 a week would cost £5–£6 today. Yet it is what so many of us want! There in a nutshell we have the problem of the average man or woman of modest means today, whether retired or about to retire. Desperate as it often looks the problem is soluble. This book is entirely devoted to finding solutions for the many problems. Fortunately a surprising number of the most frightening difficulties yield to the application of a little ingenuity.

In some ways the finding of a house or flat in the right place at the right price is the hardest task of all. There are many considerations which do not immediately spring to mind but are nevertheless important. Do you mind aircraft noise overhead? Some of the most attractive and cheapest areas from a housing angle have this disadvantage, to which some people can adapt themselves more quickly than others.

To answer the question, where shall I retire? we have first to decide what are the essentials of a happy retirement. Allowing for variations in the size of family, in hobbies and taste, it is possible to set down a dozen specific requirements one can hope to satisfy on a small income:

Scenery and surroundings that specially appeal to you.

A climate and soil that suit you.

A house or flat at a reasonable price or rent.

A garden that will not make excessive demands.

A relatively low cost of living.

Opportunity to augment one's income.

Low rates and/or low house assessments.

A friendly social circle.

Shops, cinemas, church, theatre, and pub within easy distance.

A golf-course, cricket-ground, bowling-green, or tennis-court near by.

A good bus or train service passing close to your door.
Relatively level country: old hearts don't like hills.
(In a rural area) a village hall near by.

Other more personal and specialized requirements can be added to taste, but these are usually the essentials.

I make no apology for concentrating largely on the burning question of the cost of living. Most people imagine that they can do very little about it. They see it as entirely controlled by government and mysterious economic forces. For many a man at a certain period of his life this is true. For the salesman or the civil servant compelled to live in Harrogate or Bath in the correct type of villa in the convenient suburb, there may be little chance of seriously reducing his cost of living. But the retiree is in many ways a free man. Here is his opportunity to determine and control his method and cost of living! For once the future is largely in his own hands. This may sound like a rather large statement to the man or woman facing the problems of retirement for the first time. Fortunately there is evidence to support it, as we shall presently see.

Few people seem to realize how considerably the cost of living varies over different parts of the country. The variation may reach 20–25 per cent as between a fashionable coast resort and the quiet suburb of a country town lying inland. These variations can be assessed by the use of modern statistical methods. For some fifteen years it was part of the writer's aim to develop techniques for securing this information for other purposes.

One of the factors in living costs which varies surprisingly is the cost of a house – the retiree's first requirement in so many cases. The bungalow that costs £2,500 in St Leonards may sell for £5,000 in Worthing. That is only the obvious type of variation in house prices. In five or six years the relative positions of the two resorts may be altered by exceptional skill in the management of the borough of Hastings and of the individual hotels in it, by a successful royal stay – or simply by special favours from the Clerk of the Weather.

Other factors influencing the level of prices in a town are less obvious. Some are either concealed or unknown to the average citizen. Consider the level of rates. At first glance it should be less expensive to live in a borough with a rate of 11s. in the £ than in one with a rate of 22s. But is it invariably so? Much depends on the level of valuations in the area. A rate of 11s. in the £ with a valuation of £100 on your house may cost you every penny as much as a rate of 22s. with a valuation of £50.

But house prices and rates are only two of the influences constantly at work on living costs. Others are more subtle, because they are bound up with social standards. One is how much the householder is able or willing to pay for fairly normal services and amenities. How important is it to keep up with the Joneses? Another is the density of the population in relation to housing. Where the average householder is paying a high level of rates, where the number of large houses occupied by one or two people is large, there you may look for a high cost of living. Where the number of private cars licensed is above the average for the country, where private telephones are unusually common, there life is usually expensive. A sixth test for price levels – an infallible one this, despite the National Health Service – is the death rate among children under one year of age. This factor naturally works in reverse. The lower this death rate is in any area, the higher the cost of living is likely to be.

Some years ago we combined five of these factors with two others of a more technical nature to produce an Index of Income Levels in the 145 larger towns in this country for the *Marketing Survey of the U.K.* This gave us a theoretic basis for estimating the *relative* income levels in all of these towns. In such an inquiry, however, a theoretic basis is not enough. Some influence not included in any of these factors may be affecting the fortunes of a certain area at a certain time.

An influx of civil servants to a new branch of a ministry can put prices up in a small country town in a surprising way. The decline of a small local industry will have just the opposite effect. There is no economic standstill possible in even the sleepiest of country towns. Always some influences are making for prosperity while others work to undermine it. Even in a purely farming community the appearance of tranquil economic security is purely illusory. Day and night storm, drought, pests, changes in government policy, new fashions in eating, are sapping away the gains secured by good weather, heavy subsidies, prosperity in near-by cities that buy the produce of the local farms. In economics, as in nature, 'all is flux'.

Eventually we were able to check these figures by

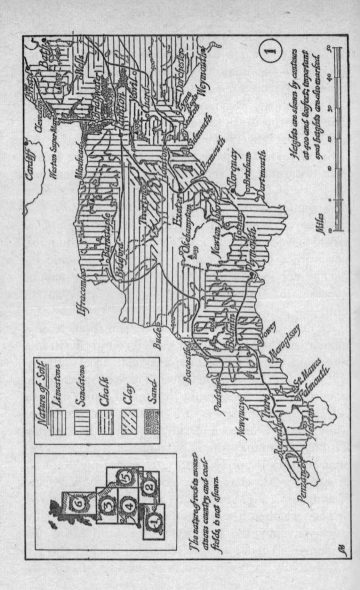

Nature of Soil

Limestone
Sandstone
Chalk
Clay
Sand

The nature of rocks in mountainous country and coal-fields, is not shown.

Heights are shown by contours at 400 and 600 feet; important spot heights are also marked.

Miles

Cardiff
Clevedon Bristol Bath
Weston Super-Mare Wells
Minehead Bridgwater
Taunton Yeovil Dorchester
Ilfracombe Tiverton Weymouth
Barnstaple Lyme Regis
Bideford Honiton Axminster
Exeter Exmouth
Okehampton Teignmouth
Bude Cheltenham Torquay
Boscastle Newton Abbot Brixham
Padstow Bodmin Plymouth Dartmouth
Newquay Lostwithiel
Redruth Truro Fowey
Penzance St Mawes Mevagissey
Helston Falmouth

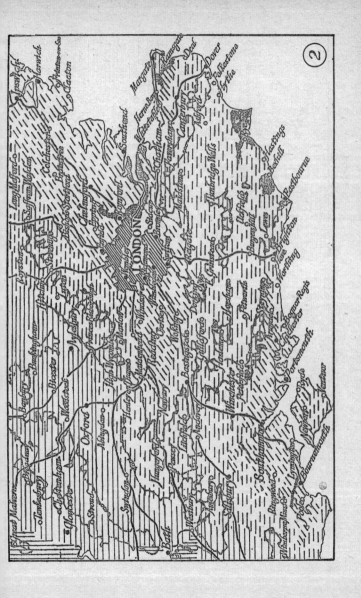

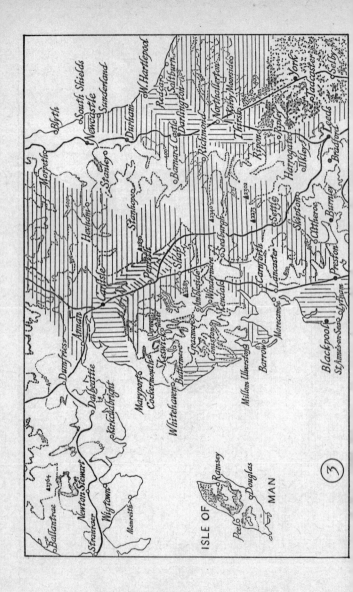

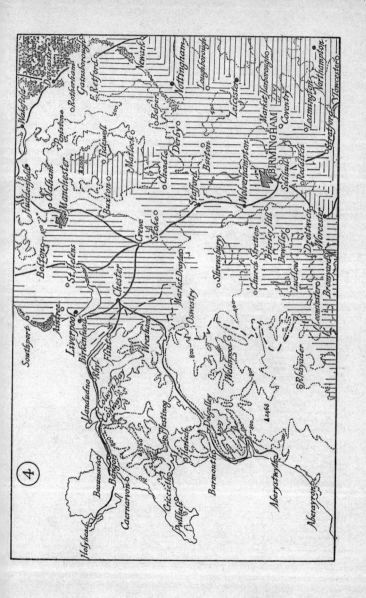

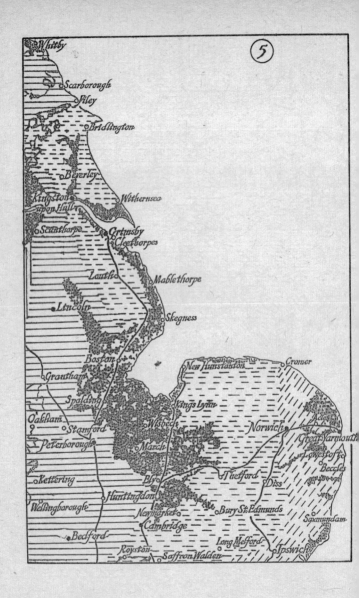

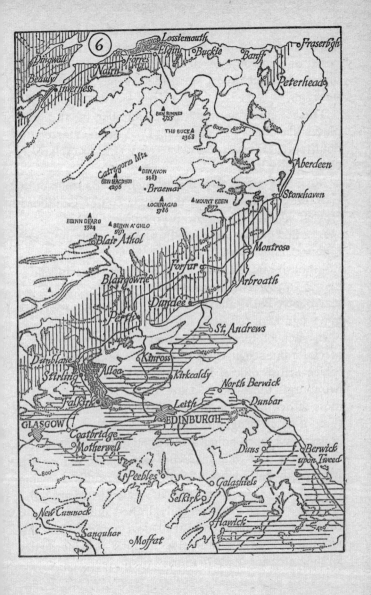

first-hand evidence of the amount of money people were actually earning in different parts of the country, based on 140,000 interviews in twenty-eight cities and towns, secured by a research agency for another purpose.

These figures showed that a number of attractive places like Blackpool, Buxton, Darlington, Harrogate, Southport, Hastings, Norwich, and York are relatively cheap to live in.

More expensive are towns such as Bournemouth, Cambridge, Eastbourne, Edinburgh, Exeter, Guildford, Hove, Oxford, Torquay, and Worthing.

At a first glance these two lists may prompt indignant protests. They seem to be far from logical. Why were Edinburgh and Exeter classed as expensive with index figures so low as 108 and 104 respectively? Were not Harrogate, Bath, and Brighton rated inexpensive with index figures of 108, 107, 106 each?

In each of the two apparent paradoxes there is a special influence at work which no index limited to our sparse British official figures can take into account. In Edinburgh there is an acute housing shortage. Over most of Scotland the housing situation is much worse than it is in England and Wales. Relatively fewer houses have been going up in Scotland, not merely for the fifteen post-war years but for eighty years past. Edinburgh has to provide for (*a*) a steadily growing population of its own, (*b*) its student colony, also growing, (*c*) the extra officials drafted into the city to control several fresh industrial developments in Midlothian. On top of all this the city must provide shelter for an increasing army of tourists in summer.

There is a further complication about Edinburgh today. The city is the administrative headquarters for the great new coal-field now being opened up rapidly in Midlothian, running southwards from Edinburgh. This means the housing of a fresh and considerable corps of officials of the Scottish Coal Board in and around the city. Further, the whole area of rich farmlands stretching to Dalkeith eastwards and beyond is scheduled for vast building estates to house the tens of thousands of miners who will be brought from the areas of the worked-out seams of Lanarkshire. While this great development, on a scale far larger than any satellite town, will clearly provide more housing around Edinburgh, it remains to be seen whether any sizeable movement to these new suburbs from the city's inner suburbs will relieve the congestion there. As the Scots say: 'I hae ma doots.'

Remember too that Edinburgh (like Dublin) provides all the civilized amenities of a great capital – without the usual mobs, the jostling, the dust, and the perpetual bus, tram, and taxi travelling of a great city. In both capitals art galleries, theatres (three of them), libraries, museums, cinemas, public gardens, and most interesting old buildings are all within a short tram ride of one another. Many are within walking distance. All these pleasures Edinburgh itself provides amid the most spectacular setting of any city in Europe. Inevitably such privileges have to be paid for. Despite an east wind worthy of the steppes in winter and a fearful housing shortage, the city draws cultured people of all ages from every part of the world. Today some people speculate on the future by buying a house already occupied at an 'assessed' rental, in order to occupy it when the tenant, aged or otherwise, passes on.

Admittedly there are borderline cases. Southport is one of them. With low rates and a relatively small payment per head, living ought to be cheap. Were other things equal, Southport should surely be an inexpensive place in which to live. But Southport enjoys special advantages. Ever since the inventions of Crompton and Arkwright began to make fortunes for Lancashire cotton spinners and weavers in the 1820s, Southport was long the adored Mecca of the successful man from the cotton towns. Retirement to Southport was a pre-taste of heaven. This explains why the shops in Lord Street vie with those of Regent Street or Princes Street. The number of luxury hotels is exceptional. Better or more elegant cinemas and cafés are not to be found outside London. Naturally all this has its effect on prices. Yet Southport is inexpensive for what it offers.

In choosing a house nothing is more important than *accessibility*. This fact is clearly overlooked by thousands of retirees. Before settling on the town you mean to live in or near, take a compass and draw circles (*a*) at half a mile and (*b*) at five miles distance from the shopping centres. This will give you a clear idea of (*a*) how far cinemas, cafés, library, theatre, art gallery are from the shopping centre, (*b*) which of the services you use are within a short bus or tram ride of your proposed new home. The results may surprise you. In Bath almost every amenity from cinemas and two theatres to library and Pump Room lies within half a mile of the city's shopping centre. In Bournemouth the cinema or café or chine you prefer may be a couple of miles away from library or bookshops.

One other factor making for economical living is sometimes overlooked. This is the wider form of accessibility. Accessibility to a great city costs money. By retiring to a resort or residential area enjoying a fast train service to a Town with a capital T (whether London or Manchester or Cardiff) the annuitant may be paying heavily for something he no longer needs. He has finished with the 8.15. It is invariably cheaper to live in the resort with a poor train service. Hence the advantages of Norfolk and Suffolk, parts of Essex, Sussex, and Kent, in the south. In the north, the same applies to part of Derbyshire, much of Westmorland, the east and north of Scotland and Northern Ireland. In both of the latter countries the one obstacle is the extreme shortage of houses.

It takes time and persistence to secure such a spacious, well-equipped, new bungalow as one of my friends (a Londoner too!) now enjoys at Liberton, Edinburgh. To make retirement a success means hard work. There are few short cuts. Luckily the search for perfection often ends in the finding of the unusual. But the task cannot be hurried.

Nor is a charming home always immediately essential. It often pays to spend a year or even two in hotel or apartment in order to find what you want – the old country cottage with possibilities, the tiny Georgian house in an ancient country town, the comfortable villa in a quiet backwater near a resort or even a city.

To suggest the spending of a year or two without a home may suggest a mere orgy of extravagance. Hotels and furnished rooms are expensive nowadays. The storing of furniture is in itself a costly item. All true, but only a part of the facts.

Do you realize that three resorts out of every four in this country endure a dreaded winter off season? Their hotels are eating their heads off from October until Easter, at least six months in every year. During this horrid period of silent bedrooms and rumbling overheads, some of the most luxurious of our resort hotels are ready to make you a bargain offer. Of the two finest hotels in a certain south coast resort, one has advertised for three years running for winter guests at five to six guineas a week with full board. The other is putting up its 'permanents' for little more. Once settled in a comfortable hotel or guest house, or in comfortable rooms, you can devote your whole time and energies to *the hunt*.

How can I endure a dull English resort for a whole winter? you ask. A reasonable objection, surely. But is it so bad in these days of better heating, busier hotels – and TV? Surely not. Simply make up your mind to relish the place in all its moods. No less an exquisite than Sir Max Beerbohm plumped for the seaside resort out of season. Partly Max liked such a retreat for a reason very near to the energetic soul facing retirement – because it alone can restore that sense of self-importance, which London takes from you. In particular Max was fond of going to L— in February. For a day or two the empty promenade, the emptier shops, the crocodiles of small girls winding sadly over the asphalt back to their school, induce a mood of melancholy. But his melancholy passes quickly.

'The very loneliness of the place', says Max, 'does but accentuate my proprietary sense. From the midst of all this lifeless monotony I stand out, a dominant and most romantic personage. Were I in London, who would notice me, no prince there? Even here in the season, I had but a slight pre-eminence over other visitors. But now I need but show myself to create a glow of interest and wonder. The blind man, standing by his telescope, knows my tread, and tries, I think, to picture my appearance. The old gentlemen see in me the incarnation of splendid youth; the shop-people a dispenser of great riches: the schoolgirls a prodigy of joyous freedom from French verbs. I could not have levied these tributes in August. . . .'

In fact Max found everything delightful. He learned to look forward to everything, even to the morning newspapers. So can you, if you will but give your mind to enjoying every moment of your new leisure. Nor had Max your incentive for enjoyment. He had no hunt before him. Nor had he your incentive for study of the place under all conditions. Better look at your district in winter or on a rainy day!

This makes feasible a winter of some comfort and at a low cost. Summer is more difficult. However if an inexpensive winter has put money in the bank, you may be able to spend a good deal more during the summer. But don't spend it in a resort hotel: spend it in an inland town or seaside village that, beautiful in itself, is not yet fashionable. There are many such, particularly in the east and north of Scotland, in Northern Ireland, in North Devon, parts of Dorset, Somerset, Berkshire, North Wales, Cumberland, and even in the Scottish border country. True, you may not want to retire to any of these places, if you have failed to find a house in the county of your choice during the previous summer. Will you *remain* of this mind?

Others have found consolation elsewhere. It is often possible to discover a house or a flat at your price in the less popular and populous areas. A home is a home, even if it stand not in the chosen spot.

Suppose we look at some of the possibilities.

4

WHERE IT COSTS LESS TO LIVE

THE first possibility you want to consider may well be London. To thousands of retirees, some born cockneys, others born a thousand miles away, the spell of London is irresistible. To many women in the sunniest parts of the Commonwealth London has become as much the centre of things as Paris to the educated Frenchman. The almost hypnotic power of London is not confined to English-women. Retiring business women will leave the gleaming skyscrapers, the glittering shop windows, the blue bay of Buenos Aires or Monte Video for a grey little flat in Kensington. 'Here I feel myself to be at the centre of it all, people, politics, sport, theatres, music', is the invariable answer of the South African or the South American to my question: 'Why on earth end up in fog when you have lived so long in sunshine?'

Not all Londoners realize the possibilities of their city for combining metropolitan amenities with country air and open landscapes. One can live within ten or twelve miles of Charing Cross with a great park or common on the doorstep. But it costs money. London is the most expensive city in Britain. Its mere size imposes excessive travelling; shortage of hotels and accommodation keeps rents high; the shops are exceptionally tempting; meals out cost more than elsewhere; West End theatres and cinemas are exceedingly expensive.

Suppose cost is not your first consideration, however,

and you decide to be near London. To get the best of
both worlds, follow the Thames. The river will lead you
to four of the most agreeable of the inner suburbs,
Wimbledon, Richmond, Kingston, and Hampton
Court. Here you have both trim, level riverside walks
and still lovely commons. If streams of traffic do rattle
through the main streets incessantly, it is always
possible to get away from the hubbub quite quickly.
The riverside towns now lay themselves out to charm
the crowd. On a bright July day Richmond and
Kingston can vie with any holiday resort. The shops are
exceptionally good, including several large department
stores, and prices are reasonable. Also Oxford Street
and Regent Street are only twenty minutes away.

Rates are about average for London suburbs, a shade
low for East England.

To avoid the high London cost of living, however,
you may be wise to go forty miles out away from
Charing Cross. If you are prepared to go so far, then
first keep on going south, making for the Surrey–Kent
border. The southern slopes of the North Downs, from
the Hog's Back, near Guildford, to their ending in the
white cliffs of Dover, contain endless miles of wind-
swept open country. If you want fresh, clean air, keep
to the top of the ridge, away from the valleys. Some of
the higher commons are exceptional in commanding
magnificent views of the country around, while being
beauty spots in their own right.

Surrey is now largely a dormitory county for the
capital. Consequently prices of houses and costs of
living are almost uniformly high in the more attractive
places like Farnham, still a perfect Georgian town,

Haslemere, the home of the Dolmetsch family and other musical and artistic groups, Godalming, with Charterhouse School on its hill, and the pleasantly open Camberley and Esher. All of these are in many ways ideal, for ex-service folk in particular, especially Farnham, with its castle and its well-preserved Georgian streets, its proximity to Frensham ponds, to the moors of Hindhead and to London itself. Two unusual merits in so small a town are a progressive art school and an enterprising repertory theatre with high standards, the latter housed in a charming sixteenth-century building. Less expensive and exclusive than Haslemere, both Farnham and Godalming offer a wide range of social activities.

It is perhaps unfortunate that Hindhead and Liphook lie on the Portsmouth road. As a result the dramatic gulch of the Punch Bowl and the Hindhead moors are lined with cars and inundated with motor-coaches the summer long. Far nearer to London, that lovely stretch of moorland, Ashdown Forest, is beautifully quiet even on a Sunday. Yet on its edge lie Crawley, East Grinstead, Tunbridge Wells, Wadhurst, Nutley, and Cuckfield, not to mention Crowborough. Although it lacks anything so sharply romantic as the Devil's Punch Bowl or so beguiling as the hills of the Devil's Jumps, Ashdown Forest has just as exquisite a range of heather and gorse-covered heath as the Hindhead moors. The quiet of Ashdown Forest is a solace at every season of the year. Prices are comfortingly low for most things from property to morning coffee in many of these small Sussex and Kentish towns.

Without much doubt the cheapest houses and the

cheapest living in England are to be found still in the
counties of Suffolk, north-east Essex, Wiltshire, Huntingdon, Radnor, north Berkshire, and Somerset. In
each some incredible bargains in housing at today's
level of prices are to be found. Probably the remoter
parts of Wiltshire and Suffolk hold the palm. (But
some parts of Wiltshire are expensive, for all their
quiet.) In the quiet places it is possible to find a pleasant
old four-roomed cottage, with a small garden, piped
water, and electric light and power for £2,500 to
£3,000. One can do nearly, if not quite as well in
Suffolk, often amid softly undulating country, served by
minor winding roads and minor railways. Here as
elsewhere, however, both local and London bus services
are improving steadily. In all these counties the disadvantages are the same: poor railway services, now
accentuated by the closing down of branch lines,
absence of cinemas and modern cafés, the lack of
social life, and the absence of many of the habitual
modern amenities.

Unless one is lucky enough to secure a house – or
land and a building licence – beside one of the towns,
migration to any of these emptier counties means
answering a disconcerting question. Do I want genuine
rural life or suburban facilities in a country setting?
Rural life demands a complete change of outlook, a
radical change in one's way of life, the ability to do
without a number of things, from the bridge foursome
to the local, from the nearby shopping centre to the
golf club. It means an hour or two in the garden most
days; a limited social circle. To keep mentally alert,
one is almost compelled to take an *active* interest in

some local business, be it the British Legion or the Residents' Association for the man, the nearest Women's Institute, or the church for the woman. Against time for reading, radio, or television and hobbies, one must set fewer friends 'looking in', often less interesting neighbours, narrow farming or sporting interests, more time to be bored.

Although it is one of our largest counties, Suffolk boasts only one town of 100,000 people. Ipswich is a busy port and an industrial centre. It is also extremely popular as a residential centre. Most of the old town has been modernized but it is still full of Elizabethan buildings. Rates are rather high and the waiting list for houses is unusually long for a town of this size.

For the rest, towns of any size are rare in Suffolk: 'rural districts' abound. Apart from Lowestoft and Felixstowe and the old town of Bury St Edmunds, there are few boroughs in the whole of the broad acres of Suffolk. One of these is Beccles, from which a country paper, the *Waveney Chronicle*, covers part of Suffolk. The whole country is covered by the *East Anglian Daily Times*. News of much property available in a wide area of Suffolk can be found in their columns. Unfortunately rates are high both at Bury St Edmunds and at Lowestoft.

In the smaller towns and villages of Suffolk, however, everything tends to be simple and inexpensive. This area of cheap living includes all the Constable country, running from Dedham, in north-east Essex, up to Long Melford. A quiet country of little hills, one slow meandering river (the Stour), of lush green meadows and small, neat woods circling hillsides.

There is a world of difference between Lowestoft and Felixstowe, the county's two largest residential resorts. Lowestoft is still a fishing town with a life of its own as well as a holiday place: Felixstowe is a smart, modern seaside resort. Fine cliff gardens and bathing beach are the chief attractions.

It is more difficult to find a combination of genuine open country with suburban amenities twenty miles north of London than the same distance south. Even thirty years ago the Watford–Bushey–St Albans area offered this. Today the huge housing estates of the various local councils are eating rapidly into the gently rolling Hertfordshire countryside. Welwyn is still one of our best planned towns but it is no longer small and the number of factories seems to increase every year. Luton too is now a very busy industrial centre, almost Detroit-like in its prosperity.

If you care to go west you can find old-world towns, pleasant scenery and comfort at Beaconsfield and in the little towns of Amersham, Great Missenden, and Chesham. Old Beaconsfield is enchanting. Go north-west and you reach the busy furniture towns, the Wycombes, and the old but now partly industrialized town of Aylesbury. (Go north and you are back in Luton.) To be truthful, the saving of these charming little towns from complete urbanization must be partly due to a deplorable railway service. To the retiree this is no serious matter.

The possibilities of the shires to the west and north of Hertfordshire are now severely limited. One hardly dares whisper the name of Hertford itself. With Oxford, Bath, and Hereford it is now one of the most overcrowded residential towns in Britain. Yet if you can plan now to secure a few years hence a foothold in Hereford, you will be fortunate. Hereford is a typical old-English episcopal see, dwarfed by the great red stone pile of the cathedral. Hereford is still relatively small. Even after the 1939–45 influx of factory workers, civil servants, and retirees, the town has still only 35,000 souls. Set in a warm, red-soiled countryside the town is within range of a hundred castles. Unfortunately rates are high, having almost doubled since 1938. The three Malverns too, on their surprisingly dramatic hills, are now very crowded places.

Coming east into Gloucestershire, we find the one English spa that can approach Bath in elegance and grace. Built largely in the Regency period by three gifted architects, Cheltenham enjoys a certain amount of planned harmony. Whole terraces and squares are built in one classical piece. Faced with cheerful stucco, or built of almost golden Cotswold stone, many of the older squares and crescents are a constant feast to the eye. Today Cheltenham is less favoured by the retired colonel and the Indian Civil Servant. Every year its streets become busier, its hotels and cafés more crowded. Population is rising at the surprising rate of nearly 1,000 a year in a town of around 70,000. Rates are high, but still only a few pence above those of Bath. As compensation there is now an adventurous theatre, some good music, and a lively social atmosphere.

'Crowded' is again the word that comes to mind when one thinks of that other midland spa, Leamington in Warwickshire. Here one seems to feel the pressure of the industrial midlands on all sides: two large factories now stand on the very fringe of the town. Built a little later than Cheltenham, Leamington too has some gracious pieces of stuccoed elegance to show. Smaller than Cheltenham (at 39,450), its population is rising at the rate of around 800 a year. Oddly enough its rates are considerably higher. Leamington's central garden is one of the most satisfying in any English town, thanks partly to its great trees. In Warwick, now almost adjoining the spa, the case is altered. Thanks to its magnificent castle, its gracious churches and hospital, the absence of factories, Warwick has even now an air of peace and far-off days. Despite its situation it remains a small country town (with low rates incidentally) and smacks far more of nearby Stratford than of its other neighbour, Coventry.

'Crowded' is again the word for Stratford in summer. The astonishing revival of interest in the theatre has packed Stratford with visitors each summer for the past ten years. Property values have soared. Building is in many cases wisely limited by the local authorities. Yet in winter this same little town is apt to seem quite dead; the commercial instinct of the Stratford city fathers has not yet focused on the possibilities of making it a winter resort. With the gracious country around and an invariably mild climate this may be considerable. Rates are about average.

To the west lie the two Worcestershire spas of Droitwich and Malvern. Droitwich is a small, successful private spa. Its spring is so rich in salt that one can sit up and balance a tea-tray on the buoyant water of its baths. The place's amenities are designed chiefly for the retiree suffering from a rheumatic or an arthritic complaint. But both Stratford and Warwick are near by.

There are few of the cities or towns of Britain which one can recommend honestly for permanent residence. Most of our cities, save Bath, Oxford and Cambridge, the cathedral towns of Ely, Hereford, Salisbury, Wells, and York, are either ugly, industrialized centres or old towns whose narrow streets are choked with traffic they were never designed to carry. Apart from its sauce, Worcester now makes everything from gloves and shoes to mining machinery. Gloucester is only less busy with the making of aeroplanes, while Chester, Durham, St Albans, and York are all crowded with traffic during most of the day. I have excepted Salisbury and York only because their attractions are so many that they outweigh the irritation of crowded pavements and hooting motor horns and because each lies in the centre of exquisite country.

Salisbury, like Hereford, is still small enough (about 34,500 population) to mix a country town freshness with the dignity of a cathedral city. A great army centre, its open spaces are not always free to the public. But from Salisbury one has the Plain as one possibility, Cranborne Chase as a second, Savernake Forest as a third.

For the retiree long in city pent, who wants to get away from his fellow men to genuine rural peace, Huntingdonshire is the county. Certainly this is the emptiest part of England. In the whole county there are but four small towns. Huntingdon, the county town, St Ives, St Neots, and the rural district of Normans Cross. Only one of these, St Ives, has a population of over 10,000. Looking very flat on the map Huntingdon is full of unexpectedly wide vistas of the broad countryside. Prioleau, that acute observer, called this the overlooked county and himself made a pilgrimage of apology. If the retiree who likes solitude can possibly wait until he gets a house built for him, Huntingdon may be a valuable discovery.

In Huntingdon we are not very far from one of the cities which one can commend with perfect safety – Cambridge. Although nearer London, Cambridge has escaped the industrialization of Oxford. With but 93,000 people it is still a university city with some of the atmosphere of a country town. Architecturally it is one of the most fascinating of our cities.

But the stone is grey, not golden, the country is flat and the sky windy, the great architecture restricted to a narrow area. In short for warmth in air and stone, for variety of vistas and a great array of noble buildings one must go to Oxford. In Cambridge rates are rather high and the level of assessment is difficult to judge. As in Oxford, the plans of the local authorities about both new streets and housing are still in debate.

Of Oxford it is difficult to speak with assurance. Its pavements are now the most crowded in Britain; you queue for almost everything; food is difficult; the city is still short of good restaurants, cafés, and snack bars. Shops, hotels, garages, traffic cops are all attempting to cope with three publics at once – the university's horde of teachers, students, and servants, the business and official community of a county town serving a wide area, the major shopping and entertainment needs of industrial Cowley. 'It is some way off from its old parents,' says an austere critic of Cowley, 'but its people, its shops, and its villas have encircled them and throttled their old throats.' A choleric overstatement, but unhappily not without truth. Apart from a few streets like the Broad, the roar of traffic is deafening. Fortunately several of the best bookshops, including Basil Blackwell's, shelter within its quiet walls. About them one can still potter at leisurely pace. Housing is extremely difficult but rates are reasonable (much lower than Cambridge) and the level of assessment moderate for the amenities provided. There are *two* first-rate theatres, any amount of interesting music, some of the finest libraries in Europe and societies devoted to every philosophy, creed and crankiness under the sun. But accommodation in Oxford is excruciatingly difficult: so difficult that one dare not recommend it.

Where can one discover a less overcrowded town with some of the grace, the social and cultural amenities that count so much in retirement? One answer is the English spas, our next quarry.

5

CLAIMS OF THE SPAS, RESORTS, AND COUNTRY TOWNS

ONE introduces the spas almost on a note of apology in these days. The modern retiree is so often bursting with health and energy that the mere idea of going to a spa jars on him. The waiting line of gouty colonels and arthritic old ladies, glass in hand at the Pump Room, is not what he wants. Only fifty years ago premature burial in Bath or Harrogate was immensely popular, deride it who will: today the special facilities of the spas for retirement seem to me to be overlooked. Worse, all spas are presumed to be expensive. This is untrue. Their peculiar advantages too are apt to be missed in a noisy age. To the retiree they are significant.

Every one of our English spas happens to lie amid lovely country. Every one of them is gracefully laid out, a few being the work of the great Georgian and Regency architects. Each attempts to provide entertainment and pleasant surroundings for people with leisure. Their atmosphere is tranquil. Medical services are exceptionally good: there are more doctors, better hospital accommodation than elsewhere.

Here let us face up to one unpleasant fact about old age. With the years, health is apt to deteriorate: in particular the wind bites more shrewdly. The spas are sheltered spots and they often provide additional shelter by way of arcaded streets, extra bus shelters, and large indoor reading-rooms, lounges, and cafés.

The number of really old people in this country who avoid every rheumatic, arterial, or chest ailment to the end is not large. In a spa one can have the correct treatment for any of these diseases easily and comfortably on the spot.

Of British spas Bath is the pearl. The one perfect eighteenth-century town in Europe, Bath lies in lovely country and is one of the best equipped and most efficient of our health resorts. Bombing did a good deal of damage to Bath during the Second World War: it has not obliterated the main pattern of this best-planned of English towns. Designed largely in its honey-coloured stone by the two Woods and by Baldwin between 1760 and 1810, Bath maintains the true Palladian style not merely in Pump and Assembly Room but in church and chapel. One or two old streets are so narrow that wheeled traffic is impossible. How delightful is their quiet!

The air of Bath may be a trifle languid, the city lying in a cup, but all around are the gentle Somerset hills for walking or motoring. If the rain be gentle, the sunshine mild, the city lies far enough west to enjoy an exceptional amount of light in the last winter months of February and March. Still a small place, Bath has everything you want at its centre. But the little city is now far too crowded for comfort. The Admiralty staffs occupy a lot of office space as well as villas and flats. Houses and flats are unusually expensive. Parking a car in the centre of the town is often impossible. It is even difficult to get an invalid really near the Baths. And the Baths are crowded with patients under the National Health Service from the surrounding area. One feels

that Bath is so fabulously prosperous that it is no
longer interested in being either a great spa or a social
centre of cultural charm.

Harrogate is even more happily situated than Bath.
One half as well designed, it has beauty and dignity in
many of its parts, but the surrounding country is unbeatable in England for variety and beauty. You are
within driving distance of the Lakes and, to the north-
east, of the vast North Riding moors. In a run of but
eighty miles you can cover hills 800 to 1,400 feet high,
endless moors, austere little towns, historic castles and
abbeys. There is every sort of scenery around Harrogate—
and a great stretch of green common (The Stray) in
the town itself. Rates are low and housing is *relatively*
easy.

Close though it be to the smoke of Sheffield and Manchester, Buxton too is situated in the midst of splendid
country. The retiree who chooses the Derbyshire spa
has the Peak country on his doorstep and he can explore at his leisure the whole of the rolling north
Staffordshire uplands. He should plan his longer trips
carefully to avoid the surrounding centres of industry:
it can be done. The little limestone town of Buxton,
struggling up its hill, has a most graceful centre, with
its limestone crescent, Pump Room, attractive theatre,
and shopping centre. The cleverly laid out gardens
run the whole length of the lower town and allow
one to cut out the streets on the way to one's abode.
As Buxton proper is a small spa, everything is most
conveniently situated. Here the authority really sets
itself out to deal with bad weather, providing a winter
garden, a concert hall, a roomy promenade, a large

café, and a theatre all under one roof – and within a
hundred yards of the Pump Room. Buxton is always
bracing; it is a winter sports venue: *per contra* it can be
bitterly cold by October and its north wind bites
shrewdly. Here too rates are moderate and housing
relatively easy, nor is the level of rating high; an
uncommon feature in a prosperous spa. Culturally
Harrogate has less to offer than it once had. The
charming Repertory Theatre has had latterly the
poorest and most spasmodic support. There are fewer
orchestral concerts and recitals. Why this setback to the
more intelligent amusements since the Second World
War? Nobody seems to know: so TV is blamed
locally.

If Bath and Buxton be the oldest spas in Britain, Tunbridge Wells runs them close. It was in 1606 that the
dissolute young Dudley, third Lord North, found that
the waters from a local well gradually cured his
complaints: in fact for his generation he lived to be a
very old man. However, Tunbridge's heyday as a spa
came in the eighteenth century when Pitt the Elder,
Dr Johnson, David Garrick, and Sir Joshua Reynolds
took their frequent 'cures' there. Today Tunbridge
still has its Pump Room and chalybeate spring at the
end of the Pantiles. But the town is now first a London
dormitory and only incidentally a spa.

Standing 400 feet up, only thirty-six miles (fifty
minutes) from London, the town is unique in having a
gorse-covered common of 170 acres running right into
its centre. Shops are attractive, especially those in the
Pantiles, the High Street, and Mount Pleasant road. An
enterprising municipal theatre and a good concert hall

are among the town's other amenities. Rates and the level of assessment are about average.

In Tunbridge Wells we are already in Kent, county of downs and apple orchards, of rich clay and light sandy soil, narrow winding roads that end so often in white cliffs and the sea. For many new retirees, however, Kent has a special appeal. Living is cheaper than in any other south coast county, saving always the remoter parts of Dorset. I recommend the retiree of limited means to study it before Sussex and Hampshire, Devon and Cornwall.

Even in Kent, however, generalization about living costs is perilous. Folkestone is one of the few seaside towns left to us in which a trace of elegance still lingers. But living in Folkestone, if not dear, is not cheap. Living in Broadstairs, Margate, Ramsgate, Deal, and Dover, however, *can* be relatively cheap. To begin with, your house costs less. Your rates are high. So is your assessment. But shop prices are exceptionally moderate. The style of living is relatively simple. Private cars are fewer. Cafés and restaurants are moderate in their charges. Yet you are among some of the loveliest rolling country in England; the air is tonic; the hours of sunshine are well over average; rainfall is well below it.

Dover was badly mauled during the war, but the town is recovering rapidly. It *is* a naval port, however, and therefore a busy, workaday little town rather than a seaside resort. Deal is still an old fishing village despite its population of over 23,000; the town is full of interesting old houses, some Georgian and Regency; but it is exposed to the full force of Channel gales;

one has so rarely seen Deal on a quiet day! While everything else is cheap, rates are high owing to the cost of storm damage and coast erosion. There is a tiny artists' colony at Deal and one or two writers have made their homes there.

Of the attractions of Margate and Ramsgate there is no need to speak. They are bits of London-by-the-sea. The air is magnificent, the social atmosphere matey, the pubs many and splendiferous. Ramsgate has placed many of its hotels and shops well above its busy beach, so that the visitor may enjoy company or quiet at will. Rates unfortunately are high at both places for the usual coastal reasons.

In some ways Folkestone is unique among English seaside resorts. Like Ramsgate it stands on chalk cliffs far above the sea; unlike most of our resorts, its designers had the sense to plan the hotels and boarding-houses far back from the edge of the cliffs. The result is the incomparable stretch of short springy turf, called The Leas, looking out on the Channel. On the edge of the cliff nestles the Pavilion, one of the most modern in the country. The sunny open balconies seem to lean out over the sea. Excellent shops, well-kept, sheltered gardens, an unusually good repertory theatre, and the busy little Channel port down below, complete Folkestone's charms. France is very near: a day trip can be made comfortably. Folkestone's one drawback is the unattractive country near by. One needs a car to come near the Downs or any other pleasant scenery easily. For the over-seventies, however, the town is almost ideal, owing to its sheltered pavilion and gardens and the level shopping streets in the centre. (It will be even better when the corporation provides inconspicuous shelters on the front. Today there are but temporary canvas wind-breaks to shelter one from Channel storms.) All this may be worth paying for by the sacrifice of some living amenities.

Sussex is the retiree's county. Today a quarter of a million people live in the Brighton area alone. There is practically no break in the buildings along the thirty-odd miles of coast between Bognor and Brighton. Too much of the building was done in the jerry-building boom of the twenties. The retiree must avoid buying the asbestos-roofed bungalow, the jerry-built villa, the wooden house (outside Kent and East Sussex where the wooden-frame house is native).

Brighton itself is still a delight to the eye. Spoiled much of the old town may be, but look what is left to gladden the soul! The show terraces and crescents still face the Channel. 'On a silvery day,' avers Betjeman, 'the reflection of the sea on to white and yellow stone, rising above wind-slashed veronica and tamarisk, lightens the heart and lifts up the rheumatic from his bath chair.'

Nominally Hove is just West Brighton; physically and statistically it may be but a part of Brighton; economically a gulf yawns between the two. Brighton's Income Levels Index is low for a seaside resort at 106: at 119 Hove's is the highest in the country, the town sharing this expensive eminence with Bournemouth. While Hove rates are below Brighton's, houses cost considerably more at Hove and most things are a little dearer. But for this expensiveness Hove has many wares to offer.

The nearest of the smaller and quieter Sussex resorts

to Brighton is Worthing (10 miles). Few seaside towns are growing faster. Since 1931 Worthing has increased its population by well over one-third. Not many smaller towns have so many would-be residents waiting to find the right accommodation. Fortunately the three less crowded villages of Goring, Angmering, and Rustington are all within easy reach of Worthing's attractions.

All of these resorts lie west of Brighton. To the east are Seaford, Eastbourne, Bexhill, and Hastings (in that order). All of these resorts are relatively inexpensive, although Bexhill is a considerably quieter and more elegant place than any of the others. Unfortunately it lacks the protection from the north winds that Hastings and Eastbourne enjoy. Bexhill's de la Warr Pavilion is the finest building of its kind in the kingdom, if not in Europe, containing a charming and technically perfect theatre, a concert room, lecture rooms, café, sun lounges, and sun terrace under one roof.

Eastbourne is of course a smaller, more elegant, and more sophisticated Brighton. With the sea before and the Downs behind, with its well-planned and colourful gardens and fine promenade, Eastbourne is one of the most amiable of all our resorts. Only about a quarter of Brighton's size, it has no proliferated sprawling suburbs: indeed Eastbourne grows slowly. Yet it possesses most of the amenities of Brighton and Bourne-mouth, two theatres, seven cinemas, many department stores. Rates are exceptionally low. But an Income Levels Index of 114 does not suggest an economical place to live. However, Eastbourne is large enough to allow of many standards of living.

As a place Hastings is the oldest of our seaside resorts; the town is just 1,500 years old. Although Hastings and St Leonards are one borough they are two contrasting places. Hastings is still an old fishing town, with its small fleet, with many a narrow winding street sprinkled with Tudor buildings. In all, 146 buildings are scheduled as of historic interest. Also it is a popular seaside resort competing with Margate and Ramsgate for the summer holiday crowds and the day tripper.

St Leonards is entirely modern in the architectural sense. Its sheltered squares and Regency terraces are largely the work of the architect, Decimus Burton, who founded the spa in 1827. (His love of Gothic is only too apparent in some of his private houses.) Rates in Hastings are average, assessments are moderate and new blocks of modern flats are beginning to appear.

Now we can turn west again into Hampshire. Today Bournemouth may well house more retirees than Brighton itself. Built in Victorian and Edwardian days the town is almost devoid of architectural charm. No resort's success and resulting expansion was ever less happily timed from that viewpoint. But timing is a complex influence in resort planning. From the angle of town design the rise of Bournemouth was perfectly timed. As a result the town is by far the best planned large resort that we possess in Britain.

The beautiful sweep of its bay, the curving line of its tawny cliffs, the miles of its gently sloping golden sands remain completely intact and untouched. The series of wooded ravines, known as chines, that run down to the sea are unspoiled. The long chain of gardens running inland are all flat, elegant, and ideal for gentle exercise.

In short, Bournemouth has everything – very low rates, sheltered position, warm climate, flat roads, magnificent shops, cafés, cinemas, a fine pavilion, an orchestra capable of the Beethoven symphonies, first-rate schools, libraries, museums, churches of every denomination, including the most esoteric. So the town is now the most prosperous in these islands, and it continues to expand in all directions.

For those who really like modern urban ways of life this is delightful. For those who happen to dislike the social round it may be less attractive. It is wise for this minority to realize that although Bournemouth counts but 145,000 people compared with Brighton and Hove's 225,000, there are now around 260,000 souls housed within a ten-mile circumference of the Square. Inevitably this makes the countryside less easily accessible from the centre. It increases necessary travel and therefore raises one's cost of living.

Into nearby Poole and we are already in Dorset. Outside Weymouth, Swanage, and Poole itself, a cheerful port-cum-seaside resort, Dorset is largely for the walker, the farmer, and the antiquarian. To the retiree looking for quiet, historical ground, literary associations, Dorset is inviting. It includes most of Hardy's Wessex. The county town of Dorchester is 'Casterbridge', Sherborne is Sherton Abbas, and so on. Corfe Castle (a ruin) and Milton Abbas are but the most famous of the county's ancient buildings. Its aged little towns like Wareham, the gate of Purbeck; Cerne Abbas; Abbotsbury, by the great swannery; Blandford, still a completely Georgian town; Wimborne, with its minster; Shaftesbury, perched 700 feet up on its hill; Sherborne on the Yeo, are all stored with antiquity. Each of these lovely old towns has a spacious setting of Dorset down, or Purbeck Hills, or Cranborne Chase itself.

This tranquil countryside is so rich in by-roads that most of its beauties can be explored without using main roads. For the retiree anxious to enjoy such quiet beauty, there is one serious difficulty. Dorset is largely unspoiled, spacious, cheap to live in, but few houses were built outside Poole, Weymouth, and Swanage between or even after the wars. With these exceptions too, Dorset towns are small. Dorchester itself has only 11,660 souls, Blandford just 16,000, Shaftesbury around 13,000, Sherborne (less its Rural District) 8,000! Finally, the building of houses, provided a licence can be obtained, is expensive. For to build of Purbeck stone, in Dorset style, means the employment of the skilled stone-mason with his chisel. Outside Poole and Wareham with their potteries, the use of brick involves considerable transport costs. Altogether the finding or building of a home in Dorset is a problem. There are signs that this situation must gradually become easier. In the larger towns rates are surprisingly high, in the smaller they are quite bearable.

Neighbouring Somerset is a big, spacious county of small, sleepy towns, and large busy farms. Everything else here is smaller, more domestic, more intimate than in Dorset. Lower hills, fewer wild, open moors, quiet rivers. The almost inevitable approach to Somerset's green lands that yield such surprisingly broad views is through Bath. Taking the road to Wells, with possibly the most picturesquely placed of our cathedrals, we quickly reach the Vale of Avalon and Glastonbury, coming south through Somerton to Yeovil. If we bear left through Crewkerne and Honiton to the tiny resort of Seaton, we have almost traversed Somerset, from north to south. On Somerset's long northern coast there is a galaxy of large resorts, chief of which is Weston-super-Mare, favourite holiday haunt of both Cardiff and Bristol folk, Burnham-on-Sea, and Minehead, on the borders of the Doone country.

On the whole transport and housing are less difficult in this prosperous farming county than in Dorset; food is exceptionally plentiful, varied, and good; rates, alas, are almost uniformly high in the large towns (for reasons unknown to me). Somerset is above all a comfortable county, rich in food, fruit, and flowers. The people are often slow of speech, cautious in temperament but friendly when they come to know you.

Most places in South Devon and Cornwall enjoy enviable temperatures in winter. Devon's moors and coast, Cornwall's wild coasts, Italianate bays and tiny rock-bound harbours on the south coast, are among the glories of English scenery. Spacious as it is, Devon is a county of crowded beaches in summer. The car has made both counties favourite playgrounds for the motorist. The most secluded of their villages and beaches are apt to be busy in the holiday season, while the great resorts like Torquay, Teignmouth, Falmouth, and Penzance are crowded to capacity from July to September. In all of the latter, rates are rather high (Torquay's stand at 20s. 10d.), houses are rather expensive yet assessments are generally low.

Torquay, conspicuously well run both by its council

and by its hoteliers, is easily the most fashionable and resourceful of our larger resorts. No coast town has dealt more rapidly or tastefully with its war damage. Torquay shops are full of enterprise. But the cost of living, if high, is not exceptionally so for the amenities provided. Also Torquay is still small enough to make all its attractions easily accessible. Only its steep hills are a drawback to the elderly or infirm: nearby Paignton, however, lies on easy, level ground.

North Wales appeals to many retirees, especially to the northerner and the midlander, whose playground it always has been. As with Cornwall both the land and the people need knowing. Most of it is up and down country, mountainous, wind-swept, dull in winter, save in some sunny sheltered valleys in the west. Here too one must not fear solitude, must respect deep religious beliefs, must be prepared to come slowly into local society. That society is often a little simple and rough: the people are none the less warm-hearted for that.

The Welsh seaside resorts, too, are crowded during summer months. This is especially true of Llandudno, Colwyn Bay, and Rhyl. The smaller places farther south, like Barmouth and Aberdovey, are quieter. Clough Williams-Ellis's model spa of Portmerion, mecca of the aesthetes of the twenties, is one of the loveliest (and warmest) spots in these islands.

Quiet and uncrowded places even today are the island of Anglesey, with its port of Holyhead, and the fortunately overlooked county of Radnor, which includes Radnor Forest and the little spa of Llandrindod Wells, but not its smaller competitor, Builth. In both areas I am afraid that too much solitude rather than too much company would be the risk, if one chose to live outside Holyhead and Llandrindod Wells.

'Why not retire to the broad open spaces of central or northern Scotland?' one is sometimes asked. A reasonable question. Scotland is not crowded, let alone overcrowded, over most of its area. Many hundreds of square miles of it are empty. Her roads have been immensely improved in the last thirty years so that access to the cities is now easy from the smallest villages. Food is often much better and more plentiful than in most parts of England. It is not, however, so varied: 'the land of cakes' enjoys its glorious scones and buns at the price of a too starchy diet.

Two reasons keep people from south of the border from migrating to Scotland. One is the acute housing shortage (see page 50), the other the severity of the weather. The first reason is well grounded. Poverty and apathy have kept back building for half a century, so that now almost every town in Scotland is short of houses. The climate is perhaps a little maligned. However much the drier east may suffer from biting winds, the moister west is far warmer and more genial than most people imagine.

The two most attractive centres for retirement in Scotland are undoubtedly Edinburgh (see page 51), and St Andrews. The latter town is as mellow as Oxford. Its fourteenth-century cathedral and its thirteenth-century castle lie all in ruins, but some of its beautiful university buildings are untouched from the fifteenth century. Still delightfully small (about 9,000), St Andrews is a seaport, a health resort, a university city, and headquarters of golf all in one. Perhaps the most exciting day in the St Andrews calendar is that on which a new captain of the Royal and Ancient Golf Club plays himself into office. In term time the short scarlet gowns of the students give a touch of colour to the always bright streets, reminding one of Grenoble. Living is *relatively* cheap at St Andrews, but not so cheap as in many other parts of Scotland. The town is too fashionable, the people too businesslike for that. Life is much cheaper in some of the pleasant little border towns like Peebles, with its huge hydro, Selkirk, and tiny Dryburgh, near its abbey. In all of these housing is still the difficulty.

Apart from the really melancholy weather, with its supercharge of mist and its eternal drizzle, the Highlands of Scotland are handicapped for pleasant living by their poor planning. There are one or two happy exceptions to the dreary rule. One is Pitlochry, a sheltered spa north of Aberfeldy. Another is Grantown on Spey, between Kingussie and Inverness, a small town built round a very broad, tree-lined street that has an almost Georgian spaciousness and symmetry. A third is the charming little spa of Strathpeffer, near Dingwall in Ross and Cromarty.

'Where can I live under a level of taxation that will reduce my inadequate pension by less than 7s. 9d. in the pound?' asks many a retiree. The obvious answer is one of the self-governing islands round our coasts. The advantages offered by the Channel Islands are plain to see: those of the Isle of Man are less obvious.

In one way the Isle is unique among favoured islands. It is not crowded, let alone overcrowded, outside the holiday months. Some 227 square miles support only

around 60,000 people, or 220 to the square mile.
Jersey packs a population of 60,000 into its 45 square
miles, about 1,330 to the square mile. So on the Isle
one never has the sense of being crowded into a corner.
There are no large towns; Douglas has but 23,500 and
the second town, Ramsey, only 4,600. These are exceptional advantages in our day.

The rate of income tax is 4s. 6d. in the pound. This
is 6d. above Jersey and Guernsey, but the allowances
are exceptionally generous. After allowances, the rates
paid by an individual are 2s. 3d. on the first £250 of
taxable income, 3s. 0d. on the next £250, and 3s. 9d.
on the next £250. Allowance for a single person is
£200, for a married person £350. Allowance for a
housekeeper is £100. There are no death duties.
Surtax was abolished in April 1961, when the necessary
Bill to abolish it should have passed its final stage in the
House of Keys.

The islanders are proud of the equable climate they
enjoy. The extreme variation of temperature between
summer and winter is only 17.1 degrees compared with
Bournemouth's 21.4 and Brighton's 23.5. Average hours
of sunshine (1921–50) are 1,562, best for the north-west
but below the top regions in the south.

In one very desirable way the Isle is probably
unique today. There is no housing shortage. For once
the would-be resident is not in a seller's market. His
needs will be carefully and helpfully considered. This
local authority is clearly anxious to attract residents,
permanent residents.

The island has three minor disadvantages only. It is
damp: yearly rainfall in Douglas (1916–50) averaged

45.17 in. Like all islands it suffers severe winter gales such as the suburban dweller inland never knows. The TT races are still held there every year, with all that involves in noise and upset. And every summer half-a-million holiday-makers and trippers descend on a few popular places.

The level of taxation in the Channel Islands is even lower. The standard rate of income tax is 4s. in the £ in both islands. Neither super-tax nor death duties are levied on property within the islands. Jersey has just (for 1961) raised the married couples' allowance to £400, and abolished Entertainment Tax and hospital charges. Tobacco and cigarettes, whisky and gin, tend to cost around half the British price. Here the property market has not broken as it did in Britain in the early fifties when the banks and the building societies sharply shortened credit. So house prices remain as high as they were in Britain at the height of the post-war boom, when so many ex-service and other retirees were attracted to the Channel Islands. At that time speculators drove some prices up above the peak British levels. There were small houses built pre-war for around £700 that changed hands for around £7,000. So it is now difficult to find accommodation at a moderate price. But Jersey offers great opportunities of saving to the heavier surtax payer and quieter Guernsey to the retiree with a modest pension. I examined the position in both islands carefully for individual chapters in my *Retire into the Sun* (1961). It must be remembered too that both the Channel Islands and the Isle of Man are exposed to heavy gales throughout the winter which are apt to rob the town-dweller of his sleep. Few city suburbs ever experience anything like the fury and the racket of the sea gales that howl across these small islands.

To retire to the Isle of Wight brings no relaxation in the income tax man's demands. Although the island returns its own member to Westminster, it is administratively merely a part of Hampshire. The devotion of yachtsmen to Cowes and of Queen Victoria to Ventnor, once made both the northern and southern tips of the island fashionable and expensive. Today Cowes is a busy seaport, with engineering, rope, and shipbuilding works on both sides of the river. Ventnor remains one of the mildest and most genial of our resorts. Little Sandown, a golfing centre on the east coast, actually holds the sunshine record for these islands over many years. To the north lies Ryde, sophisticated modern resort, with its two-mile-long promenade and its half-mile of pier. Almost everywhere the island offers more hours of sunshine and fewer cold winds than most of the mainland.

Although only 147 square miles in area, the island contains over a hundred miles of motoring roads. While living is not noticeably dear, one must remember that the trip across the Solent does add transport costs to almost everything except food and a boat. My own favourite spot is the breezy and less sheltered Freshwater Bay where the air is never languid nor August's heat oppressive.

The days in which you could live in the south or west of Ireland 'for almost nothing' are long past. Nowadays the cost of living is high in Dublin especially, partly because the Irishman prefers to pay a little more for a good cigarette made at home than for an imported article, however excellent. From the point of view of cheap living, Eire has ceased to compete. From that of an easy-going way of life and of social charm it is still unmatchable.

Now we can turn to the pressing problem of how to get the most out of one's pension at home.

6

MAKING THE MOST OF YOUR CAPITAL

by Gordon Cummings

FOR most people retirement means a cut in income. Naturally, its extent depends on individual circumstances. But, as a general rule, the number of us who will be left with more than two-thirds to three-quarters of our average income for the last few years at work is small. Apart from National Insurance pension, *your* retirement income will depend on (*a*) any pension from employment; (*b*) the investment of any lump sum from a retirement scheme or maturing endowment assurances; and (*c*) redeployment of your savings and investments to give the maximum income – with or without taking risks.

However, retirement usually has some financial compensation in a reduction in expenses. Travelling and lunches out are eliminated or sharply reduced; less may be needed for clothes; and it may be practicable, or desirable, to move to a smaller, cheaper-to-run house or flat in a less expensive and more suitable area. But for some, expenses may not fall, they may even rise; for retirement brings the chance to do things impossible while at work, such as travel, theatre- and concert-going, taking more interest in golf, bowls, and other sport, pursuing money-consuming hobbies or being simply one of those types who naturally spend more money when there is time to relax.

Whatever your circumstances and inclinations, the first financial step must be an exhaustive assessment of your resources, both income and capital, and your likely expenditure. If you have no savings or property and your only source of income will be pensions, the exercise will be simple, though possibly disheartening. As with Mr Micawber, a surplus of income over expenses will result in happiness, a deficit in misery. But if pensions can be augmented by investment income the wise use of your capital may considerably improve the position.

The vital starting-point in your financial planning will almost certainly be that of producing enough income to cover annual outlay – or to prune the latter to make the account balance. An expenditure and income budget must be drawn up. The expenditure side will have to provide for all, or most, of the following items:

Expenditure Budget

Rent (or mortgage payments)
Rates and water
Electricity, gas, and heating
Home insurance
Repairs, maintenance, and renewals
Food
Cleaning, laundry, and domestic help
Clothes
Newspapers, magazines, and books
TV licence, and running expenses
Tobacco and drink
Subscriptions and church
Entertainment and recreation
Holidays, birthdays, etc.

Life assurance premiums
Telephone and postages
Garden
Car (including depreciation)
Travelling
Miscellaneous
Emergencies

Total

You will be able to estimate some items pretty accurately. Others, like repairs and renewals, will however be spasmodic and unpredictable – which will mean trying to average them out.

Items in the income side of the budget will be relatively few and will include all, or some, of the following:

Income Budget

National insurance pension
Employment pension
Annuity
Investment income
Net income from property

Total gross income
Less Income tax

Net income

Deducting one from the other, the net amount left will be your surplus or deficit. If the latter, the gap will have to be filled from part-time work (if practicable and possible to find something suitable), by trying to prune expenses, by assistance from relatives, or by drawing on savings.

One item on the expenditure side which no amount of thought will enable you to calculate is *inflation*. Pious government hopes notwithstanding, there is little doubt that the cost of living will continue to creep upwards for as far as we can see ahead. Today's budget, however generously you try to allow for contingencies, may thus be knocked haywire in twelve months and be completely unrealistic in a few years' time. Unless you are one of the relatively small band whose employment pension is linked to the cost of living, or you have invested some or all of your capital to produce rising dividends, an awkward financial chasm may begin to open. On past performance, your national insurance pension will tag some way behind the rise in living costs.

The inflation headache rams home one vital aspect of retirement finance – *the right deployment of your savings*. What may be good and desirable investments when you are getting a good earned income liable to high tax rates may be unsuitable, even unwise, when income drops and, with it, your tax bills.

Most of us who can save money out of our earned incomes are much more, or should be much more, concerned with investments paying tax-free interest or giving promise of capital growth than with those giving high dividend yields which are whittled down by income tax and sur-tax. We concentrate therefore on Savings Certificates, with their complete tax exemption; on Building Society shares and deposits, with their freedom from further income tax; on Premium Savings Bonds, with their allure of tax-free prizes; and on the growth type of Stock Exchange securities. We also probably have endowment assurances maturing at, or near to, retirement age. Retirement changes the investment emphasis.

The second financial job therefore is to list *all* your investments, savings, and money to come from endowment assurances, lump sum payments from a pension scheme, and any other sources which will swell your capital fund. From the total you can start to work out the income which its wisest redeployment will produce and whether this will fill the gap on your expenses budget; or, if there is a surplus, provide more for non-essentials or to build up a reserve against rainy days. Your policy will be governed by the capital available, your attitude to particular types of investment and any outstanding commitments like repayment of a mortgage or provision for children, grandchildren, or other dependents on your death. Assuming that the maximum income is wanted and your capital is sufficient for manoeuvre, the first step is to weed out the less remunerative investments. The following summaries should help:

SAVINGS BANK ACCOUNTS. Post Office and ordinary department accounts in Trustee Savings Banks pay only 2½ per cent interest. While the first £15 a year is tax-free, this is not of much advantage if you pay little or no tax. On the other hand, most Trustee Savings Banks offer 4½–5 per cent on special investment department accounts in which you can put up to £3,000 and be able to withdraw on giving one to three or six months notice. As discussed later, such an account can be very useful for your emergency fund or as an easy-to-run investment.

SAVINGS CERTIFICATES. With the exception of the tenth issue, which gives the highest interest in the 6th and 7th years, it pays to cash all old issues of certificates if your tax rate is low. Apart from the eleventh issue, with an average interest of 3.8 per cent over its six year life, the maximum interest now paid on other old issues is no more than about $3\frac{5}{8}$ per cent. Income tax cannot be reclaimed on such income.

PREMIUM SAVINGS BONDS. The more Bonds held the greater your chance of winning large or small prizes in the monthly draws. Otherwise, they do not pay interest, which gives pause for thought if you want a regular income. Hence, though it may be tempting to hold Bonds for a juicy prize, it may be unwise to have too large a part of your savings in them. The working compromise if you hold a large number is to cash one-half and to invest the proceeds in something paying regular interest.

BUILDING SOCIETIES. One advantage of this type of investment is that the society pays the income tax on the interest. It does so however at a specially compounded rate which is supposed to be the average due by all such investors. A condition of this arrangement is that investors cannot reclaim any tax, even though they are completely exempt from it. When you fall below the standard rate of income tax it follows therefore that, apart from keeping some money in the society as an emergency reserve, it pays to change to investments where tax can be reclaimed from the interest.

BANK ACCOUNTS. Current accounts are useful for various kinds of payments. There is not much point however in keeping a larger balance than to cover, say, three months' needs. Though it is true that the bank charges for running accounts on which the credit balance is below a certain figure, it is equally true that the surplus can generally be invested to bring in substantially more than the corresponding charges. Deposit accounts can also be useful: but as the whole of the interest is liable to tax there are more profitable forms of investment. As a retired person, use a bank deposit account only for money which is *temporarily* not needed.

OUTSTANDING MORTGAGE. Retirement raises the question of the advisability of clearing any mortgage on your house. One key factor in the decision is how the interest paid on it compares with the interest you could earn on a correspondingly secure investment. The chances are that the mortgage rate is the higher. From this angle it therefore pays to clear the mortgage and, in the process, be free of making the monthly repayments. In fact, a good general rule is that it only pays to keep a mortgage going if you are ready to risk the corresponding capital in share investments which give the chance of capital appreciation – the theory is that you borrow money at a fixed value to invest in securities which will grow in value and thus secure a capital gain.

CHANGING HOUSES. Running costs can be saved and some cash capital provided by selling a larger house and buying a smaller one – in theory, anyhow. The major problem in this inflationary age is of course to get what you want and to be left all square or with a surplus on the transaction. Success depends on the market value of your present house, what you need in exchange, and where you wish to remove. Popular retirement places, particularly in southern England, have seen equal, even greater, rises in house prices to anywhere else. You may thus have to pay more for a smaller and less suitable house. However, if running costs will be reduced it may pay you to move, providing little or no extra capital has to be put into the new house.

Having done this important side of the investment job you can move on to the business of rearranging your portfolio. This you may be able to look after yourself. If however the amount is large or you have little or no experience of Stock Exchange operations or other financial affairs, do not hesitate to consult the appropriate experts at the earliest possible stage. Your *bank manager* can be a useful starting point; he can advise generally on your whole problem. A *stockbroker* is essential if you have more than a few hundred pounds to invest in Stock Exchange securities – although the bank can do such business on your behalf it is sometimes better to deal direct with the man who will provide the expertise, particularly if you can easily make contact with a member of the London Stock Exchange or there is a member of one of the other Exchanges near at hand in the provinces. An *insurance broker* is able to provide valuable help in any necessary rearrangement of policies and the purchase of an annuity. And if you do not have an account with one of the commercial banks but have one with the *Trustee Savings Bank* the manager of the latter may be able to assist. Your *solicitor* or *accountant* can also be consulted on appropriate matters. With these basic moves well in mind you can now consider the merits or otherwise of the main types of investment suitable for retirement.

A RESERVE FUND on which you can draw quickly

to meet a financial emergency, or through which you can accumulate money for some need a short time ahead, is virtually a must if your capital is limited. It may mean some loss of income, but on the amount which should normally be involved this is of little account compared with the freedom from worry it may give. The sum so invested clearly depends on individual circumstances. As little as £50 or £100 may do in some cases. In others it may call for several hundreds. A building society, if there is one handy, is a good choice; up to £50 can usually be withdrawn immediately, and larger sums on giving a few days' notice. Alternatively, though the interest is less, the Post Office Savings Bank may be handier; up to £10 can be withdrawn on one day and larger amounts normally within a week. The local Trustee Savings Bank also provides simple facilities for withdrawal of larger sums over the counter from an ordinary department account; and, as shown later, you can get $4\frac{1}{2}$–5 per cent on a special investment department account and know that any amount can be withdrawn on giving one to three or six months' notice.

ANNUITIES can be a good way of obtaining a high rate of income until you die. An important point however is that their purchase means the using up of capital. They should be considered therefore only if you are ready to let the investment die with you. The reason is that in return for the money paid the insurance office undertakes to pay the annuitant a regular income until death. The annual income is thus made up partly of interest and partly of a capital, an important fact which the Inland Revenue recognizes by taxing only part of the annuity – depending on age, the tax-free part is up to

two-thirds or three-quarters. Three noteworthy variations to the simple annuity are: first, you may arrange
for payments to be *guaranteed* for a minimum number of
years such as ten; second, a married man concerned
about a continuing income for his wife has the choice of
a *joint annuity* which continues until the death of both
parties, or of a *survivorship annuity* which carries on at a
lower rate on the death of one party; and three, forward
provision for retirement can be made by buying a *deferred
annuity* which does not come into operation until an
agreed age ahead. Rates offered by the insurance offices
vary. But a fair guide is that a man aged 65 could buy a
gross annual income of some £111 for each £1,000 invested, of which over £70 would be tax-free. Because of
the greater expectation of life, a woman of the same age
would get about £97 with a little over £57 tax-free.
Practical general rules are not to put all your capital
into annuities – keep some money in securities which can
be realized quickly to meet emergencies or special needs
– and if a compromise is desirable divide your capital
about equally between an annuity and other types of
investment.

GOVERNMENT STOCKS, or 'The Funds' as they
once were called, used to be looked on as the primest of
sound investments. They provided a steady income and
their market value did not fluctuate very widely. World
wars and inflation have brought drastic changes. Some
stocks like $3\frac{1}{2}$ per cent War Loan have fallen to little more
than one-half their face value and the annual income
buys only a fraction of what it did in 1938. Despite these
trends, some of these stocks can be worth consideration
for a portion of your investment portfolio. Broadly, they

fall into four categories. *Short-dated* stocks are those which are repayable at their par value within five years. Buyers thus know that they will get £100 for each £100 of stock at a certain date; and that if they buy at less than £100 there will be a capital profit in addition to the regular interest. Such issues are useful investments if you know that money will be required at a short date ahead. The market prices are the least liable to fluctuate. *Medium-dated* stocks have a life of 5–15 years and they therefore tend to fluctuate more in value. Generally however they offer higher yields and bigger redemption profits. *Long-dated* stocks have lives of over 15 years, with some repayment dates stretching into the next century. Price fluctuations are still more varied and wide, though the higher yield on market prices is some compensation. *Undated* stocks have no repayment date or are repayable only at the option of the government on or after certain dates. This small sector sees the widest fluctuations and offers the highest yields. If your main concern is an assured income it is best to stick to these issues and long-dated ones. For example, if you can buy £100 of a 3½ per cent stock at a market price of £60 the income yield is the good one of £5 16s. 8d. per cent for a long time ahead, or indefinitely in the case of an undated stock.

Local Authorities raise a good part of their loan capital through what can be called 'tap' offers to the public at large, who are invited to invest at a fixed rate of interest for periods of from, say, two to five, seven or ten years. The interest depends on monetary conditions at the time of investment, and in recent years it has varied roughly between five to seven per cent. Attractions are that you know you will get a certain income for a definite number of years, that there will be no fluctuations in market prices as with securities quoted on the stock Exchange, and that such investments are absolutely safe. Moreover, if you are fortunate enough to make your investment when interest rates are high, you will enjoy the benefits for the whole period of your loan. Contrariwise, if you invest when rates are low you will not benefit from any subsequent rise. A good rule therefore is to invest for the maximum time if you think that interest rates are at a peak, but for the shortest time if they are low and look like rising in fairly quick time. Whatever your action, it should be noted that the money has to be left for the agreed term of years; the council will only repay earlier in case of emergency. Details of current terms can be found in advertisements in local and national newspapers.

NATIONAL DEVELOPMENT BONDS are another useful type of security which does not fluctuate in value. They can be bought easily through the Savings and other banks up to specified limits; the interest is fixed for a definite number of years; at the end of this term repayment is made at par with a tax-free bonus; and, after six months, they can be cashed at their full value on one month's notice. Although the interest on the series currently on offer may be somewhat lower than you could obtain on a long-dated Government stock or from a local authority, a possible advantage of Bonds is that income tax is not deducted from the half-yearly interest; which saves the trouble of making repayment claims if you are exempt from tax. A similar tax facility applies also to $3\frac{1}{2}$ per cent War Loan and to Government stocks bought through the Post Office and Trustee Savings Banks and going on to their special registers. Subject to a limit of £1,000 a day, most Goverment stocks can be bought to qualify for this facility.

TRUSTEE SAVINGS BANKS, as already indicated, mostly have special investment departments on which a much higher interest is offered. At the time of writing it is possible, in fact, to get $4\frac{1}{2}$–5 per cent on investments of up to £3,000. The conditions are that at least £50 has to be kept in an ordinary department account and that notice of one to three or six months must be given for withdrawals. Taking account of the relatively high interest, S.I.D. accounts can be useful investments if you want to avoid tying up part or all of your capital for lengthy periods. Another advantage is that, although the interest is liable to tax in the appropriate cases, there is no such deduction from it; which avoids having to put in repayment claims if you are exempt from tax.

FINANCE COMPANIES carrying on hire purchase and similar business raise a large part of their resources by way of deposits repayable on varying terms of notice from, say, seven days to eleven months or more. Interest varies with the size and standing of the company and the withdrawal terms. While such investments can be useful and profitable for money which you do not wish to lock up for a long time, care is necessary in making a selection. In fact, this is the kind of investment where the good old rule of 'the higher the interest the greater the risk' applies. It is advisable therefore to step cautiously if the interest is more than about 1–2 per cent over Bank Rate, the pace-setter for all interest rates, and when in any doubt to take expert advice before parting with money.

Stock Exchange Company Securities provide a wide choice. You can, as with Government stocks mentioned earlier, concentrate on getting a fixed income year by year. Or, and this is where there is a chance to counter the inflationary bogey, you can invest part or all of your money in shares whose dividends depend on the success of the companies selected. First in the general line come *debentures* which, like a mortgage, are mostly secured on part or all of the assets of the company. Interest is payable whether it earns profits or not, and in the event of default debenture holders can foreclose or take other action to look after their security. Most issues are, however, repayable at stated dates or in certain circumstances. By sticking to sound, well-managed companies you can get, say, one-half to one per cent more interest than on Government stocks with similar lives. *Loan stocks*, though not usually secured like debentures, are also in the front line and give useful yields over periods which are usually up to ten or fifteen years. A variation which has become popular in recent years is the *convertible loan stock* which, as its name indicates, is a fixed interest stock having conversion rights into ordinary shares on certain terms – the investor is thus assured of a fixed income but if the company does well he has the chance to share in its future success by changing to the capital which, as seen later, takes the cream. *Preference shares* are self-descriptive. Though coming after debentures and loan stocks, they rank before other capital for dividends and for repayment if the company goes into liquidation. Dividends are payable only, however, out of profits, so that if these are not earned holders go without income. Most preference issues have some protection against such a contingency; their dividends are *cumulative*, which means that if there is not enough profit in one year to meet payments, the balance is carried forward for payment out of future profits. The greater risk is recognized in the higher dividend yields which preference shares give in comparison with debentures and loan stocks. They can therefore be attractive if you want a larger return on some or all of your capital. *Ordinary shares*, or the equity, are last in the line. They come in for all or most of the cream if the company prospers, but stand all or a great part of the losses if it does badly. Naturally, they fluctuate much more in market value than other issues and the dividend yield they offer varies in accordance with the risks involved and the future prospects of each company. Ordinary shares of, say, a stores company or one making goods in growing demand will give you less immediate income per £100 invested than a gold mine which depends for its future on how much metal can be profitably extracted. This is the type of capital which, however, gives what so many investors seek today – protection against inflation.

UNIT TRUSTS provide a practical way of spreading the risks in share investment. Under the management of experts, their funds are invested in a wide variety of shares or, with the specialized type of trust, in particular groups such as banks or insurance shares. The daily prices of the units broadly represent the market values of the investment portfolios after allowing for recognized buying and selling expenses. Unlike company securities, all the net income of the majority of trusts is distributed to unit-holders, generally half-yearly. Some trusts place emphasis on long-term capital growth and generally, therefore, offer relatively low immediate dividend yields. Others go for good immediate yields and are thus more suitable if you must have the maximum possible income.

PROPERTY can be a profitable form of investment, but only if you know something of the subject, can buy at favourable prices, and realize that against the rents receivable you will have to allow for unpredictable expenses such as repairs and maintenance. Your living expenses may be helped by the judicious purchase of a large property which can be converted into flats or maisonettes. A safety-first rule before going in for this kind of investment is to get the opinion of a chartered surveyor or other qualified and independent expert.

OTHER VENTURES may be offered to you through advertisements and canvassers. Unless you know a great deal about the type of business it will almost certainly pay you to tread warily. Seemingly attractive offers of a weekly income of several pounds from an investment of only a few hundreds may mean hard slogging or be a will-o'-the-wisp. Never commit yourself to an out-of-the-way venture until you have had the advice of your bank manager, accountant, solicitor, or some other financial adviser such as the City Editor of one of the daily or Sunday newspapers or financial periodicals.

As pointed out earlier in this chapter, the way in which you invest your capital on retirement depends on its amount and other individual circumstances. Although there cannot be any universal rule, it may help to give some general hints, as follows:

If the total is relatively small -- say £1,000 or less --

stick to easily realizable investments like Trustee Savings Bank special investment accounts, National Development Bonds, Local Authority loans, or a Building Society.

Unless you have a large capital, keep some money – at least £50 to £100 – readily available for financial emergencies in a Savings Bank or Building Society account, or in Savings Certificates.

Where the amount is reasonably large, consider investing up to one-half in a single, joint, or survivorship annuity if you are fully prepared to 'use up' such capital in return for a good and assured income until death.

Again, where there is room for manoeuvre, look after the inflationary menace by investing up to a minimum of one-half of the balance available in ordinary shares which offer prospects of growth. But unless you know your way about stock markets, be advised by a stockbroker or choose suitable unit trusts.

Do not speculate if you cannot afford to lose money. Be extra careful of propositions offering high returns.

N.B. For further information, see *The Complete Guide to Investment* by Gordon Cummings, Penguin Books 1964.

7

KEEPING FIT AFTER SIXTY
NEEDS CARE

POLITICALLY this may seem to be a desperate age in which to exist, far less to retire. Who would choose to pass his later years in the age of anxiety under threat of the H-bomb? Medically the case is different. In matters of health this is the age of achievement, the era of hope. Where for almost half a century treatment had lagged behind diagnosis, the reverse is now almost true. The change is most striking in the field of bacterial infection.

'There is in this field such a wealth of available resources in treatment,' said Lord Horder, 'that the temptation to "get busy" with one or more of the sulpha drugs or with one or other of the antibiotics, or indeed with one or other or both, before the nature of the infection is fully ascertained, is almost irresistible.'

We are living longer too. Your expectancy of life is now extended by some months every year you live. Healthier ways of living, more careful dieting, more exercise, are enabling us to enjoy our food and to use our legs to a much later age than our grandfathers.

'Age group studies tell us', says Dr Martin Gumpert, one of our best authorities on ageing, 'that the average person of 65 is now as biologically efficient as the average person of 50 was a generation ago. Physical strength and mobility climb to a maximum at 20, then slowly decline. The curve of mental potency rises sharply up to 40, more slowly up to 60, shows a slow decline to

80. The average mental standard at 80, however, is still equal to that at 35.'

In short, health is much less of a worry to the elderly than it was fifty years ago. But there is one serious new danger. We are all more health-conscious. In particular we are scared of the ills of old age. In fact there *is* no disease of old age. You will search the medical dictionary for it in vain. 'Failure of a working part is always the cause; infection, a germ assault, is the most frequent cause of that failure,' says medical research. How foolish then to worry about the effects of old age when all one's efforts should be directed to keeping fit.

Yet one of the major perils of retirement is precisely that it gives you time to think about your health. A dangerous proceeding even in these healthier days. Good health can be as elusive as happiness. To enjoy health one must almost forget it. To study the medical dictionary is to find that you have the symptoms of every disease except housemaid's knee. 'Don't worry about it' is the best advice on health that the layman can give to any retiree. Otherwise you may find yourself listening to the rumblings in your stomach and wondering what causes the noise. Which is the first step to becoming that dreariest of sights, a hypochondriac.

Yet retirement when it comes, quickly or unexpectedly, imposes a tremendous shock on the system. Sometimes possibly a greater shock than a major operation. The fact that the shock is mental rather than physical does not make it any the less weakening. 'The operation was successful but the patient died' is not merely a layman's joke: it is also a too frequent fact. The mind reacts so powerfully on the body and vice versa that the mental shock of retirement kills many men (fewer women) as we all know from our personal experience. Indeed this knowledge prevents many people from retiring at all.

What can be done to lessen the effects of the shock? 'A great deal' is the encouraging answer. One preventative today for the man or woman of limited means is the cultivation of a hobby for five years at least before retirement, better for ten. What sort of hobby a man takes up does not seem to matter very much. It may be carpentry, or bird-watching, or collecting stamps, or the study of wild flowers, or poring over philosophy. The test is whether it absorbs his attention, keeps him interested and active.

It is optimistic to expect that one will be exempt from the effects of this shock of retirement if one has been unable to taste its pleasures by instalments. Better to accept them as inevitable and prepare to offset them so far as is possible. After all, the average retiree has arrived at the age at which he must begin to give more attention to his health. The human machine runs down in a variety of ways during even the forties and fifties. During the sixties the process of what doctors call senile *deterioration* is accelerated.

'At forty', remarked Lord Chesterfield, 'a man is either a fool or a physician.' No doubt this was true of the eighteenth-century rakes: substitute 'at sixty' for at forty and you have a useful maxim for twentieth-century living. By 'physican' one means rather an observer of one's health than an active prescriber for its improvement. After sixty the human machine requires far more attention than many of us allow. Having realized this fact, the important thing is to make medicine one's servant, not one's master like Molière's *malade imaginaire*.

Normally it is not until the sixties that the arteries begin to harden seriously, the gastric juices to fail, rheumatism to visit the joint, and the respiratory system to wheeze and whistle. Many men and women in the late sixties have to contend with one or other of these chronic ailments, perhaps in a mild form.

The danger is that one may fly to panaceas. In medicine there are no panaceas, no cure-alls, no sovereign remedies. The coiners of the three most famous of all health slogans, the *daily dozen, chew your food, walk barefoot in the morning dew*, all failed to reach old age. If Gladstone chewed every mouthful of food forty times, he did it to assist a weak digestion, not as a magic formula for long life. A little muscle loosening exercise in the morning is good for many of us, emphatically not for all. To walk barefoot in the morning dew is one good way of acquiring penumonia. Behind the panacea there is always a business group out for profit. Beware of panaceas.

The same advice applies to laxatives. The use of laxatives tends to become a habit which defeats its own object, since the dose must always be increased. Some American medical men believe that addiction to laxatives should be made a crime. In particular the use of liquid paraffin calls for very special care in dosage.

Too many doctors and their patients are still infatuated with the idea that the new drugs, diets, and techniques will solve every health problem and greatly prolong life. Similarly the use of certain of the more powerful new sleeping drugs is so depressant that in time a stimulating pill must be taken. In this way the vicious circle continues until patient or doctor finds the strength of mind to break it.

Some people worry a lot about their weight. This is often futile. Your weight is partially at least under your own control. It is mainly the result of what you eat and of how you exercise (or don't). In peace-time it is astonishing how many people overeat. In war-time rationing stopped most of this with marvellous results in shapelier, slimmer figures and improved health. After fifteen years of larger meals and more varied diet, stomachs are swelling again, hips are thickening, while digestive troubles multiply.

The danger for many retirees is not too few but too many pounds. The mere fact of retirement tends to reduce one's mental and physical activity, and therefore one's need for food. One need not go out on the bad days: one sits by the fire and acquires indigestion instead. At the same time the metabolism of the body is slowing down, arteries are hardening; after sixty the whole machinery is capable of burning up only a smaller quantity of food without storing the excess as fat which increases your weight. This happens at the moment when one has time to enjoy the wife's good things! Therefore it pays to keep a wary eye on one's weight after retirement.

If one stresses the perils of fat it is because so many of one's readers are in danger of acquiring it. There is a sound medical reason for this emphasis. Fat endangers the heart and arteries and increases the hazards of high blood pressure. It overburdens the knee and hip joints and so induces rheumatism and arthritis. It hampers the lungs and aggravates the common problem of breathlessness. It leads to gall stones and other digestive troubles, and it is now judged to be the principal cause of diabetes in later life. The American life insurance actuaries have proved that any serious overweight at fifty is followed by an increase in the mortality rate and an overweight of 40 per cent at the same age by an increased mortality of 60 per cent. It looks as if any increase of weight even after the age of thirty were definitely dangerous. Of the dangers of obesity, however, the general public is blithely unaware.

8

WHY EATS, DRINKS, SMOKES
ALL MATTER

WHY devote a chapter merely to eats, drinks, and smokes when the whole subject of health is under survey? the reader may reasonably ask. Because the whole outlook on health problems is rapidly changing. The emphasis is now placed increasingly on preventive medicine in later life especially.

Probably one hundred out of one hundred of my readers over fifty have some rheumatism about them: against its on-march much can be done now. In the event, few of us will die of such complaints. Contrariwise, while few of us have arterial or heart trouble, let alone cancer, the majority of us will probably succumb to one of these diseases. Against them, too, something can be done.

Sir William Osler often talked about the soil and the seed when dealing with tuberculosis. The body was the soil, the germ was the seed. In congenial soil the seed would sprout and grow into a colony of vigorous plants. We know now that this is as true of most rheumatic complaints as it is of tuberculosis. Science has taught us much about the soil that induces rheumatism but little about the seed.

Infection may not merely plant the seed by lowering the body's resistance, but illness of any sort prepares the way for rheumatism and arthritis. One expert believes that two-thirds to three-quarters of all cases of arthritis in the United States are due to a previous infection. But earlier illness is not the only predisposing cause for rheumatic trouble. Poor circulation is another. By reducing the supply of blood to the joints it prepares the way for arthritis. Injury to a limb or joint also often paves the way for rheumatic trouble. So does fat. So does worry. Indeed it is now widely believed that any form of stress may lead to the onset of rheumatism. This reaction has been thought to apply specially to rheumatoid-arthritis.

Recent medical research emphasizes the important part played by diet in an ever-increasing range of diseases especially in arterial disease. Indeed diet may eventually prove to be the most potent single weapon in the hands of preventive medicine. This chapter is designed to assist the layman to take advantage of modern knowledge on the subject of diet and other matters and so to improve his own health in retirement.

During the sixties a great many changes take place in the body. In particular old age slows down the whole of the delicate digestive processes. Less gastric and intestinal juices are secreted to begin with: Bloomfield's experiments showed the amount secreted to be halved between the ages of twenty and seventy. Now hydrochloric acid is essential to digestion: its absence may be associated with gastritis, constipation, or diarrhoea. One medical answer is to supply hydrochloric acid artificially in a diluted form. An easier one is to give the patient a harder diet which compels him to use his teeth vigorously. This sets the saliva-producing process going naturally in the mouth and stomach, in many cases. Have you ever watched your dog tackling a bone? How freely the saliva flows, to help him in the hard digestive task ahead! Hard toast, raw carrots or shredded cabbage in salads, raw apples, nuts (in moderation) can help you in the same way in your more modest digestive tasks.

Constipation is of course *the* digestive malady that accompanies old age. The first painful step towards its cure is usually the giving up of strong laxatives entirely. The rest is largely a matter of finding the diet that prevents the condition recurring by inducing the bowels to work easily, naturally, and eventually with regularity. In one constipation, wholemeal bread, fruit and fruit juices, vegetables, and salads will probably be prominent in the diet. In another constipation, usually accompanied by cramps, the nervous condition must first be tackled. Coffee and tobacco, both nerve stimulants, may have to go. The diet will probably call for *less* bulky foods, vegetables and raw fruit.

When you are ill, allow only your own doctor to prescribe your diet. Your stomach is as individual and as idiosyncratic as your eyes or your brain. Every stomach requires its own diet tailored to its peculiar needs. This diet observation and common sense should enable you to prescribe for yourself. In health everyone is his own best dietician. Simply cut out those dishes which, however delicious, give you any form of digestive trouble.

We know now that dietary fads are peculiarly dangerous to older people. This for a simple reason. During or around the sixties, as we have seen, the stomach makes important changes in its digestive processes. This factor alone can make the fashionable diet fad which does no harm to younger folk dangerous to older people.

On the other hand you can make one or two simple decisions which should help you to elude ill health. Even at the age of seventy an intake of only 1,600–1,900 calories is probably desirable, instead of the 2,500 required even by the office worker at forty. (Gumpert estimates an average loss of basic metabolism of 10 per cent at the age of sixty, of 25 per cent at seventy.) The normal protein intake of 75–100 grams daily can be reduced by a similar amount since protein metabolism also is altered in old age. Much more of it is broken down into simpler substances, some of which are stored as carbohydrates or fat.

Here is the able American dietician, William H. Silvell's, daily basic diet to cover all our nutritional requirements:

One pint of milk.
One helping of orange, grapefruit, tomato, or other fruit juice.
One helping of green vegetables.
One helping of potatoes.
One helping of a whole grain cereal, oatmeal, or wheat.
Four eggs a week.
One helping of meat, poultry, or fish.
Wholemeal bread.
Butter.

This diet contains not merely an adequate supply of calories and of protein but also of the two essential minerals, calcium and iron. I have never seen it bettered.

What the retiree drinks is probably less important

than what he eats and smokes, save from one point of view, that of cost. Roughly five-sixths of what we pay for whisky, gin, rum, and brandy is pure tax. Ten-pence out of every shilling. Every sherry at 3s. that I drink benefits the Exchequer by 2s. 6d. There is, how-ever, one exception. The tax on French wines has been reduced to assist the French Government in its ex-change problems. So you can now buy tolerable light French (also Algerian, Spanish, Portuguese, and Yugo-slav) red and white wines at prices ranging from 6s. a bottle. Obviously none of this wine is of vintage quality nor can it be château-bottled. But you enjoy *vin ordinaire* in your French hotel on holiday, so why not with dinner at home? I now drink little else, with a great saving to my pocket and with equal benefit to my digestion.

Today with whisky and gin so heavily fined, and even beers penalized, the steady drinker of such liquors turns himself into an unpaid tax collector, which seems to me altogether too philanthropic a hobby.

The effect of alcohol on the arteries is to dilate them. As a result it is often recommended to those suffering from arteriosclerosis. Research has shown that a dose of two or three ounces of whisky may warm up toes and fingers by as much as 9–12° F. Alcohol also stimulates the secretion of digestive juices and may therefore be used against gastric anacidity. To most people alcohol in small doses is a sedative and it can often make sleep easier and sounder. The main medical action of alcohol is successively to release lower centres of the brain. Small doses release what is called 'cortical inhibitions', but large doses affect more deeply placed nerve centres, hence the difference in result between various doses. But to some alcohol is an irritant and its effects are therefore to heighten tension and not to relax it. Finally alcohol contains a heavy load of calories; as a result over-drinking tends to impair the appetite seriously: the liquid breakfast of the alcoholic is just one evidence of this. Its result is vitamin deficiency as well as gastric irritation in the elderly. If you drink hard liquor liberally every day your doctor may prescribe you some vitamin B_1 to remedy the deficiency.

Smoking presents the same problem as drinking to the retiree. He can't afford much of it. Yet probably he has been accustomed to a lot of narcotic solace. We are among the heaviest smokers of tobacco in the world: only the Americans are ahead. But our meticulous Treasury taxes every puff we draw at the same rate as every drop of alcohol we drink. Of the 4s. 6d. you spend on twenty cigarettes Excise and Customs takes just over 3s. 6d. So that the heavy smoker too has become an unpaid tax collector. The man who smokes his packet a day is collecting from himself nearly 25s. a week for the Treasury.

Unhappily there are no rebates or drawbacks in the tobacco world. Yet with care it is possible to enjoy the relaxing effect of the weed less expensively. The answer, incredible as it may seem, is not merely the pipe but also the cigar. Every experienced smoker knows that both are far more satisfying smokes than the cigarette. They take the edge off things far more effectively. Eventually too they cost less; they may cost much less.

Now it is still possible to buy a Burlington, an

Embassy, a Criterion cigar for around 2s. Any of these cigars will give you an hour to an hour and a half's smoke. A good cigarette rarely lasts more than ten minutes. In short you enjoy the full flavour of an untouched tobacco leaf for little less time than you do the shredded leaf and possibly stalk from a packet of twenty cigarettes, at under 60 per cent of the cost. Personally I now smoke only one cigar a day with a cup of white coffee, after a light supper. When working in town I smoke a second cigar after lunch, to tone things down. Total weekly expense is eighteen shillings. Result – complete satisfaction and no craving for more. The pipe smoker who is content with one or two ounces a week almost halves this, lucky man.

Medical opinion on the effects of smoking on the heart has changed radically in the last twenty years.

Apparently the once dreaded 'smoker's heart' is purely transitory and not a serious heart condition. The symptoms of palpitation, giddiness, sudden faintness, and dyspepsia which can be induced during smoking are the direct effects of nicotine poisoning and wear off if smoking is stopped. The patients with disorderly action of the heart, a phrase common in the First World War, are now regarded as purely neurotic. Indeed excessive smoking itself is regarded more as an additional manifestation of nervous tension than as the cause of permanent changes in the heart. Smoker's cough, annoying to everybody in itself, is a burden to the whole respiratory system: it can and does induce catarrh: I have several friends who have cured chronic catarrh by stopping smoking. Finally it must be accepted that nicotine distinctly constricts the smaller arteries: in other words it is another stimulant to high blood pressure and arteriosclerosis.

What is the remedy? It is quite simple. Smoke in moderation. No one who smokes five to ten cigarettes, or one or two cigars, or two pipes a day after meals (one to two ounces a week) is likely to injure eyes, heart, or circulatory system. On the other hand, he does enjoy the benefits of a gentle sedative which soothes the nerves.

If you have a medical reason, or are built on the heroic mould, you may prefer to cut out smoking. This is a painful and can be an agonizing process. The experts agree that some part of the pleasure of smoking is due to the pleasure of using the jaws and lips in the same way as a baby milks its mother. Therefore to chew gum or liquorice root (bought in little packets) gives one part of the pleasure of smoking. By keeping gum or liquorice sticks in each suit, you can start chewing whenever the desire to smoke seizes you. Liquorice is actually a good digestive, starting the essential gastric juices that change starch into sugar.

Naturally enough the problem of reducing one's weight troubles women more than it does men. Simply worrying about one's paunch does not help. Nor is a rigorous slimming diet advisable in later years. The sensible course is to organize one's diet to lose a pound or so a week: kept up for six months this means a reduction of nearly two stone. One simple method is to cut consumption of bread and potatoes. A second, known in the United States as fractional diet, is to cut the amount of everything you eat by a third. To cut one's intake of the two fiercest sources of carbohydrates, sweets and desserts, is a more heroic but equally useful method. Any one of these easy limitations of carbohydrates should of course be accompanied by a reduction in your use of oil, mayonnaise, and ice-cream. Don't overlook the fattening effect of alcohol. As Gumpert remarks: 'Alcohol oxidizes quickly and so prevents the assimilation of more valuable foodstuffs. A few cocktails or a few glasses of beer can make a well-balanced meal entirely useless.'

In adopting any reduction in diet too, one must be careful to supply enough protein (meat, cheese, milk), except in the case of a few chronic diseases.

Even on obesity, however, there can be no general rule. Anyone with tuberculosis, lobar pneumonia, or duodenal ulcer will be helped, not hindered, by a certain amount of fat. Never attempt any serious change in your diet without consulting your doctor; if you can have complete laboratory tests so much the better; when you have your doctor's advice, stick to it consistently, unless you develop some unexpected allergy.

Often closely connected with diet is the problem of sleep. Although doctors may question the facts in specific cases, retirement does appear quite often to increase the tendency of elderly people to insomnia. That tendency is surely inevitable, although we admit that the cause of sleep is still undiscovered. There are four main scientific theories on the subject, none giving a complete answer. But medical research has proved one important point. For natural, quick, sound sleep the brain must be almost empty of blood. Normally this demands some slight degree of physical fatigue. It was to cure insomnia that Gladstone felled so many trees on his estate at Hawarden, on the advice of his specialist, the late Sir Andrew Clark. The G.O.M. secured over-average sleep in his eighties as a result of his forestry. The old cure of the cold-water foot bath before bed is based on the same facts. The chill induced in the feet sends the blood rushing down from the brain to warm up the cold extremities. Hence the advice to read something dull for half an hour before going to bed. Also the danger of trying to sleep straight away after taking part in an exciting public debate or a heated discussion round the fire. Hence too the danger of taking *strong* coffee or tea after about five o'clock. In the case of good coffee or coffee and chicory which is made strong weakened by at least the same quantity of very hot (not boiled) milk, or weak tea, I find no ill results. Many of my older friends report to the same effect.

The most useful service of medicine for the elderly is prevention rather than cure. Nothing can save any of us suffering various deterioration processes after the forties. First of our senses to deteriorate is sight. The eye ages incredibly early. The exquisitely delicate lens begins to lose elasticity at the age of ten: by the age of thirty-five one-half of its precious flexibility is lost. Normally the back of the eye is the first part of the body to show signs of hardening arteries and of general fatigue. But like other parts of the body the eye deteriorates on no time pattern. The white ring round the cornea, known as the senile arc, for instance, can develop at the age of thirty in people showing no other symptoms of old age.

Like the arm and the knee, the eye is dependent on

the continual use of its muscles for health. A 'lazy eye' is one whose muscles are injured or impaired, and therefore tend to rest. This imposes an extra strain on the other eye, with the same dangers of strain as occur when the good knee is used to save the injured one. The dangers of a lazy eye, however, are greater than those of a lazy knee, since good sight is the result of the two eyes working individually but in unison, so that the picture focused by one eye is superimposed on that seen by the other. The result is a stereoscopic clarity, in which objects are seen in the round. Where both pictures are not linked, the picture shown is flat and dangerously lacking in perspective. Having had my right eye operated on successfully for squint at the age of seven, I have had to contend with this difficulty all my life. It made me hopeless at all ball games save golf, and compelled me most reluctantly to give up the driving of a car at the age of fifty.

The whole secret of preserving the sight in many cases lies in exercising the eyes to the utmost of their strength and then resting them thoroughly. The writer rarely reads or writes for more than an hour and ten minutes, but he can do this twice a day. However the eye is constantly changing: you should have your eyes inspected every three years up till seventy: after that every year.

Many elderly people live in dread of cataract. They need not. The operation to remove a cataract is one of the oldest in surgery and it is now so efficient that pain and danger have vanished and success is certain. The diseased lens is removed and with correction glasses sight remains. Far more dangerous is glaucoma, a

congestion of the inner fluids of the eye. If your eyes are
inspected for health (not merely tested for sight) once
a year after seventy, however, there is a good chance
that any early symptoms may be detected by the eye
specialist. For the rest, if you suffer from eye strain a
good deal, as I do, an occasional bath of weak, warm
boric lotion helps.

Deafness, that deadly cutter-off from human society,
that insulator of the soul, is now probably more
efficiently handled in Great Britain than anywhere else
in the world. Not merely because the National Health
Service provides free deaf aids. No, simply because this
is the one country in which the use of visible deaf aids
has become so common that the passionate resistance of
deaf people to deaf aids has been broken down: here
alone the wearing of a deaf aid is no longer regarded as
a sign of decrepitude, an astonishing revolution.

'A man is as old as his arteries,' said a great physician
long ago. A century of research has only confirmed the
truth of his finding. As we get older we depend more
and more on a healthy heart to keep us active and
therefore useful and happy. Now essentially the heart
is a pump. Its function is to maintain the circulation of
the blood. As with any other pump, the heart depends
on clean pipes to do its work. In its case the pipes to be
kept clean are the arteries, including those feeding the
heart itself.

More people die from diseases of the heart and
arteries than from any other cause. Between the ages of
forty and fifty 18 per cent of all deaths are caused by
heart disease, between fifty and sixty 25 per cent, while
after eighty the rate rises to 41 per cent. Obviously

arthritis and rheumatism, pneumonia and asthma, cancer and cirrhosis of the liver all weaken the heart; in a sense too no one is dead until the heart has ceased to beat. But the percentages quoted refer to *diseases of the heart* alone.

The phrase 'weak heart' has naturally no definite medical significance. There are a large number of defects and diseases of the heart. There may be no symptoms at all, but if there are symptoms, these are likely to include breathlessness or pain on exertion (*angina*). Often the patient's first reaction to the knowledge that he has heart disease, especially if the symptoms include *angina*, is likely to be anxiety. It is part of the doctor's job to help him to come to terms with this anxiety. In this he may be greatly helped by some of the excellent publications of the Chest and Heart Association (Tavistock House North, Tavistock Square, wc1).

The higher rate of mortality from heart disease is often put down, like the occurrence of ulcers, to the pace of modern life. The medical scientists say this is untrue. A high death rate from heart diseases, they point out, is only possible in a community that has conquered plague and the more deadly infectious diseases and whose members therefore live long enough to begin to tire or wear out their hearts.

To allow the arteries to harden prematurely is to invite arteriosclerosis, coronary thrombosis, and various heart disorders. How can one prevent this, if the tendency is already there? you may ask. The answer is by moderation in all things; in eating, in drinking, in smoking, and by taking a good amount of the gentler sorts of exercise such as walking, gardening, and bowls. Slow down the pace of your life to suit the lessened power of your ageing heart. When a serious heart defect has developed, it is a little late to go to your doctor.

Many elderly people regard cancer as enemy number one. This it is no longer, as we have just seen. But it is enemy number two, thanks solely to the fearful rise in the incidence of cancer of the lung. And of no other major disease is the average man so ignorant, says the medical profession.

Like the origin of life, the cause of the growth of the cancer cell remains a biological mystery. The human body appears to have little defence against this irregular growth of cells. Nor yet against the cancer cell's swift invasive power.

But progress in the treatment of most forms of cancer is steady. Complete removal of the cancer growth by the surgeon's knife at an early stage is the most successful preventive measure. Cancer of the skin, of the large intestine, of the tongue, can be completely eliminated by surgery. An old acquaintance of mine was successfully operated on for cancer of the tongue thirty years ago. Today she is a fit eighty and only an occasional lisp suggests that her mouth is not perfect.

But where cancer is not visible, where the cells twine round a vital organ, surgery may be impossible. In these cases other methods must be used.

The urgent need is for the average citizen to muster up courage to report any danger signal to his doctor *at once*. Danger signals include any mysterious lump, any ulcer that refuses to heal, any change in a wart or a mole, any unusual bleeding or discharge, persistent cough or hoarseness, any persistent indigestion. The thing to remember is that while, for centuries, no case of cancer was curable, today one case in three probably is, while many more can be alleviated.

Unluckily for our generation, the possible connexion between lung cancer and cigarette-smoking has entered the field of public controversy. Hence the clouding of an issue in itself only too complex.

Significantly, lung cancer is much more common among men than among women. In Britain it is now responsible for 1 in 18 of all deaths among men, but for only 1 in 103 among women at all ages. The massive Hammond-Horn Report, covering 188,000 men in the United States, proves statistically the association between excessive smoking of cigarettes and lung cancer.

Chemically the connexion is partially proven. Only in a proportion of cases, thinks the British Medical Research Council, which cannot yet be defined, may atmospheric pollution be a cause. But the identification of several carcinogenic substances in tobacco smoke provides a rational basis for a relationship of cause and effect. There seem to be no fewer than five cancer-producing substances in tobacco smoke.

The frightening fact in the situation is the speed with which the death rate from lung cancer in Britain continues to rise while the other cancer death rates fall or remain steady. *Between 1945 and 1955 alone the lung cancer death rate doubled. And it is still rising.* Both pipe and cigar appear to be less dangerous, possibly by providing a form of filter, possibly by allowing combustion at a lower temperature.

The progress made in the prevention and treatment of T.B. during the past half-century has been phenomenal. Apart from the British discovery of the fresh-air treatment, streptomycin and other new drugs are used in combination, and (in more serious cases) a series of new surgical operations are steadily reducing casualties. Today two-thirds of all tuberculosis occurs east of the Suez Canal. In course of time the disease should be exterminated in the west. Again prevention is more than half the battle. And diet, weight, circulation play a mighty part in prevention.

SELF-HELP TO FITNESS AFTER SIXTY

1. Forget your age. Concentrate on the part of you that is still young – your brain. (Dr George Lawton.)
2. Eat less. Have you cut down your diet? If not consider the step, but consult a doctor before acting.
3. Have a medical examination once a year.
4. You need more liquid in age: drink more water.
5. Cut your smoking down to one or at most two ounces a week (or thirty–forty cigarettes).
6. Never drink alcohol except at meals, preferably light wines, lager, or light ales. If you drink spirits, dilute well with water. (Dr Martin Gumpert.)
7. Get some real exercise every day: keep your midday nap to an hour.
8. See that your bowels move once daily.
9. Don't speculate. By worrying over stocks you may lose sleep as well as money.
10. Keep busy. Work for a few hours every day at some job or hobby.
11. Plan each day. Follow the plan. No two days alike. (Dr Lillien J. Martin.)
12. Make yourself useful to others, including your wife.

FORTY-FOUR WAYS OF EARNING
MONEY IN YOUR SPARE TIME

'RISING prices and wages, falling incomes and the difficulties of getting adequate domestic help have made a mockery of life in the country bungalow for . . . a large number of retired professional men . . . (and) retired members of the lower income groups,' says one expert who has studied the subject. All this is too true.

What can one do about it?

The answer is not to become frustrated and bitter because the expected fruits of your work and sacrifices have been snatched away, but to face up to the new conditions and beat them. Don't merely reduce your modest standards of living to meet the lower purchasing power of your income: instead try first to expand your income to give you the standard of living you have been accustomed to. The only sensible way to do this (forgetting the pools) is to find a means of earning extra cash in as agreeable and interesting a way as you can. We are reorienting our ideas on the subject of earning. For too long the lingering influence of feudalism made us all absurdly snobbish about work. 'The dignity of labour' has now a realistic ring in middle-class English ears: it is taking longer to reach the factory floor.

My friend E, fat, prosperous, and sixty-seven, found himself recently quite without dollars in a luxury New York hotel. His allowance had very nearly run out. It was a small matter, but it made E feel as mean as only an Englishman or a Spaniard can when he cannot pay his way. The old waiter noticed his distress. 'Say, son, you can get an evening's dish-washing in the kitchen tonight, if you want the money badly. Shall I give you a line to chef?' E was flabbergasted. Yet surely this was a sensible arrangement. That is the right spirit: it has scarcely quite reached here in such full force.

There are more opportunities for earning a little money today in retirement than you may realize. Much of the work is interesting; all of it is useful; some of it may be difficult for those who have not been in business before. To attempt the simplest form of spare-time earning does mean becoming a one-man (or a one-woman) business. This in turn means keeping simple accounts, getting a receipt for every penny spent, finding customers in your own area, selling to them successfully and taking care that, after the first year of trial, your hours of work yield a reasonable reward. It is worth nobody's while working for less than the average jobbing gardener, 3s.–4s. 6d. an hour or 24s.–36s. for an eight-hour day. Don't give credit: insist on cash from your customers.

First study the district in which you live before choosing on your new venture. Obviously you will scarcely build up a personal service business in Wednesbury but you might in Worthing. You would have a better chance with a local souvenir in Buxton or Bath than in St Helens. The selling of insurance or shares that can be done in a prosperous suburb may fail in a country village from lack of 'prospects'. If somebody is running a first-rate café in your small village already without any signs of expanding it, then the café market is probably supplied. Leave it alone.

Whatever you try out, don't look for quick results or easy success. Both are rare. The important thing is to do the job well, if possible a little differently. People are always willing to buy something fresh. The 'new look' is usually more saleable than the common, everyday look.

The easiest spare-time earning is obviously done in work similar to your old line. The trained accountant can always keep or arrange to audit the accounts of the small business man. Often this is mere play to him. But what of the retired chemist, or the teacher, or the civil servant? Admittedly they have no such easily opened door to spare-time earning; but there are a number of openings available to all of them. The acute shortage of teachers and dispensers alone provides all sorts of part-time jobs, apart from holiday spells, to men and women in both of these professions. The astonishing thing is how few retirees in these professions take the trouble to explore the possibilities for money-making through their old skills in their own locality.

We are said by the (non-American) foreigner to be a nation of advertising-conscious people. But are we? Ask the average retired teacher whether he has really taken off his coat to the job of finding a money-making opportunity and his reply is: 'Yes, I've looked all round, but there's no opening I want.' 'I suppose you've advertised in the local paper and the *Teacher's World* and advised the local employment agencies as well as the Labour Exchange?' you murmur. 'I've seen the employment agencies, yes: nothing doing. But of course it's a bit *infra dig* for a man in my position to advertise. People are apt to talk in a small place. . . .' But who is going to know, pray? The local paper is prepared to protect you completely under the anonymity of the box number. You don't need to use anything more than a short, clear statement in the correct classified column: everybody who can matter to you reads (indeed must read) the local weekly, whether yours be a suburban, small town, or rural area. Probably only the newspaper or advertising man knows all the possibilities of the shillings spent on a classified ad. A three-liner I wrote for one friend produced for him the backer with £2,000 whom he needed to start a small business.

All through this chapter therefore I assume that you use the classified columns of your local paper to get in touch with possible customers and sources of supply.

There is no need to stick to the narrow path of one's previous experience in the effort to earn money. For instance, if you have taught older boys or girls in a private or a state school, you can probably also teach adults in night classes, such as those of the W.E.A., or you can coach private pupils, or give lectures on non-syllabus subjects in preparatory and public schools, or do examination work, either supervising important exams in large schools or acting as an examiner. Marking exam papers may not be very exciting, but much of this work is now well paid, and it is apt to be more interesting when done at leisure in the easy-chair by the fire.

In some districts an occasional private school offers opportunities to a retiree without any teaching experience whatever. For the average headmaster is no business man: he has no training in keeping accounts, in buying, selling, or costing. Yet he is running a business, a complex business, to the best of his ability. A great many heads of many preparatory schools need one part-time assistant who is a cross between a bursar and a private secretary to deal with the commercial side of his work. It is true that the average head of a preparatory school cannot afford to pay much for this service. In these days of high costs he is apt to be working on narrow margins. But today he has usually plenty of pupils and he can raise his fees fairly easily in many cases.

Since the Second World War the preparatory schools have enjoyed a boom. It is estimated that over 600,000 children now attend them. A new moneyed class uses them as entrances to the public schools. To less well-off middle-class parents they are the one means of securing the extra coaching which may be needed for the boy or girl to pass the highly competitive examination for the grammar school, and avoid the unpopular modern schools. The really clever boy or girl may win a place in a public school.

But the outsider faces serious difficulties. He *is* an outsider. Teaching is a closed profession. The average head is afraid of 'a stranger' coming in and getting to know all about his business. It may well take time to win his confidence. Here, as so often, an attractive personality may be as important as business ability.

Next, such a job can only be undertaken right on the spot: you must be within easy call during term time in particular. This day-to-day job cannot be done at a distance of even five miles, let alone by post. Yet the need is there and the boom in preparatory schools should make the work of breaking-in less arduous.

Of course if you are running your own business or department you may be annoyed by having to take orders from others. Headmasters expect courtesy and quick action from their assistants. But this is merely a matter of exchanging one habitual attitude for another. If it hurts a lot, blame your lack of adaptability or your hardening arteries. Nature's unalterable biological law is *adapt or die*. So swallow your feeling of hurt dignity: recall the opulent agonies of Pooh Bah. This is true of much part-time work done in retirement.

Consider the case of my friend F, who really was demoted. F was a brilliant Hungarian editor who left Budapest in the early thirties to try his fortune as a publisher in London. He succeeded beyond his dreams and soon had a small group of papers under his own control. Eventually his lack of financial skill compelled him to sell out most of his papers to one of the large combines. Calling on him one day just before he left his old premises, I was astonished to see him enter by another door bowing deeply to an invisible being at his own desk. 'I'm practising the right way to enter his room as a very minor executive of Lord G,' he explained with a wry smile. 'My manner is far too masterful. . . . After ten years as the big boss in my own business it will be hell to be just a minor executive under another big boss.' F was a wit and this enabled him to see the humour of the situation and so almost to enjoy it.

My friend knew how to adapt even his Hungarian pride to his new situation. He had mastered early one of the laws of successful living, easily enough learned in the rough and tumble of the newspaper man's daily round. Such adaptability is a splendid asset in retirement. The number of jobs a man or woman can find to do in our highly organized modern society is legion. The secretaryship of the local golf club is indeed a sociable and enjoyable job, but it is merely the obvious and coveted plum for the retiree. Too many people covet it!

Donning the garb of the humbler aspirant, let us look first at some of the least superficially attractive of the jobs open to the middle-aged retiree. On the face of it, the rapidly growing foreign travel business looks a little repulsive. Admittedly the courier himself must be physically very fit and quite tough. Who wants to don uniform, even to be the respected 'man from Cooks'? Who wants to slave twelve hours a day in summer over fares, time-tables, and routes? True. But these are not the only possibilities. I know one or two elderly gentlemen who spend a very pleasant life as couriers of luxury coach tours at home or on the Continent during the summer months (May to September). The courier is responsible usually only for dealing with tickets and luggage, hotel and garage managers, and keeping his little family of travellers happy. Often a salesman or some other social soul in the party relieves him of much of this. You have a bed to sleep in every night (and reasonable comfort on night trains). You see the world, you eat (and often drink) luxuriously in some cases, you earn good tips and you are well paid. This job is for fit retirees only. It must take a little time to get used to the life.

Anthony Carson has immortalized the trials of the

courier. Always he must keep control of his group. This is not always so easy as it looks. A single late appearance at breakfast, one over the eight *once*, can break the spell. For women especially can foment amazing rebellions! Once I had to make myself an unofficial courier to prevent two heavyweight women executives making an able, conscientious courier's life unbearable. In both cases a curt snubbing turned these overbearing females into well-mannered ladies again overnight. The courier takes any risks of losing prestige at his peril. Just once at Venice the charming, adored Carson allegedly lost his head over a lovely American client, Leonora. In a matter of hours the authority so carefully built up over weeks had vanished!

From now on the suspicious clients held me responsible for every disaster that happened. An old gentleman was run over in Rome, and I received threatening letters. It rained heavily in Capri, and I was cut dead. The train was an hour late returning to Venice, and there was a minor revolution at the railway station.

But the first year shows you the ropes and teaches you how to do the job in real comfort. The courier I meet in Lugano or Istanbul (one is well over seventy) often has a little flat in Nice or Graz or in some inexpensive Riviera village, renting it to visitors in summer and enjoying its comfort himself in winter. A smattering of French and German is a *sine qua non* for these jobs. Tact, friendliness, patience, and some experience of foreign travel are all essential. The necessary command of languages comes quickly when you simply must make yourself understood if your flock is to have any supper or recover any passports! Necessity is a good language master.

Some of the positions open to the resident representative of a travel agency are exhausting, others are fantastically pleasant. You may spend four or five summer months in a big tourist resort like Lucerne or Florence; hard work but excitingly varied. Or you may be located in a charming little place like Igls, near Innsbruck, or beside an Italian lake. You meet the incoming trains bringing your guests, arrange their coach tours and other outings, sometimes accompanying a party of them if there is no local courier available, checking up on your flock in the evenings. Most of these jobs fall to women. There are similar jobs in Swiss and Austrian winter sports centres and on the French and Italian Rivieras during the winter. In both cases the season usually runs for only two to five months, making a pleasant break in the tranquil routine of retirement. One middle-aged vicar's wife is the best representative I have ever seen at work: she leaves her husband's parish at home about the beginning of June for the Tyrol or the Alps and returns again about mid September, with a welcome addition to a narrow stipend.

Remaining humble-minded, we may look at some other possibilities of the tourist industry. The Hotels Wages and Catering Act has revolutionized hotel work. Hours are now normal and pay is high. There is still no serious surplus of staff. On the contrary there is a shortage of clerical workers, of cooks, and of managers. These shortages are likely to continue, since the Act makes larger staffs necessary for so many hotels: in many cases the additional trained staff required does not yet exist. So a few managers are glad to have a man with horse sense and tact in the office, especially on a part-time basis. This is sometimes true of the smaller country hotels 'in season', rarely in city hotels.

While we are on the subject of catering, don't forget the possibilities of the smaller café or snack bar. The hours are shorter. Such a business can be closed down in the evening or left in charge of an assistant. There is still an opening in some towns and suburbs for a *good* little café or a smart little snack bar. Not because the opening has been neglected, but merely because so large a proportion of our small cafés and snack bars are so casually and amateurishly run. Today, with the shortage of household help, many people will pay gladly for the snack lunch, tea, coffee, sandwich that is just good, clean, fresh, well-cooked, neatly served, briefly, appetizing.

The profits on catering are good: if you can obtain a licence the profits on alcoholic liquors are more than generous; on wines, spirits (and therefore on cocktails) they are exceptional. A bottle of really good Spanish sherry costs you wholesale around 13s. to 15s. You can get 12 sherries at 2s. 6d. each from it (or 30s.), giving a *gross* profit of anything from 15s. to 17s. or well over 100 per cent. In a small snack bar your overheads are light, so that you should earn at least 50 per cent net on such business. On the other hand the number of local people in any locality who can afford a glass of Spanish sherry often is strictly limited. Mature palates are even scarcer than heavy purses: you will probably have to do most of your business in beer, stout, and gin and lime (about the cheapest cocktail after tomato juice). Licences are extremely difficult to come by today. For a number of reasons most benches are reluctant to increase the number of licensed premises in their area. It is always possible, however, to start off without a licence and eventually to earn one by proving that you are meeting a real need either among residents or tourists. This is of course a long-term policy and will only appeal to the man (or woman) who is prepared to wait. To buy an existing licensed premises usually costs a lot of money.

Oddly enough the easiest way in which to secure a licence today is to start a club. In this way we secured a licence without trouble for a provincial repertory theatre in which I was interested. It happened that we had found a beautiful and roomy sixteenth-century building which failed to comply with the Lord Chamberlain's regulations. So we were compelled to run the theatre as a club. This fact enabled us to secure a licence automatically when it might well have been refused to a mere little theatre since there was an excellent pub almost next door.

Before we leave the catering side, there is yet another opening one should mention. There are some (I emphasize *some*) families in town and country who are dying to pay someone to cook them an appetizing meal once or twice a week – out of something or nothing as the day of the week dictates. Of course one must have learned to cook thoroughly well and to clear up pots and pans as well as crockery before attempting a job of this sort. But in the wealthier suburbs of the wealthier towns there is fairly good money in it for a job that lasts only three or four hours and can be taken on just as often as it suits one during the week. Naturally women can get this sort of work more easily than men. As ever, the way to test *your* local market is to use a classified advertisement in the local paper.

Sticking obstinately to the subject of food, we come to fruit and vegetable farming. Like most forms of farming, this requires the utmost care and constant study at first if you come to it as a tyro. It also demands physique.

Actually you must work at it for three or four years before you are experienced enough to make it pay. Apart from the immense variations in the soils which govern your choice of crops and the perils of our changeable climate, there are the changes in varieties and in techniques, above all the unpredictable changes of taste in eating. Probably cabbages and cauliflowers are the safest vegetables to grow. But it is the *early* potato, the early pea, the early lettuce, the early tomato, the early cucumber that makes the higher profit. Unhappily these delicacies can equally easily make you a loss with the wrong weather, or lack of labour for lifting, or an erratic market. In fruit the very good apple, pear, cherry, seem to pay best. Again it is the early strawberry, the small, sweet melon grown under a *cloche*, the luscious peach that bring a profit rather than the common varieties or a great number of different lines. One can make a reputation more quickly for just one perfect apple and one unbeatable plum or greengage than for a variety of lines. There is an immense amount of expert manual work involved in fruit-growing. The weeding in itself can be a task. Some of the best and most resistant fruit-trees must be individually and meticulously sprayed seven times between March and September. If you can afford to buy or rent five or ten acres for this sort of fruit-farming, it may be possible to hire a clever fruit gardener as your manager. Should you be lucky enough to find a man who will take some real responsibility, it may pay you to allow him a commission on profits and so be sure of keeping him. The information you need about species, fertilizers, pests, soil conservation, prices, can only be got by careful reading of the excellent technical journals on fruit, vegetable, and flower growing (*Commercial Grower* and *Grower*). In their pages you will find full particulars about the frames, *cloches*, furnaces, and specialized equipment you will need. There too is your best employment bureau. If you happen to be situated on a main road, you may be able to sell fruit and cut flowers at their full retail prices to passing motorists. But this involves a labour problem: a youth or girl with some selling ability may be hard to find.

It is simpler for the retiree with a modest capital to go into the intensive growing of Cox's on a considerable scale than for almost any other fruit. It happens that an enterprising firm of commercial fruit-growers, W. Seabrook & Sons Ltd, of Boreham, Chelmsford, have laid themselves out to assist the prospective fruit-grower who is considering the production of Cox's Orange Pippins. This firm takes premium pupils on its 1,100-acre fruit farm at Boreham in Essex and puts them through a course in apple-growing. The fee is £50 for a year, payable quarterly in advance. In pre-war days it was possible for a pupil to 'live in' with a local family, but today very few people are willing to have paying guests. However Boreham is only four miles from both Chelmsford and Witham, both of which have small hotels at reasonable prices.

Owing to this difficulty, the firm have instituted a correspondence course in commercial fruit-growing. This can often be followed by a short course in practical instruction. For example, a week or two of practical pruning, methods of pest and disease control, or any other work can be arranged at the appropriate times of the year. Indeed this can still be done after the pupil has planted his own trees. There are slack periods in fruit growing which will allow him time for this.

For the resident abroad, who is considering taking up fruit growing when he retires home, the course obviously has a special appeal. It allows him to master the basic methods of the industry, so that the problems that arise when he faces his own trees will not be unfamiliar and strange to him. This gives him confidence.

This ten-lesson correspondence course is based on the latest edition of *Modern Fruit Growing* by W. P. Seabrook, a fruit grower of fifty years' experience. The length of the course depends entirely on the student. This should appeal to busy people whose time for reading is variable. The cost of the course is a nominal 3 guineas, to cover costs.

After training, Seabrook's give free advice on the buying of land, the optimum size, soil, water, situation, transport facilities, and necessary housing and outbuildings which a given capital sum can finance.

Finally the firm includes an after-installation service, with helpful advice and regular inspection. In many cases they have started off a colonial retiree's fruit farm for him before he actually retired!

Today (1960) Seabrook's estimate that the optimum unit of dwarf pyramid Cox's capable of being run by one man, fully mechanized, needing only casual labour for picking and packing and an occasional extra man to help during the spraying season, may be five acres, requiring seven acres of land to give enough 'head-room'. More land will demand more capital and labour. Excluding the cost of a house and the land, the cost of establishing such a five-acre unit is about £3,385. Nearly all of this capital is spent during the first year. In the third year the unit should become self-supporting, having cost an additional £200 a year during the first three years. In the fourth and successive years a profit of from £75 to £125 an acre can be looked for, more or less according to the kindness of the season. (This estimate is below Seabrook's own.) Suitable land costs anything from £100 to £200 an acre, a house roughly *anything*, from £1,500 to £4,000. In many instances a house is already on the land, in which cases the acreage cost may be higher.

This is for a minimum unit and is a quicker return than can be got from a bush plantation, which needs around thirty acres to be an economic unit and takes from five to seven years to mature. The planting and maturing of a bush plantation over six years does spread out capital expenditure but the total cost will be around £277 an acre, or £8,300. From the fifth or sixth year Cox growers expect to net at least £60 an acre, and in a few more years a net average income of from £1,000 to £2,000, varying naturally with the seasons.

The Agricultural Mortgage Corporation normally lends freely on bush plantations up to 75 per cent but to a lower percentage on dwarf pyramid plantations, owing to their small acreage. The interest on such a loan, together with annual initial expenditure other than actual capital costs, can be set against other taxable income or carried forward for a maximum of six years against taxable profits. Building societies have also been helpful in respect of house property.

From time to time poultry-keeping has been one of the easiest means of earning a little extra. At the moment of writing this is not yet the case. Years of rationing and controlled prices in a period of costly feeding-stuffs continued to lower the net profit on poultry farming, except on a large scale. Today large-scale poultry farming needs capital in order to use the battery system and other modern techniques.

Even so, if you don't mind going out twice a day in all weathers to prepare their meal and feed them and you have a deputy to do this during your holiday, it often pays the retiree to keep a few hens. You have as many eggs as you want all the year round by putting some down in waterglass during the laying season. You have an occasional good dinner from a table bird. You can sell or exchange eggs with your neighbours, and you have considerably increased the family's intake of protein, of vitamin A, of iron, and of phosphorus.

If you have some rough ground available, more than a mere run, ducks are well worth considering. Unless there is danger from foxes or the winter snows are severe, they have no need of a house. The rearing of chicks is less often necessary than with hens, as the duck lives twice as long as the hen (but the tame duck is no mother: a broody hen must be borrowed). They need but one meal a day (of bulky mash) but they need both a water trough and a bath as both their plumage and their eyes require frequent bathing. They do not fly easily and so need a wire enclosure only a few feet high. Duck eggs are increasingly popular for cooking and now fetch better prices than they did. They are economical in use since every duck's egg is equal to one and a half hen's eggs. (Yet the duck lays as many eggs as the hen.) Again ducklings are easily reared, mature quickly, and sell well. In our country districts the money-earning possibilities of ducks have been curiously overlooked.

Young turkeys are far too delicate and difficult for the average man to rear, while geese yield so few eggs that it is difficult to make them pay. So neither turkeys nor geese need be considered unless you have some past experience with them to help you.

Bees are another matter. They are fascinating creatures to watch, they keep one's interest all through the year, yet they require attention only occasionally. With honey at its present price, it is possible that they can be made to pay after the first year, during which you get your experience. Thanks to bee-keepers' organizations, it is now much easier for the beginner to avoid serious mistakes than it used to be.

While bees must be beside the flowers in summer, they are not fussy about their quarters in winter. A colony lives happily in the roof of an office in Fleet

Street using the flowers on neighbouring bomb-sites for its honey gathering. The first colony will probably cost you £15 to £17. This means normally a colony of around 30,000 bees. (It is cheaper and less frightening to start with two nuclei instead of ten.) In the old days a colony averaged 40 lb. of honey a year; today improved methods which save the bees much labour in cell-building have raised the average to 45–50 lb. of which the bee-keeper may take 25–30 lb. Later colonies cost you nothing, if you take the trouble to learn the art of catching the swarms from your own hives.

Bee-keeping requires a good deal of initial equipment apart from the hive, but most of it lasts for many years. The smoker enables you to stupefy the bees while you are extracting the honey. A bee veil and rubber gloves are necessary for this job, for feeding and for dealing with swarms. You also need a feeder to get syrup into the hive before the winter and especially during the spring breeding season. An extractor is also necessary for you to get the honey out of the closely packed hive. This can usually be hired or borrowed locally. The only materials that must be supplied freely every year are the sheets of beeswax, called comb foundations, which are stamped with the formation of the honey cells. These bees use to save them the labour of starting off each cell for themselves.

The most enticing introduction to this fascinating subject is Maeterlinck's *The Bee*. The know-how you can get from the Ministry of Agriculture's Bulletin (No. 9), *Beekeeping*; and S. B. Whitehead's *Honey Bees and Their Management* is a first-rate text-book giving all the improved modern methods and techniques. Progress in the art of bee-keeping has been so rapid in the last thirty years that pre-war pamphlets and text-books are to be avoided.

It is true that the bee is subject to an alarming number of physical ills, ranging from death through overwork to broodiness, from swarming fever to attack by an internal parasite. Today methods are available for dealing with almost every ill that bee is heir to. Prevention techniques have been developed against certain of the diseases that used to decimate the hives year after year.

Ever since genuine fur coats became so expensive there has been money in rabbits. In the colder climates more and more women demand fur coats. As a result the art of dressing pelts has been developed to the highest pitch. At the same time the rising cost of butcher's meat has made the domestic rabbit an increasingly popular food. Rabbit meat now retails at up to 2s. 2d. a pound. So rabbits can be very rewarding financially.

The fur of the Rex Rabbit is as soft and glossy as plush, and these rabbits can be obtained in the most enticing colours, including Chinchilla Grey. The very best Rex pelts fetch 15s. to £1 each, the poorer qualities correspondingly less.

At the time of writing (1960) Angora fur is not only the rage for coats, but for women's jumpers. As a result, Angora wool fetches up to 40s. per lb. for the best quality. The woolly Angora can usually be kept for three to four years. During this time, the total yield will probably be around 10 oz. on average per year. There is no difficulty about stock.

There is no longer any rationing of bran, which makes things simpler for the amateur breeder. Seven breeding does should yield at least 120–140 rabbits a year, so the economic limit is probably in the region of about twenty-three or twenty-four young rabbits per doe, and a doe will litter three to four times a year.

Bran you must have: apart from this, rabbits can be fed cheaply on vegetable trimmings, grass, thistle, roots (like carrots), etc.

These are rather the pleasant points about rabbit breeding. The drawbacks are two. First is the amount of attention the little creatures require. They must be fed at least twice a day. 'A little and often' suits the rabbit as well as the man with the duodenal. Now however, there are many systems of *ad lib* food. Indeed most of the feeding stuff firms produce pellets which can be fed to the rabbits once a day, or even once every two days. The second drawback to rabbits, unless you live in the country and have a bit of ground, is the amount of space they require. Every breeding doe requires at least four small hutches; every hutch must be cleaned at least once a week; food, apart from pellets, *must* always be fresh. If you breed Angoras, every single rabbit must have its long coat combed *every day*.

Probably the two best books on the subject, for the serious would-be breeder, are *The Domestic Rabbit* by J. C. Sandford, the secretary of the British Rabbit Council. (This can be had from the association at the reduced price of 17s. 9d. post free.) And a small book, *The Complete Book of the Rabbit*, by F. G. Woodgate.

Of course there is always money in breeding pedigree dogs. But this hardly seems to me to be a spare-time occupation. It is apt to become a full-time job. For the fit and active retiree in the country, however, who likes dogs and has a bit of land at his disposal, the care, work, and constant exercising involved appear to be largely a pleasure. Even the quite substantial amount of elementary veterinary work seems to fascinate the man or woman with the necessary flair.

One humble provider of pocket money is often overlooked. I mean the mushroom. With mushrooms retailing for much of the year at 4s. 8d.–6s. per pound, there are opportunities here for the retiree who does not mind working a good deal with manure. All you require is a border, horse manure, cow manure, and a little spawn. The bed must be carefully manured and the temperature of the compost brought to the right height, before the first piece of spawn is inserted into the bed. Correctly used the spawn lasts for five years.

There are two advantage in this crop. Apart from a few weeks in the autumn, mushrooms are *always* in short supply. Also the spent manure from a mushroom bed fetches high prices from market gardens, being an ideal manure for many forms of intensive culture. So mushrooms yield two incomes. The difficulty with mushroom growing in many areas is the scarcity of horse manure, which was essential for their culture. Fortunately an effective but expensive substitute has recently been found. It remains to be seen how changing supply and demand will affect the price later.

Some retirees add to their incomes by selling cut flowers and miniature gardens either directly to the customer or through Women's Institute stalls or the flower shops. Neither can be called a profitable line, but if there are good facilities for selling, both can apparently be made to pay.

This list covers most of the more attractive and rewarding outdoor fields for money-making. But these form a small part of the total possibilities today.

Every day the social revolution makes some new difficulty for the middle class. Each of these new difficulties opens the way to some new service. One answer to many of the servantless households is the personal service agency, often started by a retiree. The technique is to get in touch with some of the more capable young, or even middle-aged men and women who are able and willing to go out by the day or hour to do any sort of household job from scrubbing floors to cooking a three-course dinner, from spring cleaning to simple mending, from baby-minding to gardening. You then take a small single-room office and advertise your service in the local paper, by circular, by phone inquiry, and, if you are wise, by personal door-to-door canvass in the right area.

Among your clients of course you may find difficult cases. The slow payer and the cantankerous employer are merely two. Among workers the slack youth who does nothing thoroughly and the light-fingered gentleman who pilfers your client's cigarettes, gin, and silver are among the habitual risks.

Only the more prosperous residential areas seem to be capable of supporting such a service. A large number of families in the upper income bracket is essential as a basis of steady orders. The variations in effective demand for such service (at 3s. or more an hour) in nearby places is quite astonishing. A well-run service in one quite small seaside resort is able to keep over twenty men fairly steadily employed. But an identical service in a much larger resort a few miles away can barely find work for three or four. Therefore extreme care is necessary in surveying the income levels in the area before attempting to start an agency of this sort.

On the other hand here is a type of service which should expand inevitably in the better middle-class residential areas as help becomes ever scarcer, ever dearer, ever saucier. Needless to say, this is an exacting business, calling for full-time attendance. Apparently it can best be started by a couple of retirees with experience of one another's capacities, since this gives both a reasonable amount of free time. A special type of licence from the Ministry of Labour is required before such an agency can be started. Some such services are run successfully by women, thanks partly to their knowledge of the housewife's requirements.

A number of other service opportunities are open to the woman with experience of secretarial or shorthand-typing work, and (preferably) a knowledge of typewriters and duplicating machines.

For many people the field of newspaper and periodical journalism is bathed in glamour. In fact this is one of the more difficult spheres to enter *successfully*. The work is more exacting than it looks: the rewards are almost always uncertain. (I shall deal with them all in a moment.)

But for the retiree with energy and a car there is one very profitable part-time occupation open in certain areas. I mean the morning newspaper round. No raising of eyebrows, please! One publisher's salesman whom I know left publishing for such an opportunity in his fifties – and he has never regretted it. He joined a friend (whose partner had died) in an outer country area and *with half the effort and in half the time*, he is earning as much as he ever did in selling to booksellers. It is true that the paper roundsman must set his alarm clock for 5.30 in the morning. He is off on his way to pick up his papers at the train or the wholesalers an hour later. He must work fast and hard while he is on the round. But with a car *he finishes his round by ten or eleven o'clock*. The rest of the day is his own. In this business a wife with a memory for names and numbers, who can drive a little car, is just as useful as a sharing partner and may double your income.

How can one make a good living out of a newspaper round involving a car, with petrol at 4s. 3d. a gallon? For three good reasons. Because newspapers have trebled in price since the twenties: because customers are now willing to pay a delivery charge on each daily paper: because more weekly and monthly, periodical and technical journals, some very expensive, are bought today than ever before. Also in rural areas and outmost suburbs, you offer a useful morning delivery service. With a little salesmanship you can get the occasional order (and the commission) on a weekly supply of cigarettes, tobacco, and other daily necessities.

Inevitably the profitable round takes a lot of finding today. But it may still be found with diligent inquiry. The writer has happened to give three retirees (in rural areas) their first orders for newspapers. All are making a comfortable income of from £10 to £18 a week, and enjoying the leisure required to cultivate hobbies and a garden. One has developed his round into a full-scale grocery business employing a couple of assistants. Pre-war the village's grocer and general shop took the newspaper round in its stride. Schoolboys were eager to do the work for small salaries before school; parents liked – and often needed – the extra money; discipline was easily enough maintained. To-day schoolboys are no longer available for the news-paper round: older boys are expensive and irrespon-sible, since they already have jobs. There are still outer suburbs and villages, however, in which the local agent is stumbling along as best he can, short-handed and erratically served. There is nothing to prevent an independent retiree from breaking into such an area, offering a prompt and reliable service, cutting delivery charges if these are high, and generally competing to his heart's content for the business. Area agreements prevent this in all urban and inner suburban areas.

This is one of the very few businesses which really can be started on the proverbial shoe-string. Apart from an elderly second-hand car or delivery van on hire purchase no capital is needed. A five-pound note will probably cover your first week's papers and you pay for the second week with the money collected on the Saturday (or Sunday) of the first. You issue no accounts. You give no credit. You have no bad debts. Your book-keeping is of the simplest. You keep little or no stock. But it is for the younger and fitter retiree only, being very strenuous even with a partner and a car.

From the sale of papers we may now move up gingerly to the lowest rung of the journalistic ladder. You may find an opportunity to become the district correspondent to the local paper for your village or outer suburb. Today very many rural areas are poorly covered, because the small size of newspapers since 1939 has prevented the skilled correspondent from earning a living in his old district. Smaller provincial and London dailies similarly limit his possibilities when a big story breaks in his area. The district correspondent in the smaller area is paid by linage – anything from 2d. to $3\frac{1}{2}$d. a line. You cannot expect therefore to pick up a large income by such work, even after many years' experience.

No field of work is easier to enter. Simply attend meetings and report any other news that seems of local interest. The more people you know, particularly among local government, political, and association officials, the more little news stories you may be able to collect. Remember that the Women's Institute meeting, the minor church bazaar, the garden fête, social, political, or charitable, the engagement, the little car accident, even the broken leg of the chairman of the Literary Society, the village amateur show, the controversial sermon, the new post office box, even the monster marrow, are all of interest to *your* district, and the editor of the local paper is probably trying to cover it with the disjointed notes of the W.I. secretary, the screeds of the local crank, and the highly inaccurate reports of unpaid association officials and overworked clergymen.

To succeed at this most fascinating but rather arduous part-time job, you *must* be accurate about names, initials, addresses, dates, and detail of size, colour, shape of objects, and particularly of women's dress. You *ought* to learn shorthand: if you can't be bothered, learn to use abbreviated English in reporting at meetings, personal interviews, or, most ticklish of all, by phone. Errors are extremely dangerous, owing to the personal element bulking so large in small communities. People take offence at the most trifling mistake of reporting or of omission. Also the law of libel is still weighted heavily against the newspaper and in favour of the crook and the sharp solicitor who lives on earning damages for his clients out of the wrong initial or the slightly slighting adjective. You will find lots of useful tips in the excellent trade journal *World's Press News* (1s. 6d. weekly).

To be successful as a local correspondent three personal qualities are essential. You must like people, enjoy mixing with them, be a good listener to even the dreariest bore, be able to inspire confidence. You must like moving around and being where the little crowd is, however trivial its occasion. You must enjoy the hunt for news. You must be careless about hours of work, more important still, you must have a wife who allows you to go out to this meeting and that, night after night, just when she wants to enjoy a cosy chat at the end of the day's work. Finally you must be a fast but systematic worker. His card index of local personalities, officials, societies, even cranks and 'cards' is the correspondent's stand-by. Need one add that the journalist is born, not made. You will quickly discover whether you have the journalistic instinct in you or not. If not, drop it.

The other branch of journalism open to everybody is

freelance work, 'writing for the papers'. Fifty years ago it was easy to pick up a few hundred a year in this way if you had an expert knowledge of any subject from bee-keeping to yoga, from accountancy to yachting. These days are past. The Education Act of 1870 made that opportunity: the spread of secondary education is taking it away. Every day the standards demanded by editors (which means their readers) tend to rise. More research, more facts, new slants, better writing are called for. It is an unhappy fact that the editor of a national periodical is seldom able to use consistently in the sixties the contributor who wrote so valuable and lively a feature in the forties.

Almost every retiree has one or more fields of activity of which he has considerable knowledge. One is his old business or work, the other is his favourite hobby. But knowledge does not make a readable article for which an editor will pay guineas. Quite the contrary. The inevitable tendency of the expert is to become prolix, technical, wordy, in fact dull.

The question the would-be freelance must ask himself (or herself) is, Can I write? For one reason or another, the majority of people cannot. They cannot write well enough to meet the standards of a national, class, trade, or technical journal; yet these are the retiree's best quarry. The popular periodicals and newspapers, from *John Bull* to the *New Statesman*, from the *Daily Herald* to *The Times*, require immense journalistic skill from contributors to the magazine pages. Some of the simpler women's papers and a few of the more popular newspaper features covering women's interests, notably cookery, hygiene, beauty, and dress-making (*not* fashions), are the only exceptions to this rule. Save yourself endless time and labour by leaving these starry heights to the professional journalist.

There is one avenue to print and editorial contacts which demands no ability to write: instead it requires a flair for finding the human interest angles in the news and wide contacts. This is the provision of subjects for diary stories to the editors of newspaper diary features. London editors pay one or two guineas (even five if a picture can be provided) for each story and don't ask you to do any of the work. If you can provide the diary editor with an idea for a story and a contact, he will do the rest. Naturally this work needs introductions at first to prove your bona fides.

Even in the more modest field of specialized free-lancing a good deal of care should be exercised in planning your work. It is better to study carefully and eventually to satisfy the needs of the editor of one good journal than to have odd bits and pieces of work floating around a dozen offices on the off chance. . . . It is the regular feature, the longer series, the weekly or monthly article that pays best in the end. If you can become a really useful contributor to a strong paper, the editor can, and probably will, put other tit-bits in your way, surveys for his own annual reference book, articles for an associated journal, and so on. Remember that the able editor is a busy man and be merciful in dealing with him. Cultivate a curt, factual style in letters, phone calls, and especially in his office.

If you find difficulty in selling your work, it may be worth your while to invest in a course in journalism at one of the correspondence colleges. The London School of Journalism and the Regent Institute are among the most helpful and practical courses available in this country. They can give you much assistance in the technique of writing for the public; but they cannot give you the ability to write; that is inborn.

Freelance writing is no easy or quick road to extra money, as so many people imagine. Safer to regard it as a craft requiring an apprenticeship and the investment of endless time and labour before it pays off. The first year's work will be full of chilling disappointments: a small pile of curt rejection slips may be the only result of months of hard labour. Success can come very slowly and gradually indeed.

This work carries one consolation only with it. There are few thrills like the pleasure of seeing your own work in print. The mere effort to write also entails a mental training that is a tonic, makes your mind more active, stimulates your whole interest in life.

'I'm a great reader. In fact I know most of the modern novelists well. Couldn't I be a publisher's reader?' This is a common suggestion from the well-read retiree. The answer is *Punch*'s advice to those about to marry. For plodding through a vilely bad novel of 70,000 words, you will probably receive a fee of two guineas. Manuscript reading is one of the last remaining sweated industries. But don't blame the publisher who is having a struggle to make ends meet. Blame the tens of thousands of would-be authors, literate and semi-literate, who swamp him under a sea of drivel, not 5 per cent of which is worth considering, let alone publishing. (Unhappily the art of writing does not obviously demand special training, like music, painting, or ballet). Yet even in the barely average year of 1959 the publishers issued over 22,000 volumes.

But given good eyesight, a thorough knowledge of the English language, syntax, grammar, and spelling, you may enjoy proof reading for a London or provincial publisher. One or two quite elderly retired teachers enjoy this work and the little bit of money it earns.

The idea of doing illustrations for the magazines or for advertisements attracts many elderly people. The bookshops are full of excellent little primers telling you how to learn to draw in a few weeks. Commercial art studios, advertising agents, and editors are all clamouring for new artists. The rates paid for good commercial art work today are very high indeed, and getting higher. There is almost a famine in first-rate artists for this work. Work can be done at home, at one's leisure. It all sounds most attractive. But how often does any amateur find a way of earning steady sums of money by a little congenial work in his studio? Almost never. Only professional artists in semi-retirement ever seem to manage this. Why? Because to get regular work from a magazine or a commercial studio demands two qualifications. First, one should have been through an art school of some sort, have had some experience of commercial work, and often in the case of advertising, a knowledge of lay-out and a considerable familiarity with lettering work. Secondly one must be available easily and often for conferences and meetings at the office. This means living within forty or fifty miles of London or one of the largest provincial cities. Art work is only for the expert retiree.

But good work is highly paid.

The Society of Industrial Artists has published an interesting schedule of average fees for most types of commercial work. Rate for a 'rough' for a black and white ad. in a national trade paper averages 7 guineas, a rough in colour 15 guineas. A design including finished work and drawings and typographic specifications for a press ad. in black and white averages 20–35 guineas.

A quad crown poster (30 in. by 40 in.) averages 35 guineas for regional display, and 70 guineas for a National Poster Campaign. Probably the highest paid of all commercial work is the package design: a single package design may earn anything from 20–100 guineas.

Today one historic craft is attracting the amateur for almost the first time. People of all ages are taking up printing as a hobby. Hitherto the layman has regarded printing as a tiresome, dirty, and rather a dangerous job. Lead poisoning among printers has had a good deal of publicity. Many of the old printing shops were of course dirty and dangerous holes. Today many printing shops are attractive places, the floors and other surfaces being vacuumed every few hours. The craft of printing is itself a fascinating and not a very difficult one. There is the widest scope for the exercise of taste. And you see results quickly. The work is varied, including typesetting, type display, the making up of pages, and finally machining or printing them.

Like many other crafts, printing is apt to be rather a messy job. The older compositor invariably wore an apron. You can't do better than follow his example. And roll up your shirt sleeves above the elbow before you start work. Accommodation for your tiny plant, however, requires a separate small room. Printing is a hobby that you cannot pursue in a corner of the living-room!

There is still one fairly dirty job in printing; you must ink the type locked up in the frame, before taking an impression, if you are using one of the old Albion presses (costing about £20–£30 second hand). This will print you two pages of a booklet, or a small-size poster. But one smaller machine, printing postcard size, the Adana No. 2, inks its type automatically. This model has been designed with an eye to beginners: you will receive an excellent instruction book from the makers with a new Adana costing £10.

To enjoy printing you need a good eye, a meticulous mind, and deft, patient fingers. Although the process of picking your type out of the curiously divisioned type-case and setting it, letter by letter, upside down into the 'composing-stick' is at first finicky, it is not in any way difficult. All the movements are simple, you can take your own time, and you should gradually acquire an easy rhythmic movement from type-case to stick and back again.

The art of printing consists partly in the selection of a pleasant easily read type, suitable to the job, and partly in the beauty of the pattern you make on paper with your dark masses of type and your cunningly designed masses of white (blank) space. The most flexible types for the beginner, who may wish to print anything from an order of service to a menu card, from a poster for a local Women's Institute meeting to an eight-page booklet on his family's heraldry, are probably Caslon,

Bodoni, and Gill. Type faces can be bought in any fount from 6 point up to 72 point (poster). This book is set in 11 point Baskerville, the appendices in 8 point.

For the retiree with a taste for detail craftsmanship, printing is a fascinating hobby. It can be made to earn a tiny bit also. When the initial equipment is bought your expenses are little more than paper, ink, and occasional furniture. Now that professional printing has become so expensive, there are often associations, clubs, and individuals who cannot afford to pay for having menus, programmes, leaflets printed in the ordinary way. Yet they do not care to have the work duplicated. In such cases the private printer can sometimes step in and do the job at the modest price the customer can pay. Here, as always, the more social contacts you have the more likely you are to hear of the work available. Your own press will print you a business card for distribution or any other selling material you can effectively use. The Dryad Press, Leicester, sets out to help the tyro in every way. Their book, *Printing Explained* (5s.), is full of the practical advice you want.

Having considered the relatively modern craft of printing we may turn back to look at some of the really ancient crafts. Possibly because I am clumsy myself, these seem to me to be unrewarding occupations today. Nothing could be more fascinating, wet and dirty though the job may be, than spinning the potter's wheel and shaping dull clay into useful or lovely shapes on it. It involves being near a clay bed and having a kiln or the use of one. But a year's training and skill are required to produce a saleable article. Once produced the article is not often easily saleable. As more and more

British china and pottery comes on the home market through the shrinking of export sales, competition must inevitably become increasingly keen. The local shops are chiefly interested in something of local interest. Thus the W.I. stall is often the only steady outlet. They pay you retail price, less a small charge to cover their own costs. Local shops will take around 33⅓ per cent sales commission. This is a hobby for the enthusiast only.

The same applies to weaving, which is considered in the chapter on hobbies (see page 220). I mention it here as a few keen, capable workers do make a little money from it. Small useful articles like cushion covers, table mats, scarves, are more profitable than lengths of material. Many such can be woven loosely and therefore quickly.

Basketry offers little scope today. It is extremely closely competed by large manufacturing concerns. The smaller domestic basket work is partly in the hands of the blind, the crippled, and tuberculous patients. It is especially suited to the needs of all those unfortunates. Better leave it to them.

Even more severe problems arise over carpentry, more fashionably called woodworking today. Ever since timber became scarce and expensive and furniture prices soared, woodworking has become one of the most popular of home hobbies. The *Woodworker*, organ of the amateurs in carpentry, now circulates over 100,000 copies, instead of about 20,000 before 1939. This knocks carpentry out of the spare-time earning class. If you are clever with the carpenter's tools, you will have to regard your work as a favourite hobby: there is no money in it for the amateur who is not a near genius who can develop a market for a quite exceptional product in wood.

During the Second World War toys were so scarce that there was good money to be made out of making even simple rag dolls from inexpensive materials. Today the toy-making concerns are back in the field, more versatile and ingenious in their designs than ever. Even the model aeroplane, railway, motor-car is being produced in quantity with a finish and strength and at a price with which the amateur cannot compete. For women with clever fingers there is still a market for dolls with removable clothes and for outfits of dolls' clothes. These can be sold both privately and through the shops.

The toy which offers the best scope to the retiree is probably the local souvenir. The type of house common in the neighbourhood, but uncommon in city suburbs, the thatched Sussex cottage or the wooden-frame Kentish house, are often popular. But the successes in this line are usually made with quite original ideas.

Today there is quite a vogue for puppetry. All sorts of people watch puppet shows, want to see how puppets are made, how they work. Although expensive to buy, the experts insist that puppets are inexpensive and relatively simple to make when you have gained some experience. Again puppetry seems to be best started as merely a hobby. The amateur who attains to real skill in puppet making and puppet showing may, however, make a little money out of his pets eventually. Fees for a straight Punch and Judy to an elaborate puppet show vary from £5 5s. to £10 10s. You require at least three or four puppets as well as a small stage with curtains. Successful puppet work, one gathers, calls for mechanical and vocal skills as well as for flexible fingers.

The puppet-shower is well served in his tricky work by a voluntary organization of his own. The Educational Puppetry Association takes care of most of the obvious beginner's snags. For an annual subscription of 18s. (subsequent 15s. 6d.) you have the use of an expert advice service, of a specialist library, of inexpensive leaflets on technical problems and assistance if you form a local group. During school term the office at 23a Southampton Place, London WC1, is open on Mondays and Fridays from 6 p.m. to 8 p.m. Here courses for beginners and others are held, occasional demonstrations are given, and there is an annual Festival of Puppet Plays. Both a monthly newssheet and a bi-annual illustrated magazine, *Puppet Post*, are thrown in for good measure.

Puppets and equipment can be bought ready-made from Pelham Puppets, High Street, Marlborough, Wilts., along with books of instructions.

To women the crafts give some attractive opportunities of spare-time earning. The simplest is knitting. A great many of the wool shops arrange for the knitting of garments from wool bought from them. The work is usually done at fixed rates by women with some time on their hands. These rates vary from 2s. 6d. an ounce for plain knitting (vests, socks, etc.) to 6s. for more elaborate designs, such as Fair Isle jumpers.

For the first-rate needlewoman there is still a small income in fine needlework for export. But the work must be meticulously accurate and the finishing off immaculate. The Women's Industries, 41 Tothill Street, London, sw1, will advise you as to the possibilities for your work if you will send them a sample. The occasional naval or merchant navy officer who has become a fine needleman may also be able to dispose of first-rate work by taking advice from the same source.

One of the most obvious means of spare-time earning for the woman who has worked as a secretary, or run a small business of her own, is to open a typewriting office. Obviously she has all the skills required from the superficial point of view. Unfortunately skills are not enough. The smallest typewriting office is a business which requires judgement, sales ability, self-reliance, tenacity, and some capital. Unfortunately the combination of these assets is rare, while the number of women retired from business is enormous and grows every year. An experienced secretary may do best by securing secretarial work for one or two local firms.

It is often better for the retired business woman to be content with doing a little typewriting and duplicating at home. I emphasize duplicating, because the money is in the duplicating machine and not in the typewriter. The best customer of any retiree's typewriting business is the firm that circularizes regularly, be it a small department store or a turf agent. It is best to begin with a simple hand duplicator of the right sort, as power duplicators are expensive, even when bought on hire-purchase terms.

On the other hand, a middle-aged woman with either some business or housekeeping experience can often tackle one interesting if exacting job where she feels that she is doing valuable work. The capable receptionist to a doctor or a group of doctors is an invaluable asset. She also fulfils a vital social function in her neighbourhood and she meets pretty well everybody. But the job is exacting and should only be attempted by a woman who knows that she has ability, a pleasant outlooking personality, a head for detail, and incidentally that she is not a snob.

In a country district the receptionist may work for only one doctor, do a good deal of prescription copying and even a little simple dispensing. If she works for a group in a London suburb or a provincial city suburb her work may be confined purely to receiving patients, fixing appointments, keeping records. But if she has shorthand-typing this may be invaluable. The modern doctor has to keep a great quantity of records.

The salaries paid for this important and fascinating job are not high. They range from £350 to £500 a year. But there are other rewards than money, and anyone doing this job efficiently will enjoy a splendid sense of fulfilment.

While so sceptical about the possibilities of the typewriting office for the average retired business woman, I feel confident that a few men and women will do extremely well in such business in the near future. They will be people with exceptional judgement and sales ability. They will make their money in circularizing, possibly by hiring out typewriters as well, and even by selling machines. A huge new market is opening up to this business in the home. The aim of the typewriter industry in this country is now 'a typewriter in every home'. To secure this target the great typewriting firms will be compelled to use very small outlets like the typewriting office. But typewriters need sale by demonstration, a difficult type of selling.

Having considered most of the humbler and more exacting forms of spare-time earning, it may be worth while to look at some of the easier and more attractive ones. There is the golf-club secretaryship. In the country this is an unusually attractive part-time job, yielding £120–£180 a year and allowing you to meet a lot of pleasant people, with the inevitable committee crank or fusspot supplying the only fly in the ointment. A crack course near a town is of course worth a lot more, but it usually means longish hours. It is true that the finances of the average golf-course are difficult today: that gives scope for your salesmanship in finding new members to replace the losses, in livening up the service, and in keeping everybody happy. The trouble with this beau ideal of a retiree's job is its scarcity. One town, one golf-course, is the average allowance, and golf secretaries are healthy specimens. Yet you are most unlikely to pull down such a plum unless you are known and reasonably liked (certainly not actively disliked) in the neighbourhood. Still luck is a wonderful adjutant. I know two retirees who walked out of their jobs in a city, bought a house in a small coast resort, and found themselves endowed with a golf-club secretaryship within twelve months of their arrival! So we can all hope.

One well-paid new occupation open to women is private hairdressing at home. Experience is almost essential, but one man in my area who retires shortly is getting experience and buying equipment to fit himself for this unusual but profitable occupation. But find out whether a licence is necessary before you begin.

One of the easiest and pleasantest ways of earning the odd dollar is to take an occasional paying guest out in the car. One cannot make a practice of it: that requires a hackney carriage licence, a white disc announcing the fact beside your back number-plate, and it involves a heavy insurance rate covering passengers. But one or two retirees' in country districts are able to oblige their friends by an occasional lift over longer distances for an honorarium without having to acquire professional status. It is obviously impossible to do this when professional car hirers and taxi-owners are at work.

For the retiree with business training, blessed with £5,000 capital apart from his house and his annuities, a most attractive occupation is investment in and partial direction of one or more small concerns. It enables him (with ability and reasonable luck) to earn anything from 20 to 30 per cent on his money, including director's fees and expenses, and it gives him an interest in active business concerns.

To enjoy this work one must have experience of business methods and organization. Many small businesses, whether manufacturing, wholesale or retail, are poorly organized. Their owners too often lack experience of the most modern techniques of management. My friend G retired from the control of a successful north-country newspaper business at the age of fifty. He came south to an entirely new locality: today he is a director of a business selling second-hand machinery, of a book publishing house, of a textile mill, of a permanent wave, and of a mineral water concern. At sixty-seven these interests, G finds, keep his mind young and his energies engaged. Although the work involved takes him to London or the provinces for two or three days a week, he vows that it does not interfere with his golf, his gardening, his film-going, or his leisure. Such work involves risks. Most of the best opportunities for investment of this active sort are not to be found from friends. To find them demands a close study of the Business Opportunities advertisements in *The Times*, *Daily Telegraph*, and one or two of the best provincial dailies. Inevitably a few of the advertisers are cranks or incompetents, an occasional crook may get in for a day; immense care and a good accountant's help are needed in the arduous process of vetting replies. Occasionally you will make an error of judgement. G, for all his exceptional flair admits to this. But the zest of the game of business lifts most elderly director-investors quickly out of any mood of disappointment.

Today every hospital in the country is short of staff, short of nurses, short of orderlies, short of office staff. So many of the smaller hospitals are glad to take on part-time staff for all these types of work. Often some of the work is being done by women in their sixties. Naturally some earlier experience is required in every such type of work: pure amateurs are useless for it; yet many able women retirees with nursing or other hospital experience overlook this unusually useful and worthwhile way of earning extra money by part-time work. They forget too that all types of hospital work are now increasingly well paid.

Are there any openings for men and women from the serious professions? one is sometimes asked. 'We seem to be overlooked', is a common remark. The reply is surely that *all* the openings outlined are open to the retiree barrister or architect or biologist. But almost any professional or scientific training which is not too narrowly specialized gives added opportunities for occupation in retirement. A little ingenuity may work out something really original and remunerative.

A Scottish barrister of my acquaintance, the late Archibald Crawford, Q.C., retired from the Scottish Bar in 1927. In a few years he had created an entirely new profession for himself. He was training business executives in the art of public speaking or, as he would have preferred to have described it, in the technique of communicating ideas.

By 1947 he was employing 30 part-time tutors to train over 1000 businessmen every year in this difficult art.

Two different friends of mine retired from top positions in a vast East African state. Retired in the fifties, each had still youngish children whose education required finishing. Yet each was a specialist – one in agriculture, the other in modern transport. Each has made a new career for himself, in an entirely new field. By some curious accident, both men have found an identical solution to their problem. They have both applied their highly trained minds to modern biology. They have both enough humility not to scorn teaching. Today each of them is teaching that subject in a fashionable girls' school near his home. And working hard at it, believe me.

Bank managers sometimes complain of low pensions. One of them solved this problem very easily by joining a local firm of estate-agents on his retirement. His intimate knowledge of the town's personalities and business coupled with the banker's technique for assessing financial status should make him invaluable.

One job that is specially interesting to trained professional people is field work in market research. There are three concerns in London each of which uses around 200 outside interviewers on a part-time basis. Says the Field Manager of one of these, Sales Research Services Ltd, 84, Gloucester Place, London, WI : 'We employ something like 200 outside interviewers on a part-time basis, and they are in the main married women, widows, and students. From time to time we conduct surveys outside our normal territory (we operate regularly in 93 towns and villages), for which active retired men are very suitable. We have in the past used this type of interviewer very successfully for interviewing at executive level, interviewing farmers and such like. The surveys are conducted on the basis of a questionnaire and payment is around 25s. to 30s. a day, plus fares, postages, etc.' This firm is compiling a list of retired people interested in this type of work whom they can eventually contact as and when work is available, selecting those whose geographical position is suitable for the territory involved.

PICK A HOBBY THAT YOU'LL ENJOY

'No man is really happy or safe without a hobby,' observed Osler, and Sir Winston Churchill goes further. 'To be really happy and really safe,' he says, 'one ought to have at least two or three hobbies and they must all be real. . . . The growth of alternative mental interests is a long process. The seeds must be carefully chosen; they must fall on good ground; they must be sedulously tended, if the vivifying fruits are to be at hand when needed.' If this be true of a statesman seldom out of office or active opposition, how much more urgent are two or three hobbies to the retiree with all of time before him.

Today hobbies are much more intelligently cultivated than when I was a boy. At school stamp-collecting was merely the gathering together of series of stamps and the swopping or trading thereof with one's friends. Now the stamp-collector takes a lively interest in the history of the countries represented in his collection, in the politics which have influenced their history, which may have removed the heads of kings and replaced them with republican or national symbols. In the geography of these countries, their position in the world, and their influence in international affairs: in the art of the designer of these miniature national symbols. In the intricate processes of lithography and printing which produce the sheets of identical stamps. Significantly enough, that very alert newspaper, the *Daily Telegraph*, started a new hobby feature for its readers on stamps.

In recent years the services available to the stamp collector have improved immensely. Every great city has now one or more stamp shops. One of the hobbies journals, *Stamp Collecting*, publishes fifty-two issues a year full of fascinating material on stamps.

This is one of the delightful hobbies on which you can spend very little or a great deal, according to your income or your fancy. The beginner needs only one loose-leaf album, containing not less than a hundred quadrille ruled pages. When this has been in use a short time it might be better to buy one of the albums holding between 200 and 300 sheets. A good album strongly bound in cloth costs anything from 15s. to 45s. But if you want a *de luxe* binding, or an album with other refinements, you may go up to a price of £10–£12. The best book on the subject is *Gibbons' Simplified Stamp Collecting* (1961 edition).

The first question the beginner must ask himself is what stamps he wants to collect. The cost of his collection will depend entirely on what country or issues he chooses. In his first year the beginner will be unwise to spend more than £50. If this is wisely spent, he will have the nucleus of a collection.

A reasonably complete set of German stamps may have several hundred and be worth only a small sum. A collection of stamps of Newfoundland would contain fewer stamps, but if complete it would be worth several hundred pounds.

Clearly the serious collector must specialize. Generally speaking a country like Canada, Australia, and Africa has proved to be popular among specialists because a reasonable amount of material is available at fairly reasonable prices. A highly specialized collection of, say, the early classic dominions of the British Empire (New Zealand, Ceylon, Canada) can cost a collector many thousand pounds.

The collector of ability, who gives real care to the work, should be able to make a little money out of a specialized collection in about three years' time, the experts tell me. But he must develop that precious sense, philatelic acumen.

There are now no fewer than four hundred philatelist societies and Stamp Clubs in the country. Full details of these are to be found in the *British Philatelic Association's Year Book of Philatelic Societies* which costs only 2s. 6d. from the association (see Appendix IV). If you wish to take stamp collecting seriously, you can do some quiet study of the subject. This is easy in London where the British Philatelic Association holds lecture courses leading to a diploma.

Gardening is the ideal hobby in retirement, if it be taken easily. There is always something to do in a garden. Boredom is rare. Each change of season brings its change of work. You can see results quickly if you grow annuals (and accept the extra work involved).

But the wise retiree will approach his garden (old or new) – and the seed merchant's alluring catalogues – with a wary eye. English garden design *still* stems from the tradition of the Great House. It is designed to make work for the five gardeners and the boy at the Manor, for the man and/or boy at the doctor's. It is often beautifully designed in terms of space and ornamental charm: never in terms of time. The square yard of colour and not the man-hour of labour is the standard used. Today the wise retiree will plan (or replan) his garden with one eye on the man-hours required to keep it decently in order. This will mean doing away with half or more of the smaller flower and bulb beds. Cover them with turf and halve the work of the man with the mower. Put the bulbs, after careful dividing up and individual ripening in the sun, into grass or fresh ground in a sheltered corner of wild garden, where they will live a sheltered life in winter and reward you with pleasant if not remarkable blooms in many following springs. Cart away any old-fashioned, pest-breeding rockeries. A small rock garden will house all the rock plants you need. You will be surprised how much more spacious plain runs of grass make the smaller garden. You can afford to have a third of your garden down in grass, just as the old authorities used to advise.

Discard annuals for perennials, thus saving yourself no end of labour. Your losses should be slight, if you choose your perennial substitutes with care. Combine your orchard with a labour-saving wild garden of wild orchard grass, planted with daffodils, bluebells, or wild tulips. When your bulbs have bloomed, the grass will quickly cover their drooping heads with brilliant green.

Above all, begin by planning the garden as a whole on a sheet of paper. Better design most of it from an overlooking bedroom window. The average garden fails to make any impact on eye or imagination. It is simply a series of bits and pieces of colour. The garden that catches the visitors' breath is often not the big show place but a modest cottage garden designed as a single harmony of line and colour.

Most of this one has learned in designing new and re-designing old ones for oneself. But although our English garden books are easily the best in the world, they give little help in this vital problem of simplifying the garden. Only in an admirable little book by Phoebe Fenwick Gaye called *The Simple Garden* are these ideas helpfully and specifically developed.

There is one important proviso. However much you may want to save your poor back, you will never be able to leave your garden as it is, if you are a born gardener. In our sixth year in it, our eighth little garden, but a third of an acre, is at this moment in the throes of a simplification programme designed to cut down labour still further. It is a matter of temperament!

Of course, it is possible to start a garden on nothing. 'I was a married man with a garden of my own before I realized that people bought things to plant in their gardens,' says H. L. V. Fletcher.*

'In order to garden two things are essential. One is a garden and the other is a spade.' This thorough-going gardener believes that we have been spoilt by our nurserymen and a number of very keen gardeners prefer to work from seed. In fact, alpines, bulbs, roses, many kinds of fruit and ornamental trees and shrubs as well as a lot of annuals and perennials can all be grown from seed. But it is hard work. It takes a long time to see results and it calls for real skill and care. I am not a seed gardener myself and I hesitate to recommend the techniques to any but the tough and the strong-minded.

If you smoke a good deal there is one large-leaved,

* *Gardening on a Shoestring*

rather tropical-looking plant that can save you a lot of money. Tobacco-growing became interesting during the Second World War as a result of rationing.* It was a difficult business. Now it is tolerably well organized for the amateur through a Tobacco Centre and Curing Co-operative at Tilty, near Dunmow.

With the help of this body, some of my friends claim to provide themselves with 20 smokable cigarettes for 4d. These are the energetic ones with a bit of land, a small kiln, and the time and patience to care for their plants and to be meticulous in drying, fermenting, and shredding the leaves. All this you must do yourself to get down to the price of five cigarettes a penny.

But the Curing Co-operative is ready to take part or all the processing off your shoulders at a price. One of the serious difficulties about tobacco leaf is its sour, pungent smell to which the housewife may well object. Even when matured and ready to smoke it is wise to add 20 to 30 per cent of your own favourite tobacco to soften the flavour of the British-grown leaf. One or two of my friends failed to get any solace from the cigarettes they had produced with so much care. Others, however, will smoke nothing else but their own tobacco and seem to thrive on it.

What does the whole business cost them? This depends largely on how much you do yourself. It is not necessary to spend a lot on 'factory processing'. Working to their directions, the Curing Co-operative allow for an over-all capital outlay of £10 for press, shredder,

* Concessions were then given for it to be cultivated in gardens without licence or payment of duty, providing it was for the personal consumption of the grower only.

and equipment, spread over ten years. If you grow from seed your home tobacco need not cost you more than 2d. to 3d. an ounce for an average crop of 10–20 lb.

If you grow from plants, add 1½d. to 2d. an ounce. If you use special methods of heat and 'flue' curing, add 2d. to 3d. an ounce. If you send your leaf to a curing centre for fermentation, add 3d. to 6d. an ounce. Allowing for all this and still mixing with 20 to 30 per cent of a commercial brand of tobacco, your bill should still be only 1s. to 1s. 6d. an ounce, says Hugh Cuthbertson, Director of the Tilty Centre.

One hobby is often dangerous to the active-minded retiree: he may ride it to death and make himself into a crashing bore. The one-track mind is peculiarly a danger to elderly retirees who are no longer out in the world, getting the corners rubbed off in the daily hurly-burly. From the purely practical point of view two hobbies are always better than one: the first can be an outdoor hobby, the other an indoor one. Gardening and model-making seem to mix very well for the nimble-fingered, while bird-watching and stamp-collecting can make a happy combination for the elderly and less energetic.

Not that bird-watching is for the fragile. Field Marshal Lord Alanbrooke rightly described it as the ideal hobby for all young officers! But there is local, lazy bird watching and strenuous scientific bird watching, just as there is gentle hill climbing at Malvern and back-breaking climbing of the Matterhorn. Listeners to Peter Scott know just how strenuous bird-watching can be. It seems always to start with a long walk in the teeth of a nor'-wester and to end with longer hours spent wading through bog on or in which one must finally crouch for even damper hours. All this for the sight of one small dark bird winging through the night to her nest!

Yet bird-watching grows more popular every year. Unlike so many fashionable hobbies it is inexpensive. Britain is rich in birds. Only in Brazil and Australia are you likely to see a greater variety of birds than those that nest in the coasts of Northumberland, North Wales, and East Sussex. In its first nine months of existence eighty-two species have been observed from Monks House in Northumberland. The 'birder' can have his holidays settled for him quite easily by his hobby. The number of bird observatories and field study centres grows steadily. The devotee can spend a fascinating week at any one of these centres.

'The visitors who come here are a mixed bunch,' writes an observer,* 'as varied as the birds they watch, but the first shared meal of any group unites them as a flock. By the end of that meal a gentle Liverpool docker, whose schoolmistress-wife has weaned him from the study of politics to that of birds, is interpreting the benefits of communism to two energetic American ladies who are "doing" British birds. A couple of London typists discuss the courtship and flight of the tree-creeper. A lady psychiatrist and two doctors compare notes on fulmar population problems.'

Today the once fashionable hobby of butterfly collecting no longer attracts the elderly gentleman as once it did. Too many beautiful species have been collected out of existence. The same applies to bird's egg collecting

* Rosemary Wintour, *New Statesman*

outside the schools. The egg collectors have deprived us of the sight of many brightly plumaged birds and of some exquisite songsters.

Nor is the study of wild flowers so popular as it was. There are fewer nature rambles than there used to be. A pity. Botany is one of the most fascinating and the least expensive of hobbies. It takes you out of doors in all reasonable weather. It gives your walk an object and tends to lengthen it. It adds to your enjoyment of your home neighbourhood. And the new discovery is always a thrill, especially to the city-bred retiree.

'I am no botanist,' says Gissing, 'but I have long found pleasure in herb gathering. I love to come upon a plant which is unknown to me, to identify it with the help of my book, to greet it by name when next it shines upon my path.'

A very little knowledge of its wild flowers gives a new intimacy to one's feeling for the countryside. The wild flowers of no two countries are completely alike. The rarer species are often curiously beautiful. But to find the rare beauties demands a knowledge of the common varieties. Botany, with its Latin names and its technique of study, is most easily learned in a group which rambles the countryside regularly under a skilled leader. If no group exists in your district and you shun the labour of forming one, it is always possible to acquire the necessary knowledge from a good pocket textbook as Gissing did.

'I am busy with the hawkweeds,' he writes in early autumn, 'that is to say, I am learning to distinguish and to name as many as I can. For scientific classification I have little mind; it does not happen to fall in with my habits of thought; but I like to be able to give its name (the "trivial" by choice) to every flower I meet in my walks. Why should I be content to say, "Oh, it's a hawkweed?" That is but one degree less ungracious than if I dismissed all the yellow-rayed as "dandelions". I feel as if the flower were pleased by my recognition of its personality.'

There is one absorbing subject closely connected with local affairs to which curiously few retirees turn. I refer to the weather. Unfortunately the study of weather conditions, the daily concern of every citizen of these uncertain isles, is fearsomely named meteorology by the scientists. Let this deter no one from making a study or a hobby of it. Do you realize that in however small a village you live, there the Air Ministry has a reporting station. Every day some conscientious citizen measures scrupulously the amount of rain which has fallen into his recording instrument, fills in his quite detailed form, and duly posts his report monthly to the Air Ministry, once a year to a county water authority. If there is no observer in your own district, you may be able to take over the work, which is unpaid.

The technique of weather forecasting is developing fast. The increasing accuracy of our own Air Ministry's forecasts is one evidence of the rapid improvement in the techniques of forecasting weather over an ever-increasing part of the globe. An absorbing approach to the whole subject is provided by Sir N. Shaw's *The Drama of Weather*.

Best of all hobbies are surely those that can be pursued for an entire lifetime, whose possibilities are limitless. One of these is architecture. The materials for study are all around, in manors, churches, town halls, villas, cottages, and even factories. Architecture is the study of building, civil, ecclesiastical, military, or naval. Most of us prefer to study houses or churches. Oddly enough architecture remained for a century a blind spot in the British culture. The Industrial Revolution not merely made our coal, iron, cotton, and wool areas into eyesores: it seemed to rob the British public of its eyesight so far as building was concerned. Witness the mess we made of the majority of our Georgian towns, with the exception of Alnwick, Bath, Blandford, Fareham, Farnham (Surrey), Richmond (Yorks), Stamford, and one or two others. Compare even these half-dozen little remnants of our heritage with the far older yet almost completely intact medieval cities of France, Austria, Germany, Italy, or Switzerland, not to mention Yugoslavia's Split and Dubrovnik. In Split there still stands the fabulous palace to which the ailing Roman emperor, Diocletian, retired from the burden of dictatorship in the third century A.D. The palace now houses for the time being 3,500 of Tito's people!

Today the case is altered. Everybody is beginning to realize what we have lost. Our eyes are opened to the richness of our heritage remaining. Town-planning, already the rule over much of Europe in the civilized eighteenth century, has returned on a heroic, if bureaucratic, scale in the barbarous twentieth.

The materials for the study of architecture are everywhere in the older English towns. The centuries certainly jostle one another, if they do not kiss and commingle. Here is a Jacobean gateway, there a late

Norman church next to a Regency house. Everywhere
the Victorian terrace and occasionally, as at Bexhill, a
post-Gropius seaside pavilion. The material for study
is endless and usually accessible by bus or car; the few
text-books necessary are cheap and readable; and this
study takes one out into the open air a good deal without requiring much effort. There is always an objective
to make one forget fatigue.

For many elderly people the architecture of churches
has a special appeal. The leisure of many a long lifetime
has been spent happily on the study of old churches.

Incidentally one quiet, old-fashioned favourite of a
churchlover's hobby is coming back into a certain
favour. People are beginning to rub church brasses
again. At one time this was very much an art for the
elderly. Today it is being taught to children: and some
young people combine it with their strenuous walking,
cycling, and motoring. It is certainly one of the most
inexpensive hobbies there are. The often uninteresting
looking flat plate in the dark floor of an old church can
usually be coaxed to produce a figure of a knight, a
priest, or a parishioner, in all his grandeur of armour or
costume.

All you need is a roll of thin, hard paper about 3 ft.
wide (ceiling or shelf paper will do), a stick of heel-
ball, a clean duster, a clean nail-brush, transparent
sticky tape, some weights to hold down the paper.
First you dust the plate carefully with a soft cloth as
there is always grit and dust on the surface of a brass
which will show through on your rubbing unless you
clear it away. Having gently cleaned the brass, you
spread your paper over the design, weighing it down

at the corners with stones or books, then you use your
nail-brush to rub the brass over the paper as it lies
on the plate. This gives you the outline of the figure
which means that you can confine your rubbing to the
figure itself, and avoid making dark marks around it.
When you have carefully scrubbed the design, you are
ready to rub the heel-ball over the paper firmly. In the
black wax covering the paper, you will see the outline
of the design more or less clearly according to your luck.
After that you go on with your rubbing. You rub hard
so as to bring the heel-ball up into a rich black. To do
this it is best to use the flat of the heel-ball so as to avoid
the sharp edge getting down into the engraving and
spoiling the outline of your picture.

This is surely one of the quietest of all the crafts! But
it can be fascinating. I knew one elderly retiree to whom
it brought great pleasure over many years. After an
hour and a half's rubbing you may have on your paper
a really delightful design, full of interesting detail. In
deed when you become accomplished in the art, you
may be able to decorate a room with some vigorous
and unusual designs.

Nowadays those who take up architecture are apt to
find more interest in domestic than in ecclesiastical
building. A house is still home for most of us and old
houses shed all sorts of light on the way of life in earlier
ages. Architecture is an easy approach to history.

Both styles and jargon are simpler and more interest
ing in domestic architecture. Good period houses are
usually easier to find than good period churches, simply
because there are so many more of them.

For the retiree who likes to study the world about

him, archaeology has special attractions. This old science has increased enormously in scope and enterprise during the past fifty years. It has two attractive features. Very often one can study the remotest past on one's own doorstep. Flint arrows have been discovered fifty yards from my own home. Also archaeology is one of the least expensive of all hobbies. It calls for nothing more, in many areas, than a small pocket enlarging glass and a walking-stick.

The dramatic discoveries in the Near East have led many people to suppose that a lively interest in archaeology involves travel and the strenuous physical exercise of excavation. This is not so. You can start the study of archaeology in your own county in very many cases. A couple of friends of mine have already made useful discoveries in the course of their amateur work near their own homes. Often there is a county Archaeological Society which can tell you where to look for remains of past *cultures*. For archaeology is now no longer merely the study of prehistory, but has expanded its scope to cover the story of mankind from the remotest antiquity to Anglo-Saxon times. Our local museums are particularly rich in archaeological remains, and there is often a handbook to the county which contains not only a knowledgeable account of the discoveries made there but also an archaeological gazetteer indicating the chief areas of interest, as well as a list of museums in the county containing treasures.

There must be a simple beginner's handbook on archaeology, but I have never met it. You may therefore do better by reading some of the *local* material in your library before attempting any text-book. Archaeologists appear to find it difficult to write for the layman. But don't let this fact deter you from taking up this absorbing and eye-opening hobby. (All of Methuen's admirable County Archaeologies are easy reading, but as most of them are out of print you will have to rely on libraries or second-hand copies.)

Since the camera is almost as common a gadget as the fountain-pen today, I assume the retiree is at home with it. No other hobby is quite so well supplied with books, papers, expert advice.

Among the outdoor hobbies, I omit sports. Every Englishman is expert in one or another of our games: most outdoor sports, barring golf and bowls, cannot easily be taken up after fifty. But there is one delicious exception. One may take up either sea or river fishing at almost any age. Good fishing may be more difficult to find than it was, club fees may be more expensive, like rods and other tackle, yet fishing remains a relatively inexpensive hobby. Every year, they tell me, the number of anglers grows. The Sunday newspaper with the largest circulation in the world* would scarcely be so interested in anglers unless there were shoals of them.

What is the peculiar attraction of fishing for so many people? Apparently its infinite variety is one lure. Fishing can be one of the least tiring and laziest of sports, or you can make it almost as arduous as rock-climbing. The angler is at liberty to choose his own pattern of exertion, to keep his own tempo in a way impossible even in golf. His only adversary is the

* *News of the World* holds annual angling competitions in many fishing centres.

fish, and only a big one can chivvy the angler up stream and down. The fascination of fishing has never been completely explained, not even by Izaak Walton. But one Maurice Wiggin had a good shot at it.*

'Speaking as a very lazy man who is miserable if he has nothing to do, I must say that fishing gives me precisely the right amount of occupation. When I am fishing I am free to meditate and ponder, if I wish to do so, yet I am doing *something*, and that something is not sufficiently important or difficult to monopolize my attention or even to make me concentrate very hard . . . so fishing fills my bill.

'This may well be one of the many reasons why I am not a very successful angler. For catching fish is a tough business. A heart-breaking business. Fish are partial to their natural element and reluctant to leave it. To outwit a fish you must put your best foot forward. You must even concentrate. A fish is not a fool . . .' Which surely defines the double charm of fishing, the leisurely country atmosphere coupled with the thrill of the duel.

Like me, however, you may lack the energy to outwit the fish. Yet you may enjoy watching the play and the antics of fish. The invention of the electric thermostat has provided you with the answer. One of the easiest and least exacting of all hobbies is to keep a tank full of tropical fish in your lounge. These dainty creatures are very small, exquisitely graceful, and their colouring is quite spectacular. Under the right conditions, they are extremely lively and a continual delight to the eye. So lively that a bachelor friend of

* *The Passionate Angler*, by Maurice Wiggin.

mine used to summon his tank full of fish to their meal by ringing his dinner bell. The fish came to know the familiar sound and became very much excited by it.

I believe that one starts with the Guppy, a little fawn fellow, so transparent that you may watch his heart beat. Then there are brilliant Swordfish, either red or green, the male with a long, sword-like tail. For variety it is nice to have one or two sombre Black Widows. Slow-moving but extremely elegant is the brown (or beige) Angel fish, with his big, diamond-shaped body. Quite spectacular is the Neon Tetra, which darts like light-ning about the tank, showing its luminous stripe from head to tail. Unlike its name, the Fighting fish only attacks if he finds a second male in the tank. One variety of this beautiful fish is coloured a most exotic purple. The cheapest of these fish, like the Guppies and Swordfish, costs about 2s. 6d., while the Neon Tetra is twice this price, and a single Cardinal Tetra costs 17s. 6d.

Tropical fish should have live food once or twice a week. On the other days they will be very well satisfied with one of the manufactured foods like *Surgrow*. Bemax should be used sparingly as an occasional treat. Another extra that the little fish dearly love is a small chunk of raw meat, suspended on a string into the water. Very quickly the fishes' nibblings and the action of the water will change your blood-red morsel to pure white.

The great danger to the tropical fish is any fault in the thermostat. If the current should be cut off, these delicate little creatures will perish of cold. Contrary-wise, if too much heat comes through, owing to a thermostatic fault, they will be cooked alive. Friends of mine have had both calamities befall.

The keeping of tropical fish is not an expensive hobby. The smallest tank (18 in. × 10 in.) costs 25s., and the hood to fit it another 22s. 6d. But the tanks are now made in various sizes up to 42 in. × 15 in. × 12 in., a magnificent big tank costing £5 19s. 6d. The heater and thermostat keep the temperature even: each costs 10s. 6d. The only other expense is a little gravel for the bottom, a couple of dozen plants, and some fish to start you off: these should cost you around £4. The total cost is, therefore, roughly £8.

Before turning to the possibilites of drawing and painting as hobbies, may I say a word or two about a simpler craft, long neglected, that is coming into favour again. I mean good handwriting. Not three people in a hundred write well. One obvious fault is the confusion between n and u. 'The child is apparently taught at school,' says Dr Bridges, ' how to make both n's and u's; but the main motive of writing being speed, he soon finds it inconvenient to change from the one motion to the other, and decides for life whether all his n's shall be u's or his u's n's. The n-forms are called arches or arcades, the u-forms are swags. . . . The momentous decision whether you will be an Arcader or a Swagger is already some indication of character: as a matter of fact statistics show that out of a hundred writers, sixty-five plump for u's and thirty-two for n's, while only three will make both.'*

Some of the *savants* favour the Chancery script as a form of handwriting that is at once beautiful, fast, and

* *Good Handwriting and how to Acquire it,* by John C. Tarr.

legible. This script enables the letters to be formed automatically without pressure of the pen and therefore saves time. Being slightly condensed it also saves space. Really well written, it is a delight to the eye. No one is too old or too decrepit to take up and enjoy this

as quickly as I can in this script.
You've doubtless heard how Aubrey
West got interested in calligraphy
and commissioned the pen as the first
and only tool of creative craftsmanship
that can be toted around in a waist-
coat pocket or handbag!

An example of the Chancery script as written by Mrs Beatrice Warde. Her enthusiasm and encouragement of calligraphy had considerable influence on the wide adoption of the Chancery script

simple hobby that trains both eye and wrist and can be happily pursued equally well in one's arm-chair or in bed.

Every day more elderly people seem to take up painting. No doubt Sir Winston Churchill is partly responsible for making the easel a fashionable piece of furniture from Mayfair to Stornoway. But other conditions have favoured the spread of the painting art among us. The average middle-class Englishman has learned at last to lift his eyes from the ledger and the betting odds and to use them again out of doors. Now the first thing many of us want to do with a wind-swept sky or a sun-specked clump of birches is to

The quick brown

The quick brow

The quick brow

A contrasting example of Chancery script and time-wasting round hand

make a picture of them. Most people enjoy more leisure, so there is often abundant time available to take up this enchanting art even in the sixties.

Technically too the moment favours the tyro. The dyes from which the painter's colours are supplied are more plentiful. The chemists have provided a series of new dyes that fairly coruscate on the palette. Techniques have been simplified. Teaching has advanced prodigiously. The new text-books teach you how to paint with a minimum of fumbling, *assuming you possess a good eye*. This last need is a fact which too many of the new popular text-books conveniently overlook.

The fact is that four out of every five people register some part of the colour spectrum inaccurately. This does not affect their ability to draw but it can interfere woefully with their capacity to paint a picture that other people will appreciate. How many of us can distinguish green from blue? The remedy may be to paint for one's own satisfaction. For inaccurate colour perception is a defect we can still do nothing about: it remains a problem for the ophthalmic specialists.

Anyone can paint, maintains so fine a practitioner as R. O. Dunlop. Add the words 'with a good eye' – and I agree. Bitter experience with young, enthusiastic artists in commercial studios and in repertory theatres has taught me how fatal it is for anyone to attempt to deal with design in colour unless he possesses an accurate eye for colour. And don't expect to make a penny out of your drawing or painting. You won't. But your personal profit will be incalculable. You will learn to use your eyes.

'Suppose you see a person holding a wine-glass,' says Dunlop,* 'instead of thinking about what sort of liquid is in the glass – whether sherry or ginger wine, or whether the person's fingers need manicuring – concentrate on defining the shape of the glass and noting the twinkle of light in it, the curve of the fingers grasping the stem, the relation of thumb to palm and wrist. These are impersonal observations that lead directly to the desire to draw and paint the things so observed. . . .

'How do you cultivate this detached attitude? By *seeing* instead of merely looking. By making notes in

* *Painting for Pleasure*, R. O. Dunlop, R.A.

Just catch the action you remember. A quick sketch from
the note-book of R. O. Dunlop, R.A.

pen, pencil, or chalk in a small book, always carried, as
necessary as a purse. . . .'

Drawing is as easy as that in its simpler forms.
Painting is more exacting in certain directions and
demands a good deal of equipment. Nevertheless it is
far more difficult to learn to draw accurately than to
learn to paint. You have neither the canvas surface
nor the paint masses to lighten the task of eye and
hand. So go to painting with an easy mind!

For painting, even if it be taken up late in life, Sir
Winston Churchill has claimed three advantages apart
from the sheer fun of it. One can keep it up almost to
the end. 'One by one the more vigorous sports and
active games fall away. Exceptional exertions are
purchased only by a more pronounced and more

prolonged fatigue. Muscles may relax and feet and hands may become less trusty. But painting is a friend who makes no undue demands, excites to no exhausting pursuits, keeps faithful pace even with feeble steps, and holds her canvas as a screen between us and the envious eye of Time or the surly advance of decrepitude.'

The second is the heightened enjoyment of the world, of scenes, hills, trees, people, dress, tables, chairs, flowers, so soon as we begin to look at them with the painter's eye. 'Armed with a paint-box one cannot be bored.'

Last, painting is *complete* as a distraction. Without tiring the body, it entirely absorbs the mind. One's whole mental energies are concentrated on the task. Everything else fades out of the mind, as it does out of the eye. 'Time stands respectfully aside,' says Sir Winston Churchill, 'and it is only after many hesitations that luncheon knocks gruffly at the door.'

Until recent years there was very little one could do about taking up an instrument in the sixties, or even the fifties. Now the case is altered. The techniques of teaching are vastly improved, while facilities for learning and for self-help have multiplied. True, one will need a teacher, but of music teachers (alone!) there is never any dearth. One of the associations will supply you with the addresses of teachers in your district (see Appendix IV).

M. M. Scott's practical book, *What Instrument Can I Play?* will help you to make a wiser choice than your own ambitions possibly. If you affect the piano, Sidney Harrison, a professor at the Guildhall School of Music, a frequent broadcaster, has written an excellent book on self-help lines for the beginner of any age. This is *Why not play the Piano?* (Boosey and Hawkes, 6s.).

The violin is a different matter. Musicians are fond of quoting the Italian proverb: 'God preserve me from a bad neighbour and a beginner on the violin.' However the book that helps mightily, says my friend Maynard Tobin, Editor of the *Music Teacher*, is *The Violin* by Berthold Tours (Novello, 10s.) in the new edition by Bernard Shore.

These are some of the ambitious projects for middle age. Their mastery needs years of effort and concentration. But there are simpler ploys for less ambitious musicians. At the other end of the scale are the accordian, the guitars, yes – and percussion too!

An ex-London newspaper editor under whom I served found great pleasure in his retirement in playing the kettle-drums in his village's dance band. A rare taste, I imagine, likely only in one brought up to the tapping of typewriters.

Another easy instrument is the guitar. It has only six strings which are either plucked or pressed down to produce the necessary notes. Anyone can learn to play the guitar in a few weeks, as I did. While excellent for accompanying the singer, it is neither loud nor staccato enough for modern dance music. Yet what pleasure it gives to Italian, Spaniard, and Portuguese!

A third simple instrument of reed quality that has come into vogue again is the Elizabethan recorder. The revival of folk songs and of folk dancing initiated by Cecil Sharp renewed interest in the recorder. As it has only eight finger holes, and a range of about two octaves, there is nothing complicated about its management or score. For many years one of London's little theatres was able to call in the services of a small orchestra of recorders for Elizabethan music, like that of Byrd and Purcell, for its Shakespearian productions. The ages of the boys in this orchestra ranged from eight to ten. The consort of recorders includes four instruments of different pitch. The bass is a rather fearsome looking pipe four feet long, but the descant measures only about one foot. All of these instruments, even the recorders, demand long and patient practice for their mastery. But there are now easier ways of making music and of enjoying it.

In the last five years – no more – Hi-Fi and the tape recorder have made the world a sheer paradise to the music-lover with some mechanical sense. The ideal Hi-Fi enthusiast is really a mixture of an electronics engineer and a highly trained musician. Unhappily the electronics engineer is apt to get the upper hand! I can remember how the first precision camera, the Leica, created a generation of camera fiends, how the early radio receivers produced the radio maniac, the man who was only happy with a remote muttering station with a programme unutterably boring.

Now the Hi-Fi fanatic is with us – I hope only for a time. He is more interested in his machine than in the music it makes. The balancing and position of the loudspeakers, the correct placing of the chairs, absorb his complete attention. Never mind what comes out of the speaker! The thing is to have the mechanical preparations perfect. Like other fanatics, he confuses the means with the end. The end is surely music. 'What is music?' a friend asked Elgar. 'Magic in the air, my boy. Stretch out for it and grasp it.'

There was some excuse for this in the case of the Leica and the small new radio sets. In each case hard work on detail would give you astonishingly good results. There is less justification with Hi-Fi. For here too many factors are either out of your control or only fractionally controllable. You have no control over the men recording the concerto. Yet where they place their microphones, among other things, is vital to the quality of the recording. When the disc or the tape reaches you, the sounds that were recorded on magnetic tape have been through several factory processes in which all sorts of error may have been generated. From the tape, disc matrixes are made by a series of complicated processes, from these matrixes in turn discs are pressed by elaborate machines.

You yourself are dependent on three mechanical units – the pick-up that follows the grooves of the record as it revolves on the turntable; the tone-control unit and the amplifier that magnify the signal; the loudspeaker which turns the electrical signals into audible sound waves. Think of the incredible number of slight changes that may occur to distort the rendering during this series of processes! Then remember that *every human ear is itself an imperfect recorder.* Imperfect in itself, like every human eye, but further deteriorated inevitably by listening so long to poor transmissions.

Accepting all these facts, it is clear that all one can hope for with the finest instruments possible and the lavishing of untold care in their use is high fidelity. 'Perfect fidelity' is simply a myth. What a good set of Hi-Fi instruments will do for you, especially if you employ stereo, is to give you a rendering faithful enough to make you feel that you are sitting in the concert hall during the performance. But this will not always happen. These occasions are the high spots in the Hi-Fi enthusiast's life. For them you must labour and hope – and spend.

For Hi-Fi is no poor man's hobby. To get results you really must spend a lot of money. This no one contradicts. The fact is that you cannot buy a really sensitive Hi-Fi electric gramophone with a good, carefully-matched amplifier and loudspeaker for much under £100. Eventually the equipment seems to cost the Hi-Fi fan a good deal more.

On the other hand, it often provides him with almost all the entertainment he wants. He tends to give up going to concerts, operas, plays, films. So he is spending on this one hobby what he may have spread over half-a-dozen interests in the days before he became a Hi-Fi fan. And he may well become a dedicated soul!

The tape recorder is a more versatile instrument than the electric gramophone. Indeed it is probably one of the fundamental discoveries which is going to change our methods of communication like the telephone and the typewriter. For there is no end to the possibilities of a good tape recorder. Already it is the camera's essential partner in a great mass of TV work.

As a method of communication alone it is already replacing pen and printing press in many cases. For instance, there are many lonely people today whose life has been completely changed by the tape recorder. Once isolated and alone, they now have friends not only in England or the United States, but throughout the world.

One of my friends has had to buy a tape recorder simply in order to keep up correspondence with a brother abroad who uses nothing else. Needless to say, the impact of the warm human voice is infinitely more thrilling than the most carefully phrased letter. And it tells you more. The laziest man will go on talking to his tape recorder when he would have swooned with fatigue at the end of the first page.

Here are just a few of the uses to which enthusiasts put their tape recorders:

1. Recording a favourite piece of classical or popular music from the radio.
2. Recording a wedding.
3. Giving an entertainment at a party.
4. Learning a new language with a native teacher who cooperates.
5. Tape-sponding through a club.
6. Recording happy holiday memories.
7. Sound track for a cine film.
8. Writing and producing the amateur play.
9. Collecting folk lore and dialect.
10. Producing a radio play.
11. Recording for the blind.
12. Hospital programmes.
13. A programme on locality.
14. Recording bird song.

The variety of ways in which you can use your tape recorder for radio is boundless. For instance, you can record your favourite concert pieces and play them over and over again at your leisure. If friends come in just before your favourite programme is going to open, you can link your recorder to your radio set and enjoy the programme at your leisure when the guests have gone. You can record a programme like 'Any Questions' and have a session of 'Any Answers' among a few knowledgeable friends. It is astonishing how weak this team, not to mention the TV Brains Trust team, can be, on any subject of which they have not some sort of first-hand information. Anything to do with any of the arts usually foxes the 'Any Questions' team, while serious problems of finance, industry or foreign politics beat the 'Brains Trust'.

Most of the uses I have listed are fairly obvious. But apparently they all make for a lot of fun. Probably the most ambitious is the writing, rehearsal, and recording of an original play by a group. This was great fun in B.B.C. provincial studios in the early days of radio. And it will teach the keen writer or actor a very great deal about what will carry across to an audience and what will hang fire.

Simpler to do and equally fascinating is the local sound portrait of the town or village in which you live. The possibilities here are endless. Much will depend, of course, as in historical work, on getting the expert local people to put you right on detail, and to provide an interesting and coherent background. Some of the technical tricks can be used. The narrative can be recorded separately and finally spliced into the sound picture as required. Should two recorders be available, the sounds and the voices can be faded into the second machine through a mixer unit. In this way they will come into and under the narrative, getting atmosphere in a highly professional way.

There is no great problem about buying a good tape recorder. I got my own first experience many years ago through using a Grundig for dictation of letters and copy. This taught me the dangers of a monotonous delivery, the importance of the pause, and other things that one learns on the stage, but forgets in one's living room.

This Grundig was not a very expensive machine, but it was sensitive, very simple to use, stoutly built; was the most reliable speech recorder I have ever used.

Here you have the big problem of the tape receiver. The interesting-looking machines which you see advertised as Hi-Fi at 20–30 gns. simply are not sensitive enough to do more than take one or at the most a couple of speaking voices. The microphone is much too elementary to record music accurately. To get a highly sensitive and reliable recorder capable of reproducing music, background noise, and two or three voices simultaneously, you must pay about £50. When you have really mastered the machine, you may spend a good deal more quite usefully in getting even better results.

Finally, remember your living-room is *relatively small*. You will get the best results, therefore, from the single instrument, the quartet, the small chamber music ensemble, the solitary voice of a great actor reading great words. From the tent scene between Brutus and Cassius, rather than the Forum scene, in *Julius Caesar*. If you are wise, you will not attempt the magnificent and thrilling effects of grand opera, or the crowded stage, on even the best tape recorder in the largest room. The efforts to contract the whole sound picture never completely succeed. However results in the less difficult directions have been really stupendous: here the technicians go on adding conquest to conquest. So why worry about *Otello* or *Coriolanus*?

As we are toying with the dramatic stage, what about taking up acting as a hobby? Surprisingly enough an increasing number of retirees are doing so. There must be hundreds of amateur companies up and down the country with a membership averaging fifty or sixty years of age. This makes for casting difficulties but it does not deter these enthusiasts from presenting successfully plays with several young people in the cast. Surprising how presentable a stripling many a retiree of sixty or even seventy can make. Make-up is a rewarding art.

Many of these elderly groups combine some study of modern plays and acting, even some lectures on drama appreciation, with their own productions. They may arrange coach trips to a Shakespearian or any other interesting production in the nearby town. All this makes for a livelier interest in the more serious art of the drama.

On the other hand there is an infinite variety of things to be done by the retiree keen on the stage.

After all, acting is only a part of theatre work. If you have a repertory theatre within reach, there may be a number of things you can do for it. If it is not merely a dramatic multiple shop, but an independant, small and struggling, you may be able to sell programmes, to sell tickets or season tickets, to do a spell of office work, to splash paint on canvas, to serve coffee during the intervals, to work on a finance, selling, or social contacts committee if such exist. If they don't exist and the rep. is not prospering, why not offer to organize the one for which your abilities and experience best suit you? If the local theatre prospers and does not want your help on any side, you may be compelled to turn to amateur work. Amateurs also require all sorts of help in production, stage management, settings, props, and prompting as well as on the business side.

This is an exciting time in the English theatre. A happy conjunction of imaginative directors with clever young actors and the tape recorder has produced, if not a nest of singing birds, at least a brood of clever young playwrights. The angry young men like John Osborne and Bernard Kops usefully blazed the trail for quieter voices like Pinter and Wesker. And their successes gave commercial managers confidence to try out the possibly serious talents like Robert Bolt and John Whiting. Don't let us overrate this blossoming of talents, however: there is no Anouilh or Sartre or Montherlant in our team. But what a good second eleven! And what lively dialogue they write!

Here is the sincere socialist mother talking to a son whom a decade of the Welfare State (1947–56) has emptied of ideals in Wesker's *Chicken Soup with Barley*:

SARAH: There will always be human beings and as long as there are there will always be the idea of brotherhood.

RONNIE: Doesn't mean a thing.

SARAH: Despite the human beings.

RONNIE: Not a thing.

SARAH: Despite them!

RONNIE: It doesn't mean . . .

SARAH (*exasperated*): All right then! Nothing, then! It all comes down to nothing! People come and people go, wars destroy, accidents kill and plagues starve – it's all nothing, then! Philosophy? You want philosophy? Nothing means anything! There! Philosophy! I know! So? Nothing! Despair – die then! Will that be achievement? To die? (*Softly*) You don't want to do that, Ronnie. So what if it all means nothing? When you know that you can start again. Please, Ronnie, don't let me finish this life thinking I lived for nothing. We got through, didn't we? We got scars but we got through. You hear me, Ronnie? [*She clasps him and moans*] You've got to care, you've got to care or you'll die.

> [*Ronnie unclasps her and moves away. He tries to say something – to explain. He raises his arms and some jumbled words come from his lips.*]

RONNIE: I – I can't, not now, it's too big, not yet – it's too big to care for it, I – I . . . [*Ronnie picks up his case and brokenly moves to his room mumbling*] Too big, Sarah – too big, too big.

SARAH [*shouting after him*]: You'll die, you'll die – if you don't care you'll die. [*He pauses at door*] Ronnie, if you don't care you'll die. [*He turns slowly to face her*].

This is first-rate dialogue, full of energy and feeling. Grand for the actors! Our young actor dramatists give other young actors exceptional chances to display whatever talent they have. And most of their better plays are available in paperbacks.

And by a second stroke of luck, the enormous success of Stratford, one director at least, Peter Hall, had enough money to establish a permanent company in a

West End theatre (the Aldwych). Better still, he has at his command at Stratford the whole massive equipment that alone makes a producing theatre possible. Our West End theatres are merely dramatic lodging houses, one-play-at-a-time shops.

So the great talents of a young Eric Porter or Peter O'Toole have the conditions of security, variety of rôles, artistic background, and *ensemble* that they need. Also splendid actors like Max Adrian and Christopher Plummer, actresses like Peggy Ashcroft and Dorothy Tutin can stretch their powers to the limit in the great rôles.

At long last it looks as if a national theatre will rise on the South Bank in time for the summer of 1964. One hopes most earnestly that no attempt will be made to combine or confuse the work of the two Shakespeare companies with that of the national theatre. The work of these companies is distinct and different and demands far less capital than a national theatre. The cost of running any civic or national theatre is not understood in this country. The admirable little theatre of Innsbruck (population 50,000) was costing an average of £40,000 a year when I last saw the figures.

To me the thrill of the theatre is always linked with that of foreign language. It happened that I had some of my first tastes of great plays, skilled production, and fine acting abroad. Having the essential familiarity with French and German, these first performances of Molière and Racine in Rouen, of Goethe and Schiller at Hamburg and Göttingen opened new worlds to me.

Here is perhaps one reason why I believe that the study of a foreign language is almost *the* ideal hobby. It stimulates the memory, induces association of ideas, brushes up grammar and syntax, keeps the old brain active. The ability to speak a second language when abroad is much, but the key which the new language gives you to another literature, a new drama, a fresh philosophy, a different way of thinking, is much more. For to master a second language is to master a second mode of thought. Until you begin to *think* naturally in the words of a foreign language you have not mastered it. Nothing else teaches one so clearly the terrible power of words. For to think in German is for me invariably to colour my thoughts with emotion; to think in French has the reverse effect; it seems to drain the thought of emotion by its mere precision. Incidentally, no new study is more fascinating than semantics, the science of language.

Think of the new world of clear thinking and elegant expression opened out to one by Pascal and Montaigne. It has been truly said that a complete modern culture could be laid on the foundations of their thought. Montaigne's humane worldliness you can study through the equally urbane and gracious translation of Florio. But Pascal's deeper thought is untranslatable into English prose.

By far the most interesting plays are being written in France today. The Existentialist group includes both Anouilh and Sartre, whose best work is not approached by any English dramatist now writing. (Unhappily Somerset Maugham no longer writes for the stage.) In France among the elders Cocteau still originates new modes, Gide and Mauriac yet write with intense passion of modern problems. The best plays of the quite original inter-war dramatists, J. J.

Bernard, Lenormand, and Obey, are marvellously worth reading still.

The novels of the modern French school from Colette to Mauriac, from the sagas of Duhamel to the satires of Gide, are very different from those of Aldous Huxley or Elizabeth Bowen, but who can doubt the debt of, say, Graham Greene to Mauriac? The French novelists are for the moment better worth reading than any of our own, deeper, broader, more moving. For these reasons their novels are more likely to remain on one's bookshelves, paper-backed though they be.

Lytton Strachey re-educated our dull and ponderous historians in the art of bringing people and periods to life. But the French still write by far the best biographies of interesting artists, savants, statesmen. André Maurois is merely the irresistible charmer among a legion of able and witty biographers.

Of German one need merely add that it would be worth learning that far from easy language if only to be able to enjoy Goethe to the full. At his best, in some of the lyrics, in *Dichtung und Wahrheit*, he is quite untranslatable: among the moderns Thomas Mann is probably the greatest novelist of this age. *Buddenbrooks* and *The Glass Mountain* are both major masterpieces. A few critics (with whom I disagree) believe that the only *major* dramatist among us today is Bertolt Brecht, whose *Threepenny Opera* created a sensation all over Europe and whose *Mother Courage* (a tragedy of the Hundred Years War and a satire on all war) is regarded as a masterpiece. And there are always the latest German philosophers to study for an answer to the riddle of life.

After French and German, musical Italian is the language that attracts many of us. From a practical viewpoint however Spanish is surely more useful. Today it is spoken not merely in Spain, the Balearics, the Canaries, and Spanish Morocco, but throughout the whole of South America, saving Brazil. Now Italian is heard in Italy, Sicily, and Sardinia alone. Increasingly too English becomes the second language of all Europe, the Near and Middle East as well as of most of the Commonwealth areas. Inevitably the use of German and Italian must continue to shrink.

Not that I would advise any retiree to tackle more than one language. Heaven forbid! After forty one cannot hope to penetrate into the mysteries, to sense the meaning of more than one new culture.

'Choose well, choose wisely, and choose one,' as Sir Winston Churchill says. 'Concentrate upon that one. Do not be content until you find yourself reading it with real enjoyment. The process of reading for pleasure in another language rests the mental muscles; it enlivens the mind by a different sequence and emphasis of ideas.'

The learning of a language is made easier today by radio programmes always available in the major languages, by gramophone records, by simpler methods of teaching. There are fewer irregular verbs and more sprightly conversations in today's text-books.

From language it is but a step to our own literature. First get those two basic books, *An English Library* and *What Shall I Read Next?* both by F. Seymour Smith, published by the National Book League. Nothing surprises me more than the reluctance of so many retirees to lift their eyes from the fiction shelves at the local Boots. How can one get the most out of Kipling or Somerset Maugham without dipping into an occasional book about Malaya or China or the Caribbean? How much the slightest reading in geography helps with Nigel Balchin and Nevil Shute, with Bates and Hemingway. Many of our younger travel writers (like Peter Fleming on Tartary, F. Kingdon-Ward and Frank Smythe on Everest, Freya Stark on Arabia) write better than the average novelist. Never were there such companions for arm-chair travelling as today!

From travel, arm-chair or actual, comes the need to know why things are as they are in Arabia, Brazil, or just across the Channel. No lover of France can really afford to skip a page of Professor D. W. Brogan's *The Development of Modern France*.

Having studied today's probably depressing problems in, say, Scotland, it is enthralling to turn to the figures of the past who have had a hand in creating the problems as well as the amenities of the present. Here the improvement in the writing of the English historical novel in the past couple of decades gives one new and quite exciting introductions to history. There are few better approaches to Scottish history and character than Margaret Irwin's *The Proud Servant*, a novel about Montrose, the great apostate. You can check Miss Irwin's facts by Miss C. V. Wedgwood's excellent and inexpensive life of Montrose. After that you will want to get Charles I, the Covenanters and the problematic martyr, Montrose, into perspective through a good *History of Scotland*, like Hume Brown's or R. S. Rait's. And then you may relax with the literary grace of the old *History of Scotland* (1900) of Andrew Lang, and you can end up by tackling even a specialist work like Barr's *The Scottish Covenanters*.

If France and the oldest and finest culture in Europe interest you, the two greatest of nineteenth-century novelists, Balzac and Stendhal, will tell you everything you want to know about nineteenth-century France, even more about the human heart. If you want to see an even earlier France, you will find it in Arthur Young's *Travels in France*, in Smollett's *Travels through France and Italy*. Both are completely inaccurate but the latter enormously amusing. For the facts of French history there is the master, Taine, among others.

Having gone so far, I am even bold enough to recommend the reading of verse as a hobby.

Deny it as we may, every one of us is puzzled to know what this life is all about. What does it really mean? The poets have their answers as well as the divines and the philosophers. To these answers, even to some wild surmise, their art can give brilliant utterance, often a magical music.

In the twenties and thirties the poets often wrote for the few. In the fifties many poets write to be understood by the average man, not the coterie.

> We understand the ordinary business of living,
> We know how to work the machine,
> We can usually avoid accidents,
> We are insured against fire,
> Against larceny and illness;
> Against defective plumbing.
> But not against the act of God.
> We know various spells and enchantments,

> *And minor forms of sorcery,*
> *Divination and chiromancy,*
> *Specifics against insomnia,*
> *Lumbago, and loss of money.*

*

> *And what are we, and what are we doing?*
> *To each and all of these questions*
> *There is no conceivable answer.*
> *We have suffered far more than a personal loss.*
> *We have lost our way in the dark.*

This is T. S. Eliot in his least easy but most absorbing play, *The Family Reunion*. Here the language of everyday speech is given a music of its own. There are no better ushers to the great music of the masters than Eliot, Auden, and Alun Lewis.

> *Beauty, midnight, vision dies:*
> *Let the winds of dawn that blow*
> *Softly round your dreaming head*
> *Such a day of sweetness show . . .*

Is it so very far from the best of our moderns to the tragic power of Nashe's lines that, once read, haunt the memory?

> *Beauty is but a flower*
> *Which wrinkles will devour,*
> *Brightness falls from the air;*
> *Queens have died young and fair;*
> *Dust hath closed Helen's eye.*
> *I am sick, I must die:*
> *Lord have mercy on us.*

or to the enchantment of Keats's

> . . . *the same that oft-times*
> *Hath charm'd magic casements, opening on the foam*
> *Of perilous seas, in faery lands forlorn.*

One of the easy approaches to poetry is the poetic play. Eliot's *The Cocktail Party* is not even written (or printed) as verse but as rhythmically stressed prose. Much of Synge is poetry, but he prefers to write his tragic as well as his comic dialogue in prose. So does the mystic, Maeterlinck. But even the much despised and old-fashioned poetic dramatists like Stephen Phillips strike off occasional haunting lines. In the latter's *Paolo and Francesca*, for instance, Francesca is described as 'hither, all dewy, from her convent fetched', a childless widow thus:

> *I, with so much to give, perish of thrift*
> *Omitted by His casual dew.*

And Francesca's first moment of real unhappiness brings this cry:

> . . . *can any tell*
> *How sorrow first does come? Is there a step,*
> *A light step, or a dreamy drip of oars?*
> *Is there a stirring of leaves or rustle of wings?*
> *For it seems to me that softly, without hand*
> *Surely she touches me.*

If a single play by a minor Edwardian poet yield such pearls, how well worth while to read his betters, T. S. Eliot, Christopher Fry, Clifford Bax. Yes, and Masefield also, from *Nan*, which is written in prose that sometimes takes wing, to *Good Friday*, still the best written English play on a biblical theme.

With every year that passes the ultimate question:

what does it all mean? is apt to ring more insistently in the retiree's ear. An answer to the gnawing doubt 'For what am I living?' may be sought in five different directions. Every religion was founded to deal with it. You may find the answer in the Bible – or in the Koran. Both are much more illuminating at sixty than at twenty. Possibly the best of all answers is to be found in the Christian ethic of self-sacrifice. Every great religious teacher demands or implies the forgetting of self, including more specialist modern teachers like Mrs Mary Baker Eddy, the founder of Christian Science.

A second direction of approach is through philosophy. The history of philosophy from Pythagoras to Bertrand Russell is the story of man's search to find a meaning for life and therefore a final criticism for conduct. There is a wide belief that it is difficult to master the elements of philosophy. This is scarcely true. Although the modern philosophers are apt to talk complex and baffling jargon, the ideas over which they do battle are usually relatively simple. So even a big book like Bertrand Russell's *History of Western Philosophy* is not difficult to master, if one attempts only half a dozen pages at a time.

To think clearly is to write clearly. So many of the ablest thinkers have been superb writers and teachers. Plato is one Greek master of style, Aristotle another. Our own John Stuart Mill wrote clear, nervous prose which reads easily. So did John Locke and David Hume, the Scottish philosopher. And today the popular exponents of philosophical thought are both elegant and lucid in their writing. Gerald Heard and C. E. M.

Joad are two exceptionally attractive writers. Each excelled in the hard writing that makes easy reading.

A third approach to the mystery of life is through the poets. The major poets are all concerned with the eternal question, *Cui bono? Hamlet* is the greatest play ever written, partly because in it Shakespeare says almost the last word on the human dilemma. Shelley, Browning, and T. S. Eliot are all deeply concerned with the meaning of life, as are de la Mare and the older Yeats. Any one of the great poets can help one to get what one needs most in old age – a sense of perspective, an ability to see life as a whole. Nothing else helps more towards serenity and balance. Pessimistic though it be, there is no better guide to good verse and the philosophic outlook on life than the *Rubáiyát of Omar Khayyám*, as translated and possibly improved for us by Edward Fitzgerald.

How poignantly some of these minor Victorian poets expressed the pain of living. What vigour the eccentric Wilfred Scewin Blunt (who lived Muslim, complete with his stud of Arab horses) got into his sonnet on the injustice of Time:

> *I long have had a quarrel set with Time*
> *Because he robbed me. Every day of life*
> *Was wrested from me after bitter strife.*
> *I never yet could see the sun go down*
> *But I was angry in my heart, nor hear*
> *The leaves fall in the wind without a tear*
> *Over the dying summer. I have known.*
> *No truce with Time nor Time's accomplice, Death.*

*

What have we done to thee, thou monstrous Time?
What have we done to Death that we must die?

History is a humbler and less arduous approach to the nature of things. Many of the historians, too, are magnificent writers. Macaulay may be biased in favour of the Liberal tradition; his sweeping contentions may be unwarranted on occasion; later research may have disproved some of his facts. But the twentieth-century revulsion against him was carried too far; today there is a reaction in his favour. His common sense, it is realized, helped him to judgements more accurate than those of many more meticulous scholars. And Macaulay's scholarship is usually sound.

The famous third chapter of his *History of England*, 'The Condition of England in 1685', is now printed separately: it is one of the finest and most moving pieces of descriptive writing ever published. It is indeed 'as readable as a novel', like so much of Macaulay's work.

Another agreeable introduction to our island story is John Richard Green's *Short History of the English People*. Green was an accurate historical scholar as well as a lucid writer and 'fervent democrat'. His work therefore lives. From Macaulay and Green it is an easy step to the former's kinsman, G. M. Trevelyan, whose *English Social History* is a charming prelude to his *History*.

One of the minor achievements of research in the present century has been the development of economic history. The founders of the English school were Thorold Rogers, Ashley, and Cunningham: all rather dry. But the more modern and scholarly work of E. Lipson happens luckily to be vastly more readable. His *Growth of English Society* and the *Economic History of England* paint the evolution of modern industrial society in clear and significant outline.

A fifth avenue to the understanding of the nature of things is astronomy. During the past thirty years astronomy has revolutionized our whole conception of life on this planet and of its place in the universe. That universe is immensely vaster than we had conceived it. The ideas of the archaeologists as to the great age of this planet are more than confirmed. It appears probable that the entire universe is still in process of growth. Jeans's *The Mysterious Universe* and *The Universe Around Us* are still the best introduction to the dramatic new conceptions of astronomy. They are the work of a front-rank astronomer as well as of a brilliant popularizer. Jeans makes even the complex mathematics of astronomy intelligible.

Having glanced at the possibilities of some of the arts for enlivening the mind, we can now turn to the means available for delighting the belly.

Probably the most immediately rewarding hobby that any retiree can take up is cooking. Results come quickly. They are not merely visible to the eye, but delectable to the stomach. But I would cautiously advise you to cook according to your own lights and tastes, rather than copy the methods of your wife. This will make the first steps easier for you, and it will also give variety to the daily menu.

To secure the freedom of the kitchen stove is not always easy. The younger generation accepts the man in the kitchen as a matter of course: the older generation is apt to limit one's activities to the boiler and the kitchen sink. But graduation to the sacred cooker is becoming easier to win every day, thanks to the scarcity of domestic help. The great thing is to make yourself useful as an assistant. In any case you will probably have an increasing share of domestic duties as soon as you retire, because there will be more to do. Cooking can be tiring: it involves hours of standing by table or stove. But it is also rewarding. Cooking is the most fascinating of the household chores: it requires brains and imagination as well as brawn and patience.

Nor are the usual cookery books easy for men to use. They are written entirely for women who are assumed to know a great deal about it. Often a man can do little beyond boiling an egg, or making a cup of tea. What does 'Have the grill hot' mean to me? *How* hot? is the point. Worse, the average Englishwoman has had a poor chance to acquire real skill in cooking. How much does she know about herbs and their hundred subtle uses in flavouring? Or about the various appetizing curries? Or the art of marinading meat or fish? (Not to mention the mysteries of the omelette.) Her repertoire is therefore apt to be narrow, her methods a trifle routine.

Fortunately there are cookery books that meet the needs of the male novice. A perfect godsend to me is a slender, yellow-covered volume, *Cookery for Men Only*, by Wilson Midgley. The author starts at the right end, not with an elaborate recipe or a learned discourse on vitamins, but with the sensible question, What is there in the larder? Suppose there is precisely one half-loaf of bread. Mr Midgley is not dismayed. He immediately explains the simple but lost arts of making toast melba, cinnamon toast, and French toast. Then he is off into the fascinating field of sandwich making. Anyone familiar with Scandinavia knows the possibilities. And Mr Midgley adds some to the forty-nine varieties I remember on a royal occasion at Stockholm – most of them one-sided. Chopped apple with sugar or nuts, mint chopped fine, spring onions chopped fine, chopped prunes, chopped nuts and a top of marmalade, cheese with salted peanuts, lettuce and chives, bacon cut into dice-like squares, cheese and pickles, nuts and jam, cheese and chopped olives, Marmite and butter, chopped celery and cheese, honey *mixed* with butter, sardines mashed with hard-boiled egg or lemon juice, etc.

When you have mastered as much of Midgley as you need, you can find an unusually simple and fundamental guide to the principles of cooking in *Essentials of Modern Cookery* by Dora Seton, an expert. This book is meant for teachers, but Miss Seton writes so clearly that everything she says can be grasped at a first reading. She gives a basic recipe for each type of dish and from this one can go on to endless variations. Clear instructions for any number of such changes are given and the writer is surely unique in explaining tersely the reason behind every action.

Personally I do not hope to get beyond Miss Seton, but one can always have a peep at the wife's copy of the classic *Mrs Beeton* when something is wanted that Miss Seton does not provide. It happens seldom.

Absorbing as cooking is, baking has a greater fascination for me. Coming from over the border, I have the Scot's passion for scones, buns, and cakes. In baking too one can hope not merely to do the job reasonably well, but to excel. Success in cake-making especially depends largely on the thoroughness with which the ingredients are mixed. Here a strong wrist helps considerably. So does an ability to concentrate. A woman dislikes doing only one thing at a time, partly because she has many jobs to do in the home, partly because she is able easily to divide her attention between two jobs without making a mess of either. Few men can do this, but every mother must.

In baking the technique for taking possession of the mixing-bowl is the same as for capturing the cooking-stove. Make yourself useful by doing the extra jobs that come at the most vital points in the proceedings, such as sifting and weighing the flour, beating sugar and butter, mixing, getting the stove up to 400° F., greasing the paper, and lining the tin. By a gradual process of insinuation, you will soon find yourself in a position to ask on a very busy day, or a 'flu visitation, 'Shall I bake a cake for you, darling?'

For some reason Mr Midgley does not deal with baking. Happily the subject provides Miss Seton with her greatest victory over tradition. From six basic recipes she shows you how to make ten sorts of scones, not to mention the scrumptious drop scone or Scotch pancake, sixteen plain cakes, including cherry and also coffee buns, seventeen small and eight large rich cakes (with two Christmas cakes), including Swiss roll, and ending up with five separate and toothsome ginger-breads. Sixty-three tea time dainties, all different, out of six simple recipes! It sounds like conjuring but it is merely common sense applied to the technique of baking.

On baking as in cooking, the usual books are far too vague over temperatures and times. Don't pay too much attention to them on temperature. The kitchen stove, and particularly the electric stove, is a temperamental creature. It needs coaxing at all times and rarely gives the results it was designed to give. Metals vary in their resistance to heat and in their sensibility to draughts. The electric current coming into the stove varies in strength. Thermostats don't always work. Nor are stove thermometers always accurate. The temperature in the kitchen is never the same for two hours running. Yet the success of your baking depends largely on your ability to control with some accuracy the heat of your oven. One fierce stove defied me for five years, successfully denying me that last half-inch of rise that makes a cake so light that it melts in the mouth. The thermometer was untrue by 50°F.

Today baking pays a bonus. The scones, buns, and cakes we can buy in the shops are made increasingly from commercial ingredients and not always from the better types of these. These are different in quality, vitamin and protein contents and attractiveness from the butter, eggs, flours, flavourings, and dainties that one buys from the local grocer. Hence the increasing popularity of the home-made cake. Even Ye Olde Tudor Café, when it succeeds, is apt to start quietly buying commercial ingredients. They are so much cheaper.

If there be a lot of rewarding work to be done in the kitchen, there are also other ways of using your hands to advantage. If you have deft fingers the whole field of woodworking is open to you (discussed on page 160). If your fingers are all thumbs when you handle tools, like my own, then avoid it before you lose a finger.

While we are discussing woodworking, let us not forget the cognate hobby marquetry, which has recently become so popular. Everybody knows how important veneers have become as finishes for furniture. Marquetry is simply the making of a picture or panel by cutting the necessary coloured shapes from a range of veneers and pasting into position on a design already traced on a blackboard. Surprisingly good pictorial effects can be got from this technique. Obviously it is easy, demanding only patience. Marquetry can be done in bed and is therefore a possible hobby for the invalid. One firm already provides a range of no fewer than a hundred veneers. Obviously one can scarcely commend this particular hobby to the active or the vigorous minded.

If woodworking seems to you a bit strenuous, then what about model-making? Like its brother craft of fretwork, this has become an elaborate business, with its technical journals, its exhibitions, and its scores of suppliers of materials and designs. The fascination of model-making is undying. It is also a little mysterious. At one time I thought the fascination of building a model engine was to see it work. The end of making a model sailing ship to me was to make it sail on the nearby pond. But what of the exquisite ship fastened fast in a bottle, or the coronation coaches on which so many nimble fingers had worked? Often the model aeroplane or train before which an elderly gentleman will stand entranced for an hour or more will be completely unworkable. What is the attraction? I shall never know. Somewhere around the age of fourteen the model that wouldn't work ceased to fascinate. Today one can buy helpful kits and designs to model almost anything from an aeroplane (that's an easy one) or a garage (easy too) or a doll's house to a toy fort, a model excavator, or St Paul's Cathedral.

These are easy-to-learn hobbies in which results come quickly and the interest never flags. Some people prefer a more difficult and exacting occupation. Weaving is a craft that demands time, care, and some patience. It can rarely be remunerative, yet it attracts a certain number of retirees. A weaving loom is an expensive item to buy. Especially if you want a heavily built loom for weaving wide fabrics. But do you? One is probably better to start with a simple two-way loom, costing from £6 to £10. This is admittedly tiring to work, since you have no pedal to reduce the strain. On the other hand it is an ideal loom for learning the ABC of weaving. You can begin to learn the simple darning movement by using only a piece of stiff cardboard. The use of a heddle allows you to weave the weft through the warp without the labour of the darning movement.

If you master the table loom and find that you like weaving you may soon be ready to use a larger loom. This will cost you anything from £20 to £50. There are good strong looms made for around the lower figure by Dryad of Leicester, by G. and J. B. Maxwell of Burgess Hill, by Douglas Andrew. The Nottingham Handi-

craft Company also distribute most of the good models
(see page 264).

One needs merely to raise or lower the heddles as
required to create a 'shed' in the threads of the warp,
so that the weft can be woven. Two other easy movements complete the simplest type of weaving on a two-
way loom. But there are a number of more difficult
jobs involved. One of the trickier tasks is to thread the
heddle and this really requires two people. Another is
to set up the loom, putting every thread into its correct
heddle. This may be a matter not of hours but of days
when the warp is both long and wide. Once the loom is
set up meticulously, with every thread in place, the
rhythmic work of weaving is soothing, say its addicts.
(If I want to soothe my nerves I do a little bit of easy,
in-and-out stitching at a rug.)

To the possibilities of a loom there is no end: you
can weave everything from ties, scarves, and mats to
simply designed rugs, carpets, and cloth.

Of recent years the amateur weavers have done a
great deal to organize themselves. There are Guilds of
Amateur Weavers, Spinners, and Dyers in around
thirty of the chief counties and regions in the country.
They run an excellent quarterly journal full of helpful
material on both elementary and advanced weaving
problems (see Appendix).

Simple tools and a material easy to handle make
leather work appeal to many people. The results always
look most attractive. Today tasteful and well-made
leather goods are expensive Many of them can be
made at home with a little trouble for a fraction of
what they cost in the shops The number of things one

can make from leather is far greater than one imagines
Not merely blotters and handbags, purses and wallets
belts and book-holders, but comfortable shoes, cos
gloves, shopping-bags

Alas, we can no longer bind even our most treasured
books in leather. But we can bind them in boards: w
can even cover the boards with attractive cloth an
embellish them with gilding. Despite the stickiness an
the suffocating smell of glue, the drudgery of sewing
the binding of books is an interesting job for patient
painstaking people on which great skill and ingenuit
can be lavished. And your books become a joy t
look on.

To the very deft of finger, the making of soft toy
from odd bits of material, stuffed with torn scraps c
newspaper or kapok, or carved in wood, offers endles
excitement. A few progress to the esoteric craft c
puppet making. This is a double-decker of a hobby t
fill the leisure of a lifetime. The making of the puppet
provides one strenuous and exacting hobby while thei
operation affords a second, equally strenuous an
exacting. But puppet making is for the skilful finge
and the accurate eye only.

Recent revivals of old dances has provided som
retirees with a fresh interest in life and a new circle c
friends. Old-time dancing is no effort to elderly foll
since it brings back the polkas, waltzes, and lancer
they learned at school. Square dancing is often mor
tiring, but some old people revel in it. When the
want a quiet evening they go to a modern hop an
glide through two-step and tango. But they don't over
do it.

Of collecting hobbies there is no end. Most of us prefer making things or doing things to collecting them. With retirement a long way off, that may be not only natural but right. But don't sneer at the collector and don't despise the collecting hobby. It lasts after sport is impossible and the handling of tools a strain on wrist and eye. Deny it as we may, a degree of decrepitude is still the certain lot of the over-eighties. It is wise to have one hobby that can be enjoyed by the chimney corner. One remembers the despairing cry of Bernard Shaw, a dynamic genius without hobbies, in his nineties, 'If I go on writing, I shall lose any reputation I may have: if I stop writing, I shall go mad.' *Absit omen.*

Painting is not the only hobby that can be kept up to the end. There is one surprising pastime which I discovered to enthuse and even thrill thousands of retirees. This is pigeon racing. In the last week of July 1953, at eighty-eight, Mr F. Murray won the South Road Combine race from Lisburn with one of his pigeons. Generally speaking, pigeon racing is most popular in the north, particularly among miners and cotton workers. But it attracts men and women from every section of life. There are pigeon lofts at Sandringham because Edward VII when Prince of Wales raced his pigeons as Mr Jackson.

It is neither costly nor difficult to join 'the Fancy'. The sport is so widespread that I am told there is certain to be a pigeon fancier within five miles of almost any place in Britain. It is not necessary, usually, to buy one's first couple of pigeons. A local fancier can apparently be cajoled into letting the novice have a couple of young birds without any charge. All that the birds require is a loft, which many expert makers supply, or which the handy man can build for himself. Other needs are baskets and panniers. The birds' food is chiefly corn and necessary minerals, in addition to what they pick up for themselves in country surroundings.

The number of pigeon races held all over the country during the summer is quite incredible. But they are all carefully recorded in the pigeon fancier's newspaper, the *Racing Pigeon*. You have never seen this journal on your local bookstall, nor on the counter of your newsagent. Although the words 'price $3\frac{1}{2}$d.' appear on its front page, the paper's 40,000 readers are all subscribers. Many of the fanciers must be very old people. In the last issue I studied, the north-west correspondent was unable to write personally to the many readers who had written, wired, or phoned to congratulate him on his golden wedding.

The thrill of pigeon racing lies in the mystery of the bird's sense of direction. Homing pigeons have returned from as far as 1,000 miles. The work they did for the partisans in Yugoslavia in the Second World War is only one romance in their modern history, which commenced with the siege of Paris. During the same war all aircraft of Coastal Command carried at least one pigeon to fly back to its base, should the plane be forced down and its transmitter smashed.

Each club covers a considerable area, so pigeons from Bexhill or Brighton may take part in a little race from St Malo. Often the distances in the more important races are very long. But the fancier need not accompany his birds from Orpington to Aberdeen: the carriage of homing pigeons has been reduced to a fine art; the British Railways staff includes many fanciers who have a special care for pigeon baskets. You have merely to sit back in your chair and wait for a wire from the official concerned in Aberdeen. Then you wait for your copy of the *Racing Pigeon* to give you the winners on Saturday. And of course many pigeon owners back their fancy.

Collecting hobbies need not be expensive. Neither need they make excessive demands on house room. One can cheerfully collect anything from autographs or bus tickets to antiques or old pewter, knowing that a lot of other people will be interested. Nor is collecting always a costly business. There are quite a number of things which make most interesting collections at very little expense. One ingenious old gentleman had a mailing list of 200,000 names consisting entirely of people who collected inexpensive but often fascinating trifles and oddments that pour ceaselessly from the machinery of modern civilization. Here are a few of these cheap collectors' items:

Autographs	Leaves (pressed)
Beetles	Obsolete bank-notes
Bells	Press cuttings (single
Bus tickets	subject)
Cheese labels	Stamps
Coins (small	Theatre programmes
denominations)	Wine-bottle labels
Crests and monograms	

One is not suggesting the collection of signatures of film stars or flying aces but rather of well-known

T-H

politicians, writers, artists, musicians, scientists, and eminent people in any serious activity. The new approach to stamp collecting was referred to earlier (page 171). The collection of cheese labels is a new fad which has many followers. Old bank-notes, valueless in themselves, give blinding glimpses into the history of the luckless countries whom events have compelled to call in entire note issues owing to a heavy depreciation in their currencies. Witness the German mark notes called in after both the First and Second World Wars, and many other continental instances. Why collect beetles? it may reasonably be asked. Why not? is the collector's answer. There is a far greater variety of British beetles than you had imagined. One old retiree has collected over the last sixty years the majority of the 4,000 native species. The collector treats the beetle in almost exactly the same way as the butterfly, drying, stretching, and pinning each specimen in its correct position in the case. The other hobbies mentioned are so obvious as to need no comment. But one may point out that the theatre programme of a performance seen at Windsor or Perth in 1946 may carry the name of the film star of today now appearing at the local Ritz. A file of press cuttings on a subject dear to your heart, faithfully kept, can be a constant joy.

It costs a little money, however, to collect many of the most rewarding and exciting things like:

Antique jewellery	(Old) glass
Books	(Glass) paper-weights
(Horse) brasses	Pictures
(Old) China	Pipes

Clocks

(Period) costume

Crucifixes

Dolls

Etchings

(Period) furniture

Prehistoric remains

Prints

(Period) relics

Snuff-boxes

(Old) tools

Walking-sticks

On the other hand, the most successful collecting is usually done by men and women of small means who limit strictly the range of their little collection. A friend of mine who was a connoisseur of both painting and china confined his own collecting to Battersea enamels of the early nineteenth century thirty years ago. His collection then required little money or repair, yet it was unique and gave him intense pleasure in his later years. It enabled him to talk as an equal to some of the wealthiest and most important collectors in the land. No small privilege for the connoisseur of small means. To collect well always involves a considerable study of the production processes, of the period and of the history of the article collected. To collect eighteenth-century snuff-boxes is to become knowledgeable about the whole elegant world of Brummell and the Georges. To collect the works of a single, small literary school like the Victorian novelists or the (modern) Georgian poets is to acquire an understanding of a definite period in history, a literary style and theory, possibly of a philosophy or at least a way of life. Again a new world is opened to one.

One of the most old-fashioned of all hobbies is reviving in the United States. People are taking once more to the fascinating, finicky business of mending broken china and bric-à-brac. Of course, to do good work in this hobby entails patient learning of the arts of cementing and riveting china, the use of fillers, especially in the case of glass, the surgery of the more delicate dolls.

There are a number of fascinating new materials now available for this work. A little text-book published in America advocates it both as a hobby and a one-man business: possibilities here are uncertain, if they exist.

In this matter of hobbies, women are better off than men. During her lifetime a woman learns how to do so many more things than a man. She thus starts retirement with a wide range of skills, and therefore of hobbies, at her fingertips. Cooking and baking, knitting and sewing, dressmaking and dancing, gardening and fruit bottling are all within her range. In this respect I think the old-fashioned woman who has never left her village is often better off than the professional or business woman who leaves her city or suburban flat for a country cottage on her retirement. The latter may have more money to spend on herself, but she often seems to me to have few lively interests. She has lost touch with kitchen and garden and has learned to take her pleasures passively in plays, music, novels, and the office or club circle. The abler woman gives much more of herself to the job and the office life than does a similarly able man. (One excepts work like medicine or journalism, which are so absorbing and exacting that they leave little time or energy for hobbies.) Reorientation after retirement can therefore be difficult for the woman retiree also. Often the solution is to link up with a sympathetic woman friend who is domestically inclined; she will either bring the lonely woman into her own lively social circle or she will run the home so well that her companion is able to develop new hobbies and interests in the outside world.

But there are dangers in the versatility of women, if a mere man dare say so. Many men of mental ability, nervous energy, and social charm seem to run down mentally and physically after retirement. They are the less adaptable and ingenious folk who are apt to set the sights too low in view of their obvious ability: they cease to set themselves targets that require a really strenuous effort to reach. So do some able women when released from professional or executive duties. Just as the able man of yesterday may allow his days to drift into a hazy pattern of golf, meal, sleep, tea, walk or get-together with the pals, meal, television, bed, so the smartly groomed woman executive of yesterday may drift into the sloppy, slack old maid of today. The pattern of her lazy days is, however, even more negative than that of her male counterpart. She is apt to take a flat or a room in a city suburb 'to keep in touch with things'. At first she continues to keep her small home immaculate, to do a little social or public work, to read one intelligent newspaper and weekly journal, an occasional serious book. Then gradually the passion for getting excitement without effort takes hold of her. She becomes the complete onlooker. She walks round every West End store once a month or so, sees early morning film shows, queues for every 'first night', sees every free show there is in London, including weddings and funerals, the trooping of the colour, the Lord Mayor's Show, the opening of Parliament. On wet days you will find her in the magazine room of the local public library, deep in the *Tatler*. She knows the relationships of every member of the royal family by heart and she is absorbed in all their affairs. She is always bubbling over with enthusiasm: on annual visits to a few old friends and colleagues buried in the provinces, she brings all the glamour of Mayfair and Bond Street into Walsall or Oldham. But she becomes increasingly woolly, more and more scatty. She is allowing her brain cells to deteriorate quite rapidly. The eventual results of this process may be frightening. Happily such cases are relatively rare.

No need for this slackening of interest in active affairs. She could have joined the local Townswomen's Guild, worked on its committees on important matters, including schools, hospitals, and sanitation. She might have become a school governor, a godparent, a school traffic controller, or a useful worker on the Consumers' Committee. Not to mention all the work waiting to be done for her local Red Cross, W.V.S., and Friends of the Hospital group, outlined briefly below.

Many a retired professional or business woman never lets up. She becomes the salt of any community she may enter, the centre of fresh activity. I have known one single retired woman executive start up a Women's Institute, a vital Lecture and Discussion Society, and a Drama Group in a single village in a matter of a couple of years. Other professional women exercise the utmost care and skill in seeking out the most valuable work for which their specialized experience suits them. One retired woman actuary has learned the delicate and difficult technique for making the prototype from which Braille editions for the blind are embossed. This involves brains, skilful fingers, an unusually accurate eye, and the passing of a searching exam. Or you can take up the simpler job of transcribing articles and books into Braille on a special typewriter or a hand-frame. One of my correspondents finds this work fascinating – after forty years of it. A favourite remark of the able woman retiree is 'Since I retired, I don't know how I ever found time to go to work'.

To the observing journalist it always comes as a fresh surprise how many lonely older people there are in most western European countries outside those of Latin culture. One meets them everywhere, in cafés, libraries, hotels, bars. Poverty is itself a social cement: there is little loneliness in the Balkans. Actually here in Britain there is no need for anyone to be lonely in any save the remote rural areas. There are so many ways of making friends, so many ways of being useful, such a host of jobs waiting to be done.

Our hospitals in Britain are certainly run by the State: that does not mean that they do not need voluntary helpers. Many of them never needed help more. Some need one sort of help, others need quite different aids. Get in touch with the almoner of your local hospital, with any Friends of the Hospital in your neighbourhood, with the local Red Cross branch and with the W.V.S. if you are a woman. Shopping for patients is one obvious and easy job, writing letters for patients is another. You will be surprised what a number of useful things they can find for you to do. One local hospital near me has (*a*) a daily tea service for out-patients, (*b*) several sets of cheerful, light-coloured curtains for screening beds in the wards at a very considerable cost of money and work, (c) gay new pictorial screens for the children's ward, (d) a twice-a-week mobile library service, (e) regular visitors for lonely elderly patients from a distance, (f) some valuable not quite essential surgical equipment, all from their Friends of the Hospital Association. An annual garden fête in summer, a dance in winter help to raise funds for such blessings.

In country districts there is usually work waiting to be done for the county library on its weekly visit, although some knowledge of records and books is really necessary to do this work efficiently. Everywhere lonely old people are dying to be visited, talked to, read to, or taken for a walk. So are the lonelier blind people who need to have their letters written for them in many cases. Often a district nurse can advise you as to the most urgent cases. Visiting 'shut-ins' is work that retirees can do best. It is the old who understand the old. Many an old 'shut-in' is an attractive and worthwhile personality with unusual knowledge. Every charitable body in your area could do with a little extra help. Every well-run prison wants visitors for its younger inmates, often at a crisis in their lives. (Only the devoted Quaker can cope with the old lag who will try every trick of the trade on any well-meaning citizen who visits him or her out of the blue.) Prison visiting is apt to be most depressing and I suggest it only to the really tough, worldly-wise, and strong-minded retiree in the fifties or sixties.

There is always a mass of unpaid social service work waiting to be done in every community. In the Y.M.C.A., or the Y.W.C.A. for women, in the Rotary Club, in the Residents' Association, in the British Legion, in the Scout movement if you have the necessary experience, in adult education, again presuming you have specialized knowledge of one or more subjects and the ability to teach. In most cases the load of work, responsibility and leadership is being borne by a few able people. Usually intelligent help is what they are looking for. It is difficult to come by and you will find your work is quickly appreciated assuming you really take off your coat to it!

I have left local government work to the end because the present situation is so involved. It is often described by the authorities as confusion worse confounded. No expert on organization denies this. Local government is now in an unhappy transition stage. For upwards of fifty years over-centralization has been operating on the machinery of local administration. Much of this centralization was as inevitable in this field as elsewhere when transport and methods of control improved out of knowledge. But only in Scotland have intelligent modern methods of delegation and decentralization been adopted along with centralization.

In that country 'the district council, which deals with matters purely within its own area, consists partly of members of the county council and partly of directly elected local members, while in (the) burghs . . . the town council elects its own members on the county council. Moreover, the elections take place at the same time so that the same questions are at issue.' In Scotland local government work is still apparently worth while, although the powers of the authorities are much curtailed.

Compare the situation in English and Welsh areas, where the parish council has no county councillors among its membership and too often nurses a hate against 'the county' and all its works.

Can you wonder at this, particularly in a small rural area? Of the 16s. rate which a parish council may collect, only a few pence may be spent or in any way controlled by it. Around 30–40 per cent will be levied for specialist national bodies, 55–60 per cent may be handed to the county council. The hospital? That is under the local regional hospital board which reports straight to the Ministry of Health. The village school? That works entirely under the educational committee of the county council. The roads? Made-up roads were all handed over to the county authority many years ago. Unadopted roads the parish council has neither money nor power to deal with. In my own area the Residents' Association provides road gangs of its own elderly members to do the work the luckless parish council dare not attempt, having neither the money nor the power. Public assistance? This passed from the local guardians to the county in 1929. A certain number of parish councils still retain some power over housing. But the Town and Country Planning Act, 1947, removes planning powers from all districts (including the City of London) and concentrates control in the hands of the counties. Rights of way, open spaces, allotments, are practically all that is left to the English or Welsh parish council today!

The small borough does have more control over its

own affairs. It maintains any unclassified streets or roads, lighting, cleansing of streets, water supply, sewerage and drainage, refuse collection, libraries, open spaces, as well as any crumbs of control that may fall from national or county tables.

The larger towns, the cities, and the counties have still a wide range of powers. But here the smear of party politics is over most of the voting; you vote with the party on whose ticket you fought the election; your freedom of judgement is gone. As no retiree is likely to enter local government work save from a desire to serve the interests of the community, the prospect of toeing the line of party (often class) interests on every detail from the site of the new housing estate to the rightness of Graham Greene's last novel for the fiction shelf of the local library may not be attractive.

In annual visits to my small home town of D— in Scotland I was able to see the whole process of centralization at work. Both of my parents were devoted to local government. When my lively father was successively a bailie and provost between 1893 and 1903, he spread himself in every direction from a Gothenburg model pub to water trickling along the gutters, from slum clearance to electricity, not omitting a motor-bus service and a public slaughterhouse. For his final three years things fairly hummed in that Scots borough. When my mother came to the chair, thirty years later, the Local Government Act of 1929 had swept away half of the council's powers. Housing and the medical services were the only fields left open to an energetic old lady with some administrative skill. The Labour and Conservative groups voted as two obedient blocks, never differing within their own ranks in public. Not even a Joseph Chamberlain could have made things hum. Today the entire medical field and most of the housing decisions are outside the small borough's jurisdiction. Only on a city or a county council can the man or woman of ability and administrative capacity find real scope. For the county council's really interesting work on finance, highways, housing, transport, education, and other important committees it always seems to me that a car must be almost a necessity. However, county and town councillors are now allowed certain expenses.

In theory any ratepayer can stand for a parish, town, or county council if properly nominated: in practice the support of a party machine is necessary in the larger towns and in many of the counties.

However, municipal and county authorities are not the only opportunities for public service. There are a number of regional hospital boards, controlling the hospitals, clinics, health centres, and dental clinics within their area. Naturally the majority of the members of these boards are medical specialists connected with one of the units concerned. But a few laymen and laywomen serve. It is generally agreed that there is a great need for voluntary work on the problems of finance, costing, light, heat, and power supply, and the work of general management. A hospital is a factory for healing: its work calls for time and motion study and for the use of modern labour-saving devices. But only the retiree who has experience either of running an up-to-date factory or of scientific management techniques can help the medical specialists in a field in which many of them naturally seem to be rather at sea.

The Bench is still a field of public service open to many retirees. But here once more appointments to the Justices' Bench are in the gift of the Lord Chancellor, advised by local committees.

The field of public service narrows daily in this country as elsewhere. But reforms involving much decentralization are certain to come in the end.

Few people realize how absorbing a hobby ancestor tracing can be. No need to leave it to the specialist as though it were a recondite mystery, provided you are prepared to start right at the beginning by obtaining your parents' marriage certificate, your father's birth certificate, and so on for each generation, obtaining the information first from Somerset House, then from parish registers. Don't imagine a common name such as Smith will preclude you from getting a pedigree. There are many Smith family trees in existence, some of them of great length. For instance, a book was published in the early years of this century showing at least sixty families of Smith who had been sufficiently distinguished to obtain coats of arms. This list did not include the famous F. E. Smith – the first Earl of Birkenhead – whose pedigree can without any trouble be taken back six generations or so.

In their clan system, the Scots have found an excellent device to propagate family pride. The family of the chief Macpherson, Mackintosh, Chisholm, has a line of descent lost in the mists of history; various junior lines can also be traced. For the majority of people who bear the clan name a genealogy of several generations can usually be worked out, to show how their forbears came to take the particular clan name when they came under the chief's protection. In the case of the Mac-Gregors, however, says Mr L. G. Pine, ex-editor of *Burke's Peerage*, we can be fairly sure that they are all of one blood. This situation lasted until 300 years ago when they were outlawed for violent deeds done under James VI of Scotland, so that it did not pay a man to call himself a MacGregor!

There are few clubs or associations specially designed to serve the interests of the retiree. Those which do exist are apt to be concerned chiefly with the problem of finding jobs locally for their members. Nor is there any sort of printed periodical on the subject known to me except the *Sundial*, a small facsimile sheet, issued six times a year by Marsali MacCuin, 200 New Street, Horsham, Sussex, for the *Sundial Society*. The society is organized on the basis of groups centred on mutual interests such as art, discussion, gardening, etc. Its founders were interested to help the lonely retiree. For that reason local groups have been established in areas where there are sufficient members to justify meetings. The rest of the personal contacts are through corre-spondence circles. (Membership fee is 10s. a year, in-cluding the journal.)

Appendix I

———

WHAT YOU WANT TO KNOW ABOUT SOME AGREEABLE PLACES

Town	County	*Population	Soil and subsoil
Bath	Somerset	80,800	Low areas – clay. Higher – brash on Bath stone.
Bexhill	Sussex	26,610	Ashdown sand and Wadhurst clay.
Blandford Forum	Dorset	3,250	Chalk, clay.
Bournemouth	Hampshire	144,700	Sand, gravel.
Brighton	Sussex	160,000	Light variable, mainly chalk.
Buxton	Derbyshire	19,350	Part peat and gritstone; rest clay, limestone.
Cambridge	Cambridgeshire	93,140	Gravel, clay.
Cheltenham	Gloucestershire	69,490	Clay, gravel.
Cowes	Isle of Wight	16,890	Gravel with Bembridge limestone above, clay lower levels.
Deal and Walmer	Kent	25,750	Medium on chalk, Brick earth on sand subsoil.
Dorchester	Dorset	11,660	Soil light, loam; subsoil, chalk.

†Average annual hours sunshine	†Average annual rainfall in inches	Death rate Per 1,000	Hilly or flat	Type of climate	‡Rates in £
1,514	30·93	10·0	Hilly	Very mild	20s.
1,769	28·12	19·5	Generally flat	Even and mild (coast breeze)	21s. 11d.
Not known	39·23	10·2	Hilly	Mild	21s.
1,711	31·21	16·52	Partly flat Partly hilly	Mild	13s. 6d.
1,766	31·52	12·15	Hilly	Bracing	14s. 10d.
1,146	48·50	13·1	Hilly	Very bracing	24s. 6d.
1,488	21·72	10·5	Flat	Cool, subject to east wind and fog in winter	23s. 8d.
1,442	27·29	12·02	Flat	Mild	20s. 4d.
No record	29·26	14·0	Hilly	Mild and relaxing	26s. 1d.
1,708	26·62	11·23	Mainly flat	Very bracing	21s. 2d.
1,646	38·63	11·0	Gently undulating	Mild	21s. 10d.

* In all cases population figures for England and Wales are those of the Registrar General's Estimate for March 1960 or 30 June 1959.

† Majority of hours of sunshine figures are from the Meteorological Offices new thirty-year average (1921–50) and majority of rainfalls from their new thirty-six-year average (1916–50). Other sunshine and rainfall figures are for the year 1959.

‡ In most cases rates are for 1960–61.

Town	County	*Population	Soil and subsoil
Douglas	Isle of Man	22,000	Light loam.
Dover	Kent	34,680	Chalky.
Eastbourne	Sussex	57,800	Partly clay in centre of town, rest on chalk.
Edinburgh	Midlothian	469,400	Mainly clay; subsoil of boulder clay with rock at higher levels.
Exeter	Devon	77,400	Clay and gravel.
Falmouth	Cornwall	16,630	Loamy. Subsoil – shale, clay.
Farnham	Surrey	25,450	Gravels and alluvial.
Felixstowe	Suffolk	15,800	Gravel, crag, clay.
Folkestone	Kent	44,370	Sandy, some clay top; layer chalk.
Godalming	Surrey	15,850	Alluvial, bargate; subsoil, greensand.
Guildford	Surrey	51,930	Chalk, clay, and gravel.
Harrogate	Yorkshire (W. Riding)	52,890	Clay over sandstone, shale.

†Average annual hours sunshine	†Average annual rainfall in inches	Death rate Per 1,000	Hilly or flat	Type of climate	‡Rates in £
1,562	45·17	11·8	Shopping area flat; residential rising	Equable, bracing (coast breeze)	13s. 6½d.
1,721	35	10·25	Hilly	Bracing	21s.
1,828	30·82	11·77	Mainly flat	Moderately mild (coast climate)	15s. 10d.
1,385	27·53	12·8	Hilly	Bracing: cold E. winds in winter	18s.
1,678·3	31·90	11·1	Both. Most of central area flat, hilly outside	Mild. Mean temp. 50·3°F	18s.
1,672	43·30	10·8	Hilly	Mild	22s. 9d.
1,642	28	15·6	Hilly	Equable	16s. 8d.
1,720	21·38	13·7	Flat, steep cliffs to sea	Bracing (coast breeze)	24s. 3d.
1,753	30·71	11·13	Partly hilly. W. end town, plateau	Bracing	22s. 8d.
1,433·2	28·65	9·09	Hilly	Mild	19s.
1,591	28·0	11·3	Hilly	Mild	19s.
1,344	31·19	13·5	Hilly	Bracing	19s.

Town	County	*Population	Soil and subsoil
Haslemere	Surrey	12,190	Lower greensand over clay.
Hastings	Sussex	63,900	Sandstone.
Hereford	Herefordshire	34,360	Red loam: subsoil clay gravel.
High Wycombe	Buckingham-shire	45,350	Chalk.
Holyhead	Anglesey	10,370	Clay, rock.
Hove	Sussex	69,930	Chalk.
Huntingdon	Huntingdon-shire	5,960	Loam, gravel soil; subsoil, partly gravel clay.
Inverness	Inverness-shire	28,562	Sand, gravel.
Ipswich	Suffolk	114,600	Sand, gravel, and clay mixed.
Kingston-upon-Thames	Surrey	38,590	Chiefly gravel.
Leamington Spa	Warwickshire	39,450	Sandstone, clay.
Lowestoft and Oulton Broad	Suffolk	44,730	Loam sand, gravel, and chalk.

†Average annual hours sunshine	†Average annual rainfall in inches	Death rate Per 1,000	Hilly or flat	Type of climate	‡Rates in £
1,152	34·44	12·30	Very hilly	Bracing	17s. 4d.
1,786	29·11	12·41	Hilly	Mild, sheltered, coast breeze.	19s. 10d.
1,688	26·40	11·3	Hilly	Mild	24s. 6d.
No record	22·94	9·3	Hilly	Mild	21s.
1,571	34·9	No record	Hilly	Bracing (mild coast climate in winter)	24s. 8d.
1,708	29	19·13	Gradual decline to sea	Bracing, equable (coast breeze)	19s. 3d.
No record	21·75	11·9	Flat	Mild	28s.
1,239	28·44	12·7	Fairly flat in the town, hilly without	Equable, bracing	25s. 7d.
1,700	24	10·47	Undulating	Bracing	19s.
No record	23·55	10·8	Flat	Mild	17s. 10d.
1,343	24·60	11·1	Slightly undulating	Mild	24s. 2d.
1,650	23·61	11·4	Very flat	Bracing and dry	23s.

Town	County	*Population	Soil and subsoil
Malvern	Worcestershire	24,960	Red and grey marl and rock outcrops with clay and limestone subsoil
Margate, inc. Cliftonville	Kent	43,660	Light, chalky.
Oxford	Oxon	104,000	Gravel, clay.
Paignton	Devon	27,270	Soil – medium alkaline loam. Subsoil – red shale.
Pitlochry	Perthshire	2,383	Alluvial.
Poole	Dorset	89,400	Sand, gravel. Some chalk on high ground.
Ramsey	Isle of Man	4,607	Varied.
Ramsgate	Kent	36,100	Chalk.
Richmond	Surrey	42,330	Clay to 200 ft, then sandstone to 900 ft.
Rothesay	Buteshire	10,145	Average.
St Andrews	Fifeshire	10,000	Top soil, black; subsoil, clay, sand, rock.
Salisbury	Wiltshire	34,520	Chalk. Gravel in valleys.
Stratford-on-Avon	Warwickshire	15,270	Top soil, gravel. Subsoil, red marl and gypsum, sandstone.

†Average annual hours sunshine	†Average annual rainfall in inches	Death rate Per 1,000	Hilly or flat	Type of climate	‡Rates in £
1,531	29·50	11·3	Hilly	Equable, inclining to high humidity	21s. 10d.
1,771	21·25	12·0	Flat, no hills	Very bracing. Dry	24s. 9d.
1,482	25·66	10·74	Flat. Hilly on outskirts	Mild	20s.
1,678	38·54	10·67	Hilly	Mild and relaxing	22s. 1d.
1,186	32·7	No record	Hilly	Bracing, sheltered	19s. 9d.
1,798·7	32·19	13·0	Mainly flat	Equable and mild	20s. 8d.
1,588·6	39·63	No record	Mainly flat, hilly in parts	Equable	14s. 9d.
1,720	21·68	11·5	Mainly flat	Bracing	24s.
1,460	27·66	9·7	Flat. Hilly in parts	Enervating	19s. 7d.
1,264	56·19	11·4	Flat round coast, slightly hilly inland	Mild and equable (coast breeze)	26s. 2d.
1,437	28·06	13·57	Town centre flat, outskirts hilly	Bracing	19s.
1,517	30·06	14·72	Undulating	Mild	19s. 10d.
1,394	24·74	12·1	Undulating	Mild	20s. 10d.

Town	County	*Population	Soil and subsoil
Teignmouth	Devon (South)	10,760	Red conglomerate, flint filling.
Torquay	Devon	51,160	Mainly clay on limestone.
Tunbridge Wells	Kent	38,810	Sandstone and clay; subsoil, sandy.
Ventnor	Isle of Wight	6,540	Varies; most greensand and chalk with outcrops of clay.
Wareham	Dorset	2,840	Black earth, gravel.
Welwyn Garden City	Hertfordshire	31,270	Boulder clay, gravel.
Weston-super-mare	Somerset	41,150	Limestone, sand.
Woking	Surrey	63,600	Bagshot sand.
Worthing	Sussex	75,260	Soil – rich loam overlying all areas except chalk. Subsoil – mainly brick earth and coombe deposits.
York	Yorkshire	104,900	E. of river – heavy soil, clay subsoil; W. of river – light sandy top; gravel subsoil.

†Average annual hours sunshine	†Average annual rainfall in inches	Death rate Per 1,000	Hilly or flat	Type of climate	‡Rates in £
1,711	33·23	11·7	Centre of town flat, remainder hilly	Mild	21s. 10d.
1,733	34·98	16·15	Hilly	Mild	20s. 10d.
1,655	30·26	11	Hilly	Mild	23s. 2d.
1,831	32·4	11·7	Hilly	Very mild	26s.
No record	34·93	9·9	Mainly flat	Temperate, mild	20s.
No record	25·59	10·5	Flat	Bracing, cold winds	18s. 10d.
1,539	32·40	11·6	Southern portion flat, northern hilly	Temperate, equable (coast breeze)	20s. 10d.
No record	25·13	12·89	Mostly flat	Mild	17s. 4d.
1,838	27·49	13·4	Flat	Mild and equable	18s. 2d.
1,310	24·70	12·0	Flat	Relatively dry	21s 6d.

Appendix II

TABLE OF AVERAGE HEIGHTS AND
WEIGHTS AT DIFFERENT AGES

(Drawn up by the Metropolitan Life Insurance Company)

Height	MEN								
	Age and Weight								
	15–19	20–24	25–29	30–34	35–39	40–44	45–49	50–54	55–59
ft in.	lb.	lb.	lb.	lb.	lb.	lb.	lb.	lb.	lb.
4 11	111	117	122	125	127	130	132	133	134
5 –	113	119	124	127	129	132	134	135	136
5 1	115	121	126	129	131	134	136	137	138
5 2	118	124	128	131	133	136	138	139	140
5 3	121	127	131	134	136	139	141	142	143
5 4	124	131	134	137	140	142	144	145	146
5 5	128	135	138	141	144	146	148	149	150
5 6	132	139	142	145	148	150	152	153	154
5 7	136	142	146	149	152	154	156	157	158
5 8	140	146	150	154	157	159	161	162	163
5 9	144	150	154	158	162	164	166	167	168
5 10	148	154	158	163	167	169	171	172	173
5 11	153	158	163	168	172	175	177	178	179
6 –	158	163	169	174	178	181	183	184	185
6 1	163	168	175	180	184	187	190	191	192
6 2	168	173	181	186	191	194	197	198	199
6 3	173	178	187	192	197	201	204	205	206

Height	WOMEN								
	Age and Weight								
	15–19	20–24	25–29	30–34	35–39	40–44	45–49	50–54	55–59
ft in.	lb.	lb.	lb.	lb.	lb.	lb.	lb.	lb.	lb.
4 11	110	113	116	119	122	126	129	131	132
5 –	112	115	118	121	124	128	131	133	134
5 1	114	117	120	123	126	130	133	135	137
5 2	117	120	122	125	129	133	136	138	140
5 3	120	123	125	128	132	136	139	141	143
5 4	123	126	129	132	136	139	142	144	146
5 5	126	129	132	136	140	143	146	148	150
5 6	130	133	136	140	144	147	151	152	153
5 7	134	137	140	144	148	151	155	157	158
5 8	138	141	144	148	152	155	159	162	163
5 9	141	145	148	152	156	159	163	166	167
5 10	145	149	152	155	159	162	166	170	173
5 11	150	153	155	158	162	166	170	174	177
6 –	155	157	159	162	165	169	173	177	182

Appendix III

——————

HOW TO START ON SPARE-TIME EARNING

The Job	How to start	Qualifications, training
INDOOR Accounting and/or book-keeping work (private).	Advertise local weekly. Circularize local firms and shops if necessary.	Experience in book-keeping and/or accountancy work essential. Knowledge of income tax regulations helpful.
Advertisement copy writing (free lance).	Contact in provinces generally through local agencies, industrial firms, department stores, etc.	Previous experience essential for London, Manchester Agency work and largest cities.
Coaching, spare-time at home.	Contact local headmaster *re* help for backward pupils for exam. Advertise local weekly.	Experience of teaching essential. Knowledge of subjects for well-known exams valuable.
Commercial art.	Submit work through artist's agent to commercial studios and journals using free-lance work.	Art school training essential for commercial art studios.
Courier for tourist agency.	Apply leading (and also minor) tourist agencies.	Several languages. Experience foreign travel and countries. Liking for people. Strong, fit physique. Even temper.
District correspondent local newspaper.	Supply reports of local events on spec.	Shorthand and typing desirable. Local knowledge. Good mixer. Accurate memory.
Doctor's Receptionist/ Secretary	Write giving experience to local doctors.	Business training or household management equally useful. Shorthand and typing valuable.
Exam supervisor (state or private school).	For state school apply County Education Officer. Private – headmaster of local school.	Experience of teaching essential.

Equipment	You may earn
	By arrangement either a round fee or on time basis. Charge at least 5s. per hour.
	Vary with type of work, size, etc., client and his expenditure. Generally well paid (See p. 156).
	Private lesson 10s. 6d. to 15s. an hour on specific subject. Group fee by arrangement.
	All expenses paid while touring plus small salary.
	3d. to 6d. per line used.
	You may earn £350/£500 a year, and pro rata for part-time. Hours worked usually leave afternoon free.
	Varies with type of subject and importance of exam.

T—1

The Job	How to start	Qualifications, training
Genealogical research.	No course. Study at libraries. Apply membership Society of Genealogists, Chaucer House, Malet Place, London, WC1.	Knowledge of (and liking for) history. Ability to read Latin, old English writing and records. Ability to assess evidence and follow clues.
Hairdressing (private).	Start work with local acquaintances.	Previous experience essential.
Half-commission broking.	Contact local broker and introduce new clients' business.	Previous stock-exchange experience essential.
Hospital part-time orderly (women).	Apply local hospital's almoner or manager.	Good physique essential. Experience sick nursing valuable.
Journalism (free lance).	Send in work to suitable journals on approval.	Journalistic experience helps. Knowledge of one or more fields. Ability to write interestingly, lucidly, accurately.
Lecturer at evening classes.	Write County Education Officer.	Usually degree in academic subject. Long experience in scientific and technical subjects. Expert knowledge of one subject may suffice.
Lecturing to public and preparatory schools.	Write County Education Committee or Director of Education.	Previous teaching or writing experience. Degree helps.
Printing.	Study *Printing Explained* (Dryad Press, Leicester).	Good eyes, steady hand, ability to work to detail. Small, well-lit room necessary for equipment.

Equipment	You may earn
A large number of standard works like *Burke's Peerage*.	Varies immensely. £10–200 gns. per case.
	Rates relatively good but essential to keep step with local level of prices.
	Per cent of total broker's commission on sales, shares, etc.
	Varies with hours of work, etc.
Copy should be well typed.	£4 4s. to £15 15s. per 1,000 words according to market.
	According to qualifications and subject. Average 13s. 3d. (crafts) to 30s. 6d. an hour.
Slides or film for epidiascope often essential.	£3 3s.–£6 6s. per lecture plus expenses.
Small printing press, type etc., £20–£30.	Small fees can be earned for printing for local societies.

The Job	How to start	Qualifications, training
Private cooking.	Advertise locally.	Expert cook, either diploma or good experience.
Publisher's reader.	Secure introduction one or more publishers. Approach direct.	Knowledge of languages and literature. Ability to summarize and assess taste of specialized publics.
Publishers' translation.	Write publishers direct. Market overstocked with German and French: opportunity with less common languages.	Literary ability required as well as languages.
Representative for tourist agency abroad.	Apply agencies for whom you have worked as courier.	Fluency in at least one foreign language. Familiarity with tourist centres of one country. Experience as courier. Liking for people. Even temper.
School meals supervisor (women).	Apply local education authority.	None for small county schools. Experience of teaching and disciplining essential town and large schools.
Secretarial work (women).	Advertise locally. Contact local typing office.	Experience genuine secretarial duties. Shorthand, typing. Experience special or professional field useful.
Secretary (state school).	Apply Divisional Educational Office.	Knowledge simple bookkeeping essential. Typing, shorthand not usually necessary.
Sitting up with old people (women).	Apply local w.v.s. in first instance.	Some nursing experience.

Equipment	You may earn
	Payment as arranged: £1 1s. to 30s. an evening, with dinner.
	£1 1s. to £2 2s. for reading and reporting on each book. Novels 30s. to £2 2s.
	Common languages around 30s. per 1,000 words. Higher rates for rarer languages.
	All living expenses paid while abroad plus salary (around £10 per week, good agency).
	3s. 3⅛d. per hour (average 7½ hours per week)
Typewriter helpful.	4s. an hour, local work, to 6s. 6d. an hour where travel or other extra expenses required.
	2s. 11½d. an hour, first 30 hours, plus 6d. a day up to 20 hours. 1s. 9½d. an hour between 30 and 38½ hours a week.
	2s. 6d. an hour; 10s. an evening (4 hours).

The Job	How to start	Qualifications, training
Space selling.	Apply local newspaper or printer, selling guide books, etc.	Experience of selling essential. Good appearance. Ability to talk well and to mix.
Teaching (evening classes).	Apply positions advertised by local educ. authority, May or June, local press.	Experience in industry or commerce, recognized technical qualifications and teaching experience preferred.
Teaching, part-time (state schools).	Write Divisional Education Officer.	Must hold Ministry of Education Teacher's Certificate and have teaching experience. Specific qualifications demanded and specialist knowledge valuable.
Teas in own home.	Apply local Food Office for licence.	Catering licence necessary.
Translating.	Advertise local weekly and national weeklies. Specialist journals if specialist knowledge.	Expert knowledge of one or more foreign languages, of English idiom, syntax, grammar.
Typing and duplicating (at home). Women.	Advertise local paper. Contact local stationer and typing agency.	First-rate touch typist. Ability to decipher manuscript, etc. Good spelling and grammar essential.
OUTDOOR Bee-keeping.	Write British Bee-keeping Association, Roes, Eastchurch, Sheerness, Kent.	Strong back and arms for heavy lifting. County Association can introduce expert to you; may provide course. Several years experience necessary for success.

Equipment	You may earn
	Small allowance or salary in advance of commission. Earnings vary enormously according to rates charged, area, ability to sell.
Own tools of teaching craft. (Educ. authority also provides.)	Depends on size of class, etc. Av. 13s. 6d. to 30s. 6d. an hour.
	Around $\frac{1}{200}$ of annual salary for which qualified a day. Around $\frac{1}{40}$ of annual salary for which qualified for full week.
Spacious room or separate hut, crockery, furniture, etc., ability to bake daintily in quantity, control costs, build sales.	
Less common languages pay best owing to intense competition in French and German.	£1 1s. per 1,000 words. More for technical or specialist material, or less common language.
Typewriter – second-hand machine may be bought for £10 15s. Hire 20s.–25s. per month. Duplicator £10–£20 (hand), £70–£100 (power).	Rates: 2s – 3s. per 1,000 words. First 2 carbons half price, others quarter price.
1 hive, 1 nucleus (small colony). Veil, smoker, etc. Bottling tank. (Settler). Cost around £22. Full colony (10 combs) £6–£7 10s.	Depends on local market facilities: £16–£20 from 6 colonies in good area.

The Job	How to start	Qualifications, training
Cox's Orange Pippins, growing.	Write to W. Seabrook & Sons Ltd, The Nursery, Boreham, Chelmsford.	Good physique. Preferably used to outdoor work. Strong arms for pruning.
Gardener.	Contact local garden owners, advertise in local weekly.	Experienced gardening, preferably both vegetables and flowers. Good physique. Limit hours of work to physical capacity.
Golf club secretary.	Local contacts essential to get news of such vacancy.	Good mixer and golfer. Knowledge of book-keeping helps.
Poultry keeping.	Write Domestic Poultry Keeping Council, Osborne House, 12a Palmerston Rd, Walthamstow, E17.	Experience very useful.
Rabbit-keeping.	Write Secretary, British Rabbit Council, 273 Farnborough Road, Farnborough, Hants, for address local rabbit club.	Membership local rabbit club essential to secure bran for breeding does. More than seven breeding does make you a commercial breeder; you can then secure bran direct.
CRAFTS Leather work.	Study *Leatherwork*, by I. P. Roseaman (Dryad Press, Leicester).	Skilful fingers, strong wrist.
Pottery.	Write for leaflet: *Notes on Pottery and the Once Fired Method*. A. T. White (Dryad Press, Leicester).	Good eye, neat hands, colour sense.
Weaving.	Write local School of Art re course.	Good eyesight, supple fingers, strong wrists.

Equipment	You may earn
Cost of establishing and equipping 5 acres of dwarf pyramids £3,385 and additional expense for the first three years £600.	This should be self-supporting in the 4th–5th year. Profit of £50 can be expected per acre thereafter.
Few easily carried tools, less generally owned by householder, e.g. strong secateurs, modern clippers, etc.	3s.–5s. an hour.
	£200–£400 p.a.
Ground must be given for adequate hen house and run. Average cost of 6 young pullets £6–£7 10s.	Price of eggs varies according to season. If you wish to sell table poultry you can find cost from V.P.A.P. Club, Women's Institute.
Each breeding doe requires one large and four 2-ft square stock hutches.	Pelts are sold wholesale through club or may be utilized for making slippers and gloves.
Set of tools (approx. 20), skins, leather cloth or manufactured leather (pig grain).	Rather better market than other crafts. Craft, drapery, leather-goods shops best sales avenues.
Near clay field, clay. Wheel to kiln for firing.	Show and sales may be obtained from high-class arts and crafts shops. Difficult field.
Elex Loom (4 shaft, 6 pedal, foot-power) £24 12s. 6d. Dryad foot-power, 42 in. reed, £40. Dryad Two-Way (Table) Loom (2 shaft, 24 in. wide), £8 17s. 6d. Hideaway Loom (4 shaft, 26 in.) £21 10s. (Douglas Andrew, Canterbury, Kent).	Depends on skill, contacts and ability to sell. (Very difficult market, especially poorer areas.)

Appendix IV

A GUIDE TO CHOOSING A HOBBY

The Hobby	How to start
I. ARTS Amateur acting.	Write secretary of local amateur group.
Art appreciation.	*Read *Meaning of Art*, by Herbert Read (Penguin Books).
Drama appreciation.	*Read *Drama*, by Ashley Dukes (Home University Library).
Drawing.	Write secretary, nearest art school or evening institute.
Hi-Fi.	*Read *Hi-Fi for Pleasure*, Burnett James, (Phoenix House).
Modelling in plastics.	*Read *Work with Plastics*, by G. A. Lomax (Dryad Press, Leicester).
Music.	
Music – Accordion.	Write editor *Accordion Times*, Somerset House, Cranley.
Music – Piano.	
Music – Violin.	
Musical appreciation.	
Painting.	Write secretary, nearest art school or evening institute.

Equipment	What to read
	Teach Yourself Amateur Acting. A Textbook of Acting. Susan Richmond. Later – join British Drama League, 9 Gordon Square, London, WC1. Membership gives use of library, quarterly journal, inquiry service, etc.
Opera glasses.	Shaw's Plays and Players (World's Classics).
	†British Drama, by Allardyce Nicoll (Harrap).
According to type of work undertaken.	*Teach Yourself To Draw (English University Press).
	*Sketching Out of Doors (Foyle Handbooks).
Electric gramophone of quality. Pre-amplifier. Amplifier. Loudspeaker.	Records Magazine or Popular Hi-Fi (monthlies).
Tools. Small vice as used for metal work. Drills, files, saws, etc.	*Plastics (Foyle Handbooks).
	*What Instrument Shall I Play? by M. M. Scott.
Accordion may be purchased from second-hand shop.	Accordion Digest, Somerset House, Cranley.
Piano (rented?).	*Why Not Play the Piano? (Boosey & Hawkes).
Violin.	*The Violin. Berthold Tours (Ed. Shore).
Penguin Scores of classics.	*Observer Book of Music (Warne). The Orchestra Speaks, by Shore (Longmans).
Canvas, easel, palette, knife, brushes, and paints.	*Teach Yourself Painting for Pleasure, by R. O. Dunlop, R.A. (English Universities Press).

Books marked thus * are essential reading, first-rate text-books costing 1s. 6d.–10s. 6d. Books marked thus † are more expensive, being standard works on their respective subjects, costing 12s. 6d.–42s.

The Hobby	How to start
Tape Recording.	Read *Tape Recording Year Book*, and *Advice on buying a Tape Re order*, by J. F. Ling (Print and Press Service).
Writing in script.	*Read *Good Handwriting*, by John Tarr (Phoenix House).
II. COLLECTING Antiques.	
Beetles.	
Books.	*Read *The Personal Library*, by Lionel McColvin (Phoenix House).
Brasses.	
China.	
Cigarette cards.	
Coins.	
Period arms.	
Period clothing.	
Period furniture.	
Stamps.	Subscribe to *Stamp Collecting* (weekly), 42 Maiden Lane, London, WC2. Read British Philatelic Association's Year Book (3 Berners Street, London, W1) for branches.

Equipment	What to read
Tape recorder of quality.	*Amateur Tape Recording* (monthly). *Tape Recording Fortnightly.*
Pen nibs.	
Cabinet.	*Antique Collector* (monthly), 16 Strutton Ground, Victoria Street, London, SW1.
	*British Beetles, by N. Joy (Warne). *The Reader's Guide.* Ed. Sir W. E. Williams (Penguin Books).
Simple shelving, preferably in adjustable units, with glass front for protection against dust and sun.	**Readers' Guides on Book Collecting* (National Book League).
Roll of paper, heel-ball.	*†Monumental Brasses*, by H. W. Macklin (Allen & Unwin).
†Chaffer's Marks of Monograms on Pottery and Porcelain (Reeve).	*†English Pottery Porcelain*, by W. B. Honey (Black).
	*All About Cigarette Cards, by A. J. Cruse (Perry). *†Cigarette Card Cavalcade*, by A. J. Cruse (Vawser).
Display cabinet.	**Coin Collecting*, by J. G. Milne and others (Oxford University Press).
	†Arms and Armament, by C. Ffoulkes (Harrap).
	There are innumerable histories of costume.
	*English Period Furniture, by C. H. Hayward (Evans). *†English Furniture Illustrated*, by H. Clifford Smith (Benn).
Strongly bound album and good small magnifying glass. *Gibbons' Stamp Catalogues.*	*Gibbons' Simplified Stamp Collecting* (1961 ed.) **Teach Yourself Stamp Collecting* (English Universities Press).

The Hobby	How to start
III. CRAFTS Basketry.	*Read *Rush Baskets and Mats* (Dryad Handicrafts, Leicester).
Canework.	
China and bric-à-brac.	
Cooking.	*Read *Teach Yourself to Cook* (English Universities Press). *Cooking for Men Only*, by Wilson Midgley (Newnes).
Furniture making.	*Read *Woodwork for Boys* (English Universities Press).
Model making.	
Printing.	*Read *Printing Explained*, by H. Simon and H. Carter (Dryad Press, Leicester).
Puppetry.	Write Educational Puppetry Association, 23A Southampton Place, London, WC1, or Department of Further Education of local authority.
Soft toy making (women).	*Read *Felt Toys*, by E. Mochrie and I. P. Roseaman (Dryad Press, Leicester). Gives designs.
Wood carving.	

Equipment	What to read
Supply of materials to be used.	*Make these from Raffia* (Dryad Handicrafts, Leicester).
Frames and cane (Dryad Handicrafts, Leicester).	*Canework*, by Charles Crampton (Dryad Press, Leicester). *Cane Work on Simple Frames* (Dryad Press, Leicester).
Potter's wheel, clay, etc., from Dryad Handicrafts.	*Pottery Making* (Studio). †*A Potter's Book*, by B. Leach (Faber). *Simplified Cookery*, by Dora Seton (Evans).
Set of wood-working tools.	Subscribe to *Woodworker* (monthly) (Montague House, Russell Square, London, WC1).
Set of model-making tools.	*Model Engineer* (monthly) (Percival Marshall & Co. Ltd, 23 Great Queen Street, WC2). *Model Aircraft* (monthly) (Percival Marshall & Co. Ltd, 23 Great Queen Street, WC2).
A small hand press, type, stick, etc. Cost £20–£30. Write Adana Ltd, 15–19 Church St, Twickenham, Middlesex, for catalogue.	
Equipment varies with type of puppet, i.e. marionettes (string puppets), glove puppets. Course run by E.P.A. L.C.C. and others run evening classes.	*Hand Puppets and String Puppets*, by Waldo S. Lanchester. (Dryad Press, Leicester.) *Your Puppetry*, by John Wright (Sylvan Press). † *The Complete Puppet Book*. Ed. Wall and White (Faber).
Felt squares (Dryad Handicrafts). Unbleached linen, thread, beeswax, needles, and adhesive.	*Circus Toys*, by Peggy Tearle (Dryad Press, Leicester). Gives full-size patterns.
Write Dryad Handicrafts, Leicester *re* necessary tools and materials.	†*The Art of Woodwork and Furniture Making*, by A. Gregory (Dryad Press, Leicester).

The Hobby	How to start
Wooden toy making.	*Read *Wooden Toy Making*, by W. Horton (Dryad Press, Leicester).
IV. OUTDOOR Bird-watching.	*Read *Book of Common Birds* (Oxford University Press). *Read *Watching Birds* and *Bird Recognition*, by James Fisher (Penguin Books).
Botany.	
Fruit growing.	
Gardening.	*Read *Teach Yourself Gardening* (English Universities Press). *Read *The A.B.C. of Gardening* (English Universities Press).
Gardening from seed.	
Meteorology.	*Read *Understanding Weather*, by O. G. Sutton (Penguin Books).
Rock gardening.	
Simplified gardening.	
Vegetable gardening.	
Photography.	*Read *Photography for Boys and Girls*, by S. Bowler (English Universities Press). Later join local camera club.
V. RECREATIONS Chess.	*Read *Teach Yourself Chess* (English Universities Press).
Conjuring.	

Equipment	What to read
Assemble a set of toy-making tools from Dryad Industries or elsewhere.	*Small Carved Animals.* *Carved and Jointed Animals* (Dryad Handicrafts, Leicester). * *Wooden Toy Making* (Foyle's Handbooks).
Good pair of binoculars.	†*Bird Book for the Pocket*, by E. Sandars (Oxford University Press). †*Bird Watching.* Hickey and others (Oxford University Press).
Good small pocket glass, specimen case.	†*Flower Book for the Pocket*, by M. Shere (Oxford University Press). * *Soft Fruit Growing* and * *Tree Fruit Growing* (Penguin Books).
Assemble garden tools gradually, one by one as needed.	*Amateur Gardening* (weekly). * *Gardener's Pocket Book*, ed. C. Wallace (Evans Bros).
One or more glass frames helpful.	* *Gardening on a Shoestring*, by H. L. V. Fletcher (Phoenix House). †*Drama of Weather*, by Sir N. Shaw (Cambridge University Press). * *The A.B.C. of the Rock Garden and Pool* (English Universities Press). * *The Simple Garden*, by Phoebe Fenwick Gaye (Phoenix House). * *The A.B.C. of Vegetable Gardening* (English Universities Press).
Camera. Start with cheap box camera.	If seriously interested, read *Amateur Photographer* (Dorset House, Stamford St, London, SE1). *Cine-camera Journal.*
Chessboard and pieces (cheap portable miniatures now available).	Read *Chess Monthly* (Sutton Coldfield). * *Chess*, by L. Hoffer (Routledge). * *Conjuring.* * *Card Conjuring* (Foyle Handbooks).

The Hobby	How to start
Dancing (including Old Time and Square).	Join local dancing class. *Read *Teach Yourself Modern Dancing* (English Universities Press).
Fishing.	*Read *Teach Yourself Fishing* (English Universities Press).
Pigeon racing.	Join local Pigeon Fanciers' Club. First birds easily obtained without charge usually from local fanciers.
VI. CULTURAL, SCIENTIFIC Anthropology.	
Archaeology.	Write nearest archaeological society. *Read *Prehistoric Britain*, by C. and J. Hawkes (Penguin Books).
Architecture.	*Read *Teach Yourself Planning and Designing* (English Universities Press). *Read *Architecture*, by M. S. Briggs (Oxford University Press).
Astronomy.	*Read *Teach Yourself Astronomy* (English Universities Press).
Biology.	*Read *Teach Yourself Biology* (English Universities Press). *Read *Biology*. Home University Library (Oxford).

Equipment	What to read
	Read *Modern Dance Monthly* (2 Norfolk House, Brixton Oval, London, sw2).
	Modern Ballroom Dancing, by Victor Silvester (Jenkins).
Rod, lines, artificial baits, etc.	*Mr Crabtree Goes Fishing (Daily Mirror)* (gives fishes and their habitats in British fresh waters).
	Fishing for Beginners, by M. Wiggin (Phoenix House).
Pigeons, pigeon loft, baskets and panniers, corn and minerals.	Subscribe to *Racing Pigeon* (19 Doughty St, London, wc1).
	History of Anthropology, by A. C. Haddon (Watts).
	†Later: *Early Man*, by Allan Houghton Brodrick (Hutchinson).
	†*Beginning in Archaeology*, by K. Kenyon (Pheonix House).
	†*Archaeology in the Field*. Cranford (Phoenix House).
	†Later read: *Meet Your Ancestors*, by Roy Chapman Andrews (John Long).
	†*Gods, Graves and Scholars*, by C. W. Ceram (Gollancz).
Consult *The Buildings of England*, by N. Pevsner. 21 vols. (Penguin Books).	†*Architecture – An art for all men*, by T. F. Hamlin (Oxford University Press). Books published by Batsford (Architectural Press).
Second-hand telescope or use of telescope.	†*Universe Around Us*, by James Jeans (Cambridge University Press).
	Introduction to Biology, by E. J. Hatfield (Oxford University Press).

The Hobby	How to start
Tropical fish aquarium.	See local aquarium, or Preston Aquarium, 44 Beaconsfield Road, Brighton.
Cosmology.	*Read *Size of the Universe*, by F. J. Hargreaves (Penguin Books).
Economic history.	*Read selected period in *Pelican History of England* (7 vols.).
Genealogy (heraldry).	*Read *Trace Your Ancestors*, by L. G. Pine (Evans).
Geography.	*Read *Teach Yourself Economic Geography* (English Universities Press). *Read *First Introduction to Geography* (Oxford University Press).
History.	*Read *Teach Yourself the Use of History* (English Universities Press). *Read *History*, Home University Library (Oxford). *Read *The Condition of England in 1685*, by T. B. Macaulay (Bell).
Local history.	Contact local museum (women consult local WI).
Philosophy.	*Read *Teach Yourself Philosophy* (English Universities Press). *Read *Philosophy*, Home University Library (Oxford).
Politics.	Attend regularly meetings of local political parties.
VII. SOCIAL WORK Hospital work (voluntary).	Join local Friends of the Hospital League (women), local branch of W.V.S. or British Red Cross Society.

Equipment	What to read
Tank with hood. Heater with thermostat. Plants and gravel. Selection of fish. Total cost, smallest tank, around £8.	*How to Keep and Breed Tropical Fish*, by Dr C. W. Emmens (T. F. H. Publications).
	*The Mysterious Universe, by James Jeans.
	†*Growth of English Society* and †*Economic History of England*, by E. Lipson (3 vols.) (A. & C. Black).
	†*The Economic History of Britain*, by W. W. Meredith (Pitman).
Cf. Appendix III (for serious student).	*Heraldry* (Foyle Handbooks).
	Grammar of English Heraldry, by W. H. Hope (Cambridge University Press).
Good atlas and glass.	†*The World*, by L. Dudley Stamp (Longmans).
	A Junior Outline of History, by I. O. Evans (Denis Archer).
	Short History of the English People, by John Richard Green (Everyman).
	†Later read *English Local History* (Oxford University Press).
	Greek Philosophy, by M. E. J. Taylor (Oxford University Press).
	Recent Philosophy, by John Laird (Oxford).
	Modern Philosophy, by C. E. M. Joad (Oxford).
	†*A History of Western Philosophy*, by Bertrand Russell (Allen & Unwin).
	Introduction to Politics, by Dorothy Pickles (Sylvan Press).
	English Parliament, by K. R. Mackenzie (Penguin Books).
	Public Health and Social Services, by Geffen and Browne (Edward Arnold).

The Hobby	How to start
Visiting old people.	Contact nearest local Old People's Welfare Committee. (Address from N.O.P.W.C. 26 Bedford Square, London, WC1), or local Social Welfare Officer.
Visiting prisons.	Consult governor or chaplain nearest prison. Later contact Central After-care Association, Artillery House, Artillery Row, London, SW1, or Prisoners' Aid Society.
Volunteer librarian.	Contact local Library Committee in town; County Library in country.
VIII. MUNICIPAL GOVERNMENT County Council.	Contact local county councillor for advice. Write county office for information.
Borough Council.	Contact local councillor. Apply town hall for information.
Parish Council.	Contact local parish councillor and local office.
Education committee.	Consult local education office.
Hospital Area Group Management Committee.	Get experience as governor of local hospital first. Contact member of local hospital group management committee.
Hospital governor.	Consult local hospital governor.
Ratepayers' Association.	Join local Ratepayers' Association. If none, assist to form one.
Residents' Association.	Join local Residents' Association. If none, assist to form one.

Equipment	What to read
	Social Therapy, by M. B. and S. W. Hale (Williams & Norgate).
	The Magistrates' Courts, by F. T. Giles (Penguin Books). †*Who Lie in Gaol*, by Joan Henry (Gollancz) (women). †*The English Prison and Borstal Systems*, by W. Fox (Routledge & Kegan Paul).
Car is almost, but not quite, essential for visiting different towns.	*Your Local Authority*, by C. Barratt (Pitman). *Local Government in England and Wales*, by W. E. Jackson (Penguin Books). Later subscribe to *Municipal Journal*, 4 St Clements Inn, London, WC2.
Considerable experience of social work and/or administration necessary. Appointments are made by Ministry of Health.	*Hospital*, 15 Charterhouse Street, London, EC1, also *Hospital and Health Management*, 9 Catherine Place, London, SW1. Later subscribe to the *Hospital*, 15 Charterhouse Street, London, EC1, or *Hospital and Health Management*, 9 Catherine Place, London, SW1. *Teach Yourself Local Government* (English University Press).

INDEX

PENGUIN BOO
BBC BOOKS

STORM FROM T

Praise for the television series

'As spectacle and history it's fascinating' – *The Times*

'The battle cry of 5,000 Mongol soldiers brings a haunting vision of thousands of highly trained killers on horseback . . . The result is stunning' – *Daily Mirror*

'A handsomely presented four-part series telling how the 13th century Mongols conquered and ruled the largest empire in history' – *Sunday Telegraph*

'Robert Marshall's epic documentary series is story-telling at its most evocative . . . Gripping, romantic, appalling' – *Time Out*

'This is the TV of superlatives – big names, big spaces, epoch-making battles and ancient legends. Gilded places such as Samarkand and Bukhara provide the mythic settings' – *Observer*

ABOUT THE AUTHOR

Robert Marshall is a television producer whose credits include: *Vichy France and the Jews*, *All the King's Men*, *Light in the Dark* and *Summer of the Bomb*. He was the Series Producer of *Storm From the East*. His previous books are *All the King's Men*, *Shadow Makers* and *In the Sewers of Lvov*.

ROBERT MARSHALL

STORM FROM THE EAST

FROM GENGHIS KHAN TO KHUBILAI KHAN

PENGUIN BOOKS
BBC BOOKS

To the memory of Bruce Norman

PENGUIN BOOKS
BBC BOOKS

Published by the Penguin Group and BBC Enterprises Ltd
Penguin Books Ltd, 27 Wrights Lane, London W8 5TZ, England
Penguin Books USA Inc., 375 Hudson Street, New York, New York 10014, USA
Penguin Books Australia Ltd, Ringwood, Victoria, Australia
Penguin Books Canada Ltd, 10 Alcorn Avenue, Toronto, Ontario, Canada M4V 3B2
Penguin Books (NZ) Ltd, 182–190 Wairau Road, Auckland 10, New Zealand

Penguin Books Ltd, Registered Offices: Harmondsworth, Middlesex, England

First published by BBC Books, a division of BBC Enterprises Limited, 1993
Published in Penguin Books 1994
1 3 5 7 9 10 8 6 4 2

Printed in England by Clays Ltd, St Ives plc

CONTENTS

MAPS

ACKNOWLEDGEMENTS

This book is largely a product of the work done by a great many people who came together to work on the television series *Storm from the East*, the inspiration for which came from my colleagues at NHK Television in Japan. Over the course of the last two years we have shared and learnt a great deal together, and I want to give credit to their contributions. First of all Mr Takashi Inoue whose determination ensured the project happened at all. I would also like to acknowledge the work of Hisashi Anzai, Sanji Eto and Nobuya Yamamoto. I especially want to thank my colleague and now friend, Tomohito Terai, for his dedication, enthusiasm and indomitable spirit of co-operation.

I am, of course, deeply indebted to everyone who worked on the series here in London. Their contribution has been enormous. I want to mention, in no particular order, John Slater, Vivianna Woodruff, Jo Langford, Susan Vogel, Angela Moonshine, John Adderley, Ron Brown, Paul Dawe, Mike Burton, Sheila Ableman, Martha Caute, Joanna Wiese, Paul Snelgrove, Harry Green, and, especially, Habie Schwarz for her invaluable scholarship and imagination.

Naturally I have relied a great deal on the contribution of our academic advisers, and their enthusiasm for the series has been a great encouragement. I want to acknowledge the work of James Chambers for his insight into Mongol military matters, Dr Morris Rossabi for his work on Khubilai, and Drs Reuven Amitai-Preiss, Peter Morgan and Judy Kolbas for their advice on the Mongols in the Middle East. My deepest gratitude goes to our series consultant, Dr David Morgan, author of *The Mongols*, for his guidance throughout and for patiently reading my manuscript.

Robert Marshall
London 1992

For their kind permission to use copyright photographs in this book the publishers wish to thank the following: 1–4, 8, 10, 15, 16 Akira Soda; 5, 6 The Trustees of the British Library; 7 Robert Harding Picture Library; 9 Bildarchiv Preussischer Kulturbesitz; 11 Werner Forman Archive; 12, 13 Collection of the National Palace Museum, Taiwan, Republic of China; 14 The Trustees of the Victoria and Albert Museum, London (C.8–1852); 17 Robert Marshall/BBC Enterprises.

DYNASTIC TABLE

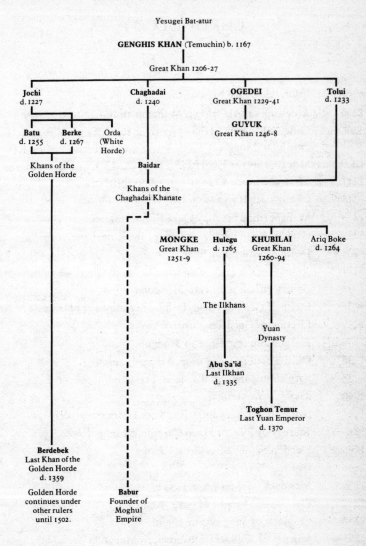

Yesugei Bat-atur

GENGHIS KHAN (Temuchin) b. 1167

Great Khan 1206-27

Jochi
d. 1227

Chaghadai
d. 1240

OGEDEI
Great Khan 1229-41

Tolui
d. 1233

Batu
d. 1255

Berke
d. 1267

Orda
(White
Horde)

GUYUK
Great Khan 1246-8

Khans of the
Golden Horde

Baidar

Khans of the
Chaghadai Khanate

MONGKE
Great Khan
1251-9

Hulegu
d. 1265

KHUBILAI
Great Khan
1260-94

Ariq Boke
d. 1264

The Ilkhans

Yuan
Dynasty

Abu Sa'id
Last Ilkhan
d. 1335

Toghon Temur
Last Yuan Emperor
d. 1370

Berdebek
Last Khan of the
Golden Horde
d. 1359

Golden Horde
continues under
other rulers
until 1502.

Babur
Founder of
Moghul
Empire

CHRONOLOGY

?1167	Birth of Genghis Khan
1200	Accession of 'Ala' al-Din Muhammad II, Khwarazm Shah
1206	Genghis Khan proclaimed supreme ruler of the tribes at *quriltai* in Mongolia
1209	Mongols invade Hsi-Hsia
1211	Mongols invade Chin empire of north China
1215	Chung-tu falls to Mongols
1218	Mongol troops occupy Qara Khitai empire
1219	Genghis Khan invades empire of the Khwarazm Shah
1221	Death of Khwarazm Shah
1221–3	Journey of Ch'ang Ch'un from China to Genghis's camp
1223	Genghis Khan returns to Mongolia
1227	Death of Genghis Khan. Definitive conquest of Hsi-Hsia
1229	Election of Ogedei as Great Khan
1234	End of Chin resistance to Mongols
1235	Ogedei builds Qaraqorum, Mongol capital
1237–42	Batu's campaigns in Russia and eastern Europe
1240	Kiev falls to Mongols
1241	Battles of Liegnitz and River Sajo. Death of Ogedei
1245–7	Journey of John of Plano Carpini to Mongolia
1246	Election of Guyuk as Great Khan
1248	Death of Guyuk
1250	Mamluks seize power in Egypt
1251	Election of Mongke as Great Khan
1252	Conquest of Sung empire begins
1253–5	Journey of William of Rubruck to Mongolia

1253	Hulegu's forces set off for Persia
1255	Death of Batu, first Khan of Golden Horde
1256	Hulegu takes Assassin castles in north Persia
1257	Accession of Berke, Khan of Golden Horde
1258	Fall of Baghdad to Hulegu. Death of last Abbasid Caliph
1259	Death of Mongke
1260	Hulegu invades Syria, then withdraws. Battle of Ayn Jalut. Rival *quriltais* elect Khubilai and Ariq Boke as Great Khan: civil war ensues
1261–2	Civil war betwen Hulegu and Berke
1264	Khubilai victorious over Ariq Boke
1265	Death of Hulegu, first Ilkhan. Accession of Abaqa
1266	Building begins at new Mongol capital of China, Ta-tu (Peking)
1267	Death of Berke, Khan of Golden Horde
1272	Khubilai adopts Chinese dynastic title, Yuan
1274	First Mongol expedition against Japan
1276	Hang-chou, capital of Sung empire, falls to Mongols
1279	Sung empire defeated
1281	Second Mongol expedition against Japan
1287	Rabban Sauma sent to Europe by Ilkhan Arghun
1294	Death of Khubilai
1295	Accession of Ghazan as Ilkhan. Mongols in Persia become Muslim
1304	Death of Ilkhan Ghazan. Accession of Oljeitu
1313	Accession of Ozbeg, under whose rule Golden Horde becomes Muslim
1335	Death of Abu Sa'id, last Ilkhan of line of Hulegu
1346	Outbreak of Black Death in Mongol force besieging Kaffa, in the Crimea: from there it spreads to Europe
1353–4	Major outbreak of the disease in China
1368	Mongols driven from China by Ming forces
1370	Death in Qaraqorum of Toghon Temur, last Yuan emperor

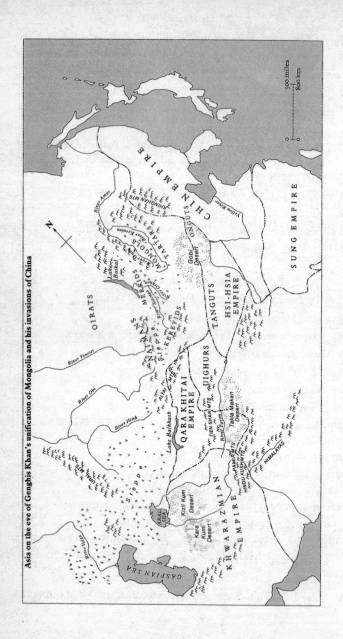

Asia on the eve of Genghis Khan's unification of Mongolia and his invasions of China

1

BIRTH OF A NATION

In the centre of the main square in Cracow stands St Mary's church, considered one of the most important churches in Poland. Every hour on the hour, a trumpeter from the Cracow fire department presents himself at the balcony of the main tower and blows an alarm. This ceremony has taken place each day, almost continuously since the middle of the thirteenth century. It commemorates the destruction of the city, for the trumpeter is blowing a call to arms, a signal that the enemy has been sighted and is at the gates. As the trumpeter sounds his haunting melody he comes to an abrupt halt midway through the call – at precisely the moment, so legend has it, when the Mongol arrow struck.

When the alarm was being sounded on that first occasion, more than 700 years ago, the population of Cracow were already abandoning the city, making for the forests beyond the city walls. Some days before, the Polish ruler Duke Boleslaw the Chaste had sent his army out to meet the invaders; but they were ambushed and the small Polish force was decimated under a hail of arrows. When the news reached Cracow, Boleslaw and his family gathered up all the wealth they could carry. With the remaining contingent of soldiers they fled for Hungary, leaving the citizens to fend for themselves. When the main body of the invading army reached the city, they found the streets strangely quiet, and on 24 March 1241, Palm Sunday, Cracow was put to the torch.

THE FURY OF THE TARTARS

To the rest of Europe, the news of the sacking of Cracow seemed a terrible omen; an unearthly storm was sweeping away everything in its path. From Cracow the invader moved west to confront an allied European army of local mercenaries, Teutonic Knights, Knights Templars and Hospitallers – the very flower of Europe's chivalry. For the Europeans the battle was a complete disaster and within a few days a second great Christian army was destroyed. Bewildered medieval chroniclers could make no sense of it; confused by the lightning tactics of the invader, they consistently estimated his strength at four or five times their actual numbers. However, for the European commanders the experience had been a devastating lesson in warfare. At every major battle the invaders had been outnumbered and yet their generals constantly out-manoeuvred, out-thought and out-fought the Europeans. Their armies had operated like disciplined machines, co-ordinating a complex series of tactical moves with extraordinary precision. In the grand scheme of things, the Mongol armies had conducted a brilliantly complex campaign, carefully planned and executed from first to last – from Poland to the Hungarian prairies.

News of these disasters swept through the rest of Europe, bringing predictions of utter destruction and damnation. Rumours spread of diabolical atrocities committed by inhuman monsters, of creatures with the head of a horse that devoured their victims, possessed supernatural powers and had been unleashed to bring retribution upon an ungodly world. In Germany this superstitious hysteria generated stories that the Mongols were actually one of the lost tribes of Israel and that Jewish merchants were smuggling arms to them across the borders. As a result many innocent Jews were summarily and pointlessly executed at frontier posts. The Hungarians described the invaders as 'dog-faced Tartars', while a French monk living in Austria wrote that, after the Mongol soldiers had raped European women, they tore off their victims' breasts and delivered these 'delicacies' to their 'dog-headed' princes, who devoured them.

The Church was not above regurgitating ancient myths and legends in a vain attempt to explain the disaster. A Dominican monk, Ricoldo of Monte Croce, explained that the name Mongol was derived from Mogogoli, the sons of the legendary Magog. Gog and Magog, so the legend goes, had been a pair of marauding giants who had terrorized Europe in ancient times. They had been defeated by Alexander the Great and locked away behind massive gates in the Caucasus Mountains. Now their descendants were loose and bent upon the destruction of civilization. Only by invoking the name of Alexander could these monsters be subdued. In packed churches across northern Europe sermons were being conducted before a terrified population, while prayers were offered up pleading: '. . . from the fury of the Tartars, oh Lord deliver us'. The only sizeable army that might stand in the path of the invader was that of the French King, who was prepared for the onslaught but expected martyrdom. To the Pope it seemed that all of Christendom would be destroyed: 'When we consider that through these Tartars the name of Christian might utterly perish, our bones shudder at the thought.'

Europe had been struck and left reeling by an alien force that might just as well have come from Mars. The Mongols, or Tartars as they called them, were a race that had emerged from a land which, to Europeans, was on no known map. Narrow and inward-looking Europe had no knowledge or experience of the territories beyond the Urals. Indeed, European ignorance of who the Mongols were or what they had accomplished persisted for centuries. This was not just because of the limits of European knowledge, but also because the sheer breadth and scope of the Mongol conquests beggared the imagination. Never had so much territory been conquered so quickly. The sudden and overwhelming devastation that shook Europe to its core had already been visited upon the entire expanse of Asia. From the Korean peninsula to the River Danube, nearly a third of the world's land surface lay under the command of one single family – and all this had been achieved in less than fifty years.

3

Yet still they continued to expand. No more than thirty years after their armies had stood on the frontiers of Germany, the Mongols had completed the conquest of all of China and were launching invasions upon Japan and Java. By any standards it was a breathtaking achievement.

The storm that swept across the world during the thirteenth century changed the political boundaries of Asia and Europe, uprooted entire peoples and dispersed them across the continent. It transformed the ethnic character of many regions, while at the same time permanently changing the strength and influence of the three major religions: Islam, Buddhism and Christianity. Most important, the Mongols opened up the East to the West, expanded our knowledge of the world and in so doing created for the first time one whole world.

MOUNTED HERDSMEN

All of this is remarkable enough, yet when one considers the Mongols' humble beginnings it is almost beyond comprehension. At the end of the twelfth century, the Mongols were one of a number of small nomadic tribes that inhabited an isolated plateau in the heart of Central Asia. To the west lay two massive and converging chains of mountains, the Altai and the Tien Shan; to the north were the vast frozen Siberian forests; while the Gobi desert lay to the south and the Khinghan Mountains to the east. Though technically the Mongolian Plateau lies within that vast expanse known as the steppe which extends across the breadth of Asia from Manchuria to Hungary, in reality it is locked behind natural barriers that kept the inhabitants safe from invasion for centuries.

The plateau lies some 1200 m (4000 feet) above sea level and is subject to dramatic extremes of climate. In the summer the temperature often rises above 40°C (104°F) and in winter drops well below − 40°C (− 40°F). The soil itself varies from a loose gravel to a thin clay and is frozen hard during the winter. By

November all the streams, rivers and lakes are also completely frozen and water has to be got by laboriously cutting and dragging large blocks of ice to the nearest fire. Nothing stirs until April. Add to the extreme climate a low rainfall, and it is clear that the steppe makes poor agricultural land. However, during the summer it is carpeted by a luxuriant blanket of grass that gives the countryside the appearance of a gently undulating billiard table. Even during the winter months, the more sheltered valleys retain a hardy turf that provides reliable pasture for the herds of sheep, goats, cattle and horses that nomads have kept here for centuries.

The life of the Mongols is therefore a constant cycle of seasonal migrations from the flat open summer pastures to protected river valleys for the winter. These migrations are not arbitrary. Each tribe or clan would return to their traditional pastures year after year, and would only alter this pattern if the growing size of their flocks obliged them to search for more land, or if they were forced off their traditional territory by other nomads. Maintaining control of traditional pasture or seeking out better pastures was a common source of conflict between the Mongol tribes. The need for good grazing land for their herds was a primary preoccupation, for their survival depended on it. Today, the life of the average Mongol herdsman has changed little in 800 years. Sheep still provide the main staples of life: meat, milk, cheese, leather and wool for clothing and the manufacture of felt from which they still build their tents. Cattle are also kept for meat, but are more commonly used as beasts of burden. During the autumn months each Mongol family slaughters a number of their sheep, prepares the mutton and then freezes it, usually by simply burying it in the ground before the snows arrive. Mutton is the major source of protein, and through the long winters it sustains the population on meals that are usually produced by melting a block of ice in a cauldron and then boiling frozen slabs of the stuff until it forms a thick stew. Another useful food during the long winters is *ayrag*, a mildly alcoholic and somewhat bitter fermentation made from mare's milk.

Today, extended nomadic families live on large collectives of land controlled by the state. Any number of families may share these tracts of land, herding their sheep or horses, which are bred both for riding and for their milk. Eight hundred years ago, the Mongols lived not on collectives but in loosely defined tribes or clans. They tended not to live together in a single large encampment; instead, the tribe would be scattered amongst any number of smaller encampments that might be spread across two or three different valleys. These encampments had to be mobile enough to be struck and loaded on to wagons for the annual migration. An essential aid to this mobility was the *ger* or *yurt*, the Mongol tent which is still made by stretching a piece of thick woollen felt across a squat cylindrical framework of thin wooden struts. The floor is usually covered by simple planking while beds, cupboards and chests containing the family heirlooms are arranged in a circle against the wall. Beside the centre pole stands a stove which is vented through a hole in the roof. Although the average *ger* can be dismantled and re-erected in under an hour, it was not uncommon for clans simply to lift the entire structure on to the back of an ox-cart. It must have been an extraordinary sight, the migration of vast herds of sheep and horses and, in their midst, three or four mobile *gers* sailing across the steppe.

The key to the nomads' dominion over the steppe was the horse. Since its domestication in southern Russia during the second millennium BC, the horse's remarkable speed and stamina has been exploited by steppe nomads. It became an essential element of daily life, the primary means of transport, an aid for tending the herds and of course an invaluable asset for the hunt. All steppe nomads were exceptional hunters. Their principal weapon was the compound bow, made from alternate sections of horn and bamboo, bonded together by silk and resin. They developed stirrups (perhaps borrowed from the Chinese), which enabled them to ride without using reins. As a result they could fire arrows or use the lasso while at full gallop. It was these skills that were to contribute to the emergence of a great military power from the heart of the Asian grasslands.

From around 800 BC onwards, the settled societies to the south began encountering nomadic horsemen who appeared periodically, sometimes attacked and pillaged the towns and villages, and then disappeared again. But what set these people apart from their predecessors was their exclusive use of cavalry: a swift and lethal force of men on horseback, able to direct a withering barrage of arrows at their enemies from a distance. They became the scourge of most settled societies. Indeed, historians have recorded that wave upon wave of nomadic horsemen have charged out of Asia through the low passes of the Tien Shan and Altai Mountains into Europe or down into the Middle East, from the days of the Scythians in the fifth and sixth centuries BC right up to the Mongols.

The relationship between the steppe nomads and settled societies was never an easy one. Living in their pastoral wilderness for century upon century, trapped within a perennial struggle against climate and the fluctuations of tribal power, the nomads developed no technologies, produced no manufactures nor even learned simple mining. The demands of seasonal migrations made this impossible. So the nomadic societies soon developed a traditional dependency upon the settled societies that had developed in the Middle East and China. Wrought metals and products such as swords, armour, silks, gold and silver were bought, traded or stolen. In terms of the exchange of materials it was a very one-sided relationship, for the nomads had little to offer in return but woollen goods and animal skins.

Be that as it may, the nomadic horsemen never saw themselves as inferior to the settled societies. Quite the opposite. For more than 2000 years the people of the steppe confronted the largest agrarian society in the world, China, without ever being politically or culturally absorbed by it. Indeed, these two societies surveyed one another with mutual arrogance. China's deeply rooted cultural traditions had led to a perception of itself as historically superior to all other societies and states. Its ancient name of Chung-kuo (Middle Kingdom) implied that it was the very heart of civilization, and because of the resilience of its cultural traditions the Chinese also have a long history of absorbing other civilizations that hovered along its border – or heavily influencing the more distant cultures of such fiercely independent societies as Korea, Japan and Vietnam. Virtually all of eastern Asia adopted Chinese calendars, cuisine and literacy. All, that is, except for the nomadic horsemen of the steppe.

They not only rejected Chinese culture and ideology, they also refused to see any value in it – except for the few material goods that it could provide. From their perspective the vast majority of the Chinese population spent their lives on their hands and knees scratching away at the soil. To the nomadic horseman, the peasant farmer was regarded with the utmost contempt, and was of less value than a horse. The contempt was mutual. Chinese government officials writing about how to deal with the bands of horsemen on their borders argued that it was impossible to have proper relations with people who migrated to and fro like birds and beasts. So the relationship between these two peoples developed along simple lines: the Chinese saw the periodic incursions as a blight, not unlike a natural disaster such as flood or famine, that had to be dealt with as and when it arose, usually by means of large bribes in return for being left unharmed; while the horsemen, on the other hand, saw the Chinese as little more than a resource to be plundered.

EARLY NOMADIC EMPIRES

The first major empire to be forged by nomadic horsemen was that of the Turks, the people who eventually colonized Anatolia. From around the sixth and seventh centuries AD they controlled an exclusively steppe empire that extended from the Chinese frontier to the Black Sea. After the collapse of the Turkish empire the eastern steppe came to be dominated by the Uighurs, a semi-nomadic people who had their capital in the Orkhon valley, in what is now Hentiy Province in modern-day Mongolia. The Uighurs were a cultured people, natural traders and sophisticated artists. After the collapse of their empire in the ninth century they migrated southwards and westwards to settle along the Tarim River, in what is now Sinkiang, at the most western extremity of modern China. Here the Uighurs established themselves and flourished for another 300 years. They adapted an alphabet from the people in eastern Persia and were the first semi-nomadic people to become literate, going on to develop a sophisticated legal system and a civil service.

The Uighurs had been forced out of their original domain in western Mongolia by the Khitans, another semi-nomadic people who conquered most of Mongolia and northern China. In the tradition of all conquerors of China, the Khitans were soon tamed by the resilience of Chinese civilization and absorbed into the great Chinese melting pot. To assume control of China it was expected that the invader would adopt a Chinese name and establish a new dynasty; this the Khitans did, calling themselves Liao. With the Sinicization of the Khitans, their invasion actually became a reverse conquest, effectively extending Chinese control westwards into Mongolia. The Liao established a new frontier, forcing the remaining Turkish peoples and any others who would not submit further to the west. It was the Liao Dynasty's occupation of this part of the eastern steppe that provides historians with the first evidence of the appearance of a people that eventually became known as Mongols.

By the early twelfth century the Khitans themselves were forced out of northern China, displaced by yet another semi-nomadic invader, the Jurchen from Manchuria. These new people were less interested in the lands beyond the traditional Chinese frontier, and left the eastern steppe to the tribes that had traditionally inhabited them. The Jurchen were more concerned with securing control over China proper, which they managed to do far more successfully than had the Khitans. But the Khitans, like the Uighurs, didn't simply disappear. One of the Khitan princes, together with a large group of his followers who were unwilling to submit to Jurchen rule, migrated westwards deep into Central Asia to establish a new empire called

Qara Khitai. They settled even further west than had the Uighurs, near Lake Balkhash close to the eastern frontiers of the great Persian empire. Meanwhile the Jurchen, having conquered northern China, adopted the dynastic name Chin and it was this dynasty that was fated to encounter the emerging Mongol empire.

SECRET HISTORY

However, at this time the Mongols were still an emerging people struggling along with other tribal groups for control of the eastern steppe. Historians find it impossible to account for Mongolian history before the thirteenth century. Most early descriptions of nomadic empires come from the literate civilizations like the Chinese or Persians, whose own histories describe the frequent encounters they had with nomadic invaders. Apart from the Uighurs, most nomadic groups, and certainly the Mongols, were illiterate. So, whether by design or circumstance, Mongol history begins with Genghis Khan, because it was he who commanded that the Mongols adopt the Uighur script and adapt it to the Mongolian language. After Genghis's death his successor commissioned the famous *Secret History of the Mongols*. In a curious mixture of myth, legend and apparent fact it describes the rise of the Mongol people, the early life and struggles of Genghis Khan and his breathtaking world conquests. Scholarly opinion varies on whether it actually does provide a reliable account of Mongol history. For some it is no more reliable than the Nordic sagas, a collection of legends brought together to enhance the reputation of Genghis. But others disagree. There was once an official history kept at the Mongol court known as the *Altan Debter*. Substantial portions of it survive in Persian and Chinese histories, and these scraps make certain things clear. The *Altan Debter* and the *Secret History* are two completely separate works, compiled independently of each other; and yet they describe the same events in roughly the same

10

way. So it is more than probable that at least some portions of the *Secret History* can be assumed to be fact.

It has to be said, however, that the *Secret History* begins quite solidly in the realms of myth, as it describes the genesis of the Mongols.

> There was a blue wolf which was born
> having [his] destiny from heaven above.
> His spouse was a fallow doe.
> They came, passing over the Sea.
> Batacaciqan was born when they camped
> at the head of the Onon River,
> at [Mount] Burkan Qaldun.

In the traditions of Old Testament genealogies, the *Secret History* then goes on to recount how Batacaciqan begat Tamaca and Tamaca begat Qoricar Mergan ... and so on until it quickly arrives at the twelfth century, where at least some events can be corroborated by Chinese sources. The most important subject that the work covers is the early life and struggles of Temuchin, as Genghis was known before he assumed the title Great Khan. Here again historians speculate about its value as a reliable account. The description of his rise to power becomes something of a litany of betrayal and revenge, as one after another of the tribal rulers proves to be disloyal and the young Temuchin is forced to take reprisals. His motives are always above reproach, his methods ruthless but justified. Because of this repetitive cycle of events it is tempting to see the *Secret History* as merely a panegyric; a more sober view might suggest that it was Temuchin who had been less than straight with his rivals, and his struggle nothing more than the most ruthless scramble for absolute supremacy. But that is too simple, for the *Secret History* also produces at times a very unflattering picture of Temuchin. Would a panegyric mention that the young Genghis Khan was afraid of dogs, or describe how he murdered his half-brother and was then bitterly rebuked by his mother? Although it is an extremely difficult work to classify, it

11

is at least invaluable in one respect: it is a wholly Mongol account of Mongol history and life. It vividly presents a Mongol perspective of the importance of their conquests and their place in the world at that time. And whether it is historically accurate or not, it does present an extremely dramatic profile of one of the greatest generals of all time.

The political scene in Mongolia during the twelfth century was characterized by a struggle amongst all the tribes to fill the vacuum left by the defeat of the Khitan by the Jurchen. These tribes are perhaps more correctly described as Turko-Mongol, in that they all spoke either Turkish or Mongolian and intermarried. Indeed it was forbidden for any male to marry within his own tribe. The most powerful of the tribes during Temuchin's youth were the Tartars, who lived alongside the Mongols in eastern Mongolia. Other tribes that play a part in the saga are the Kereyids, who lived in the very centre of Mongolia, the Merkids who were to the north of them, and the Naimans, to the west. It is often confusing that the term 'Tartar' seems interchangeable with 'Mongol', when originally they were two separate tribes and in fact were sworn enemies. It is even more confusing since, during the early civil wars, the Mongols eventually exterminated virtually the entire Tartar tribe. The explanation lies in the fact that, up to the point when the Mongols gained supremacy, the Tartars had been the most prominent of all the steppe tribes; in addition, their name appears in Chinese registers dating back to the eighth century. Consequently, the name was employed by both Chinese and others to refer to all the steppe tribes of central Asia. The Tartars enjoyed this pre-eminence over the other tribes because they were supported by the Chin Chinese.

It was the traditional tactic of the Chinese, of whatever dynasty, to develop an alliance with one of the nomadic tribes on its frontier and encourage them to sow unrest amongst the remainder. Should another of the tribes appear to be gaining the upper hand, the Chinese would abandon their ally and take up with the emerging new tribe. The purpose was, of course, to foster internal strife, for as long as the tribes fought amongst themselves they were unlikely to pose a threat to anyone else. This was the background against which Temuchin rose to greatness. But the task of uniting the tribes under his leadership and maintaining that leadership against the usual fluctuations of steppe politics would be an extraordinary achievement. Temuchin emerged from an extremely marginal position within the clan hierarchy. Although born of a clan that had provided leaders in the past, there was no tradition of leadership being passed on through a hereditary title. Mongol clan or tribal leaders were chosen because they had demonstrated particular qualities in battle or in some other field – and leaders were also as easily abandoned if they failed to maintain those leadership qualities. There were loose confederations of clans, structured around a unique Mongol concept known as the *anda*: a boon companion who has sworn his brotherhood to another. However, none of these confederations had ever succeeded in permanently dominating the others, and there was definitely no history of all the Mongol tribes ever having been united under a single leader in the past. Besides, the Chin were extremely successful at exploiting the enmity that arose towards any leader of these confederations. If all this suggests that Temuchin had the odds strongly stacked against him, then it is hardly surprising that his conquest of the steppe tribes and the establishment of order consumed most of his adult life.

TEMUCHIN'S RISE TO POWER

Temuchin was probably born in 1167 of the Bjorjin clan. His father, Yesugei Bat'atur, was the leader of a small clan that had been caught up in the relentless feuding between the Mongol and Tartar tribes. Yesugei had arranged a marriage for his nine-year-old son Temuchin with a girl from his wife's tribe, the Unggirad. According to Mongol custom, he had left his son with his future in-laws. During the journey home he encountered some Tartars. Unaware of their identity, Yesugei asked them for a drink. The Tartars, on the other hand, recognized their old rival and gave him a draught of a slow-acting poison. By the time he reached his family *ger* his life was already slipping away, and he died before nightfall. Temuchin was summoned home. His mother, Ho'elun Ujin, attempted to keep her late husband's people together but a rival clan, the Tayichi'ud, incited them to desert the family. Ho'elun and her children were forced to migrate to the mountains near the River Onon where, friendless and in constant danger, they survived on wild berries and by hunting and fishing. In this harsh environment Temuchin grew into adolescence, during which time he befriended a boy named Jamukha, who came from another clan and who became his *anda*. Their lives would later become closely entwined.

It was in this period of harsh hand-to-mouth existence that Temuchin is known to have quarrelled with his half-brother over some birds they had shot, and in a moment of uncontrolled temper shot him 'as though at target practice'. It seems unlikely that they were merely arguing over the spoils from a hunt, but rather that Temuchin was already exercising the rudiments of clan politics by eliminating a potential rival for the head of the family. In any case, according to the *Secret History*, Temuchin's mother recoiled in horror, branding him a murderer. She went on to lament:

> At the moment when you have no companion other than your
> shadow;
> At the moment when you have no whip other than your tail,
> At the moment when you are saying, 'By whom shall we take
> vengeance?' you do this to each other. Saying, 'How shall we
> live . . .'

Soon his mother's distress turned to anguish as Temuchin was carried off by the Tayichi'ud clan, the people who had incited the late Yesugei's men to abandon the family. Some scholars claim it was in revenge for the murder of Temuchin's half-brother, who had been related to the Tayichi'ud. Others suggest it was simply a pre-emptive strike for fear the young Temuchin might later seek revenge for the hardship his mother and family had been forced to endure. According to the *Secret History*, Temuchin remained a captive for some months but managed to escape during the celebrations of a local festival. He was helped by a number of characters, all of whom are rewarded in later episodes of the *Secret History*. What seems to be emerging in these accounts of Temuchin's development is a picture of a young man who, although of noble birth, is familiar with the life of the peasantry, has learnt from his elders how capricious and faithless they could be, and how true loyalty was often found outside the clan or tribe. At the age of sixteen he returned to the Unggirad clan to marry his betrothed, Borte, as arranged by his father. Soon after the wedding, Temuchin, thinking he might need the help of a patron if he was ever to reclaim his birthright, sought out a friend and former *anda* of his father, To'oril, the leader of the Kereyids, a Turkic people living by the shores of the upper Onon River.

The Kereyids were nomadic horsemen, not unlike their Mongol neighbours except in one respect; they were Nestorian Christians. Christian communities were not uncommon, even this far east; they were the product of a great wave of evangelical monks that had spread from the Middle East during the eleventh century. When Temuchin arrived at To'oril's camp, he presented him with gifts and was repaid with To'oril's promise to support Temuchin in his struggle to recover his father's people. But before he could begin, Temuchin's camp was raided by a party of Merkid and his wife, Borte, carried off. To'oril responded to the news by immediately raising an army to attack the Merkid, which he placed under the command of Temuchin's childhood *anda*, Jamukha. The campaign was a complete success; Borte was rescued, and in the course of it Temuchin distinguished himself in battle. The only disappointment was that Borte returned pregnant; her first child, Jochi, was forever haunted by the stigma of possible illegitimacy.

For eighteen months after the successful campaign against the

Merkid, Temuchin and his followers rode with Jamukha. Although the two men had enjoyed good relations, an unspoken rivalry had developed between what were clearly two very ambitious young princes. One evening, sensing that they no longer saw eye to eye, Temuchin and his followers left Jamukha's camp and rode off into the night. In the morning they discovered that they had been followed by a detachment that had decided to change their allegiance – apparently because, of the two, Temuchin inspired greater loyalty and confidence. The generosity with which Temuchin treated his followers soon earned him high regard. According to the *Secret History*, the would-be converts declared, 'The Prince dresses his people in his own clothes, he permits them to ride his own horses; this person could truly bring peace to the tribe and rule the nation.' Soon afterwards, Temuchin was elected Khan of the Mongols, though this title had scant practical value as he had actual command over only a small fraction of the Mongol population. However, tales spread which were soon taken up and embellished by the shamans that held the Mongol audiences in such thrall, telling how Temuchin had received a heavenly mandate to rule the steppe. Temuchin certainly knew how to exploit these tales. He is said to have proclaimed, 'My strength was fortified by Heaven and earth. Foreordained [for this] by Mighty Heaven, I was brought here by Mother earth.' Soon the clans were flocking to his banner.

Temuchin's apparently effortless rise incited Jamukha's jealousy, and it was not long before he decided to confront Temuchin in battle. He launched a surprise attack against his childhood *anda*, from which Temuchin only just managed to escape. It was now Temuchin's turn to seek revenge, and his appetite was further whetted when he learned that the men that had been taken prisoner after the ambush had been executed by Jamukha, who had boiled them to death in seventy large vats. But before Temuchin could have satisfaction, his patron, To'oril, the leader of the Kereyids, called upon his vassal prince to come to his aid. A faction within the Kereyid confederation had risen up and deposed the old man, casting him out to wander the Gobi Desert with no protection. When Temuchin heard the news he raised an army and led it into battle against his patron's enemies. His stunning success only further enhanced his growing stature within the steppe tribes, and he soon went on to further victories when he repelled an attack from the Merkid who had hoped to exploit the temporary instability within the Kereyid confederation.

Meanwhile, larger political moves were afoot. In typical Chinese fashion the Chin, having become irritated by their Tartar clients' growing insolence, enlisted the help of To'oril and Temuchin to act as mercenaries and remove the Tartar nuisance. The Mongols, eager to avenge themselves on their old enemy, threw themselves into the task. The subsequent defeat of the Tartars not only bathed Temuchin in further glory, but also dramatically altered the balance of power on the steppe. In gratitude for a job well done, the Chin honoured those responsible, bestowing a nominal title upon To'oril and renaming him Ong (Wang) Khan. (As the histories of this period of Mongol history were written and corrupted with stories from other cultures, Ong Khan soon became the best-known Christian prince of the East, and the name Ong or Wang later became confused with the word 'John', which helped nurture the seed of a great Christian myth.) Temuchin was also ennobled, receiving a minor title.

Although he was by now something of a military celebrity, he was content to remain in Ong Khan's service. Together they waged campaigns across the steppe, from the Altai to the Khinghan Mountains. But their growing power and influence soon attracted enemies, and Jamukha, whose enmity towards Temuchin had only intensified, was quick to exploit this. He gathered round him an alliance of discontents – the Merkids, the Naimans, what was left of the Tartars, the Tayichi'uds and even Temuchin's mother's tribe, the Unggirad. The war that followed, an apparently uneven match between the armies of the Ong Khan and virtually all the rest of the steppe tribes, was fought during the winter of 1201–2. Jamukha's confederation was badly organized, and sections were easily picked off and dispersed. The campaign came to a climax with the massacre of virtually the entire Tartar army in the foothills of the Khinghan Mountains, a revenge attack for the murder of Temuchin's father, Yesugei.

SUPREME COMMANDER

As a result of these wars Ong Khan's Kereyid confederacy, staunchly supported by Temuchin's Mongols, had successfully taken control of the eastern steppe. Yet as the campaign continued, the trust between the Ong Khan and his protégé began to disintegrate. After the elimination of the Tartars, Temuchin had felt the time was right to seek a marriage alliance with the Ong Khan: Temuchin's eldest son Jochi would receive the Ong Khan's daughter as wife. The Ong Khan, irritated by his vassal's impertinence, not to say his ambition, dismissed the idea outright. But the old man had also begun to fear Temuchin's growing importance and it soon became apparent that, when on campaign, the two men no longer fought so well together. On more than one occasion Temuchin found himself almost overwhelmed by the enemy, with the expected relief from the Ong Khan's troops having failed to arrive.

Gradually the clans began to sense that Temuchin was no longer in favour, and they started to desert him. It was another painful lesson about the realities of steppe loyalty. After an appalling encounter with an overwhelmingly superior Kereyid force, in which Temuchin's second son Ogedei was badly wounded, they were forced to retreat with 4600 men and found refuge on the shores of Lake Baljuna. He tried to make contact with his former patron, but was rebuffed. This period in the wilderness, thought to have been around 1203, is regarded by the early chroniclers as the greatest test for both Temuchin and his followers. In the years to come, those who could claim to have been with Temuchin at Lake Baljuna were assured of high honour.

Eventually the Kereyid confederation, now under the inferior command of the Ong Khan's son, showed signs of fragmenting. More and more of the clans swung back to Temuchin's side and, when finally he felt his strength adequate, he struck back – catching the Kereyid unguarded. The ensuing battle against superior forces was apparently an epic engagement that continued for three days. Victory finally came to Temuchin; the elderly Ong Khan fled the field, but was captured by a neighbouring tribe and executed. Temuchin, keen to refocus the loyalties of the enemy commanders, ordered that they should not be punished; he even went so far as to praise their heroism in public. But now the Kereyid were defeated they had to be absorbed into the Mongol nation, and to encourage this he took a number of Kereyid princesses whom he gave as wives to his sons. One of the Ong Khan's youngest nieces, Sorghaghtani Beki, who was given to Temuchin's youngest son Tolui, later became one of the most powerful figures in the empire and the mother of some of the greatest khans.

It might be assumed that by now Temuchin enjoyed absolute supremacy throughout the eastern steppe, but in fact as a result of his victory over the Kereyid he now faced even more determined opposition. The last remaining significant power in the region was the Naiman, a tribe that lived north-west of the traditional lands of the Kereyids – between the Selenga River and the Altai Mountains. It was here that an army of fugitives from the other defeated tribes had gathered. It was here, too, that Jamukha had sought refuge and was now plotting Temuchin's downfall.

Temuchin realized the inevitability of this final encounter and so he called a *quriltai*, a meeting of the tribal leaders in his command, to plan the campaign. He wanted it to be a decisive confrontation, a victory that would spell either the end of all tribal conflicts – or oblivion. In preparing for this encounter, Temuchin restructured his army into groups of thousands, hundreds and tens. He also reorganized the command structure. When all this was complete he consecrated his battle colours on the day of the Feast of the Moon, in the Year of the Rat (1204), and then began his march on the Naiman armies. By the time they encountered the enemy, an overwhelmingly superior force, the Mongol horses were exhausted. He decided to make camp and by lighting hundreds more fires than were necessary, successfully convinced the enemy scouts that his army was far greater than in fact it was. When the two armies finally stood before each other in the field, Jamukha studied Temuchin's new battle order and, perhaps because it confused his own calculations, slipped quietly from the field even before battle was joined. The Naiman marched forward to meet the Mongols, but as Jamukha's forces fell away behind their master the Naiman lost heart and were soundly crushed. The Naiman king died of his wounds, his son fled to the west and Jamukha, who had also taken flight, was finally captured and, according to the *Secret History*, was executed at his own request. Temuchin was now absolute master of all the tribes of Mongolia. At a *quriltai* in 1206 he was finally proclaimed as such, and invested with the title Genghis Khan.

THE NEW MONGOLIA

This account of Genghis Khan's epic rise to power describes a struggle through a seemingly endless nightmare of alliance and betrayal. For historians who have attempted to bring to life the personality of one of the most important figures in world history, these events seem to supply some insight. Certain facts are unique. He emerged from an extremely marginal position within steppe politics and therefore had no firm base of support from which to launch his bid for outright leadership. Moreover, that support which he was able to gather invariably slipped through his fingers at the first hint that the tide seemed to be turning against him. This fickleness, it is argued, shaped his ideas not only about military strategy, but also about how to organize the political structure of the newly united Mongolia. Bitter experience had taught him that he could trust neither the individual clans nor even his close relatives, for even his uncles and brothers had at some time allied themselves with his enemies. They were just as likely to elect him khan one year and desert him the next. He understood that these ancient habits had to be broken and that the narrow interests of each tribal group had to be subsumed into the greater needs of the union. The traditional view is that Genghis Khan's ideas about the future political structure of Mongolia were part of some vision of a nation that would eventually begin a campaign of world conquest. But a more recent view suggests that this new structure was the only possible answer to the problem of maintaining control over an army of nomadic horsemen that in 1206 probably numbered fewer than a hundred thousand men.

The traditional loyalty to tribal lords, or *tus*, had always been conditional and unreliable. According to the *Secret History*, the most formative experience in Genghis Khan's early life was the period when he and his family were deserted by his father's men after his death. Left to fend for himself, Genghis learned that the only reliable support was that which grew out of his own personal following. This group became the backbone of the army command, and consequently of the political powerbase. There were two basic relationships that developed. The first was the *anda*, the sworn brotherhood, which was effectively an alliance between equals as the respective partners swore both loyalty and support in times of trouble; support that included the men and families under the command of the respective 'brothers'. This relationship withered somewhat under the new imperial structure, which replaced it with the *nokor*, someone who had sworn personal allegiance. Those who swore themselves as *nokors* were subservient to their patron and had proved themselves faithful in battle. A *nokor* could expect to be rewarded by being given command of a division of the new army which, apart from bestowing prestige, also entitled him to a larger proportion of booty. However, anyone who betrayed his *nokor* could expect no mercy. When Genghis Khan came to set up the command structure of his army, the most remarkable aspect was the absence of most of his family members. There were no uncles, cousins, brothers, nephews or sons – with the exception of Jochi. Later, when the Mongol army had grown, he grudgingly distributed small units amongst his family. But he was always reluctant to entrust important affairs to his family and extremely suspicious – one might even say paranoid – about family motives. Throughout his struggle for supremacy Genghis Khan executed or threatened to execute about a dozen members of his family because of plots, real or suspected, to overthrow him or exploit some influence over him. On the other hand he was extremely trusting and generous to those to whom he was not related and had proved themselves loyal in battle.

Genghis Khan also developed the *keshig*, or personal body-guard, made up of seventy day guards and eighty night guards. As his power grew this expanded to some ten times its original size, and when finally he was proclaimed master of Mongolia it had expanded to about 10 000, made up of ten units of a thousand. Its leaders were recruited from the sons or younger brothers of his divisional commanders, thus reinforcing the new imperial loyalty. The *keshig* also provided a group of young warriors whose advancement would be tied to the new imperial government, and not to traditional tribal loyalties. Their duties, apart from the protection of the sovereign, included providing units of hand-picked warriors and messengers for special imperial duties. The development of this new model army often meant removing the traditional commanders of tribal armies and replacing them with commanders from another tribe. Genghis was even prepared to break up and scatter entire tribal armies within the ranks of other units, especially if they had been particularly unreliable in the past. So effective was this strategy that, as time passed, the old tribal divisions gradually disappeared. No one was allowed to move from one unit to another, on pain of death, without explicit permission. Discipline was strict and subject to central authority, and the men were regularly trained to fight as a large unit and not as individuals. Those who broke rank to loot or who engaged in private feuds were severely punished. Genghis's aim was to make the army the focus of each individual Mongol warrior's loyalty – and himself the focus of the army's loyalty. Hard experience had taught him that the nation would have to be founded upon a personal following. Absolute autocracy was the key.

The reputation that Genghis Khan earned as a great general was based upon the fact that he had always been prepared to take greater risks than his enemies. He did so because he had no choice, he had nowhere else to go, and he needed the victories because failure would have meant being abandoned again. Victory brought him loyalty. In 1206 the newly proclaimed Genghis Khan, now aged thirty-nine, was, in terms of the Middle Ages, past the prime of his life. Yet now he stood at the head of a nation that, just a few years before, had not even existed. More importantly, he stood at the head of an army that needed some greater purpose. But what that purpose might be was by no means immediately apparent. All that he could possibly have understood was that he had to go on from there.

2

FROM CHINA
TO THE CASPIAN SEA

Soon after Gengis Khan was made master over all 'the people with felt tents', he is said to have set down his great *Yasa*, a promulgation of general laws. It was customary whenever a new steppe empire was inaugurated for the leader to 'mark the foundation of his polity' by establishing certain decrees. Genghis Khan's famous code came to be regarded so highly that it set him above any previous nomadic chiefs as a great administrator and law-giver. The *Yasa* was supposed to have been set down soon after the *quriltai* of 1206, and entrusted to Genghis's adopted brother, an orphan of the Tartars, Shigi-Qutuqu, who was made a kind of chief justice. It enshrined Mongol attitudes towards religious tolerance, exempted priests and religious institutions from taxation, prescribed the death penalty for espionage, desertion, theft, adultery and, in the case of a merchant, being declared bankrupt for the third time. It also forbade washing or urinating in running water, as streams and rivers were thought to be alive. The *Yasa* became the institutional foundation of the empire, evidence of Genghis's wisdom and his vision of how the future empire should be governed.

However, modern historians cast doubts upon whether there was such a vision of a future well-governed empire, and suggest that a large proportion of what we know as the *Yasa* is really a

24

body of case histories – accounts of judgements which became precedents for future cases. There is also an account from the great Persian historian, Rashid al-Din, of a large number of decrees uttered by Genghis. These maxims, or *biligs*, were recorded and have been mistakenly assumed to be fragments of the *Yasa*, but they were not a code of general laws. In addition to Genghis's decrees and the body of case law, there is an inheritance of Mongol customs and traditions. In other words, the *Yasa* is no longer seen as the great foundation stone of the empire, but rather as a mixture of enlightenment and superstition that is as much an account of Mongol lore as law.

REVITALIZING THE ARMY

There was, however, a far more influential institution which was structured and regulated by Genghis Khan and which strictly governed the way most Mongols lived their lives – the army. All men over the age of fourteen were expected to undertake military duty. Only physicians, undertakers and priests were exempt. Upon being summoned, the men were expected to leave their flocks, take with them four or five changes of horse, and travel to wherever their unit happened to be based. Wives and children were expected to follow, and if the army was abroad the family travelled with the herds. As new arrivals rode into the *ordu* (military camp) they would find it laid out along standard lines, so they knew exactly where to find the physician's tent, or the armoury to collect their allocation of weapons. They would then move out to join their unit, which might be an *arban* – a simple unit of ten; a *jagun* – ten *arbans* or 100 men; a *minghan* – a regiment of ten *jaguns* or 1000 men; or a *tumen*, a division of ten *minghans* or 10 000 men. The *ordu* was run by quartermasters, or *jurtchis*, who secured supplies and organized the running of the place.

A soldier was responsible for making sure his equipment was kept up to standard and was regularly inspected by officers.

Failing to look after one's equipment usually meant being sent home from the regiment. A soldier's equipment began with a silk undershirt, a novelty learnt from the Chinese. If he was unlucky enough to be hit by an arrow, although it might pierce the armour it was unlikely to penetrate the closely woven silk shirt. What tended to happen was that the silk was dragged into the wound with the arrow head. Removing an arrow embedded in flesh creates a much larger wound than when it entered, but with the silk wound tightly round the arrow head this became easier. By gently pulling the silk around the wound, the soldier or physician would turn the head of the arrow and remove it without ripping further flesh.

Over the silk he wore a tunic, and if he was part of the heavy cavalry he was given a coat of mail and a cuirass made of leather-covered iron scales. Each soldier carried a leather-covered wicker shield and a helmet of either leather or iron, depending on his rank. He was armed with two composite bows and a large quiver containing no fewer than sixty arrows. Light cavalry carried a small sword and two or three javelins, while the heavy brigade carried a scimitar, a battle axe or a mace and a 4 m (12 foot) lance. Soldiers were also equipped for travel. They were expected to carry on the horse clothing, cooking pots, dried meat, a water bottle, files for sharpening arrows, a needle and thread and other useful little items. The saddlebag itself was usually made from a cow's stomach which, being waterproof and inflatable, also provided a useful float when crossing rivers.

One important institution Genghis Khan developed was to transform the nomadic horsemen's favourite sport, the hunt, into a military drill. Whether the quarry was wolf, wild boar or deer, the hunt became a way of instilling into the minds of his soldiers the virtues of working and acting as part of a large single entity. These hunting exercises were conducted during the winter for about three months and every soldier participated. A variety of techniques were employed, depending on the size of the unit.

A small party would be ordered to deploy themselves at

various points in an arc. The quarry would be herded or drawn towards the most advantageous ground by a series of carefully orchestrated strikes. Sometimes the quarry might even be goaded into attacking one or two horsemen, who would gallop away, drawing the quarry after them into a trap. The use of the feint became a standard tactic of the Mongols and was employed successfully again and again. Once the quarry was in the intended place, the waiting circle of horsemen would move in for the kill.

Another approach was to string an entire division of the army along what might be described as a starting line, sometimes 130 km (80 miles) long. On a signal the entire complement, fully armed as if for battle, would ride forward at a walk towards a finish line hundreds of kilometres away. This was usually situated at a point in the shadow of a hill, where the proceedings could be watched by the khan and his entourage. Over the following days the massed cavalry would march forward, sweeping or herding before them all the game they encountered along the way. Something approaching this sport is still practised today in Mongolia during Naadam festivals – modern-day tourneys where traditional Mongol skills such as archery, a particularly moribund form of wrestling and horse-riding are celebrated. The horse race takes place over 30 km (20 miles) or more, often involving as many as 500 riders who begin the race at a leisurely walk, only gradually spurring their horses towards a gallop as they approach the finish.

During the hunt, as the riders approached the finish line the flanks would begin to ride ahead of the centre, and so slowly describe a massive arc. Still further on, the flanks would turn and ride towards each other, thus trapping all the game that had been herded over the hundreds of kilometres of countryside. During the march it was forbidden to kill anything, but it was even more of a disgrace if a rider let some beast escape the net. Throughout the exercise officers rode behind their men, shouting orders and directing their movements.

The Mongols also employed an extremely effective and

reliable system of signals, through flags, torches and riders who carried messages over great distances. This eventually provided them with one of the greatest advantages they ever took into the field: reliable and effective communications. It enabled all the Mongol units to remain in constant contact with each other and, through their remarkable corps of couriers, under the control of a single commander.

At the end of this elaborate piece of hunting choreography, the men were given the chance to show off their individual fighting skills. Once the flanks had met and the circle tightened, the khan would ride down from his vantage point into the circle and take his pick of the game. This was doubtless a somewhat daunting exercise, as the khan's own skills would be on public show before the entire company. When he had finished and returned to the hill, it was the turn of the soldiers. Now it was the opportunity for each individual, in front of his officers, to show off his skill with sword, bow and arrows or lance. Many wrestled the beasts by hand and tried to kill them with nothing more than a dagger, and it was not uncommon for some soldiers to be torn to pieces by frenzied packs of wolves. Eventually, the elderly and the youngest in the party would beg the khan for the lives of the animals still left in the ring, and once that was granted the great hunt was formally finished.

With exercises like this the Mongols developed a regime that enabled them to train and maintain an extremely professional army – something of a novelty for the thirteenth century. Alongside the skills of riding, shooting and swordsmanship, each Mongol warrior learned the importance of discipline, co-ordination and obedience. Although their tactics in the field were no different from those of any other nomadic tribe, their strategies became masterpieces of originality and daring. The pursuit of the quarry became the pursuit of the enemy; and soon commanders began developing strategies that were to leave their enemies nonplussed. What was being forged, under Genghis Khan's direction, was a modern cavalry that would have no equal anywhere in the world.

FOREIGN EXPANSION

It was not for some three years after the *quriltai* of 1206 that Genghis Khan began any campaigns abroad. The political situation on his borders presented no threats; the various sedentary empires were stable and largely uninterested in the internal politics of the Turkic Mongol tribes. China at that time was divided into three separate kingdoms. South of Mongolia, in what would be the most western extremities of modern China, was the Hsi-Hsia, easily the weakest of the three; its people were largely Tibetan Buddhists. To the east of Mongolia, northern China was under the domination of the Jurchen, the semi-nomadic people from Manchuria who, like the dynasty before them, had conquered and established their own dynasty, the Chin. South of the Chin was the real heart of China, governed by a pure Chinese dynasty, the Sung, that traced its heritage back hundreds of years. To the west of Mongolia lay the empire of the Qara Khitai and the Uighurs, and beyond them the vast lands of the Khwarazm Shah, the northern Persian empire.

In many traditional accounts it is assumed that, once all internal resistance had been thoroughly put down, Genghis turned his attention to building his empire. It is also assumed that the first and most likely conquest would be China, as this had always been the country into which nomadic horsemen had ventured when seeking to extend their influence. But this explanation only holds good for the semi-nomadic horsemen who had periodically ridden out of Manchuria. These people had always shown an interest in exploiting and governing an agricultural nation like China. Having established themselves as the legitimate rulers, they were particularly adept at handling the illiterate bands of horsemen that occasionally came thundering out of Mongolia to raid Chinese towns and settlements. The Chinese referred to the Mongols as the 'uncooked'. These raw horsemen had never shown any interest in conquest before; terror and extortion were their ambitions – not government. The conquest of China was the last thing the Mongols set out to do. China had always been, and particularly to the horsemen from the eastern steppe, simply a rich quarry to be plundered at will – and it was exactly so under Genghis Khan. China was a raid that turned into an occupation.

The first expansion of the Mongols' influence came when the Uighurs abandoned their relationship with the Qara Khitai in 1209 and offered their submission to Genghis Khan. They were welcomed as a 'fifth son'. As such, the Uighurs' state remained autonomous throughout Genghis's life; later it became the most valued client state in the empire. It became the preferred policy, wherever possible, to seek out alliances with local rulers who, in return for their acknowledgement of the Mongols' supremacy, would be granted a kind of vassal-like autonomy. A similar arrangement was extracted from the Tanguts, the rulers of Hsi-Hsia; however, the latter had to be encouraged to accept Mongol terms. Genghis had launched a raid into Hsi-Hsia in 1207, and then again in 1209. The first of these was a typical raid intended to gather booty with which to finance the new nation, but the second was a far more serious affair and found the Mongols placing the Tangut capital under siege. The experience was a salutary one for the Mongols, just as it had been for all previous nomadic empires when they encountered enemies that preferred to fight from behind large fortifications. The Mongols had no immediate answer to these tactics, but nevertheless were able to force the Tangut king to accept their terms. In addition Genghis also extracted a promise that the king would send troops to aid the Mongols, should they ever be requested. Finally the Tangut king gave his daughter in marriage to Genghis, thus cementing the relationship. In return he was not required to renounce his sovereignty.

THE INVASION OF CHINA

But the Tanguts and Uighurs were relatively small kingdoms, and Genghis really made no impression on the international stage until the campaigns against the Chin, which began in 1211. They started with the time-honoured practice of extorting money and other concessions out of the wealthy Chinese. What went wrong, however, was that the Chin decided to respond to the Mongol initiative with military force. To begin with the Chin had constructed a chain of intimidating fortified cities to protect the empire from invasions from the north; they also maintained a large and powerful body of cavalry plus an equally large army of foot soldiers, which they had every intention of using if provoked. Genghis marched into Chin territory with a sizeable force which divided into smaller units and rode in all directions, systematically laying waste small towns and villages which they found in their path. They intended to avoid the larger, fortified cities and were happy to continue in this fashion until they eventually encountered a vast Chin force at Huan-erh-tsui. Instead of beating a hasty retreat, Genghis decided to attack. In their first serious engagement with a large foreign army, the Mongol cavalry proved devastating. They completely outmanoeuvred the Chin, virtually destroying a force of some 70 000 within a matter of hours. Nine years later, a Taoist monk on his way to visit Genghis travelled through this area and reported that the battlefield was still littered with human bones. Jochi, Genghis's eldest son, went on to the very gates of the Chin capital, Chung-tu, near the site of modern Peking, but since he had no knowledge or experience of siege warfare he withdrew. Although the Mongols had also gained control of the key passes into China and a number of small fortifications in the Chin defensive perimeter, they had no use for these; so in February of the following year the invaders rode back to southern Mongolia. They had failed to extort much out of the campaign, and the Chin quickly reoccupied those towns that had been destroyed by the Mongol raiders.

The Mongols returned to their homelands having learnt one important lesson: even though they had routed a huge Chin army, they would never extract a submission from the Chin emperor so long as he and his government remained safe inside

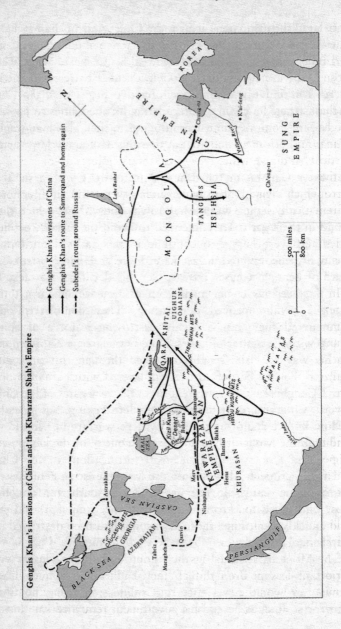

Genghis Khan's invasions of China and the Khwarazm Shah's Empire

→ Genghis Khan's invasions of China
→ Genghis Khan's route to Samarqand and home again
--→ Subedei's route around Russia

their large fortified cities. It had never occurred to the Mongols to stay and occupy the lands they had conquered, so the campaign achieved almost nothing – either by their standards or by those of any other conqueror. However, once back in Mongolia Genghis sought to strengthen his hand before conducting any further raids. He effected an alliance with the Khitans, a small neighbouring kingdom who had been ousted from northern China by the Jurchen less than a century before. They were not particularly powerful, but because their territory lay north-east of the Chin the new alliance would make the Chin feel almost surrounded. Genghis then launched another campaign, with the Khitans, across the Chin's northern frontier. On this occasion the Mongols were more successful at capturing fortified towns, but the campaign was brought to an abrupt end when Genghis was wounded by a stray arrow. The Mongols decided to take as much booty as they could and depart.

In the autumn of 1213, the Mongols returned for the third time. They marched in three large columns, with Genghis in command of the largest while his sons Jochi, Chaghadai and the youngest, Tolui, shared command of the others. When they reached the outskirts of the Chin capital, Chung-tu, they again realized it was far too formidable, so they turned south and marched across the North China plain towards the Yellow River. In the process they crossed the fertile plain north of the Yellow River, seeing for the first time some of the vast area of land that lay under cultivation, and, of course, the huge numbers of peasants who worked it. Throughout 1213 they rode back and forth across Chin territory and in the process slaughtered countless thousands of the population. They also gathered the most prodigious amounts of booty: massive quantities of silk, gold and silver, plus hundreds of young boys and girls who were marched back as slaves. However, as the campaign dragged on the Mongols became victims of an outbreak of the plague that periodically swept through these lands. When the three columns reunited to lay siege to Chung-tu, Genghis's force had come to resemble a much reduced host of rag-tag ruffians rather than a conquering army. He had neither the skill nor the men to take Chung-tu, nor was he inclined to stay and try to starve the city into submission. However, internal disputes within the Chin court brought things to a conclusion when the Chin emperor suddenly indicated that he wanted to make peace. Genghis responded by asking what the Chin might offer in return for the siege being called off. When the negotiations had been concluded, the Mongols departed with even more silk and gold, together with another 500 children to be added to those already headed for slavery. Once again the Mongols turned and rode back towards their homeland: 'Our soldiers laden [with] satin and goods as many as they could carry, tied their burdens with silk and went away.'

Genghis also accepted a marriage with a Chin princess, assuming, as his shabby army departed China, that the Chin now took him to be the pre-eminent sovereign in the region and that this situation would not be challenged. From a Mongol perspective the campaign was a great success, and Genghis's status was much enhanced by the enormous quantities of booty to be shared out. But from the Chin perspective the outcome could also be seen as a success, for once again they had survived simply by paying off the invaders. Once the Mongols were gone, the Chinese would return to their lands and continue where they had left off. As ever, the Mongols had shown not the slightest interest in permanently occupying or supplanting Chin control of northern China.

In the meantime the Chin emperor, thinking that Chung-tu was a little too close to the northern passes that led to Mongolia, decided to move his court to the city of K'ai-feng, south of the Yellow River. According to a Chinese account, having assumed that the Chin had accepted his supremacy, Genghis interpreted this as a breakdown in trust. 'The Chin emperor made a peace agreement with me, but now he has moved his capital to the south; evidently he mistrusts my word and has used the peace to deceive me!' It seems likely that, had the Chin still been prepared to appease the Mongols, they might have escaped destruction. In the autumn of 1214 the Mongols returned to the siege of Chung-tu, this time with a much larger army that included Chinese and Khitans as well as Mongols. This time the city was invested by a force prepared to stay for as long as it took. The inhabitants, distraught that their emperor had deserted them and terrified of the retribution they expected at the hands of the Mongols, remained behind their walls and suffered appalling deprivations. As the months passed they even turned to cannibalism, and the longer they held out the greater Mongol retribution would be. In the spring of 1215, as there seemed to be little progress, Genghis left the campaign to one of his generals and returned to the northern frontier. So he was not present when finally, in the early summer, the Chin commanders abandoned the city and the Mongols entered unopposed.

Once the Mongols were inside the city walls, the inhabitants' worst fears were realized. Chung-tu had been one of the largest cities in northern China, and it was utterly laid to waste. News of the destruction must have sent a shiver of dread through all the courts in the region. For the first time the Mongols were seen not merely as a significant military force, but as a force capable of appalling levels of destruction. Squadrons of Mongol horsemen rode the streets firing incendiary arrows into the wooden houses, while others put thousands of the civilian population to the sword. Entire districts were reduced to ash, and a visiting ambassador from the Khwarazm Shah, the leader of the great Islamic empire in western Asia, reported that, after all the slaughter and the fires, the streets were greasy with human fat and littered with carcasses.

There was, however, some method in this madness. Genghis preferred to secure submission from his neighbours without resort to warfare, so the military successes were clearly meant to send a signal to others. In 1218 the Koreans, no doubt heavily influenced by reports of the fate of Chung-tu, made their submissions to the Mongol court along with substantial payments; and so they avoided destruction. The annihilation of the former Chin capital was both an act of appalling retribution and a warning to others, for the singular fact appreciated by all Mongol commanders was the enormous discrepancy between the size of the Mongol nation and that of other nations that lay on its borders. Slaughter on a grand scale, or the threat of it, was the only way to get their own way. Those that accepted Mongol terms, like the Uighurs, Tanguts, Khitans and Koreans, could expect clemency; those that did not or – worse – who reneged on their agreements could expect no mercy.

With the fall of Chung-tu large numbers of Chinese, Khitan and Chin troops surrendered, along with the administrators and officials responsible for the government of the northern part of the Chin empire. Under their influence, the Mongols took their first hesitant steps towards assuming responsibility for the administration of a conquered land. It was a role for which they had little enthusiasm, but it was being forced upon them. Even so, the Chin were unconquered and remained so for nearly twenty years.

THE PUNISHMENT OF GOD

But by now Genghis had already lost interest in the campaign in China, and had become absorbed in matters further west. Reports of the fall of Chung-tu had inspired the Khwarazm Shah to open a dialogue. Khwarazm Shah 'Ala' al-Din Muhammad II had inherited an empire founded by a Turkish mercenary, Qutbeddin Muhammad, in what is today Uzbekistan. 'Ala' al-Din also took over a massive army largely made up of Turkish mercenaries from the tribes west of the Aral Sea, and with this force he had expanded his empire south into the Persian territory of Khurasan. In reality it had been little more than an easy annexation, given the size and reputation of his army, yet it was enough for him to declare afterwards that he was 'the chosen prince of Allah'. Indeed, so impressed were his own sycophantic courtiers that they proclaimed him the second Alexander. To the north-east of Khurasan lay the empire of Transoxiana with its grand cities of Bukhara and Samarqand, and beyond that the powerful Buddhist empire of the Qara Khitai, which stood between the Muslim world and the expanding empire of the Mongols.

Following the neighbouring Uighurs' submission to Genghis Khan in 1209, the territory of Qara Khitai seemed far less powerful, especially as it was currently being ruled by a survivor of the war between the Mongols and the Naimans, the hated and despotic Kuchlug. 'Ala' al-Din chose this moment to march into Transoxiana, which he finally conquered in 1210. These lands lie between the rivers Oxus and Jaxartes and are on the whole fairly barren. But it was across these lands that the caravans of both the East and the Middle East had crossed for centuries, and they had brought extraordinary wealth to the cities that produced or traded in carpets, silk, woven cotton and silver lamé. The greatest of these was Samarqand, which the Khwarazm Shah had made his capital. By some accounts it was a magnificent city of some 500 000 inhabitants, a community of craftsmen, merchants, Chinese artisans, leather workers, goldsmiths and silversmiths. In the fields beyond the city walls aubergines and melons were grown, to be packed in snow inside lead-lined boxes for export. The streets were lined with shady trees, cooled by fountains and decorated with gardens, and under the Khwarazm Shah Samarqand became one of the most magnificent cities in Asia.

Since the Khwarazm Shah had found conquest a somewhat effortless exercise, he had given serious consideration to conquering China. However, his plans had been halted by reports of the Mongol victories against the Chin – hence the presence of one of his envoys at the sacking of Chung-tu. He had been sent to report on the new power that had emerged from the steppe. Genghis would have long known of the Khwarazm Shah's reputation. Now they were both aware of each other.

In 1216, Genghis sent to Samarqand three envoys bearing magnificent gifts of gold, jade, ivory ornaments and cloaks spun from the wool of white camels. They were delivered with a letter:

> I send you these gifts. I know your power and the vast
> extent of your empire and I regard you as my most
> cherished son. For your part you must know that I have
> conquered China and all the Turkish nations north of it;
> my country is an anthill of soldiers and a mine of silver
> and I have no need of other lands. Therefore I believe that
> we have an equal interest in encouraging trade between
> our subjects.

The letter was sealed 'God in heaven, the Kah Khan, the power
of God on earth. The Seal of the Emperor of Mankind'. Opinion
varies about the real motives behind the letter, given the ambigu-
ous language; but its ostensible purpose seems clear. It was an
acknowledgement that he, Genghis Khan, was lord of the East
while the Khwarazm Shah was lord of the West, and that
perhaps it would be a good thing if there was a trade agreement
between their respective empires. In due course an agreement
was established allowing the free passage of merchants and
traders through their respective territories.

Nevertheless, Genghis's intentions must be questioned in view
of the barely veiled insult in his letter, describing the vastly more
powerful Khwarazm Shah as his 'son'. Could he possibly have
been trying to incite trouble with his great neighbour? Even
though he had just won some important victories in northern
China, the war there was a long way from being concluded.
Indeed, it had only just begun. The Mongols had been absorbing
new territories to the east and the west, and their meagre
manpower was sorely stretched. To have undertaken another
campaign at this juncture and against such an adversary would
have been reckless in the extreme. Yet to judge from the Mongol
chroniclers who recorded these events some time afterwards, it
was only a matter of time before Genghis Khan struck out in the
west. In the event, however, it was 'Ala' al-Din Muhammad II
himself who took the initiative.

In 1218 a caravan of some 450 Muslim merchants, travelling
from Mongol territory, arrived at the frontier town of Utrar to

inaugurate the trade agreement. The Khwarazm Shah's governor in Utrar, Inalchuq Khwadir Khan, suspecting that the merchants were spies – which they almost certainly were – had them all killed and their property confiscated. When Genghis sent three envoys to the court of the Khwarazm Shah to demand reparations, he responded by killing one of the envoys and burning the beards of the other two. This was tantamount to an act of war, for the Mongols always accorded ambassadors the greatest respect and assumed that the persons of their own ambassadors were sacrosanct.

The Khwarazm Shah must have realized that such contempt would lead to war. Perhaps he had come to believe his own courtiers' claim that he was, indeed, the new Alexander, and calculated that a swift and effortless encounter with this pagan horseman would render him undisputed master of all Asia. After all, it is thought he had a massive army of some 400 000 men in Transoxiana alone, with reserves scattered throughout the empire – there was no other army to match it anywhere. Whatever his motives, this vain, arrogant, self-deluding individual succeeded in bringing down one of the most appalling disasters ever to befall the eastern Islamic world.

But before Genghis embarked upon a war with the mighty Khwarazm Shah there were a number of irritating issues that had to be settled closer to home. First he had to deal with an old enemy named Kuchlug, a survivor of the Naimans, who had set himself up as ruler of the Qara Khitai. The second was the threat of insurrection from the survivors of the war against the Merkids, whom Genghis had defeated in 1208. To contend with these problems he despatched two of his leading generals. The first was Subedei Bat'atur of the Reindeer people, an obscure tribe that still exists today in north-western Mongolia. They still ride and herd reindeer and are regarded by the rest of the Mongolians as the most unsophisticated barbarians. The other was a man named Jebei Noyan. As soon as Kuchlug had been dealt with the kingdom of Qara Khitai fell into the Mongol dominion, which meant that Genghis's frontiers now abutted those of the Khwarazm Shah. First blood was drawn when Subedei's detachment, while in pursuit of the remaining Merkids, had a somewhat bruising encounter with a force led by the Khwarazm Shah's son, Jalal al-Din, in the Fergana valley, below the Tien Shan Mountains.

Unlike his father, Jalal al-Din had natural gifts as a military leader and would have been a match for any of the Mongol princes had he been given command of a force of significant size. Having assumed that war with the Mongols was now inevitable, Jalal al-Din had counselled his father that the best strategy was to deploy their massive force in a series of highly mobile corps that could be despatched to encounter any invading Mongol troops. Instead, his father had elected to spread the entire force in a thin line along the River Syr Darya. Jalal al-Din argued that the line was not strong enough to withstand a determined assault, and that the best thing would be to launch a pre-emptive strike before the Mongols could put together any kind of substantial force. Again, he was ignored, although he was given permission to patrol the frontier in case of any incursions.

It was Subedei's ill-fortune to be leading some 30 000 exhausted Mongols, doggedly in pursuit of renegade Merkids, through the passes in the Tien Shan Mountains and straight into 50 000 of the Khwarazm Shah's soldiers led by Jalal al-Din. Although the battle was inconclusive and both sides suffered heavy losses, the Mongol column was forced to retreat with its wounded back across the passes. The encounter served as an object lesson. Jalal al-Din would be a serious obstacle to any invasion, and his whereabouts would have to be carefully monitored.

To help him plan this expedition, Genghis called a great *quriltai* of his most senior generals. It would not be like a raid against the Chin; this would be the largest military expedition the Mongols had ever conducted. As he became more involved in the planning, Genghis was urged by one of his wives to give some thought to the succession of the empire. He was already fifty-six, and the outcome of the adventure was by no means certain. In considering the problem, he examined the qualities of each of his sons. Despite his obvious qualities as a general the eldest son, Jochi, was ruled out because of doubts about his paternity. His mother, Borte, had given birth to him after being rescued from the Merkids, who had captured and raped her soon after her marriage to the young Genghis. His second son, Chaghadai, the so-called guardian of the *Yasa*, was a scrupulously fair administrator; but Genghis was not fond of him, regarding him as a somewhat narrow-minded and obstinate character. Ogedei was clearly the most intelligent and educated of the sons; an able if not distinguished commander, he was extremely generous, fond of good company and good alcohol, and, although far less athletic than his father, he seemed the most open to new ideas. The fourth son, Tolui, even more of a drunkard than Ogedei, was already regarded as a brilliant general but was also thought to be too quick tempered. Genghis struggled over the choice between his two youngest sons, and finally settled upon Ogedei. The other three were made to promise that they would not oppose Ogedei's succession, and with this matter resolved Genghis returned to planning the campaign.

In the meantime, from right across the eastern steppe tens of thousands of men were being summoned from their herds and ordered to report to Genghis's *ordus*. Gradually the army swelled to perhaps something between 150 000 and 200 000. It represented the largest concentration of Mongol power that had ever been mustered – yet it was still less than half the size of the opposition. Given these hard facts, it was decided to co-ordinate an attack against the Khwarazm Shah on a number of different positions at the same time. The Mongol force was divided into four corps: the first commanded by Genghis and Subedei, the second by his sons Ogedei and Chaghadai, the third by Jebei and the fourth by Jochi. Still conscious of his meagre forces, Genghis decided to call in the agreement he had made with the Tanguts, that they would furnish him with soldiers whenever and wherever he requested them. The Tangut king's reply was disappointing: he said that if he [Genghis] didn't have enough men of his own, then he didn't deserve to be khan. Stung by this response, Genghis grimly set forth alone on the campaign in the west.

The first move was in the autumn of 1219 against the city of Utrar, where a force of some 50 000 Mongols led by Chaghadai and Ogedei advanced on the city walls. The governor knew he could expect no mercy, so he poured scorn on the Mongol demand to surrender and, with his 80 000-strong garrison, settled down to a long siege. Meanwhile, the forces under the command of Jebei and Jochi moved south. Jebei had command of 20 000 men, with whom he was ordered to draw off any major enemy force guarding the southern approaches, and then advance into Transoxiana. While all eyes were on him, Genghis and Subedei moved their contingent quietly out of Mongolia, crossed the Syr Darya River into Transoxiana and then, instead of riding south, turned due west and promptly disappeared. It was as though they had ridden off the map. Meanwhile Jochi's force roamed up and down the Syr Darya with orders to attack the Khwarazm Shah's strongholds at Khojend, and to harry their defences before also crossing the river.

Genghis and Subedei were in fact leading their forces on a secret route through the Kizil Kum Desert to the north-east of the Khwarazm Shah's territory. This region was thought to be impenetrable, but the Mongols had a guide to show them the way. Genghis knew the Khwarazm Shah's spies could not follow his progress; as far as the enemy were concerned, the entire division did not exist. It emerged, however, in March 1220 some 650 km (400 miles) behind the enemy lines, when the people of Bukhara sighted the Mongol force on the outskirts of their city. Stunned by this remarkable apparition, the Turkish garrison burst from the city gates and attempted to fight their way free. They were slaughtered to a man. According to the Persian historian Juvaini, the plain 'seemed to be a tray filled with blood'. Totally demoralized, the inhabitants surrendered without a fight.

Once Genghis had entered the 'cupola of Islam', as Juvaini described Bukhara, he rode into the largest mosque thinking it was the Sultan's palace. When it was explained that it was a house of God, he ordered it to be converted into stables and the cases that held the Koran to be used for mangers. As copies of the Koran were thrown to the four winds, Genghis mounted the pulpit inside the mosque and lectured the citizens about the treachery of their Sultan. 'I am the punishment of God,' he told them. 'If you had not committed great sins, he would not have sent a punishment like me.' Genghis, determined there would be no hindrance to the plundering of the city, ordered the entire civilian population to abandon everything and leave with nothing but the clothes they stood in. As the city was being sacked, a fire broke out and swept through the closely packed wooden houses. When the fires were out all that was left were the most prominent stone structures; the rest had become 'a level plain'. Juvaini estimated that upwards of 30 000 had been slain, while thousands more women and children were led off into slavery in Mongolia along with cartloads of booty.

However, the majority of the population had been allowed to escape, to roam the countryside and seek refuge where they could, and take with them terrible accounts of the fate of Bukhara. The object was to terrify and demoralize the inhabitants of Samarqand, the Khwarazm Shah's capital. When Genghis approached that city he forced prisoners from Bukhara to march ahead, which swelled the ranks of his army and, of course, provided shields against the enemy's arrows. Samarqand was expected to hold out for a year; it capitulated after five days. Neither Genghis Khan nor any of his army had ever seen anything quite like it. They roamed the streets and avenues, drinking at the fountains and gorging themselves on the exotic fruits and sherbets. The Turkish garrison, all 30 000, were put to the sword. The population was divided into sections: women were set apart to be raped and then sent off as slaves; the clerics

43

were all spared; while the entire population of craftsmen and artisans were also transported to the Mongol homeland where they would be employed at Genghis's court.

While Genghis and Subedei had captured the jewels of the Khwarazm Shah's empire, Chaghadai and Ogedei had still been engaged in the siege of Utrar. It had taken five months before the walls were breached, and another month to take the citadel where the garrison and most of the inhabitants had taken refuge. When the citadel walls too had been breached almost the entire garrison and most of the citizenry were slaughtered, but Genghis had sent orders that he wanted the governor, Inalchuq, taken alive. He and his wife, knowing they were doomed, had taken to the roof of the armoury from where his wife ripped off tiles which he then hurled at his pursuers. The Mongols began demolishing the building stone by stone, until they had Inalchuq in their grasp. They took him to Samarqand, where he was executed by having molten silver poured into his eyes and ears. Utrar was then put to the torch, and later levelled to the ground.

FUGITIVES FROM MONGOL WRATH

Although Inalchuq had been dealt with, the Khwarazm Shah had escaped Genghis's troops. The Sultan had ignored his son's appeal to stay and carry the fight back to the invader, and instead took flight in the hope of finding refuge in Mesopotamia. Genghis sent Subedei and Jebei in pursuit. They followed him from town to town, from province to province – and the Khwarazm Shah found no refuge. Jalal al-Din had also departed Samarqand, but it was his intention to stay in the field and harass the Mongols in an attempt to halt their progress. In the event, however, he too became a fugitive, and for as long as he remained at liberty the Mongols were prepared to burn and slaughter everything in their path in their efforts to capture him. Genghis and his son Tolui took up this task themselves. They rode south across the Oxus River, pursuing Jalal al-Din down through south-eastern Persia into what is now Afghanistan, then into Pakistan and across the Indus River. The destruction that was wrought along the way was on a scale never before experienced in steppe warfare. When Merv fell in 1221, the Persian chroniclers claim that Tolui slaughtered 700 000, sparing just eighty craftsmen. Nishapur suffered just as badly, as did Balkh; once one of the greatest cities of the age, filled with magnificent mosques, hospitals and palaces – a place where Alexander had visited and Zoroaster had once preached. Today it is an empty arena of walls guarding a windswept plain.

Jalal al-Din evaded capture throughout the campaign and in so doing became, in Persian chronicles, a figure of epic qualities. His exploits stirred the citizens of a number of cities to revolt, but this only brought down Mongol wrath on an even greater scale. For a week the Mongols devoted themselves to the slaughter of the inhabitants of Herat, after which most of the city, bar the citadel, was levelled to the ground. Jalal al-Din continued to trouble the Mongol forces for years to come, but was never able to concentrate his forces into any significant size and was never again a serious threat. His father, on the other hand, was hunted into ignominy.

Subedei and Jebei pursued the Khwarazm Shah through Tus and Rayy up to the western shores of the Caspian Sea. Subedei had been ordered to finish off the Khwarazm Shah, and in the process was given leave to carry out a reconnaissance in force of the lands between the Caspian and Black Seas. The Khwarazm Shah was eventually pursued to Astara on the shores of the Caspian, where he discarded his fine clothes, took up the rags of a beggar and, with a small group of followers, attempted to slip out of the town unnoticed. Penniless and anonymous, he boarded a small fishing boat just as a Mongol troop raced to the shores, firing their arrows in vain after the little boat. The mighty Khwarazm Shah made it to the tiny island of Abeskum, where he finally died of pleurisy in January 1221. He had fallen from the greatest heights to utter poverty, and was buried in a torn shirt borrowed from one of his servants.

The rest of Subedei's campaign has entered the annals of military history as one of the greatest adventures in cavalry warfare. His contingent continued through Azerbaijan and into the Christian kingdom of Georgia, then around the western and northern shores of the Caspian Sea into Russia. Once he had made his way through the pass at Derbent, his column emerged on to the plain north of the Caucasus. Here they were confronted by an alliance of Turkic tribes from the western steppe: Alans, Cherkes and Kipchaks. Though both sides suffered serious losses, these Western tribesmen proved no match for the easterners and Subedei continued his 'Great Raid' across the Russian steppe. When the Russian princes heard news of the foreigners' progress through their territory they put together a united force to challenge what had by now become a much weakened detachment – it was no longer an army. But again the locals came off worse in a crushing defeat at the battle of Kalka in 1223. It was now five years since the Mongols had gone to war.

FINAL REVENGE

As far as the main army was concerned, military operations ceased once Genghis reached the waters of the Indus. Messengers had brought news of the Khwarazm Shah's death: his army had been decimated, and Jalal al-Din was no longer thought to be a threat. Almost as if he had suddenly had his fill of carnage, Genghis retired to pastures south of the Hindu Kush and from there summoned a famous Taoist sage, Ch'ang Ch'un, to leave his monastery and come to the Great Khan's side. In an uncharacteristically philosophical vein, Genghis had become preoccupied with questions of his own mortality and was anxious to know if the sage knew of any elixir that might postpone death indefinitely. The learned one knew of no such potion; nevertheless Genghis was so impressed with Ch'ang Ch'un's wisdom that he granted the Taoist sect valuable privileges. In this somewhat reflective mood he travelled, during the autumn of 1222, back to

Transoxiana where he stayed for some time in Bukhara. Here he listened to the clerics expounding upon the virtues of Islam. He remained attentive throughout their lectures, but admonished the imams over the annual pilgrimage to Mecca, insisting that God could not exist in a stone but was present throughout the entire world. In Samarqand he ordered the imams to pray for him in their mosques, but was not content to stay and, in the spring of 1223, began the long journey back to Mongolia. He was apparently in no hurry, having taken up with a young and attractive new consort along the way. But it was not her charms that caused him to dawdle. He had learnt that his first wife, Borte, was furious that he had taken up with a new wife; and so, as the conqueror of the world approached Mongolia, he sent forth emissaries to report on Borte's temperament.

It was 1225 before his great caravans, laden with booty and trailing long lines of slaves, finally returned home. Subedei and Jebei had by this time completed their march through the Russian principalities and had brought a great deal of intelligence about the lands that lay in the western steppe and beyond. Genghis was by now nearly sixty, and new campaigns into these lands were beyond even his remarkable faculties. However, his soldiering days were by no means finished; there were a number of problems that he would deal with now that he was back. During his absence from the Chin campaign, the general he had left in command had died and the small contingent that he had commanded had returned to Mongolia; the Chin had therefore been able to reoccupy much of the territory that Genghis had taken from them, ten years before. But before an expedition could be mounted for China, there was even more pressing business closer to home.

Seven years earlier, the king of the Tanguts had refused to supply Genghis with soldiers for the campaign into Transoxiana. According to the *Secret History*, before setting out to deal with this miscreant, Genghis had been troubled by a number of bad omens. The Mongols were a deeply superstitious people and even the most learned of them were easily ruled by the vagaries of a shaman's wisdom or the encoded messages in the charred shoulder-bone of a sheep. Yet, despite these omens, revenge had always been the most vital motivation, and so in 1226 he set out at the head of his army. From a military aspect everything proceeded according to plan, yet in other respects the years spent on this campaign were dogged with misfortune. After just a few months he was badly thrown from his horse during a hunt. When he returned to his camp, the surgeons discovered that he had suffered serious internal injuries and pleaded with him to give up the war until he had recovered. Genghis refused, struggling to hide his pain from his soldiers. He was determined to stay with the army at least until the Tanguts were vanquished.

Chinese chroniclers echoed the accounts written by Persians about the war in Transoxiana, describing dreadful scenes of slaughter, destruction and fields littered with bones. At times the Mongols employed ingenious tactics against the enemy cities; like damming up rivers and then letting loose the flood to engulf a city and the surrounding countryside. On one occasion a battle took place on the frozen Yellow River, when the Tangut commanders saw an opportunity for a full-scale charge across the ice. But the Mongols coped with frozen rivers all the time in their part of the world, and the Tanguts were hopelessly out-classed. Their horses slid and crashed into one another, losing their mounts which were then picked off by Mongol archers. The Mongols had taken the precaution of scattering grit over their section of the ice and tying felt around the unshod hooves of their horses. But it was a victory that gave Genghis little comfort. Some weeks before he had learnt that his son Jochi had died. On hearing the news he had retired into his tent and remained there for some days, unwilling to let his soldiers witness his grief.

By the summer of 1227 the war against the Tanguts was nearly over, but by then Genghis and his surgeons knew that the life of the Great Khan was ebbing. He summoned his sons before him, and when Ogedei and Tolui arrived they found their father wrapped in blankets and shivering before a small fire. He was delirious with pain, and ranting: 'My descendants will wear gold, they will eat the choicest meats, they will ride the finest horses, they will hold in their arms the most beautiful women and they will forget to whom they owe it all.' Gradually he rallied and found the strength to explain to his youngest son how the campaign ought to be completed. 'A deed is not glorious until it is finished.' He extracted a promise from them to continue the war against the Chin, and they discussed how that campaign ought to be waged.

Some time in August 1227 Genghis Khan finally died, but in accordance with his orders his death was kept a secret from his army. The Tangut capital had not yet surrendered, though its inhabitants had sent word of their wish to sue for peace. When the city gates were opened at last the Mongol soldiers were told of Genghis's death. They swept inside with their swords drawn and showed no mercy. Every living thing inside the city walls was put to death.

The procession carrying their commander back to the steppe took many weeks. Anyone who met the bier along the road was instantly dispatched 'to serve their master in the other world'. He had chosen to be buried on a mountain named Burkhan Kaldun, in a range that rises near the Onon, Tuula and Kerulen rivers. According to tradition, it was near this mountain that the original forebears of the Mongol nation, the Blue Wolf and the Fallow Doe, had mated. It was, and for most Mongolians still is, the spiritual heartland of the nation. Genghis's body lay in state for three months while princes and ambassadors travelled to pay their respects. At his burial, forty jewelled slave girls and forty of the finest horses were sacrificed and buried alongside him. Then a thousand horsemen rode over the ground to disguise the site. Within less than a generation the mountainside was covered with fresh undergrowth and Genghis Khan's final resting place was devoured by the steppe.

3

THE PROMISE
FULFILLED

The campaigns of Genghis Khan were far and away the most far-reaching in world history; never had so much territory been conquered by a single man. At the time of his death the empire was four times the size of Alexander's and more than twice the size of the Roman empire; yet it had barely even begun to expand. Moreover, just like the Greek and Roman empires, it would have a tremendous impact upon world history even though it survived less than two hundred years. All of this was forged around the genius of a single figure, born within an insignificant nomadic tribe which for hundreds of years had anonymously tended its sheep and horses in the eastern Asian steppe.

By any standard Genghis Khan was a major figure in world history, and yet the true scale of his success has never been properly recognized in the West. Here his name has largely become synonymous with scenes of unbridled barbarism, the rape of civilization and the threat of pagan hordes. He has never enjoyed the status of great empire builders like Alexander, Tamerlane or Napoleon. Nevertheless, his accomplishments greatly outshine these more familiar names, and not simply in terms of scale. For one thing the Mongol empire was far more enduring. When Alexander died his empire was divided up amongst his generals, who then descended into a series of petty quarrels which quickly led to the collapse of the fragments that remained. The Mongol empire did not lose its sense of purpose once the charismatic figure at its heart was gone, as was the case with the empires built by Tamerlane and Alexander. Genghis had ensured a secure succession and at the same time established the beginnings of an administration that would grow with the empire. Like Napoleon, he had been blessed with generals of great calibre – men who were promoted through the ranks of a modern army where talent and ability were rewarded. In most armies of those days, nobles and princes of the blood automatically assumed military command regardless of their competence. Another quality that Genghis shared with the little Corsican was his ability to provide his army with a seemingly endless string of victories, and with it incredible wealth, which was repaid with uncompromising loyalty. But unlike Napoleon, Genghis never abandoned his armies nor sacrificed them for his own vainglory. Nor did Genghis ever meet his Waterloo. His victories were won through brilliant strategy, organization, discipline and courage. There are simply no comparisons in military history with the breathtaking conquests undertaken during the last twenty-five years of his life. The whole of Asia resounded with the name Genghis Khan – though at an enormous cost.

A TERRIBLE PRICE

The unprecedented slaughter, particularly of civilians, that occurred throughout his campaigns has always given historians reason for pause. Yet it is too simple to dismiss the huge degree of carnage as unbridled barbarism. In his favour it has to be said that Genghis never employed murder as a political weapon, as Tamerlane and other more recent tyrants did, and indeed the death penalty was used for very few crimes. During Genghis's reign conquered subjects were immediately emancipated, and there was never any form of political or racial tyranny. The Mongols were extraordinarily tolerant of other religions and this was a tradition that they maintained for most of the history of the empire – a rare quality in a world where Christians and Muslims had been at war with each other for nearly 500 years.

Yet, in the words of the historian Dr David Morgan, these highly enlightened attitudes must always be seen in context: 'Assuming you survived your first encounter with the Mongol armies,' he once mused, 'it was highly improbable you would be subsequently persecuted for your religious beliefs.' Before the how and why of Mongol war-making policies are examined, it is important to try and grasp the scale. No one suffered more than the people of Transoxiana, Khwarazmia and Khurasan. There was nothing in living or recorded memory that compared with the catastrophe, and one Persian chronicler writing a hundred years after the event described the parlous state of the country in these words: '... as a result of the eruption of the Mongols and the general massacre of people which took place in those days ... there can be no doubt that if for a thousand years to come no evil befalls the country, yet it will not be possible to repair the damage, and bring the land back into the state it was formerly.'

All the chroniclers seemed to vie with one another in trying to capture the sheer scale of the disaster. They make grim reading. One writer claimed that when the town of Herat suffered Genghis's terrible retribution, having rebelled and challenged Mongol rule, the Mongol general Elchidei is supposed to have exterminated no fewer than 1 600 000 people. Another chronicler puts the figure at 2 400 000. At the destruction of Nishapur, the death toll was supposed to have reached 1 747 000. The heads of their victims were stacked in three pyramids: a pile each for men, women and children. When the bones had been picked clean the piles of skulls stood as macabre warnings to anyone who might challenge Mongol supremacy.

No modern historian takes these figures as a realistic account of the death toll. For a start, no one has any idea what the populations of these areas were in the mid-thirteenth century, though it seems unlikely that any city there could have matched the population of a Chinese city like K'ai-feng or Hangchow, both of which numbered over a million inhabitants. Even making allowances for people from the countryside who sought refuge behind the city walls, these figures are certainly exaggerations. But even if they cannot be taken literally, they do begin to suggest the enormous psychological shock that had swept through the population. There is no precedent for these figures in Persian histories, which suggests there was no precedent for the amount of death and destruction that had been endured. Throughout Khurasan, the Mongols continued the same policy. At Bamian, Balkh and Merv the entire populations – even domestic animals – were slaughtered. The generals Jebei and Subedei brought similar disaster to Azerbaijan, destroying the towns of Rayy, Qum, Zanjan, Qazvin and Maragheh. Interestingly, nearly all the cities dealt with this way had been those whose inhabitants had rebelled against Mongol rule. It is also worth adding that not all the inhabitants were thought to be expendable; officers and nobles were invariably spared, as were artisans, craftsmen, scribes, clerics, merchants and occasionally administrators – all of whom the Mongols held in high regard. The opposite was the case, however, when it came to peasants, the majority of human life in the thirteenth century. Whether in China or western Asia, the peasants who worked the land were regarded without exception as having no greater status in life than a flock of sheep. When the order came to put the population to the sword, they were herded together like sheep – and dealt with as such. Being pasture-based horsemen, the Mongols viewed men and women who worked on their knees in the soil as the basest form of human life. Even a horse was far more valuable.

But as we know from more recent experiences of mass extermination, one cannot believe that the soldiers of a conquering army would go to all the effort required to slaughter many hundreds of thousands of people simply because they had a loathing for agricultural labourers. It is quite clear from the evidence that the Mongols preferred to gain submission without having to resort to mass-murder. Their strategy was to avoid Mongol casualties whenever possible, so any city that surrendered without resisting was spared – and the Mongols usually kept their word. However, any sign of resistance was met with merciless retribution; the resulting massacre was intended as a warning to others. Judging by the large numbers of cities that surrendered upon the Mongols' demands the tactic seems to have worked.

But the slaughter that went on during the fighting was nothing compared to the destruction wrought in its wake. The Persian plateau does not have many great rivers, and so agriculture had always been supported by a very sophisticated and widespread system of artificial irrigation known as *qanats*. This consisted of an elaborate system of underground channels constructed to carry water from the mountain sources across – or under – the land to the fields. From the surface this system appears as a long line of shallow wells from which are dug long trenches that carry the water at right-angles to the line of wells, irrigating the land on either side. All irrigation systems, and *qanats* in particular, need to be regularly maintained. Unless they are regularly dug out they silt up and the entire system collapses. With the population either dead, or frightened away, the *qanat* system gradually broke down and the land dried up. Agriculture ceased to be possible and the cities of the region that had depended upon it withered, or, like the city of Bukhara, were not rebuilt to anything like their previous size and opulence. The Mongol legacy lasted for centuries.

These devastating consequences lead one to wonder why an army bothers to conquer a place if in the process there is nothing left worth ruling. The answer is that, under Genghis Khan, the Mongols were not really engaged in a campaign of conquest. As soon as fighting came to an end, the armies withdrew from all the territories except Khwarazmia which was put under the control of Mongol-appointed administrators. There was no real interest in occupying and exploiting the lands through which they had swept like a juggernaut. Despite the vastness of his conquests, Genghis's vision of the world at the time of his death was still centred upon the steppe. While Mongol territory had expanded to include all the lands previously controlled by all the other Turko-Mongol tribes, it was almost coincidental that it also consumed some of the lands of sedentary peoples that surrounded its frontiers. Genghis Khan's invasions of northern China and Khwarazmia were designed to gain submission, not so that he could rule the world. He had set out originally to gain control of the steppe, and from his perspective the sedentary territories on his frontiers were of marginal importance.

This was quite the opposite view to that of the new ranks of advisers and administrators that had joined the Mongol court; for them, of course, the steppes were of marginal importance, lying as they did between the frontiers of one civilization and another. It was this fundamental distinction between the nomadic and the sedentary view of the world which had led to the most devastating effects on the populations of farmlands and cities.

But there was another crucial factor that influenced Mongol attitudes towards the sedentary populations, and that was the Mongols' inferior numbers. They simply didn't have the manpower to station garrisons in the territory they had conquered, so they relied upon a country's collective memory of the most terrifying and brutal assault upon one or two cities to ensure loyalty in the absence of the main army. Though it lasted for seven long years, the entire campaign through Khwarazmia, Khurasan and the Russian steppes was really one gigantic raid, intended to terrorize the massive populations in those regions into submission. Any sign of revolt was, from the Mongols' point of view, much better dealt with by wiping out the entire population.

Through all these considerations of Mongol attitudes, there was one singular principle that informed all their ideas – their almost total lack of contact with sedentary civilizations. Their proud nomadic traditions had led them to look contemptuously upon the great agricultural producers like China. They had traded for centuries with border posts and had received, indirectly, gifts and money from the Chinese courts, but China was seen as nothing more than a vast treasure house to be plundered.

Perhaps the most chilling statistic that illustrates this stunning disregard for their sedentary neighbours comes from their own records. A census taken by the Chin empire in 1195 showed a population in northern China of fewer than 50 million people, yet when the Mongols took their first census of their newly won domain in 1235–6 they counted fewer than 9 million. Even assuming that enormous numbers of people may not have been counted because of the general state of chaos in northern China, this kind of discrepancy in the numbers suggests that Mongol policies of terrorism were akin to genocide. As was pointed out earlier, although the population of western Asia was far lower than that of China, the effects of the Great Raid were, if anything, proportionally much worse.

China's recovery from these disasters took longer than necessary because of the Mongols' unwillingness to assume responsibility for their conquests. They continued to be more than satisfied with the regular payment of tribute: silk, grain and precious metals, as well as sophisticated war machinery built by captured artisans. Though they had acquired rights over vast areas of land in China and Persia, both with long traditions of complex and sophisticated self-administration, the Mongols saw no immediate need to rely upon these traditions in the running of their new domains. Indeed, for some time they saw no need for an official government structure at all; and when pressed to deal with a crisis they would respond in a somewhat *ad hoc* fashion, usually delegating responsibility to a foreign official who carried out his job under distant Mongol supervision.

So although at the end of Genghis Khan's life it cannot quite be claimed that he had forged an empire, nor is it accurate to suggest that, having withdrawn their armies, the Mongols took no further interest in the conquered lands. Quite the opposite; and it is in this particular respect that the legacy of Genghis Khan differs dramatically from, say, that of Alexander, Attila, Tamerlane and Napoleon. It is clear that Genghis believed he had established a dynasty that had won the submission of most of western and central Asia and northern China – and that he expected it to endure long after his death. But it was also clear that no steppe nation had ever conquered this much territory before and that the Mongols would have to employ new policies with regard to it. Quite what those policies would be was not yet certain, but the Mongols were above all things practical and were never too proud to learn from others.

THE GOLDEN CLAN

As the empire expanded, eventually to encompass all of the Middle East and China, the Mongols became much more sophisticated in their methods of government, though initially they were not seduced by the obvious sophistication of either the Chinese or Persian administrations. They preferred to employ the administrative experience of people who had an acceptable nomadic pedigree, like the Uighurs, who occupied the lands to the east of the Tien Shan Mountains, and the Khitans, who had been the rulers of northern China before the Jurchen Chin. From the Uighurs, of course, the Mongols had adopted an alphabet and their traditions of commercial law, while from the Khitans they borrowed such intangibles as concepts, vocabulary and institutions.

The most significant institution they took from the Khitans was the *darughachi*, a sort of all-purpose Mongol official who was stationed in conquered territory and became, in effect, a kind of provincial military governor. It was his responsibility to ensure that the local communities did not renege on the submissions they had made to the Mongols. These officials had a swift and reliable line of communication with the Great Khan, and any hint of revolt was dealt with immediately. However, the *darughachi*'s most vital responsibility was to ensure that the appropriate taxes were collected and forwarded to the central chancellery in Mongolia. *Darughachi* had been recruited from the ranks of the *keshig,* the imperial guard, whose allegiance was to the life and wellbeing of the Great Khan. All lines of communication led to him – or the aristocracy that had been created around him. This aristocracy, or the Golden Clan as it was known, was the families that could trace their lineage to Genghis Khan himself. The most important of these were Genghis's four sons born of his first wife, Borte. It was only they and their descendants who had the right to rule.

These four – Jochi, Chaghadai, Ogedei and Tolui – formed the bedrock of the dynasty. To ensure the Golden Clan's endurance Genghis had devised a system of appanages, or *ulus*, that were distributed amongst the members of his clan and honoured commanders who had distinguished themselves in warfare. These tracts of territory extended only over lands where nomadic peoples tended to dwell and provided the holder with a source of wealth, for along with the land came a contingent of army units plus animals, artisans and artists. The holders of these *ulus* also shared in the tax revenues from other parts of the empire. The *ulus* varied in size, depending upon the age of the recipient and the esteem in which he was held, and his subsequent wealth reflected his status within the Clan. The majority of *ulus* were of the order of many hundreds of square kilometres; however, those distributed to Genghis's sons were much larger.

Before he set out on the campaign into western Asia, Genghis had already settled the question of succession, and before he died he had also set out the geographical shape of the future empire through the *ulus* he designated to his four sons. It was Mongol tradition to pass to the eldest son the lands furthest from home. Jochi, the eldest, had died some months before his father, and so all the lands 'to the west as far as the hoof of a Mongol horse trodden', were divided amongst his sons. The eldest, Orda, was given possession of the land from the northeast shores of the Aral Sea and the districts around the Sari Su River. This was later called the White Horde, and precious little is known about it. His younger brother, the able but youthful Batu, received land to the north-west, stretching from the northern shores of the Caspian as far west as the Volga and east as far as the Irgiz River. This became known as the Golden Horde, and would in time prove extraordinarily extensive. Chaghadai, a kind of Lord Chancellor, was given the lands in Central Asia that had previously been the land of the Qara Khitai, to which was later added Transoxiana. Ogedei received the lands north-east of Chaghadai's – the Ala Kul, the Tarbagatai Mountains, the Kara Irtish River and the region extending from the Altai Mountains to Lake Baikal. Tolui, the youngest son, received the Mongol 'heartland', the traditional inheritance of the youngest-born.

Although Genghis had already decided upon Ogedei as his successor, it was two years before he actually assumed the title of Great Khan. Some suggest it was because Ogedei himself was reluctant, feeling that Tolui might perhaps have been better suited, while other sources suggest it was Tolui who was unhappy about being passed over. At any rate, a *quritai* was called in 1229 at which the issue was finally settled.

THE GREAT KHAN OGEDEI

Ogedei was, by all accounts, the most intelligent and certainly the most generous and tolerant of the four brothers. Judging from the number of stories that have survived about him, it would seem that he spent a great deal of his time devising expedients by which those who had fallen foul of Chaghadai's stern judgements might escape the death penalty. Ogedei was also a great *bon viveur*, having a well-developed taste for wine. After being admonished by his elder brother for his excessive drunkenness, Ogedei is supposed to have meekly forsworn his past behaviour and promised to restrict himself to a specific number of cups of wine a day – though not before taking the precaution of obtaining the most enormous wine goblet!

But these accounts of Ogedei do not paint his full character. Under his control the proto-empire established by his father expanded into a commonwealth of the most prodigious size. The first and most important action undertaken was the long-overdue conquest of the Chin. This campaign, begun by Genghis in 1211, had been continuing for more than twenty-five years. Ogedei was determined to bring matters to a swift conclusion, but first he had to make up lost ground. After the death of Muqali, the general whom Genghis had left in charge of the campaign, the Chin had reconquered a large tract of territory around the Wei valley and in Shensi. Genghis had always known that defeating the Chin would not be easy and he had advised his sons that they would probably need the aid of the Sung empire, to the south in the traditional heartland of China.

In 1230 a new Mongol offensive began, but it was soon repulsed. In 1231 they returned under the command of Subedei and, although they made some ground, they were again repulsed from the Wei valley. Ogedei finally decided to take his father's advice and make a supreme effort to court the Sung. The Mongols' aim was to try and approach K'ai-feng, the current Chin capital, through Sung territory. If they could also exploit a hundred-year-old hatred between the two dynasties and actually recruit the Sung armies to their cause, then that would be a bonus. Ogedei took command of the bulk of the Mongol army and marched it in an easterly direction along the banks of the Yellow River. Tolui took a contingent of 30 000 in a large sweeping movement down into Sung territory, taking the city of Hang-chung, then moved south towards Szechwan. There he turned and moved north-west again, crossing the Han River and suddenly appearing inside Chin territory. By early 1232, his forces depleted from disease and malnutrition, he had joined up with Ogedei Khan's army again. Almost immediately the Mongols were confronted by a Chin army led by one of their most able generals, Wan-yen Yi.

The battle was hard fought, with the outcome turning many times, but eventually the Chin were defeated. Wan-yen Yi was captured and the Mongols, impressed by his ability, tried to persuade him to join their side. He refused, preferring death to dishonour. The Chin, in the meantime, had withdrawn their forces to K'ai-feng, abandoning the rest of their territory. The subsequent siege of K'ai-feng was undertaken first by Ogedei; but, when the Chin emperor refused to submit to Mongol rule, the inevitable long-drawn-out campaign against one of the largest and best-fortified cities in China was left to Subedei. It turned out to be a far more difficult exercise than any other that the Mongols had faced. According to a Chinese account, it seems that the Chin were employing a new weapon that was having a devastating effect on Subedei's forces: '. . . great mortars that roared like thunder in the heaven'. The Mongols were confronted by what is thought to have been their first experience of gunpowder and their forces were in danger of being destroyed at the very gates of the city.

While Subedei was left to get on with the investment of K'ai-feng, Ogedei and his brother Tolui returned to the mountain passes to spend the summer. While they were together, both Ogedei and his brother became seriously ill and news reached Subedei that the Great Khan was not expected to survive. There are many different stories about the events at the mysterious summer retreat. One legend has it that Ogedei's illness caused so much concern that the great Lord Tengri, the Mongol God, was called upon to come to his aid. The Lord God in heaven agreed to take the life of another in place of Ogedei's, and Tolui volunteered. This particular legend was developed amongst the later rulers of the empire, who were to be descendants of Tolui. It is far more likely that the story was invented to enhance the circumstances of Tolui's death, which was probably caused by nothing more mysterious than alcoholic poisoning. The two of them had perhaps partaken of a less than wholesome brew, and only Ogedei recovered.

In the meantime, Subedei's own situation was becoming desperate. As he was losing men at an alarming rate he had to find a quick way of bringing the military stand-off to an end. He took the initiative and approached the Sung for help. The Sung emperor agreed, in return for a couple of Chin provinces – Honan and K'ai-feng. Soon 20 000 fresh Sung troops arrived at the gates of K'ai-feng, and the city collapsed shortly afterwards.

The destruction and plundering of K'ai-feng in 1234 was followed by the execution of all the male members of the Chin Dynasty, while the women were deported to the Mongol court. These scenes were witnessed by the Sung generals and would haunt them in the years to come. Subedei was about to set upon the rest of the population when one of Ogedei's advisers, Yeh-lu Ch'u-ts'ai, intervened.

LIBERAL INFLUENCES: YEH-LU CH'U-TS'AI

Yeh-lu Ch'u-ts'ai already had a reputation at the Chin court at Chung-tu even before he entered Mongol employment, where he later shone as a great statesman. A Khitan by birth, he was related to the old Liao dynasty, though his father and grandfather had been functionaries in the Chin court. Educated as an astronomer/astrologer, he was brought up with Buddhist ideals though his future lay as a typical Confucian administrator. After the fall of Chung-tu, Yeh-lu Ch'u-ts'ai was amongst the prisoners brought before Genghis Khan. When Genghis asked if he was not glad that his forefathers had been avenged now that the Chin were defeated, Yeh-lu Ch'u-ts'ai reminded Genghis that both his father and grandfather had served in the Chin court. 'How can I, as a subject and a son, be so insincere at heart as to consider my sovereign and my father as enemies?' Genghis was impressed with the young man's strong sense of loyalty and immediately recruited him into his budding administration. Before long Yeh-lu Ch'u-ts'ai was recruiting others from the ranks of the Chin, Khitan and Chinese prisoners. He rescued libraries from the torch, gathering up documents and books wherever the Mongol armies travelled, and along with his growing staff fashioned a makeshift, mobile civil service. After Genghis's death he was inherited by Ogedei and became one of his closest advisers.

It is Yeh-lu Ch'u-ts'ai who is credited with having moderated the Mongols' worst excesses, and in particular with radically altering their approach towards gathering revenue. But it was after the fall of K'ai-feng and the conquest of the Chin that he is said to have made his most important stand. It had been seriously proposed by Subedei and the other generals that, after the artisans, merchants and scholars had been rounded up and sent off to Mongolia, the rest of the population should be put to the sword – not the population of K'ai-feng, but the entire population of north China.

The millions of Chinese peasants had been a source of concern to the Mongols for some time, not just because their labour seemed incomprehensible, but because their sheer numbers were so disquieting. They made utterly useless soldiers; besides which, the vast amounts of good land they occupied might be better used as pasture for the Mongol herds. As mass extermination was being seriously debated, Yeh-lu Ch'u-ts'ai energetically argued against it. He pointed out that if the peasants were left alone and allowed to prosper, and he was granted permission to introduce a fair and progressive system of taxing the product of their labours, the Mongols' income from north China would be massively enhanced. Yeh-lu Ch'u-ts'ai's scheme was to try and introduce a proper budget for the running of the Mongol court and army. This meant raising a tax that would be uniform throughout the empire. A settled population would pay 10 per cent of its harvest, while nomadic people would provide one animal for every hundred owned. In particular he wanted to do away with the Mongols' unproductive methods of gathering tax. Yeh-lu Ch'u-ts'ai's reforms came slowly, though once the increased revenue and produce started flowing Ogedei became more sympathetic and talk of mass extermination ceased.

Although Genghis held Yeh-lu Ch'u-ts'ai in high esteem, his influence within the Mongol court as a scribe, astrologer and principal minister was not really felt until the reign of Ogedei. The second Great Khan was more open to foreign ideas and prepared to practise foreign methods, although by comparison with his principal minister he was still a determined nomad. It had been Genghis's great wish that the empire should remain largely steppe-based – that, however large it grew, the centre of power would not shift to any of the settled societies but remain firmly in the Mongol heartland. However, with the empire now expanding on all sides, a burgeoning administration struggling to keep pace, coupled with an ever-increasing traffic of suppliants and envoys arriving to pay tribute to the Great Khan, the traditional encampment of tents and *gers* was inadequate. The Mongols had to have a capital.

CAPITAL OF A NOMADIC PEOPLE

Rather in the manner in which cities like Washington, DC, Brasilia and Canberra were constructed out of nowhere, Qaraqorum emerged from the midst of a great grassy waste to be the notional focus for the greatest land-based empire in history. After the collapse of the empire it quickly fell into decay, and the majority of its permanent buildings were plundered for materials during the construction, in the sixteenth century, of a nearby Buddhist monastery. The location of Qaraqorum was subsequently lost to history until it was rediscovered in the nineteenth century, and excavated by the Russians during the first half of the present century. Evidence from these excavations suggests that the site had been used by a Buddhist community long before the Mongol empire, and that during the time of Genghis Khan it was a kind of tent city, being both a military camp and a trading centre for commerce and handicrafts.

In some respects it was a curious location for the seat of government. It was not in original Mongol territory but in the border regions, roughly midway between Ogedei's and Tolui's *ulus* in the Orkhon valley – territory that had once been occupied by the Naimans. However, for the steppe peoples the location had great significance. It was close to the crossroads of a series of traditional highways that had been used by migrating nomads and merchants' caravans for centuries. Forest-dwelling nomads passed through the area during their annual migrations to and from the south, while Islamic merchants journeying to and from China passed through the same valley in an east–west direction. These ancient highways were still being used, so it made great sense for the capital to be placed at this important point.

Work began on the city while Ogedei was still on campaign against the Chin, and the first walls went up in 1235. According to the archaeologists, it was constructed on an artificial hill composed of alternate layers of sand and clay. The city itself was surrounded by an earthen wall about 1 km (1100 yards) across the northern face, 1.5 km (1650 yards) down the western side and about 2 km (2200 yards) down the opposite wall. These were only about 1 m (3 feet) high but some 15–18 m (50–60 feet) thick. To the west of these, in the south-western corner of the site, was Ogedei's palace area, which was itself a walled compound. At the southern end of this compound there were two massive gates, set one in front of the other; an outer gate was some 30 m (100 feet) high. Inside the compound were two large halls used for audiences, banquets and the reception of guests. The larger was more than 80 m (250 feet) long and was described by Friar William of Rubruck, a French friar who went to the Mongol empire as an evangelist:

> And the palace is like a church, with a middle nave, and two sides beyond two rows of pillars, and with three doors to the south, and beyond the middle door on the inside stands the tree [a fountain that produced a selection of liquors], and the khan sits in a high place to the north, so that he can be seen by all; and he himself sits up there like a divinity. There are twelve idol temples of different nations, two muhummeries [mosques] in which is cried the law of Mahomet, and one church of Christians is in the extreme end of the city. At the eastern end is sold millet and other kinds of grain; at the western one, sheep and goats are sold; at the southern, oxen and carts are sold; at the northern, horses are sold.

Within the palace compound, behind the main halls was a low, circular mound where the Mongols erected large residential tents. Despite the existence of numerous large buildings, they preferred to sleep under canvas. The major buildings seem to have been built on a Chinese model, with high-pitched, tiled roofs. The halls were supported off the ground by regularly spaced pillars. In public places stone tortoises formed the bases of imperial stelae. By all accounts the Mongols lavished considerable sums on the decorations of the buildings, and yet the site itself was not that imposing. One European traveller compared it with a French village.

> As for the city of Qaraqorum I can tell you that, not counting the Khan's palace, it is not as large as the village of Saint Denis, and the monastery of Saint Denis is worth ten times more than that palace. . . . There are two quarters in it; one of Saracens [Muslims] in which are the markets, and where a great many Tartar gather on account of the court, which is always near this [city], and on account of the great number of ambassadors; the other is the quarter of the Cathayans, all of whom are artisans. Besides these quarters there are great palaces, which are for the secretaries of the court.

Despite having created a permanent seat of power, Ogedei did not forgo the traditional seasonal migrations. He would be at Qaraqorum from February through to the spring, when he travelled north of the capital to the lakes and marshes of the Orkhon River. He would stay there for a month or six weeks, return to Qaraqorum briefly and then, to escape the baking summers, move to the high ground in the mountains to the south-east. By the end of August he would move once more, this time south to the Ongin River, where he had his hunting grounds and winter residence, and there he would stay until returning to Qaraqorum to begin the cycle over again.

Nevertheless, Qaraqorum did provide a focus for the expanding empire, and a place to house the administration. Yeh-lu Ch'u-ts'ai was instrumental in strengthening the authority of this medieval Brasilia. The Treasury was located there, as were the taxation and revenue-gathering services; and Chaghadai, the Lord Chancellor, held court there. But most importantly, it was the place to which foreign envoys, wealthy merchants and prominent clerics travelled for an audience with the most important man in Asia. It became the hub of all political and commercial life in the continent.

In order for this to be so, the empire had to develop a system of communication that would bind all the spokes to the hub. The great *Yam* was forged by Ogedei from a simpler system that his father had employed for keeping in touch with his generals. Its essence was a network of riders whose purposes were varied: they could act as escorts for visiting envoys, ensuring their safe passage over the thousands of miles of open steppe; or the system might be used to transport materials, especially along the roads from China. They might also be used for the gathering of intelligence from the far reaches of the empire and beyond. However, the most important use of the *Yam* was the swift transmission of royal orders across the length and breadth of Asia.

Ogedei established the system first in his own *ulus*. At regular stages along the roads, roughly 40–50 km (25–30 miles) or a day's ride, post stations were constructed that provided messengers with food, shelter and fresh horses. These horses were provided by the local population, while the system itself was maintained by the army. The messengers carried with them a form of identification, known as a *paiza*, that established under whose authority they travelled. Each *paiza* was about 50 cm (18 ins) long and was usually made of wood, though *paizas* representing someone of high authority might be of silver or even gold. They were also highly decorated, bearing engravings of tigers or falcons – which also testified as to the rank of the holder.

There are reports of couriers covering some staggering distances through the *Yam*; Marco Polo claimed 300–500 km (about 200–300 miles) a day. These express couriers galloped day and night from one post station to another, swathed in a garland of bells that signalled their approach. The custodian at the station would hear the courier and have fresh horses saddled and ready. On one occasion, when a message was sent from the court at Qaraqorum to Russia, the couriers covered 1600 km (1000 miles) a month.

EXPANSION INTO WESTERN ASIA

As Ogedei set about constructing the fabric of the empire, there were still military objectives that had to be met. Genghis's campaign through Khwarazmia and Khurasan had left appalling ruin and destruction in the countryside and swept away all remnants of central government control. In the anarchy that reigned, Jalal al-Din, who had fled to Delhi in 1221, had gradually clawed his way back to power in an attempt to fill the vacuum. It was precisely the same situation that had occurred in northern China, after Genghis had lost interest in that campaign. As the Mongols had not left garrisons to hold the territory they had conquered, it was only a matter of time before someone else moved in.

Jalal al-Din had a great deal to avenge and found no difficulty gathering supporters. By 1224 he had won back a large slice of territory, which he extended into Azerbaijan by the following year, and soon he was also launching raids into Christian Georgia. By 1228 he had virtually restored the empire his father had occupied, and included with it the provinces of Fars, Kirman, Iraq-Ajemi, Azerbaijan and Mazandaran. In his obsession to reconquer his birthright, Jalal al-Din had no hesitation in conducting a murderous campaign no less terrible than that of the Mongols. Though he was clearly a commander of some distinction, he had no political skills; having reconquered most of Persia, he failed to unite the kingdom against any outside threat. This came in the form of a new Mongol invasion in 1230, when Ogedei sent an army to put an end to the unexpected restoration of the Khwarazm sultanate. The Mongols moved swiftly through

Khurasan and up to Azerbaijan, where they completely surprised the defenders at Tabriz. Jalal al-Din fled from his old enemies and led them on another chase, though on this occasion he found no sanctuary. The Mongol commander, Chormaghun, kept up a relentless pursuit, and the longer he continued the harder it was for Jalal al-Din to hold on to his support. He fled north-west towards the plains of Mughan, west of the Caspian Sea. He was crossing territory that his father had crossed when he too was being pursued by the Mongols ten years before. Eventually, just like his father, Jalal al-Din found himself bereft of allies and he died around 1231, probably murdered by Kurds.

The Mongol general who had led the campaign, Chormaghun, remained as *darughachi*, or military governor, in the areas of Persia he had conquered, and established his residence in the plains west of the Caspian Sea. Over the next ten years Chormaghun worked his way through the many small states of the Caucasus, subduing them all before turning towards the kingdom of Georgia in 1236. The reputation of the Mongols had already reached these lands, so that by the time Chormaghun and his army arrived the famous Queen Rasudan had already fled to the neighbouring province. Thus Georgia too became a vassal state. Another *darughachi* was despatched to govern the lands to the south-east, Khurasan and Mazandaran, and gradually the Mongols extended more effective control over western Asia. This policy of strengthening the Mongol presence in western Asia would soon pay dividends when decisions to expand the empire even further west were taken.

THE DECISION TO INVADE EUROPE

Following the destruction of the Chin empire in 1234, Ogedei had returned to Qaraqorum to supervise the construction of his city, which was now well advanced. With the capital still rising out of a grassy wilderness, in 1235 he called a *quriltai* at which the Golden Clan and its advisers took stock of the state of the empire. It was perhaps one of the most important *quriltais* in the history of the empire, setting down a number of institutions that survived for many generations, and also directing the empire on a new course that would dramatically transform the history of the rest of the world.

Yeh-lu Ch'u-ts'ai used the *quriltai* to impose his taxation reforms and establish a number of new institutions that would serve the expanding empire. Having instructed Ogedei that 'although the empire had been conquered on horseback, it would not be ruled on horseback', he established a set of rules and precedents for the running of the Mongol court and established libraries for the precious books and documents that he had rescued from the remnants of the Chin capital. He also built schools where Mongol children would be taught to become civil administrators.

It was also at the meeting in 1235 that the formal establishment of the *Yam* took place. The order was given for the construction and supply of staging posts throughout the empire, but especially along the route between the main residences of Ogedei, Chaghadai and Batu way out in the west. Wells were dug at regular intervals to supply water, while Yeh-lu Ch'u-ts'ai saw to the provision of grain, horses and cattle for every outpost.

When the discussion came round to military activity, the generals reported action on a number of different fronts. With the conquest of northern China complete, Ogedei could now contend with one or two annoying problems. Since 1211, when Genghis Khan had first extracted a submission from the Korean rulers, the Mongols had been irritated by the Koreans' persistent streak of independence. In 1231 a Mongol army had crossed the Yalu River, not to conquer but to raid and terrorize the Koreans into submission and the payment of tribute. Having succeeded, the Mongols left seventy officials behind to gather the revenue they had exacted. However, it was reported at the *quriltai* that in the absence of Mongol forces most of these officials had been murdered.

Ogedei, determined to deal with the Koreans once and for all, despatched an army across the Yalu. After three years of war that took a heavy toll upon the local population, the Korean rulers finally agreed to .negotiate with their conquerors and peace came in 1241. Ogedei also decided to entrust his two sons, Koten and Kochu, with an army which they were to lead in a separate campaign against the Sung empire. This was in retaliation for some territorial infringements that had occurred following the collapse of the Chin. In the meantime, there were reports of General Chormaghun forging his way towards the kingdom of Georgia. In a sense, this operation was the vanguard for what was to be the most critical decision taken at the *quriltai* of 1235.

Batu, the orphaned son of Jochi, had inherited the westernmost reaches of the empire, though in fact these lands had never been conquered. They had, of course, been reconnoitred by the great General Subedei during his extraordinary Great Raid around the Caspian Sea and through Russia. Subedei saw great opportunities in these lands, but he also saw that the western steppes were the weakest point in the empire's defences, occupied as they were with numerous volatile nomadic groups. He argued that the Mongols ought to extend their empire west to the edge of the steppes and to protect their flank. Once that had been accomplished, the Mongols could push forward into Europe – conquering the separate nations one by one, just as they had done in China. As Subedei pressed his case it was greeted by growing enthusiasm, especially from Ogedei who became so enamoured of the idea that he suggested leading the army into the west himself.

Fortunately Yeh-lu Ch'u-ts'ai tempered Ogedei's enthusiasm, arguing that, unlike the situation in his father's time, the Mongols now had an empire which required someone at its head; his place, therefore, was in Qaraqorum. It was agreed instead that, since the proposed expedition was meant to conquer lands bequeathed to Batu, it was only appropriate that he should lead the campaign. It was the decision to invade Europe that above all else distinguishes the *quriltai* of 1235 from all others, and it quickly became the only real issue of discussion for the rest of the session. It would require an immense amount of planning and time; the campaign, Subedei estimated, would take eighteen years.

4

THE INVASION
OF EUROPE

PREPARATORY FORAYS

The first objective of the operation that emerged from the meeting at Qaraqorum was to secure the lands up to the banks of the River Volga. This meant taking the city of Bulgar, which stood at the confluence of the Volga and Kama rivers and dominated all commercial life between these rivers and the Ural Mountains. The Bulgars themselves had once been nomads, but had long since given up camp life for the city, growing rich on the fur trade. They had also taken up the word of the Prophet and were, at that time, the most northerly converts to Islam. In the seventh century those Bulgars who had not converted emigrated across the Danube, where the nation they founded eventually bore their name. Apart from the Bulgars, the Mongols would also have to subjugate the nomadic tribes that inhabited the lands to the south, along the banks of the Volga. Then the Mongol armies could cross the Volga safely, knowing their flank and rear could not be threatened. But before any military operations could commence, there would be a great deal of preparation.

The great push west was going to require enormous resources, and these were not immediately to hand. Batu, who had been given nominal responsibility for the campaign, had a miserably small army of some 4000 men. A form of conscription would have to be introduced. Subedei had estimated that the armies should be ready to move by the winter of 1237, which would give them two years to recruit men from subjugated tribes, train them and prepare their *matériel*. By the spring of 1236, a formidable army had already been gathered: it consisted of 50 000 men from the main Mongol army, plus several corps of Chinese and Persian engineers and some 20 000 conscripts. No fewer than ten princes of the blood had joined the growing ranks, including Batu's brothers Orda, Shiban, Berke and Sinkur; Chaghadai's sons Baidar and Buri; Ogedei's sons Guyuk and Kadan; and Tolui's sons Mongke and Budjek.

With things advancing so well, Batu and Subedei set out northwards with an expeditionary force to attack the Bulgars, while Mongke and Budjek moved south to tackle the tribes along the lower Volga. The pursuit of the southern tribal groups turned into a classic Mongol hunt, with Mongke and Budjek spreading their forces out into a great arc and then sweeping along either bank of the river. The middle ranks floated on 200 barges down the river itself. The hunt led them to an island in the centre of the river, where fugitive tribal warriors and their princes thought themselves safe, given the swift currents and choppy waters. But they had not noticed a sandbar that ran from the river bank to the island, shallow enough to allow horses to cross. Within an hour all were slaughtered and resistance in the south put to an end.

Meanwhile, in the north, Batu and Subedei were working their way through the Bulgar territories. By the spring they had smashed all Bulgar resistance and turned yet another nation into a vassal state. Little is recorded of that campaign, except that the city of Bulgar itself was so utterly destroyed that it was never rebuilt. Before returning to Mongolia, Batu and Subedei charged through the foothills of the Urals, gathering up further conscripts for the great new army. By the winter of 1237, just as Subedei had predicted, a Mongol army of 120 000 stood ready to cross the frozen Volga into Russia.

TWO ARMIES, TWO CONCEPTS OF FIGHTING

The army that had been forged under Genghis Khan and then tempered during the campaigns in China and Persia was by now easily the most formidable military force in existence. Its command structure and tactics were more advanced than any other army at the time, and would not be unfamiliar to soldiers of today. By comparison, however, the armies of Russia and Europe had evolved tactics that would seem hopelessly unimaginative to a Mongol officer. Though they were just as dependent as the Mongols upon the cavalry, or knights, as the most potent element of the army, the Europeans had neglected the mobility of the horse in preference to a host of head-bashers, for that is what the knights had become.

This may seem an unlikely description of European knighthood during the age of chivalry. But chivalry was rather more a state of mind than a period of great military accomplishment. Thought to have emerged around the turn of the thirteenth century, the era of heroic European knighthood takes its name from the French word *chevalier*, meaning horseman or knight. Chivalry originally referred to the process of recruitment and training of knights, but it soon came to refer also to the curriculum of training that a young man underwent when learning to fight, hunt, serve his lord and govern his vassals. Ultimately it evolved into that courtly ideal in which the true knight was not only courageous and skilful in war but also generous, pious and courteous. He was a defender of the weak, often a poet or musician, and dedicated to serve some lady of his choice.

The other important aspect of the great flowering of European knighthood was the number of military–religious orders, such as the Knights Templar and Hospitallers and the Teutonic Knights. Their lives were bound by religious ritual, celibacy, vows of poverty, devotion to the Church and the restoration of the Holy Land to Christianity. In short, they were monks who were also professional soldiers. So the ideals of European knighthood were aesthetically quite sophisticated. But as an army they employed terribly crude methods.

The most important difference between European and Mongol horsemen was the development of armour. By the first half of the thirteenth century the northern European knight wore heavy steel mail that covered virtually every part of his body. Over his bare back he wore two separate linen undershirts, plus one that was padded called an aketon. On top of this he wore a long mail tunic, called a hauberk, that hung down to about mid-thigh. Underneath the skirt he wore thick woollen hose and then mail leggings that laced up to his crutch. Over his head he put on a linen hood called a coif, then a heavy mail coif, and on top of that the distinctive bucket-shaped helm. On top of his mail hauberk he wore a simple linen surplice or surcoat that bore the emblem of his order, or coat of arms. The entire outfit, including broadsword, lance and shield, weighed well over 45 kg (100 lb), and with the rider himself it was an enormous burden to place on the back of a horse. In consequence the European horseman was far less mobile than his Mongol counterpart. He could not manage delicate or intricate manoeuvres; the day was usually decided on the basis of a rather basic head-on clash. Once the charge had taken place, most knights dismounted (or were brought down) and combat continued with blade and shield in ferocious hand-to-hand combat. First lance, then sword and axe were wielded against shield and mail in very close fighting, for the essence of knightly combat was a vicious duel to the death with an opponent.

Behind the cavalry would be the infantry, usually a mob of untrained and badly equipped peasants who had been forced into the army to serve the knights and usually got cut down by the enemy's horsemen. The knights themselves were not trained officers, and their individual combat skills were of no use when leading men into battle. The size of their retinue was an indication of their wealth, not their ability, and there was no clear chain of command down from the commander-in-chief.

The only area in which the Europeans excelled was in the

construction of fortifications (the ultimate defence against horsemen) and in siege warfare. But nothing in the European experience had taught them any other form of warfare. Even during the Crusades most European armies were engaged either in the defence of fortified towns or in laying siege to them. Yet, in the event, these skills proved of little consequence when the encounter with the Mongols finally took place.

By contrast the Mongols were a tightly disciplined fighting machine, in which each soldier knew his place and his responsibilities. He did not fight as an individual, but as part of a massive formation that was led in and out of well-drilled manoeuvres. When the Mongol army advanced they approached as a series of long single ranks, made up of a number of units. The first two consisted of heavy cavalry, followed by three ranks of light cavalry. Out on either flank and up front were further, smaller, detachments of light cavalry.

An encounter with the enemy was rarely a surprise because there were scouts out in the field who were able to communicate with the main body through a system of flags and messengers. When the enemy had been engaged, either on the flank or in front, the outer detachments quickly became the vanguard and were soon reinforced from the rear. Once the enemy's position and disposition had been discovered, the three rear ranks of light cavalry would move up through the ranks of heavy cavalry and gallop up to the line. Rarely would any of these detachments engage the enemy in close combat. Instead they would detach small squadrons of some ten or twenty riders to gallop across the enemy's line, pouring in a deadly shower of arrows.

The Mongols also preferred to manoeuvre the enemy's ranks to exactly where they wanted them. They did this by deploying the *mangudai*, a corps of 'suicide troops' that charged straight at the enemy line. As they approached within range of the enemy, they would suddenly break ranks, turn and flee. The sight of the Mongols in flight was a temptation that most enemy commanders could not resist. With the enemy cavalry in hot pursuit, the *mangudai* galloped to a prearranged spot – where the rest of the army lay in wait. By the time the enemy had reached the killing ground, their ranks were already spread out and made easy targets. From 200 m (180 yards) away the Mongol archers would let loose a hail of arrows until the enemy's ranks had been shredded, and it was time for the heavy cavalry to be deployed. This was summoned by the sound of the *naqara*, a huge drum carried into battle on a camel. The heavy brigade would begin at a walk, gradually breaking into a trot – and then, on a signal from their commander and the appropriate beat of the drum, a terrifying shriek would rend the air, lances would be lowered and the horses spurred into a gallop.

But there was more to the Mongol army than cavalry. Following their long campaigns in China and Persia, they had acquired a great deal of expertise in siege warfare and artillery. From China they had taken up the rather lightweight Chinese siege machines and adapted them to the battlefield. There was a light catapult which could launch a 1 kg (2 lb) missile over 100 m (100 yards), and a heavier machine that would fire an 11 kg (25 lb) projectile over 150 m (150 yards). The advantage of the lighter device was that it could be dismantled and carried with the main body of the army. Both of these machines could be used either to launch rocks at walls or gates, or to hurl naphtha or burning tar into the enemy's lines. But their range was not very great, and it was not until the Mongols had adapted machines captured from the Khwarazm Shah's army that they really had a formidable artillery. The Islamic designs were adapted to the lighter Chinese models to create something similar to the European catapult or trebuchet, with a range of more than 350 m (350 yards). They also adopted the ballista, which looked like a giant crossbow and fired a heavy arrow over the same range as a catapult, but with far more accuracy. These were light enough to be carried on to the battlefield, and could be used to push back the enemy's front line, which was often set up before the army's advance.

But perhaps the most important war-making invention that the Mongols adopted was the Chinese discovery of explosives, which they probably first encountered during the wars against the Chin. They were used either in the form of rockets, which, fired *en masse* into the enemy's ranks, caused little damage but much alarm; or as grenades – clay vessels packed with explosives and hurled either by catapult or by hand. It might also have been possible for the Mongols to use cannon, as the Chinese had used them since the eleventh century, but there are no accounts of their doing so.

Virtually every new military invention was taken up and used by the Mongols and with these machines they quickly developed the modern principles of artillery. A prolonged battering from rocks, burning tar, grenades and fire bombs into the enemy lines would be followed up by an attack from mounted archers. These carefully rehearsed manoeuvres depended on great mobility and discipline. Although the bombardment was not nearly as accurate as the mounted archers, it spread fear and confusion amongst the enemy and made the archers' job much easier.

The image of the Mongol army on the march must have been an inspiring sight. Each *tumen* (roughly 10 000 men, but it was rarely up to that strength) was equipped with additional supplies of weapons and equipment carried on packhorses behind their ranks. Way off in the rear amongst the artillery and reserves was the main baggage train, made up of vast numbers of camels and wagons. Some of the wagons would be carrying supplies and equipment, but many would also be supporting mobile *gers*. In the midst of huge clouds of dust it would have seemed like a convoy of tents floating through the countryside; and behind it trotted flocks of sheep and goats that would provide food and drink for the thousands. Twentieth-century military historians have described the Mongol army as the precursor of the modern military force made up of tanks and artillery, and it is hardly surprising that two of the greatest exponents of tank warfare, Field Marshal Rommel and General George S. Patton, were both students and admirers of the legendary Subedei. The European armies of the thirteenth century were ill prepared for what was emerging out of the East.

In the winter of 1237, the great Mongol juggernaut crossed the frozen Volga and set out, according to Subedei's plan, to drive swiftly deep into the heart of Russia dividing the dozen principalities that ruled the region and reducing the risk of a united opposition. The prospect for that was at any rate slim. Over the previous thousand years the Russians had gallantly withstood invasions from Swedes, French and Germans; however, the Mongols now found a nation perilously unable to produce a joint concentration of military force – even under the most critical circumstances. Their internecine rivalry made Mongol victory that much more likely.

Nevertheless, the Mongols' objective was total conquest and with that in mind they were not prepared to take any risks. The most powerful of the Russian princes were Grand Duke Yuri of Suzdal and Prince Michael of Kiev. The plan was to drive between the two and isolate Suzdal and Novgorod from the lands of Chernigov and Kiev. Having crossed the Volga, the Mongols rode north through thick forests to disguise their arrival. A woman ambassador was despatched with two riders to confront the first obstacle, the principality of Riazan which lay on the eastern frontier of Russia.

The citizens were so surprised at the sight of a woman at their gates that they were certain she was a sorceress and refused to let her in. But she had probably been chosen because she spoke their language. At any rate, the two sides were forced to conduct their business by shouting at one another. The Mongol demand was for submission, a tax of 10 per cent and reinforcements for their army. The Riazan prince replied contemptuously that, if the Mongols were prepared to wait, once the inhabitants had all gone they could have everything.

Subedei had already decided to make an example of Riazan. The city was surrounded by thick forests from which the Mongols now cut timber to construct a stockade that encircled the city walls. From behind this, Subedei's artillery could fire upon the city with impunity. After five days of relentless bombardment the city was taken, then systematically razed to the ground. The prince and his family were all slaughtered – some impaled, others flayed alive. The entire population of young women was raped including all the nuns, while others were forced to watch. As was intended, a few survivors were allowed to escape so that the warning spread elsewhere.

From Riazan the Mongols moved on to Kolomna and then into Suzdalia, where they took the town of Moscow. After Moscow they turned back again and rode east towards the city of Vladimir, where they also employed the stockade technique. After Vladimir they divided their forces and criss-crossed the countryside, bringing terror from one town to another, in an attempt to flush out the main army of the Grand Duke of Suzdalia. By February they had located it and, without the hapless Grand Duke ever being aware, managed to surround the entire army before bringing down on it a deadly shower of arrows.

While Subedei was slaughtering Suzdalians, Batu had marched on to Novgorod. But his progress was delayed; he was caught out by the approaching thaw which turned the countryside into a maze of impassable marshes and the attack of Novgorod city was abandoned. Batu joined up with Subedei again and they rode south-west towards what is now the western Ukraine. Along the way they were held up at the city of Kozelsk. Here the defenders were prepared and had decided to ride out to meet the Mongols rather than find themselves besieged and bombarded as their neighbours had been. Their garrison managed to catch the Mongol vanguard unprepared and inflicted a great many losses. Unfortunately, this only meant that Batu and Subedei halted their march to the green pastures of the Ukraine and dealt with the upstart city of Kozelsk. The defenders' resistance was by all accounts heroic and lasted no less than seven weeks, but when it finally fell the population was put to the sword and there were no survivors. The slaughter was so great that the Mongols themselves renamed Kozelski the City of Woe.

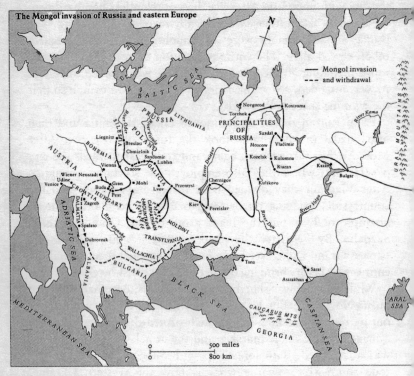

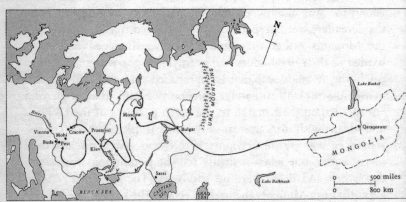

By now the army was sorely depleted and in need of rest. They continued south and finally made their encampment in the great breadbasket that is the Don Basin. Reinforcements were summoned from across the various vassal states, fresh horses were driven from Mongolia and for a whole year the army rested and rebuilt its strength. Small detachments were sent off on raiding expeditions to subdue the various nomadic tribes that inhabited southern Russia and north Caucasia – and in the process to gather in further recruits. This time it was the turn of the Circassians, Alans, Kipchaks and Cumans. Although most of the Cumans and Kipchaks were captured, their leader, Khan Kotian, managed to escape with a force of some 40 000 through the Carpathian passes into Hungary.

Nevertheless the Mongol raids were so successful, especially those conducted by Batu's young brother Berke, that they actually gathered up more slave-soldiers than they could employ. Many were sold off for gold, in particular to the new Sultan of Egypt who was keen to establish himself as a power within the Middle East. It was an ironic transaction, since it had tremendous repercussions for the Mongols in the years to come. These Turkic nomadic slave-soldiers soon became the most powerful element of the Sultan's army. By 1250 one of their leaders, Aybak, had married into the Egyptian royal line, created the Bahri regime and become the first Mamluk Sultan of Egypt. The Mamluks and the Mongols were destined to meet again and again throughout the second half of the century.

MONGOL RIVALRIES

By the spring of 1240 the Mongol army had reassembled and was ready to continue the campaign. However, before it got under way a rift developed amongst the Mongol princes that was to have consequences later. Although Batu had been given nominal command of a large and powerful army, it was made up of elements from every corner of the empire. With a vast array of resources and at the express will of the Great Khan, Batu's own personal realm was being expanded further and further west, adding very significantly to his own wealth and prestige. This situation apparently irritated a number of the princes in his entourage, but nothing was said until a trifling incident during a banquet to celebrate the recommencement of the campaign. It was the Mongol custom at a celebration for the most senior to have the privilege of drinking first. Batu, without thinking otherwise, lifted his glass and drank before any of the other princes. Although he was perfectly entitled to do so, he had shown not the slightest hint of offering to defer to any of his nephews or cousins, and some of the princes felt insulted by his presumption of superiority. They expected to be treated as equals.

Princes Guyuk and Buri, the son of Ogedei Khan and grandson of Chaghadai Khan respectively, were so incensed that they stormed out of the tent. Batu then complained to Ogedei Khan that he had been insulted in public by his cousins, who had since both returned to Qaraqorum – to the great embarrassment of the court. Ogedei was now placed in a difficult position: his son Guyuk was already the focus of a campaign to become the next Great Khan and, unless Batu's charges were answered, Guyuk's chances might be jeopardized. Rather than be seen to chastise his son and nephew in public, Ogedei referred to the Yasa for a solution. There they discovered that Genghis Khan had once declared that any transgressions committed in the midst of a campaign had to be dealt with by the commander in the field. Batu himself would have to decide on the punishment. The two princes set out on the ignominious return to the western steppe, where it seems that Batu was only too glad to see them take up their commands again. There is no record of any punishment. However, the incident was not forgotten and beneath the surface animosity continued to brew.

With the campaign under way again, it was the turn of the principalities of Chernigov and Kiev to face the Mongol onslaught. For the past year most of the Russian princes had had time either to ponder the magnitude of the Mongol catastrophe or to dread the prospect of it. Once again Mongol progress seemed relentless and the cities of Chernigov and Pereislav fell in quick succession, causing Prince Michael of Kiev to decide that resistance was useless. He and his entourage fled to Hungary and from there to Silesia in what is now western Poland. The defence of Kiev, the political and religious capital of Russia, was left to the governor, Dmitri. Batu had entrusted the offensive to his cousin Mongke, the eldest son of Tolui; Mongke, conscious of the city's great importance to the Russians, attempted to take it undamaged. Unfortunately, Dmitri refused to surrender and sealed the city's fate by murdering Mongke's envoys. Russian chroniclers recorded how 'clouds of Tartars' approached the town, and claimed that the thundering sound of wagons, bellowing cattle, the hooves of thousands of horses, war cries and so on were so loud that people within the city walls could barely make themselves heard without shouting.

The bombardment began once Batu had arrived to oversee his cousin's efforts. The Mongols concentrated their attack upon the so-called Polish or Western Gate, where the battlements were made of wood. It fell quickly, and within a matter of days the outer wall had been breached. Since Kiev had no citadel the final battle was fought at the church of the Virgin, which had been hurriedly fortified. But the work had been in vain as the entire structure collapsed under the weight of hundreds of terrified citizens who had climbed up on to the roof. Dmitri was captured but, because he had remained to defend his city while his lord had fled, the Mongols set him free. Again the destruction was appalling, and the only major structure to survive was the magnificent Cathedral of St Sophia. Six years after the disaster a European traveller described the once-splendid city: 'Many valuable artistic relics and architectural monuments were reduced to rubble.' Kiev, 'the mother of Russian cities', lost its place as the principal city of all Russia; henceforth the focus of political power would lie in the north-east.

From Kiev the Mongols marched west to the Russian border

into the foothills of the Carpathian Mountains. Along the way they over-ran the country of Galicia, taking the cities of Volhynia, Cherven, Lvov and Przemysl. It was near Przemysl, on what is now the Polish border, that Batu established his winter encampment – his springboard into Europe. The question was, where to attack and when? The logical approach would have been to wait until the spring and ensure the expedition had the best of the weather. Poland was the obvious target, because there was nothing but open country between it and the Mongols. But Batu and Subedei had a far more sophisticated campaign in mind, and in any case an issue had developed between Batu and the Hungarian king that required attention.

THE SWEEP INTO POLAND AND HUNGARY

A great many refugees had fled west into Poland and Hungary to escape the Mongol storm. Among the numerous princes and bishops that had taken flight were a large number of Cumans and Kipchaks, nomadic peoples that had escaped from southern Russia. The rest of their countrymen had made submission to the Mongols, but the Cuman leader Khan Kotian had fled with 40 000 soldiers and found safety in Hungary. The Hungarian King, Bela IV, had shown great promise as a leader since his accession in 1235, though in the months to come his reign came to resemble an exercise in survival. He already had one of the most powerful armies in Europe, made so by a first-rate cavalry that had no equal west of the Urals – provided, of course, he had the cooperation of all his nobles who commanded each detachment. In the past, during times of national threat, the Hungarian horsemen had successfully repelled nomadic raiders – in fact many of the Hungarian ranks comprised steppe horsemen who had drifted, or were pushed, west and settled in Hungary. So in 1240, when a large army of Cumans and Kipchaks suddenly appeared looking for asylum, Bela was only too glad to grant it – provided the heathen converted to Christianity, which they were only too glad to do. Forty thousand horsemen would make a significant difference to the King's army – a thought that had not escaped the Hungarian nobility, who strongly advised against it. They claimed, somewhat disingenuously, that by harbouring refugees fleeing from the Mongols the Hungarians might incur the wrath of the great Eastern invader. They were right, but their actions did nothing to improve the situation.

When the Mongols learned of the Cumans' exodus to Hungary, Batu wrote to Bela: 'I have heard that you have taken the Cumans, who are my subjects, under your protection. I command you to send them away, for by taking them away from me you have become my enemy. It is easier for them to flee than it is for your people. They live in tents, while you live in houses and cities. . . .' Along with his letter Batu had sent no fewer than thirty envoys to Hungary, not all of whom arrived; but those who did were murdered. In allowing this to happen Bela had sealed his country's fate. But in any case the Mongols had already decided upon an invasion, because the terrain was the best in which to pasture their herds before the push into central Europe.

As the Mongols settled down for the winter near Przemysl, Subedei unveiled his extraordinary plan for the conquest of eastern Europe. Having established that Hungary was the primary objective, Subedei proposed that the expedition be put into operation as soon as possible, in the very depth of winter. The ground would be frozen and hard under hoof; but, more to the point, a winter expedition would provide the element of surprise. The Mongol army stood at around 130 000, since 30 000 troops had been left in Russia to maintain control. It was by no means a massive force, and yet Subedei's plan called for it to be divided into separate detachments. Before the conquest of Hungary could be certain, Subedei wanted to deal with any threat of a counter-attack from any of Hungary's neighbours; so he planned an invasion at several points along a front of no less than 1000 km (600 miles). By modern standards it was an extraordinary idea, but for those times it was positively majestic.

Twenty thousand men were to be sent into Poland under the command of the princes Baidar and Kadan. Their function was to sweep through Poland and Lithuania and draw off any substantial force from the north that might threaten the campaign in Hungary. Meanwhile, the bulk of the army under Batu would cross the Carpathian Mountains into Hungary, seek out Bela's army and draw it into battle. While this happened, the 20 000 in Poland, having crushed any opposition there, were to sweep down into Hungary to support the rest of the army. The two forces would be at times 650–1000 km (400–600 miles) apart, and to ensure success they had to remain in constant communication. Chains of horsemen would have to be assigned across the front, and the entire manoeuvre would have to be choreographed down to the day.

Poland had been a divided nation since the death of King Boleslaw III a hundred years before. The King had split his kingdom among his four sons and their lands were broken up again by later generations until the country had fallen into civil war among no fewer than nine separate principalities. By 1240 the struggle was between four dukes: Conrad of Mazovia, Miecislaw of Oppeln, Henry the Pious of Silesia and Boleslaw the Chaste of Sandomir. The latter also ruled Cracow, was married to the daughter of King Bela of Hungary and saw himself as the rightful king of Poland. The Polish dukes were curiously unmoved by the events that had been taking place in Russia. Though they had received countless warnings from Russia and from Bela of Hungary, they seemed little concerned that the Mongols would ever cross the Vistula. Even Conrad, who had sheltered one of the Russian princes, Michael of Chernigov, seemed barely conscious of the terror encamped on his doorstep.

In Hungary, things were markedly different. King Bela was making desperate preparations for the expected onslaught. Since his accession Bela had been obsessed with redeeming the authority of the Crown and the character of the Hungarian court, left in a parlous state by his father. However, a series of quite ruthless reforms had led to his being isolated by the majority of barons, who saw Bela's policies as an attack upon their freedoms. Without their support, Bela had no hope of putting into the field an army at full strength; hence his enthusiasm for the presence of Cumans. But the sight of this uncivilized soldiery trampling the crops wherever they camped inflamed the barons even further. They demanded that the newcomers should be expelled; but Bela was determined to defend his realm and, if he had to employ nomads to help him do it, it was a price he was prepared to pay. He refused to submit to the barons' demands and urgently set about constructing defences at the various passes through the Carpathian Mountains.

By January 1241 the Mongols had begun to deploy their armies according to Subedei's plan. Princes Baidar and Kadan were marching with their 20 000 men towards Lublin and the Vistula. Meanwhile Batu and Subedei had broken up the remainder of the army into no fewer than three separate detachments. Batu led 40 000 men himself; Prince Shiban, his brother, led another 10 000 through a pass on the northern flank; while Subedei and Guyuk took 30 000 through passes on the southern flank.

Reports began arriving at Pest, the Hungarian capital, that the Mongols were on the move. Having inspected the defences Bela called a council of war, to which the Cumans and all the barons were summoned. By now the barons were prepared to gather their separate armies, but they were still not prepared to lead them into battle alongside the Cumans. In an attempt to placate the barons, Bela offered to hold the Cuman leaders hostage for their followers' loyalty. Still the barons were not satisfied, making even further demands for financial reward in return for the support of their armies.

The situation was becoming desperate by 10 March when Bela received reports that the Mongols had begun to attack the defences in the Carpathian passes. Four days later the commander in charge of the Carpathian defences arrived bloodied and exhausted, to report that the passes had fallen and that the Mongols were advancing steadily towards Hungarian territory.

Six hundred and fifty kilometres (400 miles) to the north, a separate drama was playing out. In Poland the inhabitants were taken completely by surprise. Baidar and Kadan had attacked the city of Lublin in early February and soon afterwards had crossed the frozen Vistula. Having done so, they laid waste Sandomir, destroying the Cistercian monastery. After Sandomir the two princes split their already meagre force and set off to spread alarm and destruction over as wide an area as possible. The purpose, according to Subedei's plan, was to draw off any of the northern armies that the Mongols expected would come to the aid of the Hungarians. In particular, the Mongols were concerned about the large number of Christian knights that had built garrisons along the Baltic coast.

The Order of the Teutonic Knights of St Mary's Hospital in Jerusalem had been formed in 1198. Though the order was originally established in the Middle East like the two older orders, the Knights Templar and Hospitallers, the Teutonic Knights soon moved to northern Europe where they established fortifications in Prussia and Lithuania, along the Baltic. Their strength grew as more and more German nobles flocked to the order, gradually turning their outposts into large independent estates loyal to the Pope. These Knights had developed relations with the Polish dukes, especially Conrad and Henry the Pious. The former, somewhat over-awed by the Teutonic Knights' growing power, had handed over one of his provinces; while the latter had allowed German immigrants to settle on his own territory in the hope that he might earn support for his own ambitions. The gradual intertwining of interests between the Teutonic Knights and the Polish dukes created the potential for a formidable alliance of northern European powers. Once the Mongol presence in Poland was confirmed, this alliance began to pull itself together. Duke Henry of Silesia was gathering together an army, enlisting support from the Teutonic Knights.

They had in turn enlisted support from a small number of Knights Templar and Hospitallers from France. Altogether they would number almost 30 000. In addition, King Wenceslas of Bohemia was riding to join them with an army nearly twice that size.

The Mongol force in Poland, now divided into two, had set about burning and pillaging wherever they went. Baidar's force, not having encountered any serious resistance, proceeded towards the Polish capital, Cracow. Duke Boleslaw the Chaste had established his garrison there and might have presented a formidable barrier to the Mongols had he not thrown caution to the wind. A vanguard of Baidar's force had ridden to within a few kilometres of the city walls. When they were sighted, Boleslaw's commander responded by putting together a large force and chasing after them. The Mongols turned and fled. When the invader failed to return in strength, Boleslaw commanded that they should be hunted down and forced into battle. The forces of Cracow and Sandomir marched forth in dogged pursuit – but it was a trap. Having lured virtually the entire army out into the countryside, Baidar ambushed them at a place called Chmielnik, about 18 km (11 miles) from Cracow. There they were cut to pieces under a shower of arrows.

When stragglers from the battle reached the city walls they raised the alarm. Boleslaw and his family packed all the treasures they could carry and set off for Hungary. Most of the citizenry followed their example and began leaving in droves. While the streets were filling with horses and carts loaded with belongings, a trumpeter had been at the balcony of St Mary's church, sounding the alarm. A small Mongol reconnaissance force arrived at the city gates even before the battle at Chmielnik was concluded. One of their number, realizing the alarm had already been raised, took an arrow from his quiver, laid the hilt against the string of the bow, drew back and took careful aim. Again and again the trumpeter blew his refrain, while beneath him the streets teemed with thousands of people doing their best to get out of each other's way. Suddenly the trumpeter's call was silenced, and when the crowds turned to look up at the steeple the horn was already somersaulting towards the ground. The trumpeter was staggering backwards, an arrow through his throat. When the main Mongol force reached the city walls, Baidar found the streets virtually empty. The city was burnt to the ground on 24 March.

In Hungary, Transylvania had already been ravaged, as had Moldavia and Wallachia. The princes from these regions never had the opportunity to shift their armies to Buda, so swiftly were they overwhelmed. While Guyuk continued the destruction throughout south-eastern Hungary, Subedei swept north around and behind them towards Tiza, where he rejoined the main force under Batu. They were reported to be covering no less than 100 km (60 miles) a day, heading south between Uzhgorod and Mukachevo. There they encountered a Hungarian army, sent forth to turn the Mongols back, and swept it aside on 12 March.

Three days later, the Mongols had reached the Danube and were in sight of Pest. Batu brought his column to a halt in sight of Bela's army, which was camped on the other side. Batu was in no mind to advance until he was joined by Shiban's contingent; and Subedei too was still some distance away. Communications between the various commanders were critical over the following weeks as they manoeuvred towards the big encounter that would decide the fate of the Hungarian invasion. Shiban was advancing at a terrific pace along the upper Vistula on his way to the rendezvous. On 17 March he took the town of Vac, further up the Danube. While Batu awaited Shiban's arrival he watched the Hungarians' camp fires a few miles off, but he saw no sign of Bela being tempted to take advantage of the Mongols' relative weakness.

There were growing problems within the Hungarian camp that prevented Bela from making a move. The barons were still intent upon ridding Hungary of the Cumans and were trying to foment an uprising against them. The Hungarians had captured a small Mongol reconnaissance column which had contained a number of Cuman horsemen – a perfectly likely occurrence, given that thousands of Cumans had been pressed into the Mongols' service. The Hungarian barons declared that the presence of Cumans within the Mongol ranks was proof that the refugees were actually fifth columnists. In the midst of the uproar the Cuman leaders were assassinated and the rest took flight, burning and killing everything in their path out of Hungary. Bela was now in dire straits, with the barons steadfastly refusing to unite with him unless it was on their terms.

It would seem that the Mongols knew little of the chaos within the enemy camp – otherwise they might have tried to take advantage of it. Batu knew that the Hungarians would be the hardest challenge of the entire campaign and he was not about to proceed until he was certain of victory. The weeks passed and eventually Shiban's columns arrived, but instead of proceeding to advance upon the Hungarian camp they packed away their *gers* and began to withdraw.

When news arrived at Pest that the Mongols were retreating, the barons, sensing that victory was now possible, threw their support behind the King. On 7 April, the Hungarians marched out from their positions. Batu moved his army eastward, drawing the Hungarians after them. Subedei, although some distance away, shadowed Batu's manoeuvre so as to confirm the impression that the Mongols were withdrawing. A day later they drew to a halt at a spot they had already chosen near where the Hernad River flows into the Sajo. Nearby, on the Mohi plains, Bela drew up his army of nearly 100 000 and made camp. Even without the Cumans he still outnumbered the invaders by 20 000. Mongol scouts reported that Bela was camped in an area far too small for the size of his army. He had also encircled them with a ring of wagons and tents, making it impossible for them to escape in the event of an attack. Although the Hungarians were formidable horsemen, their commander was somewhat inept.

In the meantime, the Mongols under Kadan and Baidar rode deeper into Poland, crossing the Oder River before the end of March. Their scouts had located Duke Henry's army some days' march to the west. On their way, Kadan and Baidar took the town of Breslau and burned it to the ground. The inhabitants had taken to the citadel, but the Mongols were in too much of a hurry and left the citizens unmolested. Duke Henry's army outnumbered the Mongols by 10 000; and a few days' march away was another army of some 50 000, belonging to Henry's brother-in-law King Wenceslas of Bohemia. Among Duke Henry's 30 000 was a large contingent of Teutonic Knights, plus small numbers of Knights Templar and Hospitallers from France, some of the most formidable contingents in northern Europe. Though the knights made a dramatic sight, with pennants flying and helms glinting in the sunlight, most of the army was made up of infantry, dragooned from the local peasantry and armed with little more than pitchforks and scythes. It was to delay forces such as these that Kadan and Baidar had been sent into Poland.

DESTRUCTION OF THE EUROPEAN KNIGHTS

On 9 April, the two armies met at a place called Liegnitz (now Legnica), in western Poland. Having given each other a good sight of their respective ranks, the following day the Mongols began their well-rehearsed manoeuvre. A thinly armed vanguard rode up to the Europeans, then turned and began to gallop away from the Polish archers. Duke Henry fell into the trap and sent his cavalry, the flower of European chivalry, into a suicidal charge at the Mongol lines. Under the weight of their armour, lances and helms, the Europeans galloped after the fleeing vanguard.

Once the cavalry was separated from the infantry, the Mongols let loose a smokescreen that cut the two units off from each other. Then the cavalry suddenly found themselves surrounded by Mongol archers who had been lying in wait. The Knights Templar, Hospitallers and Teutonic Knights swirled round and round in search of the enemy so that they could engage them. If they saw anything of the Mongols through the smoke they would probably have been more than 100 m (100 yards) away, pouring a lethal shower of arrows from the brow of a hill. Meanwhile, another detachment of Mongols had moved round in an arc and come upon the infantry standing unprotected in the middle of nowhere. Neither of the two forces could see what was happening to the other, but the results were identical. The Mongols, able to stand back from their victims, fired volley upon volley into the hapless knightly ranks. Mail provided an effective defence against sword cuts, but was utterly useless against arrows and spear thrusts.

The slaughter continued until it was time to send in the heavy cavalry. When Mongol heavy cavalry met European knights in hand-to-hand combat it was a ferocious and bloody affair, and the Mongols took heavy casualties. But by then the outcome had already been decided and Liegnitz was a complete disaster for the Europeans. Duke Henry was killed trying to escape: his body was decapitated and mutilated almost beyond recognition. To taunt the inhabitants, the Mongols carried his head round the city walls on the end of a Mongol spear. Again the invaders were in no mood to lay siege and were content with the slaughter they had inflicted on the battlefield. To prove the scale of their success, Kadan and Baidar ordered that an ear be cut off every victim. They sent nine sacks of ears as a tribute to Batu.

After Liegnitz, the Mongols were expected to push further west; instead they turned south. When King Wenceslas heard the news of Liegnitz he headed back towards Bohemia for reinforcements. The Mongols, despite having been badly mauled, chased his army most of the way. But rather than risk another encounter with a large army, the Mongols broke up their force into small raiding parties and set about terrorizing the countryside. As they dashed from village to town, causing mayhem and destruction, the Poles could only conclude that they had been completely over-run by a massive host. The Mongols seemed to be everywhere and nowhere with no clear objective. But that was not the case at all; their objective was Hungary.

GATEWAY TO THE ATLANTIC

On 10 April, on the banks of the River Sajo, Batu's army had received word of the battle at Liegnitz. That night, it began its attack. Batu and his brother Shiban moved forward, thinking to cross the river and engage Bela from the front, while Subedei took his contingent north in search of a ford so that they could outflank the Hungarians and attack from behind. Unfortunately they found no crossing and were delayed while his engineers built a bridge between the villages of Girines and Nady Czeks. Before light, Batu's force approached a stone bridge that led across the Sajo and straight to Bela's army on the far side. The bridge was too narrow to let more than a few horsemen across at a time, making it impossible to advance in any strength. It looked as though the Hungarians could hold the bridge indefinitely. Then Batu brought up a battery of seven catapults and began to hurl curious-looking missiles across at the Hungarians, 'to the accompaniment of thunderous noises and flashes of fire'. The Hungarians drew back from the explosives, allowing the Mongols to cross the bridge in sufficient numbers. Every so often the catapults were brought up closer, sending the Hungarians back further and allowing more Mongols across. It is known in modern artillery tactics as a 'rolling barrage'.

Eventually, Batu and his army got themselves on to the opposite side of the river, but they were no longer fighting a typical Mongol encounter. Batu's force stood at no more than 40 000, while the Hungarians numbered 100 000, and it was beginning to look as though the sheer weight of numbers would eventually take its toll. The Hungarians mounted one mass charge after another against the Mongol lines, but each time they were beaten back by fire bombs and hails of arrows. Nevertheless, for the finest cavalry in Europe it was beginning to look as though victory would be only a matter of time. Subedei's force was long overdue and Batu's situation was becoming desperate. The only manoeuvre Batu could employ was to try and turn the Hungarians' flank; so like a rugby scrum the

Mongols wheeled round, forcing the Hungarians to turn with them. In doing so Batu succeeded in turning the Hungarians' back to Subedei's approach – when and if it arrived. After two hours of debilitating attacks, Batu suddenly ordered his men to fall back against the river and spread out into a single rank. As the puzzled Hungarians watched, awaiting the next opportunity to charge, the Mongol ranks fanned out into a massive semi-circle that appeared to embrace the entire Hungarian army. Behind the Hungarians, Subedei and his army had just arrived on the scene and were doing precisely the same thing. Only when it was too late did the Hungarians realize they were about to be surrounded; but, more to the point, they had suddenly lost the advantage. They were minutes from being encircled by a deadly ring of mounted archers who were about to loose their arrows. It was like the conclusion of a hunt.

Doggedly, the Hungarians closed ranks, spurred their horses and charged out of the circle, making their way straight for their fortified camp. Worried that his soldiers might not be up to a chase, Batu signalled to call off the attack. But Subedei was made of sterner stuff. He quickly roused the army, led them in hot pursuit and soon had the camp surrounded. When he eventually had his artillery in place he sent a concentrated barrage of exploding missiles into their tents and wagons until the camp was in ruins. Those left standing were finally cut to pieces by the heavy cavalry.

A small group of Hungarians succeeded in escaping the attack, and fled in a thin column through a gorge back towards Pest. But they had fallen into another trap. Mongol light cavalry pursued them on either side, cutting them down with lethally accurate archery. The road to Pest was described as having been littered with bodies, 'like stones in a quarry'. The Hungarian dead were estimated at 60 000. Bela managed to outride his hunters, swim the Sajo and scramble into one of the forests on the other side where he found somewhere to hide. Meanwhile the Mongols reached Pest and put it to the torch. Then they rode along the Danube, making threatening lunges at Buda on the other bank. It had been a long day, and at times an uncertain one; but at the end of 10 April 1241 an army that had travelled nearly 10 000 km (6000 miles) from the eastern steppes of Asia was now in complete command of the Hungarian plain, and no power between it and the Atlantic Ocean seemed able to stand in their way.

5

FROM PRESTER JOHN TO ARMAGEDDON

CULTURAL STRANGERS

More than 700 years after the event it is still difficult fully to appreciate the massive geographical scale upon which the Mongols had fought their campaign; how, with such extraordinary precision, they co-ordinated so many separate army corps, developed and maintained long and complicated supply lines, operated communications systems over hundreds of kilometres, and then fought with courage and imagination against an enemy defending its own territory. The Asian armies – Mongol, Chinese and Persian – were unquestionably the masters of the art of war during the medieval period. Europe could barely comprehend what had happened, and was left in thrall as to what would follow.

Europe's first military encounter with the Mongols had been no more one-sided than that of the armies of China and Persia during the first half of the thirteenth century. However, the psychological impact was in every sense far more traumatic and long-lasting. Civilizations in both China and Persia had a long history of encounters with nomadic armies, whereas Europe had lived in blissful ignorance of the rest of Asia and nothing had prepared them for the Mongols. Europe in the thirteenth century was completely ignorant of the lands to the east of the Urals. Although there had been trade with the East dating back to the pre-Christian era, this had always been conducted through merchants who plied between the Latin world and China without ever enlightening the one about the other.

The best-known product from the East was of course silk, which the Romans were convinced had been combed from the leaves of trees. India was a country that was only vaguely known, and even this chiefly because of Alexander's legendary march into the great subcontinent and the many weird and wonderful tales that had been spun about his exploits there. These tales, probably invented by merchants to enhance the exotic quality of their wares, were taken up by historians and were perpetuated right up until the time of Marco Polo (1256–1323). India, which was then synonymous with most of what we call Asia, became a land occupied by men with the head of a dog (Cynocephali), or a single foot (Monopodes), or whose feet pointed backwards with their heels facing the front (Antipodes). There were creatures with neither neck nor head, but with a face set into the middle of their chest. There were wild hunters who lived on the mere smell of flesh. And there were curious pygmies who were supposed to live a thousand years, Satyrs, Amazons, Brahmans and Gymnosophists, enchanted mountains, unicorns, griffins and ants that dug for gold. It was also the land of rare jewels, pearls, aromatic woods and spices.

All these fantastic creatures became a feature in medieval art and literature, and their likenesses were carved in perpetuity on the exteriors of Gothic churches. We know them today as gargoyles, but 700 years ago they were imaginative stone likenesses of the inhabitants of the East.

Europeans were not unique in depicting such fantastic creations; the Chinese had a remarkably similar pantheon of creatures which they believed inhabited the unknown West. These included the creatures with the head of a dog, the single-footed beings and the headless beasts with their faces in their chests. The Chinese also had fanciful notions about the origins of cotton, a commodity they imported from western Asia, and which was supposedly clipped from the fleece of 'water sheep'.

The reasons why these curious fantasies survived for so long was the complete lack of cultural exchange between the two hemispheres. The Roman empire had never extended further than the River Euphrates, beyond which were fierce nomadic horsemen, rugged mountains and deserts – a realm the Romans failed to penetrate. It is claimed that the Chinese made a number of attempts to contact the civilizations in the West, though there is a record of only one: Kan Ying, an envoy despatched in AD 97. He reached the Persian Gulf but was warned by his Arab hosts, keen to maintain their privileged position as international go-betweens, that the rest of his voyage would take two years and that most who ventured into those uncharted lands perished. Kan Ying turned back. By the seventh and eighth centuries, with the rise of Islamic power in the Middle East, both land and sea routes had fallen under the control of the Muslims. Islam's inevitable confrontation with the Christian West led to Europe becoming even more isolated; though trade in silks and spices continued at higher and higher prices through Arab middlemen.

It was not just ignorance that sustained ideas of a land populated with monsters and fantastic beings; they were also given credence by the writings of early Christian scholars. St Augustine had written about the existence of monsters, declaring their creation to have been an important part of God's great plan, so that man would not be perplexed by the birth of the malformed or insane. Under the authority of Christian teaching the regions to the east also became associated with certain biblical localities, like Terrestrial Paradise and the land inhabited by Gog and Magog – the latter being the land beyond Alexander's Gate (the Derbent Pass in the Caucasus Mountains) where Alexander is said to have imprisoned the two foul giants, Gog and Magog. According to the Book of Revelation, they would be released by Satan to destroy Jerusalem and bring destruction upon the world. It is hardly surprising, therefore, that contemporary chroniclers, reporting the Mongol attacks, laced their accounts with flesh-devouring monsters, and that congregations were told to expect the imminent apocalypse. The tall tales of travelling merchants became part of the Christian view of the real world.

But there was another Christian fantasy, a far more recent one, that both disarmed and confused European monarchs about the origins and purpose of the invader. This had its origin in the story of the Magi – the three wise men from the East invested with the dignity of kings, as described by St Matthew. This was supported by stories which claimed that St Thomas had journeyed to India, where he had preached the gospel, met the Magi and baptized them. Out of these stories developed the conviction that, somewhere in the vast uncharted Orient, ruled a number of Christian kings. Add to this rich brew the great literary tradition that developed around the heroic exploits in India of Alexander, who had become an important figure in the world of chivalry and courtly love, and you soon have a medieval picture of Asia as a land inhabited by grotesques, and in some part of which there reigned heroic Christian kings who performed romantic deeds.

THE LEGEND OF PRESTER JOHN

By the eleventh century, with Europe locked in a war with the Islamic world over the possession of the Holy Land, these centuries-old tales were given some contemporary relevance with the creation of the extraordinary character of Prester John, or John the Presbyter, the legendary Christian king of the Orient who was bound to come to the aid of Christendom in its hour of need. With the Crusades going badly, that hour was at hand. The legend has its origins in a visit to Rome in 1122 by a prelate named John. He claimed to have come from India and was possibly from a Christian community on the Malabar coast, part of a flourishing community of eastern Christians whom the Roman church referred to as Nestorians. Since Rome had severed relations with the Nestorians, and with virtually all the Christian communities east of Constantinople, Europe lost a golden opportunity to develop contacts with Asian civilizations and expand its knowledge of the world. Rome simply had no idea just how much Christianity had flourished in the East.

In the early sixth century the Nestorians moved from a strong base in Persia into west Turkistan, and from there progressively east to China. At the beginning of the eleventh century there were Christians even among the Mongol tribes, and by the height of the Mongol empire Christianity was expanding throughout Asia.

Given that contacts between Rome and the eastern Christians had been extremely rare, a visit of a prelate from the East was guaranteed a fascinated audience. Accounts claim that he lectured the Roman cardinals about life in India and the extraordinary miracles that regularly occurred in that kingdom during the great Christian festivals. Historians today believe that the prelate was probably an impostor, yet at the time of his visit the stories he told seemed plausible to medieval scholars because they appeared to confirm St Matthew's account of the Magi; that is, that there existed an Eastern kingdom ruled by the descendants of the three wise kings who had visited the holy family in Bethlehem.

Twenty years later, when the memory of the prelate's visit was still relatively fresh, a bishop in Syria reported the existence of a powerful Eastern king named Prester John who had inflicted a heavy defeat upon the Muslims. He also reported that this monarch, who was descended from the Magi, had decided to come to the aid of the crusaders in Jerusalem, in emulation of his illustrious ancestors, but had been prevented from doing so because of the untimely flooding of the River Tigris. It is now · thought that the report was a garbled account of the wars fought against the Muslim rulers of Persia by the Qara Khitai empire in the twelfth century. So here we have a suffusion of the best medieval legends – a wise king with impeccable antecedents who was also heroic and therefore in the best traditions of Alexander. Whatever the claims for Prester John's ancestry, the mere fact that he was reportedly killing Muslims virtually guaranteed his Christian credentials.

Then, in 1165, a letter purporting to be from Prester John began circulating in Europe. From here on this character is clearly exploited for political reasons. The letter came in many forms, addressed to many different European notables: the Byzantine Emperor Manuel I Comnenus, the Pope, the Holy Roman Emperor and other monarchs. In his letter Prester John claimed to rule over a vast kingdom that extended from the tower of Babel to where the sun rises. He declared his intention to rescue Jerusalem from the Muslims, defeat the enemies of Christ and visit the Holy Sepulchre. He then went on to catalogue his treasures and the marvels of his kingdom. The letter was, of course, a complete fabrication, though it proved an enormous fillip for the crusading movement – which was probably the author's intention.

The figure of Prester John gained further verisimilitude when in 1177 the Pope despatched an envoy to seek him out in the lands east of the tower of Babel. Although the envoy disappeared, the crusading movement had received the necessary boost. However, for thirty years the next three Crusades met with one disaster after another until enthusiasm began to waver again. In 1217, with remarkably good timing, during the preparations for yet another Crusade, fresh news began to circulate about the legendary Prester John and other 'Christian kings living in the Orient'. The Bishop of Acre, conducting a vigorous propaganda campaign for what would be the Fifth Crusade, had decided to employ the legend in many of his letters to the Latin settlers in the Levant. The Bishop claimed that Prester John and his Oriental colleagues had heard that a new Crusade was imminent and were about to set forth to help sweep the Saracens from the Holy Land.

Three years later, these claims were given further credence when a somewhat apocryphal document appeared called the 'Report on King David'; a description of the victorious advance into Persia of 'King David, Christian King of India, sent by the

Lord to crush the heathen and destroy Mahomet's teaching'. There are many accounts of this letter; some of them equate King David with Prester John himself, while others claim he was his son or grandson. Again the letter affirmed prophecies that Prester John's arrival was imminent. It is at this point that Christian propaganda becomes entwined with historical fact, for what undoubtedly provided the basis for this report was Genghis Khan's breathtaking campaign against the Khwarazm Shah. The Church had taken a harbinger of disaster and transformed it into a prophecy of salvation.

The irony couldn't have been more bitter. During the following months, as further reports arrived, the Pope announced repeatedly the victorious progress of 'King David' through Persia and predicted the forthcoming liberation of the Holy Land. Even when this failed to occur, it did not diminish faith in the existence of Prester John. In 1223, when Subedei's army was engaged in the great raid through Georgia and the Russian states, the King of Hungary sent a letter to the Pope claiming that 'a certain King David or, as he is more usually called, Prester John' had recently entered Russia with a vast army and slaughtered 200 000 people. This terrible work was explained at first as the great Christian King setting upon the heretical Georgians, followers of the Greek Orthodox Church, with the same vigour as he had attacked the Islamic Persians. So firm was the belief in this character that, even when Queen Rusudan of Georgia sent an accurate account of the Mongol armies, it was dismissed in preference to the semi-fictitious reports of 'King David'.

Nevertheless, given the growing contradictions from various sources, there is no doubt that the Christian West was becoming a little alarmed and confused, especially by accounts of the most incredible amount of slaughter. Clearly Prester John was no longer quite the pious Christian so beloved of those early prophets, despite his hatred of the Muslims. As Europe pondered these contradictory reports, the great Novgorod Chronicler recorded a more accurate account of the 'Great Raid' through the

Russian principalities: 'They turned back from the River Dnieper and we know not whence they came, nor where they hid themselves again; God knows whence he fetched them against us.' Their sudden disappearance left a great many questions unanswered, but these preoccupations disappeared as Europe soon became more deeply concerned with its own internal problems.

CONFLICT BETWEEN CHURCH AND STATE

The single most important issue that exercised most of the courts during the 1230s was the growing enmity between the Pope and the Holy Roman Emperor. It was a conflict that had its origins in the Investiture Conference of the eleventh century, when Pope Gregory VII formulated the doctrine that the Church exerted universal rule over the whole of Christendom and over all Christian kings and emperors. It was a split between the successors of St Peter and Charlemagne that turned from a political issue into open warfare under the Emperor Frederick II. He was an extraordinary figure, sometimes described as the *enfant terrible* of medieval Europe. He had been educated at the Norman court at Palermo in Sicily, where he had absorbed the *mores* of an exotic society that combined the sternness of the Norman court with heavy influences from the Middle East. Frederick combined brilliant intelligence with a taste for the cruel, the sensual and the strange. He had a deep love of Arab culture and great sympathy for Islam. His failure to take part in the Fifth Crusade almost certainly caused its failure, for which he was excommunicated by the new Pope in 1227. In spite of that he sailed to Palestine the following year, in the wake of the Sixth Crusade, and through some stunning diplomatic moves secured control of Jerusalem, Nazareth, Bethlehem and the territory between Jerusalem and Acre without spilling a single drop of blood.

Frederick's intimate knowledge of Middle Eastern politics

enabled him to conduct negotiations with the Sultan of Egypt at the best possible time. Following the destruction of his father's empire, Jalal al-Din had escaped to India from where he emerged in 1223 to reconquer those lands. His campaign had been short-lived, following the Mongols' return to reaffirm their control. Nevertheless, during a brief period in 1225 Jalal al-Din was proving a serious threat to the current rulers of the Muslim world, having won control of western Persia and Azerbaijan, invaded Georgia and launched an attack on Baghdad. In other words, Frederick had caught the Sultan at a bad moment and was able to exact a heavy price for peace with the Europeans. But although the Sixth Crusade had been a success, and as a result Frederick was absolved of his sins and taken back into the Church, the rift between Church and Empire had been too deep to be easily resolved. Hostilities had broken out again by the late 1230s, dividing Europe into two separate camps just at the time when Ogedei Khan had set in motion the conquest of Europe.

INTELLIGENCE IGNORED

When Batu's army first rode into Russia, Europe showed very little interest. Russia's remoteness, the tenuous relationships between the various principalities and her adherence to the Eastern Church meant that she had remained somewhat estranged from the rest of Europe. The flight of the various Russian princes alerted few to the true nature of the approaching threat, but among those taking note was the Hungarian King, Bela IV. It had been Bela's practice to send out Christian missionaries to try to convert the various nomadic tribes in the western steppe and perhaps even entreat them to accept him as their king. In 1237 he sent forth the most famous of these missionaries, the Dominican Friar Julian, to eastern Russia with instructions to gather information on the invader from the East. The monk's journey was interrupted by the Mongol advance;

nevertheless he returned with a great deal of intelligence, much of it extremely accurate.

Julian produced a detailed account of how the Mongol armies relied upon great mobility, and of their strategy for conquering fortified towns. He claimed that the Mongol invasion had its origins in a conflict between two of their chieftains, one of whom is supposedly the young Genghis Khan and the other an older and more powerful figure who had refused the younger man permission to marry his daughter. This story had been in circulation for some time and in fact survived long after the European invasion, to be picked up again and again by Western travellers in the years to come. In more detailed versions the 'powerful chieftain' is identified as Prester John of India, or his son King David, and is apparently killed by Genghis Khan in the ensuing conflict over the issue of the daughter. At a Papal Council held in Lyons in 1245, a version of this story was presented in a report containing a general account of the Mongols. In this version, 'the King of the Tartars' (Genghis) is supposed to have killed Prester John and then married his daughter, and their son was presumed to have been the present 'king'. The story is probably based upon accounts of the civil wars amongst the steppe tribes during Genghis's rise to power; the Prester John figure is Wang Khan, chief of the Kereyids and an eastern Christian or Nestorian, who was defeated by Genghis in 1203 and whose niece the Great Khan later married.

Julian's report managed to keep dimly alive the spirit of Prester John. On the one hand, according to the account, Genghis Khan was supposed to have killed Prester John, and so then destroyed Christendom's great saviour; yet on the other hand the Khan, Genghis's son, had maintained the Prester John bloodline. European chroniclers were still clutching at stories of saviours, even when the bulk of Julian's intelligence formed alarming news for King Bela. The Mongols' declared ambition, Julian reported, was nothing less than world domination, with Rome as their ultimate goal. It is thought that Julian was the first European writer to use the term 'Tartari' to identify the

Mongols, a name he had probably picked up from the Cumans and which was eventually taken up by Westerners because of its similarity to the Latin word Tartarus, meaning hell. In the accounts that appeared a little after the Mongol invasion, they are depicted as devils released from hell.

Julian also brought back with him the message from Batu demanding that Bela hand over the Cumans to whom he had granted asylum, which was, in reality, a demand for the Hungarian King's unconditional surrender. Although Julian's report was quite widely disseminated, it is remarkable how little notice seems to have been paid to its contents by other monarchs. It seems that Frederick, the Holy Roman Emperor, even received a specific order of submission from Batu, which was accompanied by an offer that if he agreed, then he, Frederick, would be rewarded with some high office under Batu's rule. Frederick is reported to have replied, somewhat contemptuously, that as falconry was one of his favourite sports, perhaps he might be suited to the role of the Khan's chief falconer. The distinct impression is that Frederick would not have been too distressed about an invasion from the East, and that it was certainly not something he would have been interested in trying to prevent. The Pope too had received accounts of Julian's report, but he was too involved in his dispute with Frederick and paid very little attention to the threat, or to requests for help from Queen Rusudan of Georgia, or later on from Catholic Poland and Hungary. The image of Europe at this stage is of a land cocooned within the limits of its own imagination, and heedless of reliable evidence that disaster approached. Even when the reports clearly identified the approaching armies as having caused unimaginable death and destruction, there still persists a vestige of hope in some tenuous link with Prester John.

In 1238 Europe again received word of the Mongols, this time from a most unlikely source. The chronicler Matthew Paris gives us this account:

About this time, special ambassadors were sent by the

Saracens, chiefly on behalf of the Old Man of the Mountain, to the French King, telling him that a monstrous and
inhuman race of men had burst forth from the northern
mountains, and had taken possession of the extensive, rich
lands of the east; that they had depopulated Hungary
Major [the region between the Volga and the Urals], and
had sent threatening letters, with dreadful emissaries; the
chief of which declared that he was the messenger of God
on high, sent to subdue the nations who rebelled against
him. . . . This powerful and noble Saracen messenger, who
had come to the French King, was sent on behalf of the
whole of the people of the East, to tell them these things;
and he asked assistance from the Western nations, the
better to be able to repress the fury of the Tartars: and he
also sent a Saracen messenger to the King of England
[Henry III], to tell these events and to say that if they
themselves could not withstand the attacks of such people,
nothing remained to prevent their devastating the countries
of the West.

The 'Old Man of the Mountain' was Hasan-i Sabbah, the chief
of the Ismailis or Assassins, an Islamic Shia sect which had its
headquarters in northern Persia and a branch in Syria. They had
been at war with the Sunni Muslim leaders for some time, but
had also fought against the crusaders. The reason behind their
unexpected appeal to the West was the Mongol campaign under
Chormaghun, which had been sent to pursue Jalal al-Din and
reconquer Persia and the Caucasus. The Assassins, having been
cast out as heretics, could expect no help from other Muslims.
However, in view of the fact that another Mongol army was
attacking Christian countries to the north, the Assassins naïvely
assumed that Westerners might join with them in common cause
against the Eastern threat.

Once again it was an opportunity for Europe to gain hard
information about the new emergent Eastern power; however,
the approach of the 'Saracens' was greeted with utter contempt.

The Bishop of Winchester, Peter des Roches, able to see the world divided into just two camps, replied: 'Let us leave these dogs to devour one another, that they might be consumed, and perish; and we, when we proceed against the enemies of Christ who remain, will slay them, and cleanse the earth, so that all the world will be subject to the one Catholic Church, and there will be one shepherd and one fold.'

But not all of Europe was unmoved by the accounts of slaughter that were filtering through. One of the most fascinating stories connected with the Mongol invasion, also recorded by Matthew Paris, was of the fate of the Yarmouth herring industry. As the Mongols were making their approach on Novgorod, during the winter of 1237–8, word of the destruction they were causing penetrated a number of fishing communities in northern Europe.

> The inhabitants of Gothland and Friesland [the Baltic Islands and the Netherlands], dreading their attacks, did not, as was their custom, come to Yarmouth, in England, at the time of the herring fisheries, at which place their ships usually loaded; and owing to this, herrings in that year were considered of no value, on account of their abundance, and about forty or fifty, although very good, were sold for one piece of silver, even in places at a great distance from the sea.

It would seem that ordinary folk in northern Europe had received abundant warning from the communities in Russia, and although their response was typically superstitious, it would also seem that their lords and masters were still untroubled by the same intelligence.

Having devastated the northern Russian principalities, Batu rested his forces in the lower Don throughout 1239 and the following year moved on Kiev. As has been seen, during the winter of 1240–41 Batu's army gathered near Przemysl, ready to launch out upon Europe. Within three months the political map of Europe had been torn in half. The disasters at Liegnitz in

Poland and Mohi in Hungary, fought within two days of each other, had transformed the European perception of the Mongol threat. The last remnants of hope that these invaders might somehow be the armies of Prester John, or of his descendants, were finally and utterly extinguished. With the sudden and absolute destruction of two great Christian kingdoms, Europe was propelled from a state of naïve hope into an abyss of utter incomprehension.

PANIC AND CHAOS IN EUROPE

Within a week of the battle at Liegnitz, the Mongol army in Poland had rejoined the main force in Hungary which then moved on to secure the eastern half of the country, thus making it impossible for King Bela to muster a new army and renew the struggle. The invaders moved swiftly to gather up the reins of power and encourage the local people to return to their farms and trades. Though there was a great deal of looting and Pest itself was almost stripped to the bone, Batu's army did not engage in the wholesale slaughter and rape of the countryside that had been the hallmark of his grandfather's campaign in Khwarazmia. Nevertheless, Hungary was in a parlous state. Bela and his family had taken flight through the Carpathian Mountains on their way to Austria. While staying overnight at the monastery at Thurocz the Hungarian King encountered another fugitive, Boleslaw the Chaste, who was heading south from Poland. With Hungary abandoned and still reeling, Boleslaw's domain was at the mercy of the fates.

The population was no less bewildered by the storm that seemed to have swept across their country, and for a long time the Poles simply could not comprehend what had happened nor why. This state of confusion was made worse by the crude and fanciful reports that were being spread in the aftermath. The Mongols' mobility was something that Polish chroniclers never understood; the only way they could explain the speed and vast distances the enemy covered was to over-estimate the size of the Mongol army by some five times. The staggering defeat at Liegnitz was explained by the heathens' vile use of some foul-smelling gas that incapacitated their soldiers. The Mongols' sudden departure from Poland was explained not by the events in Hungary, but by the notion that Polish armies had finally beaten them off. Polish chroniclers perpetuated these fallacies long afterwards, and Polish histories still include fictitious accounts of gallant victories fought and won against the invader. Even the battle of Liegnitz itself is regarded in some central European histories as a Pyrrhic victory for the Europeans.

During the second half of 1241 Europe was on the verge of chaos. The chronicler Vincent of Beauvais vividly described the atmosphere when he claimed that the Mongols had let loose a series of evil spirits to destroy their enemies: 'the spirit of fear, the spirit of mistrust and the spirit of discord'. Having at first been stunned into complete inactivity, an aging and nervous Pope Gregory finally gathered sufficient presence of mind to declare a Crusade against the Mongols. In an uncharacteristic show of solidarity the Holy Roman Emperor, Frederick II, announced he would lead it. He despatched letters to all the courts of Europe, calling for their support: '. . . to Germany ardent in war, to France who nurses in her bosom an undaunted soldiery, to warlike Spain, to savage Ireland and to frozen Norway'. The response was varied. In numerous northern European castles, great caches of arms were stockpiled in preparation for the great united counter-attack. However, at the other extreme the Duke of Austria, whose borders ran with Hungary's, seemed supremely indifferent to the Mongol menace. He was more preoccupied with taking advantage of Hungary's plight, having demanded an enormous indemnity from Bela in return for granting him and his family protection. The Duke also took the opportunity to annex three Hungarian departments that lay against his borders. During their march into Hungary, the Austrians came face to face with Mongol reconnaissance patrols that were probing unexplored territory. One of these was repulsed by the Austrians; from this evidence the Duke was convinced that the Mongol threat had been greatly exaggerated, and he boasted to those who would listen how his soldiers had killed hundreds of Mongols in hand-to-hand combat. The Duke's accounts did little to pacify the alarmists.

Elsewhere in Europe there was little evidence of any united crusade, and there were other ambitious monarchs who, like the Duke of Austria, tried to take advantage of the chaos wrought by the invaders. In Russia the Swedes, allied with contingents of the Teutonic Knights, landed at Neva in an attempt to take Novgorod. They were beaten off by the legendary Alexander Nevsky, who, though subsequently acclaimed as a Russian national hero, was nevertheless one of Batu's vassal princes. Frederick II, having agreed to lead the crusade, proved utterly ineffectual – he claimed that his ongoing conflict with the Pope prevented him from taking any significant action. Such were the internecine intrigues throughout the European courts that even the Pope himself was rumoured to be in league with the Mongols against his rivals.

By the winter of 1241–2 it had dawned upon the rest of Europe that neither the Church nor any individual Christian nation was powerful enough to withstand the next inevitable onslaught. Messages laced with portents of doom and bitter recrimination flew from one court to another. This letter from Count Henry of Lorraine to his father-in-law is typical: 'The dangers foretold long ago in Holy Scripture are now, owing to our sins, springing up and erupting. A cruel tribe of people beyond number, lawless and savage, is now invading and occupying our borders, and has now reached the land of the Poles, after roaming through many other lands and exterminating the people.' It seemed that the servants of Satan had finally been let loose, that the apocalypse was at hand, retribution for the sins of mankind would soon follow, the collapse of Western civilization and the extinction of Christendom itself were expected – if not the end of time itself.

Within this apocalyptic atmosphere, chroniclers drew freely

upon their imaginations to provide the most gory accounts of Mongol practices. The arrival of the Mongols in medieval Europe was akin to an invasion of extra-terrestrials. The narrow, intolerant Christian world could only interpret the unknown in terms of salvation or damnation. Having been deprived of their hoped-for Prester John, chroniclers explained the harsh reality of the Mongol attacks by fantastic references to Armageddon. To the Hungarians they were creatures with the heads of dogs who, not satisfied with merely defeating their enemies, were intent upon devouring the corpses as well. Here are Matthew Paris's sadistic imaginings of Mongol destruction.

> For touching upon the cruelty and cunning of these people, there can be no infamy [great enough]; and, in briefly informing you of their wicked habits, I will recount nothing of which I hold either a doubt or mere opinion, but what I have with certainty proved and what I know. . . . The Tartar chief, with his dinner guests and other lotus-eaters [cannibals], fed upon their carcasses as if they were bread and left nothing but the bones for the vultures. . . . The old and ugly women were given to the cannibals . . . as their daily allowance of food; those who were beautiful were not eaten, but were suffocated by mobs of ravishers in spite of all their cries and lamentations. Virgins were raped until they died of exhaustion; then their breasts were cut off to be kept as dainties for their chiefs, and their bodies furnished an entertaining banquet for the savages. . . .

Matthew Paris had never seen a Mongol nor, from all accounts, ever met someone who had. Even the more informed reports were not without some embellishment. Friar Jordan of Giano, a Franciscan vicar in Bohemia, described in some detail the Mongols' fighting practices yet also claimed that the army contained large contingents of women. 'She who fights best is regarded as the most desirable, just as in our society she who weaves and sews best is more desired than the one who is beautiful.' No account could be too gruesome: 'They eat frogs, dogs, serpents, and all things alike. The men are inhuman and of the nature of beasts, rather to be called monsters than men, thirsting after and drinking blood, and tearing and devouring the flesh of dogs and human beings. . . .'

The Mongol invasion had transformed vague Christian ideas about retribution into an almost obsessive conviction that the end of the world was nigh. In northern Europe, the churches were filled every day of the week with terrified congregations whom the clergy led in hysterical prayers for deliverance. Flagellants trailed across the country spreading predictions of the approaching apocalypse, while in Germany those ubiquitous scapegoats, the Jews, were slaughtered in large numbers because it was believed they were somehow smuggling arms across the border to the Mongols. To Matthew Paris the end of the world was so certain that he confidently prophesied the year 1250 would be the advent of the Antichrist and the end of the sixth and last age. Even powerful monarchs like Louis IX of France were already resigned to martyrdom. 'We have this consolation from heaven,' he told his mother. 'If these people whom we call Tartars come against us, either we shall send them back to hell where they came from, or else they will send us to heaven, where we shall enjoy the bliss that waits for the chosen.'

FURTHER POWER STRUGGLES OVER THE MONGOL SUCCESSION

As Europe awaited the sound of the last trumpet, the Mongols settled down during the summer months to rest and recuperate, allowing their herds to fatten and enabling reinforcements to arrive, receive training and be absorbed into the ranks. During those months another dispute broke out amongst the Mongol princes – or more likely it was a continuation of the same dispute that had alienated Batu from Guyuk and his followers.

There is no account of what precipitated the incident, but suddenly the princes Guyuk and Buri returned to Qaraqorum. In the absence of anything concrete, some historians have speculated that Guyuk's sudden departure was part of some obscure manoeuvre to secure his succession. Ogedei Khan had in recent years become an alcoholic, his days spent in blind stupors, oblivious to the world around him. His fierce and somewhat rapacious wife Toregene had become the effective authority at Qaraqorum and was utterly dedicated to the promotion of her eldest son, Guyuk. Ogedei had nominated his grandson, Shiremun, but his declining faculties meant that there was little support for the young man.

Far away in Hungary, Batu's fabulous victories brought him immense power and influence. Six years earlier he had left Qaraqorum as the weakest and least significant of Genghis's princes; now his realm surpassed in area the empire in both China and western Asia. It is probable that, as news of Ogedei's decline filtered down to the imperial army in the West, Guyuk felt it wise to take advantage of the lull in fighting to return to court and lobby for his cause. But he was not the only Mongol prince concerned with the succession: Mongke, son of Tolui and one of Batu's staunchest supporters, also departed for Qaraqorum. He had gone not to present the case on behalf of Batu – who had no ambitions to be Great Khan – but to effect an alliance between Batu and the opposition at Qaraqorum who were determined to prevent a dynasty forming out of Ogedei's descendants.

RECONNAISSANCE FOR THE CAMPAIGN IN THE WEST

Meanwhile, in the capitals of Europe, the absence of any further Mongol advances meant that the impetus behind the Crusade against them dissipated and the great counter-attack itself was postponed. In August Pope Gregory died; his successor, the eighty-year-old Celestine IV, lasted only seventeen days. The

Vatican, hampered by Frederick's interference, soon descended into a protracted struggle to elect a new Pope.

As winter approached, the Mongols prepared the next stage in their campaign. The number of reconnaissance patrols was increased, gathering valuable intelligence on the strength and disposition of nearby armies and looking for the safest point at which Batu could get his army across the Danube. But before he had decided, he was granted a stroke of good fortune when the Danube froze hard. On Christmas Day Batu led his army into western Hungary and immediately attacked Gran (Esztergom), the ecclesiastical capital. This beautiful city, complete with royal castle and cathedrals, was stormed after the gates had been battered down by catapults. Vast quantities of Hungary's state treasures were captured and removed to Qaraqorum. A separate force led by Kadan entered Buda, sacked it and moved on to the next city, Gyor.

Throughout these encounters the Mongols were again little interested in prolonged sieges; if they met any serious resistance they preferred to ride on to the next objective. As western Hungary was being dealt with, Batu despatched a *tumen* ahead of the main force across the border into Austria. This force tore through the south-eastern territories, laying waste the country-side as far as Wiener Neustadt. The Duke of Austria, suddenly shaken out of his complacency, pleaded for support from his allies abroad – but none was forthcoming. The Austrians grew frantic when during the spring of 1242 a Mongol force attacked Klosterneuburg and scouts were sighted on the outskirts of Vienna.

It was during this reconnaissance in force into Austria that one of the most fascinating episodes of the European story took place. One of the Mongol reconnaissance patrols was attacked and eight of its number were taken prisoner. Amongst the prisoners was an Englishman, a knight who had been exiled for some unknown crime. Very little is known of this man, except that, having left Britain, he had journeyed to the Middle East where he had gambled away his wealth and soon afterwards joined the services of the Mongols. He is said to have spoken several languages and claimed to his captors that he had been in the Mongols' diplomatic service. If he had tried to secure diplomatic immunity by this claim, it failed; the Austrians executed him, as they did the other seven.

Mongol forces also swept south-west, towards the Adriatic. About the same time that they were in Austria, Kadan was in command of a *tumen* engaged in pursuit of Bela who had fled from Austria into Croatia and Dalmatia. Patrols attached to this force were sighted as far away as Udine, just 100 km (60 miles) from Venice. Kadan moved on to Zagreb, sacked the city and then headed towards Spalato (Split) and Trogir, where Bela was in hiding. But Kadan's force had been badly mauled during this tour of the Dalmatian coast and, having reconnoitred the defences, passed Spalato by and moved on to Dubrovnik. By May, the *tumen* that had entered Austria had returned, having compiled a good account of the Austrian armies.

Batu was now prepared to begin the next stage in his campaign, the thrust into central Europe. The only thing that might stop him reaching the Atlantic would be a united European army of overwhelming numbers. No such army existed. Batu knew this and was impatient to get on with the task.

THE KHAN IS DEAD

Then, one morning in May 1242, quietly and with little warning, the Mongol encampment gathered itself together and prepared for action. But instead of heading west the armies turned east, recrossed the Danube and moved back into the territory they had just recently conquered. In the process they set about the most appalling campaign of slaughter and destruction that had yet been witnessed in Europe. This was not part of some elaborate manoeuvre designed to confuse and disable the enemy; this was a complete and total withdrawal. In the process, Batu was determined that the Hungarians and anyone else in his path would not soon forget the Mongols. Prisoners were released and then hunted down and slaughtered like rabbits, while whole villages and towns were erased from the map. Leaving in his wake a land turned to ashes, Batu rode back into southern Russia, towards Sarai, a base camp that stood near Astrakhan. He decided to make this the capital of his new empire, while Subedei took the imperial *tumens* back to Qaraqorum. Europe was abandoned. What had precipitated this dramatic change in strategy was news from Qaraqorum that the Great Khan Ogedei had finally died.

There was also news of great political confusion at the capital. Ogedei's widow was at the heart of a series of conspiracies to ensure Guyuk's succession. Against her the opposition was working away in support of their candidate, Mongke, son of Tolui. Although Batu had already thrown his support behind the opposition, Toregene, who was ruling as regent, had tilted the odds in her favour by dismissing all her late husband's advisers and replacing them with her own sycophants. There was even a rumour that Toregene and her fellow conspirators had grown impatient with Ogedei's slow decline and had despatched him with poisoned wine.

Batu realized immediately that under Toregene's regency there was no question of his continuing the campaign in Europe. The imperial *tumens* would have been recalled, had they not already been sent back to Mongolia. Should Mongke succeed as Great Khan, it was certain that the conquest of Europe would be continued. In the meantime Batu's best strategy was to consolidate the lands he had already conquered east of the Carpathians and west of the Urals – a vast expanse by any standards. The future of the house of Batu was already assured. The future of Europe would be decided in Qaraqorum.

6

MISSIONS TO TARTARY

PAPAL ENVOYS

The sudden withdrawal from eastern Europe was initially regarded as something approaching a miracle, though it was also assumed that it was merely a respite and that the Tartars would inevitably return to complete their work. This view was encouraged by the Church, which was now more convinced than ever that the Tartars were the tools of a vengeful God bent upon retribution and so had renamed them the 'Hammer of God'. The Mongols were clearly the descendants of Gog and Magog, released from their prison behind the Caucasus Mountains, and thus heralded the coming of the Antichrist and of Armageddon. Indeed, there was a great deal of theological debate about the Tartars, their origins, purposes and the very meaning of their attack upon Europe.

But the Church was in no state to formulate a policy to cope with the end of the world so long as it remained without a head. Pope Celestine IV had died in September 1241 and Christendom was left to drift without a spiritual leader for another two years. In addition to the constant threat of a renewed attack from the 'Hammer of God', there also came news that Jerusalem had fallen to the Muslim armies and Christian authority in the Holy Land seemed shattered. A new Pope, Innocent IV, was eventually elected in 1243 and almost immediately Frederick II renewed his attacks upon the Pope's territory in Italy. With internal quarrels in Rome and even the threat of rebellion, Innocent, fearful for his safety, left for Lyons and the protection offered him by the devout young King of France, Louis IX. From Lyons, Innocent immediately called what was to be the Thirteenth Ecumenical Council, which would be convened in June 1245. The new pontiff declared that the most important issue to be dealt with was the future security of Christendom, which most people understood to mean how it would cope with the 'Hammer of God'.

Innocent IV, a Genoese jurist before he had been elected Pope, took a far less superstitious approach to the problem than most people. A year before the Council was due to be convened he summoned to Lyons all informed persons or reports that could be gathered from Russia, Poland and Hungary. From these he learned a little about Mongol religious practices, a good deal about their methods of fighting and, perhaps most significantly, the fact that they accorded great respect and reliable protection to official envoys. Armed with this information, Innocent decided a few months before the Council to send forth a number of exploratory missions. They had instructions to travel to the Mongol court bearing greetings from Christendom, coupled with a somewhat audacious invitation to accept Christianity and be baptized. However, more importantly, the missions were charged with gleaning information about the Tartars and their intentions. A further objective was to extend invitations to the Eastern Russian and Greek Orthodox Churches and the eastern Christians to unite in common cause against the Mongol threat, and at the same time return to the bosom of Rome. Innocent chose to send monks from the newly founded Dominican and Franciscan orders for his mission '*Ad Tartaros*'. These were both new and highly enthusiastic orders; the Dominicans in particular were friar-preachers, full of religious fervour.

There were a number of legates despatched with letters from the Pope – Lawrence of Portugal, Ascelinus of Lombardy, Andrew of Longjumeau and Dominic of Aragon – all of whom took the route through the Levant. Their instructions were to deliver the letters to the first Mongol chieftain they encountered, and request that the letters be handed on to the Mongol king. One of the first missions to depart was that undertaken by the

Franciscan John of Plano Carpini. His was by far the most difficult mission. He was instructed to take the overland route into eastern Russia first travelled by the Hungarian Julian in 1237, then continue all the way to the Mongol court – wherever that was – and deliver letters to the Mongol king in person.

This was a terribly arduous journey for a man already in his sixties and somewhat overweight. No doubt he had imagined he might see out his final years in quiet contemplation amongst other monks of his order. But he had been carefully chosen because of his experience in diplomatic circles, and because he knew personally a number of monarchs in eastern Europe who would be important contacts along the way. John had been born some time around the end of the twelfth century at Plano Carpini, a small town near Perugia in northern Italy. He was an early disciple of St Francis and had been sent by him in 1221 to Saxony where he established a number of monasteries, converted a great many friars to the new order and then sent them forth into northern Europe to spread the movement.

On Easter Day, 16 April 1245, Carpini left Lyons with a small party of companions that included Friar Stephen of Bohemia, and journeyed into Bohemia, Silesia and Poland where he was due to have consultations with the monarchs there. While in Breslau the party was joined by a Pole, Friar Benedict, who was fluent in Slavonic languages. From there they travelled to what was left of Cracow where they sought out Conrad, the Duke of Mazovia and Lanciscia, who was known to favour a union of nations and churches against the Mongols. It was also thought that Conrad's family links with the Russian princes, especially with the current leader Prince Daniel Romanovich, might exert some influence around the idea of an anti-Mongol bloc. Unfortunately, Daniel and the other Russian princes were already vassals of Batu and, so far as they were concerned, a rebellion against their Mongol overlords would have been suicidal.

At least the Franciscans did not depart for Kiev entirely empty-handed. They had learnt that it was the Mongol tradition to expect envoys to come bearing gifts, and so Carpini and his party purchased with what money they had a large collection of furs. In the depth of the Russian winter they travelled through a land firmly in the grip of the Mongol army towards Kiev, where they encountered a *tumen* commander. According to Carpini's own account, it was as they approached Kiev that they saw, in the most appalling detail, the worst evidence of the Mongol invasion three years before. The ground was still littered with the bleached bones of countless victims, and there were ruins all about them. Carpini's party, which by now had grown to about ten, was escorted south through Cuman country to where they first encountered Mongol camps. At the sight of Europeans 'some armed Tartars rushed upon us in a horrible manner, wanting to know what kind of men we were'. Struggling through a number of translators, Carpini explained the purpose of their mission and was eventually allowed to proceed. They would be escorted to Batu's camp, and it would be up to him to decide their future. Before proceeding further they were required, as was the custom, to leave a hostage, and so Stephen and some of the servants remained behind.

While the Franciscans made their way towards their first encounter with a Mongol prince, in the Middle East the Dominicans were making their way slowly through the Levant towards Mongol settlements in northern Mesopotamia. The Frenchman Andrew of Longjumeau, accompanied by another monk of his order, journeyed through Syria trying to get to a Mongol outpost. They had little assistance from the various Sultans, who suspected the monks' real mission was to help form an alliance between the Mongols and Rome against Islam. To the papal envoys it must have seemed a most unlikely suspicion, yet it would prove remarkably prophetic in the years to come. So Andrew continued unassisted into northern Mesopotamia and then into Armenia, which was under the control of a Mongol military governor named Baiju. Toregene had sent Baiju to replace Chormaghun in 1242, as part of her policy of sweeping away her late husband's officials.

As the Dominicans made their way through Baiju's territory they encountered a number of Christian communities and eventu-

124

ally the prelate of the area, Simeon Rabban-ata, who had been appointed by none other than Ogedei Khan. Andrew discovered that the eastern Christians enjoyed a great many privileges under the Mongols and consequently were flourishing. Simeon had built many new churches, and the faith was spreading beyond northern Persia into Mongol-controlled western Asia.

The eastern Christians trace their history back to Thaddeus, one of the seventy evangelists sent forth by Thomas at Jesus' bidding shortly before his crucifixion. Thaddeus journeyed to the city of Edessa, now called Urfa, in modern Turkey, and from there the gospel spread to the East. From the outset the eastern Christians had an independent nature; their language was neither Greek nor Latin but Aramaic, said to be the language spoken by Jesus, and their script Syriac – or biblical Aramaic. The Church spread into Persia where it flourished for the next four centuries, growing stronger and ever more independent. Following a series of wars between the Byzantine Roman empire and Persia, the eastern Christians sought to distance themselves from the Western Churches. The separation became permanent in 431, after most eastern Christians supported a Greek prelate named Nestorius who had been condemned as a heretic for teaching theology divergent from that of Rome; ever since then the eastern Christians had been regarded as followers of Nestorius – hence Nestorians. Eastern Christianity continued to develop in its own way, such as rejecting the doctrine of celibacy of the clergy. Over the centuries they became renowned as physicians, having gathered a great deal of knowledge from the Arabs, and churches were built in Merv, Nishapur, Samarqand, Bukhara and Herat. Eventually their faith spread to the nomadic horsemen of the steppe and the Onghuts, Kereyids and Uighurs were converted.

AUDIENCE WITH BATU KHAN

During the spring of 1246, as Carpini was still making his way through the Ukraine towards Batu's camp, in faraway Qaraqorum the question of the succession was finally resolved. The regent, Toregene, with the support of the Chaghadai clan, had finally succeeded in winning sufficient support to ensure the election of her son Guyuk. This was apparently an unpopular decision; Guyuk had few devotees amongst the other Mongol princes, being even more addicted to drink and debauchery than his late father. Although the Mongke candidacy had been defeated, the opposition were far from satisfied and Qaraqorum continued to seethe with discontent.

Into this political maelstrom rode the portly John of Plano Carpini. He arrived at Batu's capital, Sarai, on the banks of the Volga, on 4 April 1246. As was the custom, John and his party were required to pass through various purification rites, such as walking between two fires to purge themselves of any evil intentions, and then bowing before a stuffed felt image of Genghis Khan. Batu made a deep impression on Carpini and his party, as did his magnificent tent city. They had numerous audiences in a particularly beautiful white linen tent that had once belonged to the Hungarian King, Bela IV. Inside the tent, lined in gold brocade, Batu Khan sat with his wives and officials offering his guests the best of their food and wine, to be eaten and drunk from gold vessels. Unfortunately, as it was the middle of Lent the good monks were obliged to refuse everything but gruel and water.

Batu had established himself as the supreme power throughout Russia and had received the submission of most of the Russian princes, starting with Yaroslav of Novgorod and followed by the princes of Chernigov and Galicia. Batu became adept at working the Russian princes' mutual animosities to his own advantage and succeeded in extending his rule from Bulgaria to Novgorod, even though his armies were rarely deployed further west than Kiev. Within a few years his power and prestige were unmatched anywhere outside of Qaraqorum. Seated on silk carpets, surrounded by beautifully adorned women, the simple Franciscans awaited Batu Khan's wishes. Having had the papal letters translated and read out to him, Batu decided the monks should carry them personally all the way to Qaraqorum, where they could be delivered to the Great Khan himself. Batu saw no reason for interfering in the relations between Europe and the empire, even though he had opposed the rise of the new Khan. Guyuk was due to be enthroned within a few months, and Batu was keen that the Europeans should have the opportunity to witness the full splendour of Mongol wealth and ceremony.

So the envoys set off, under escort, towards the most important capital in the world. Qaraqorum was no longer the oasis of civilization that Ogedei and his Chinese architects had envisaged; the court had changed during the reign of the regent. For a start the great and wise chief minister, Yeh-lu Ch'u-ts'ai, had been replaced by a Muslim merchant by the name of Abd al-Rahman, who had immediately doubled the taxes in northern China. The royal house itself had become a den of intrigue. Toregene had become infatuated with a Persian slave named Fatima, whose influence upon the regent had caused great resentment – especially as a great many old favourites were purged from government. Virtually all the Chinese or Uighur officials were hounded out of the administration and some of them actually executed. Yeh-lu Ch'u-ts'ai himself left Qaraqorum a broken man and died in 1243, while even the military governor of Transoxiana found himself being pursued by a unit of imperial guards and had to seek refuge in Batu's domain.

Although the significance of these developments was probably not appreciated by Carpini and his party, he was nevertheless aware of some form of division within the empire. To get to Qaraqorum they were led along the pathways of the now well-established Yam system; changing horses at each station, they sometimes arrived so late that they had no time to eat before collapsing into bed with exhaustion. The envoys followed a route that took them north of the Aral Sea through Khwarazmia, passing a number of towns including Utrar, the scene of the beginning of Genghis Khan's great westward expansion. They reached the Altai Mountains in July, entered former Naiman country, then proceeded eastward across the Khanagi range and arrived at Guyuk's *ordu* on 22 July. They had covered 5000 km (3000 miles) at a blistering 50 km (30 miles) a day, having arrived at their destination a little more than three months after leaving Batu's capital. The man from Plano Carpini had ventured further eastward than any European before him, and in the process had seen lands and people no European had ever dreamt of. His account of his travels includes a great deal of detail, filling countless blank pages in European knowledge. Yet there were still vast areas of Asia that the party did not explore, and in trying to fill in the blank areas on their maps Carpini fell back on traditional European geographical folklore. Hence there were still creatures 'who are said to have faces like dogs and live in the wilderness along the shores of the oceans'. His colleague Benedict also produced an account of their journey in which he claimed that northern Asia was populated by 'the dog-headed Cynocephali' and creatures called the Parossies, who, he claimed, ate no solid food on account of their having such narrow mouths.

A NEW GREAT KHAN IN QARAQORUM

On 24 August Carpini and his party were very much part of the real world, standing amongst a vast host gathered at a tent city at Sira-ordu, a few miles from Qaraqorum near Lake Koku-nor, for the enthronement of Guyuk Khan. Envoys, princes and other vassal lords had gathered from the four corners of the empire to be present at the enthronement. Grand Duke Yaroslav had travelled from Christian Russia; Sultan Kilij-Arslan IV from Seljuk Rum (Asia Minor); Constable Sempad from Armenia, the Egyptian Sultan's brother; an envoy from the Caliph of Baghdad; royal princes from Korea; and Prince David IV, son of Queen Rusudan of Georgia. There were representatives from northern China, from the Sung empire in the south, holy men from Tibet, shamans from the mountains and armies of retainers. All the Mongol aristocracy was present – except, that is, for Batu Khan, who preferred to remain in Sarai. This was a tremendous insult to the ruling family, and only served to widen the rift amongst the Mongol princes.

The ceremonies continued for four days, and on each successive day the colours worn by the court were changed. Carpini made particular note of the harnesses and breastplates that adorned the Mongol officers' horses, which he claimed had been made of 'about twenty marks' worth of gold'. He and his party were also greatly impressed by the vast quantities of silk, brocade, furs and jewels that had been brought as tribute for the new Great Khan. At the actual enthronement Guyuk was carried on a litter by four princes, so that he could be seen above the heads of the gathered host, to a large solid gold and ivory throne, encrusted with pearls and other gems, that had been made by the Russian goldsmith Cosmas.

Following the ceremonies the Mongol court remained at Siraordu, as did Carpini and his party, waiting patiently for their audience with the new Khan. In fact, Carpini never managed to get to Qaraqorum, though that doesn't seem to have deprived him of things to see and write about. He presents a curiously flattering picture of Guyuk the man, describing him as a somewhat formidable man in his mid-forties. In fact he was considerably younger, of a sickly complexion, certainly an alcoholic and well on his way to an early grave. Nevertheless, Guyuk had sufficient presence of mind during the first months of his rule to make some dramatic changes to the court.

One of the first to go was Abd al-Rahman, the Muslim merchant whom his mother had made Prime Minister, and in due course it would be the turn of Baiju, the military governor in northern Persia whom his mother had promoted. Guyuk also dealt with his mother's confidante, Fatima, whom he had convicted of witchcraft and sentenced to be executed by suffocation – a peculiarly Mongolian practice. According to shamanistic tradition, blood contains an individual's spiritual essence; if the blood of a noble is spilt, it has an evil effect upon the ground on which it falls. Consequently, it was a form of respect towards enemy leaders or members of the aristocracy who had fallen from grace to be executed either by being wrapped in carpets until they were asphyxiated, or crushed under planks of wood. In Fatima's case, to make doubly sure her blood was not spilt, all her orifices were sewn up before she was rolled in a sheet of felt and then thrown into a river. Though the coming of a new reign seems to have brought with it the usual violent purge, Guyuk was also responsible for returning to power many of the former ministers who had previously been persecuted by his mother.

A FRANCISCAN VIEW OF MONGOL SOCIETY

Carpini described in some detail the comings and goings within Guyuk's administration, and in particular the return of an extremely able Uighur Christian named Chinqai, who had been Yeh-lu Ch'u-ts'ai's deputy. Carpini describes him as 'proto-notary' or chief secretary, though he was more of a Chancellor or Prime Minister. It was Chinqai who acted as an intermediary in their efforts to arrange an audience with Guyuk. But the Great Khan was in no hurry to see the Europeans, partly because he already knew the content of the papal letters, which had been passed on by Batu, and partly because these so-called envoys from the Pope had arrived without any tribute or offering to make to the new Khan – a dreadful lapse in etiquette. Carpini had disposed of all the furs they had purchased in Russia as tribute to Batu. Indeed, not only was Guyuk prepared to let the monks wait, he was also prepared to let them suffer. He was so disappointed with them that he ordered them to be given hardly any food during their stay at his camp, and the wretched monks probably would have starved had not Cosmas, the Russian goldsmith, come to their rescue.

In reality, Carpini's request for an audience with Guyuk was little more than a formality. He already had private information concerning the Great Khan's intentions towards Christendom,

1. The Onon River in north-eastern Mongolia, said to be the birth place of the Mongols. According to legend, a blue wolf and his mate, a fallow deer, settled here to raise their offspring, who became the tribe known as the Mongols.

2. The Mongolian plateau is subject to dramatic extremes of climate. From above 40 °C (104 °F) in the summer, the mercury plunges to −40 °C (−40 °F) in the winter, causing the lakes and rivers to remain frozen for nearly six months of the year.

3. Most steppe nomads still live in the traditional *yurt* or *ger*. Made of felt stretched across a wooden frame, it can be dismantled and loaded on to an ox-cart in under an hour.

4. Genghis adopted as his standard the 'Nine Tails' made from yak hair. It later became the imperial standard and even today stands as a symbol of Mongolia's past glories.

5. Genghis pursuing the Chin through the mountains, from a manuscript of Rashid al-Din. At the beginning of this campaign, the Mongols captured many of the Chin fortifications that guarded the mountain passes.

6. Genghis berating the citizens of Bukhara: 'I am the punishment of God,' he told them. 'If you had not committed great sins, He would not have sent a punishment like me.'

7. Once the fabled city of Balkh, in what is now northern Afghanistan. A thouand years before Christ, Zoroaster preached here; seven hundred years later, Alexander passed this way. Then came Genghis Khan.

8. *Qanats*, the Persian system or irrigation. Underground channels drew water down from the mountains across the plains to fill lines of shallow wells and trenches in the fields. After the Mongol attacks the *qanats* were neglected, the system silted up and Persia reverted to a desert.

9. These large pieces of stone ordnance were carried by Hulegu's army up the mountain slopes, along with the catapults that would fire them, to attack the walls of the Assassin's fortress at Alamut, in what is now northern Iran.

10. The remains at Qaraqorum. There is a number of these large stone tortoises, which are thought to have supported imperial *stelae* – official pronouncements from the court carved in stone.

11. The citadel at Aleppo. The Mongols were so impressed with the way in which the garrison defended its post that they spared the life of the commander, Turan Shah.

12 and 13. Portraits of Genghis Khan (top) and Khubilai Khan, from the National Palace Museum, Taipei.

14. Yuan Dynasty porcelain vase, 1320–50. Knowing that Chinese ceramics were potentially a valuable export, Khubilai encouraged potteries to open up across the country. Artists were allowed a free hand to develop new styles, and some wonderful work was produced.

15. The Gaocheng Observatory in Henan Province, one of the twenty-seven observatories established by Khubilai to recalculate the Chinese calendar in an effort to improve agricultural production.

16. In the sixteenth century the Ming forces built these defences, creating what became known as the Great Wall. They were determined that a Mongol invasion would never again trouble the people of northern China.

17. The Taj Mahal. Built by the fifth Mogul emperor Shah Jahan, for his wife Mumtaz, it is the very antithesis of its barbaric origins.

and it was not encouraging. In the meantime he made careful observations of the Mongols and their way of life, knowing that his report to the Pope was now even more vital. Yet, given the gloomy prospect that would underline his report, Carpini's account remained remarkably even-handed and in many cases extremely flattering. He devotes considerable space to describing Mongol religious practices: the making and worshipping of felt idols, particularly of Genghis Khan, horse sacrifices and so on. He briefly describes certain shamanistic rituals and the worship of Tengri, the Eternal Heaven or sky god.

As for his mission to convert the Mongols to Christianity, he seems to have swiftly concluded that any efforts in that area would be somewhat premature. Nevertheless, he does note the large number of 'Nestorian clerics' at the Mongol court and the fact that most of the royal family were either already Christian or heavily influenced by them. He also claimed that there was some hope for future evangelizing in China, of all places. Although he and his party got nowhere near China, there were a great many Chinese at Guyuk's court and, perhaps because most of these were Christians, they seem to have given him a distorted impression. Although the Church of the East had sent missions to T'ang China since the seventh century, Christianity had been in decline in China for more than a hundred years. Nevertheless, from his enquiries Carpini concluded that the Chinese have 'an Old and New Testament, and lives of Fathers and hermits, and buildings made like churches, in which they pray at stated times; and they say they have some saints. They worship one God, they honour Our Lord Jesus Christ, and they believe in eternal life, but are not baptized.' Although none of this was even remotely accurate, in what was the very earliest European account of the Chinese he goes on to give a very good description of their physical appearance and their marvellous craftsmanship.

When he comes to piece together a history of the Mongol tribes he is forced, again, to rely upon a mixture of fact and legend. Carpini is armed with his own thorough knowledge of the histories of the East, the Alexander romances and other

European texts. With these in hand he is forced to make sense of the accounts gathered from Uighur scribes, travellers and any others that might shed light on the Mongols' origins. He provides Europe with an authoritative account of the importance of 'Chingiscan' and couples it, almost inevitably, with a further reference to that ubiquitous figure Prester John. In his account Carpini makes it clear that Genghis Khan was not Prester John, nor King David, but the founder of a great pagan empire. Prester John, on the other hand, is identified as the Christian king of Greater India, who is supposed to have defeated Genghis Khan by using Greek fire (burning sulphur that was catapulted at the enemy) and manikins tied to horses.

This is a mixture of certain elements from the accounts of Genghis's campaign against the Khwarazm Shah, combined with legends surrounding Alexander's defeat of the Indian King Porus. Carpini heard these stories at a time when the Mongols were developing their own Genghis romances, having already elevated him to something approaching a deity. The Mongols were already familiar with the Oriental version of the Alexander romances and had blended themes from this with facts from Genghis's exploits. As for the account of Genghis's defeat, Carpini received this from Russian captives at the court, who had probably concocted the story as a way of ridiculing their masters.

By far the most important section in Carpini's account is that describing the Mongol army, its decimal structure, discipline and manner of fighting. It is an accurate and in parts detailed picture of a modern fighting machine. He ends this part by emphasizing that Europe's only hope of countering this formidable threat is to unite in common cause: 'Therefore, if Christians wish to save themselves, their country and Christendom, then kings, princes, barons and rulers of countries ought to assemble together and by common consent send men to fight against Tartars before they begin to spread over the land.'

It was November before Chinqai managed to secure Carpini a series of audiences with Guyuk Khan. At those occasions the contents of the papal letters were read out, chiding the Mongol Khan for the great destruction his armies had created in Christian Europe, entreating him to make assurances that these attacks would cease and offering him and his people the gift of baptism. Guyuk Khan's response was unequivocal. Chinqai was at great pains to record it accurately for the envoys to take back to Europe; a copy was made in Latin and another in Persian.

To the Pope's complaint about the destruction carried out in Europe, Guyuk replies: 'I do not understand these words of yours. Tengri [Eternal Heaven] has slain and annihilated these peoples, because they had adhered neither to Genghis Khan nor to Khagan [Ogedei], both of whom have been sent to make known God's command.' Mongol notions of political diplomacy had probably been borrowed from the Chinese, and Guyuk's response was completely in character with Chinese principles. The fundamental concept was that the founder of a new dynasty clearly held the mandate of heaven; that is to say, the unquestionable proof that a leader held this holy mandate was his very success in seizing power. The spectacular achievements enjoyed by the Mongol armies had led them to see their holy mandate not simply in terms of a dynasty, but in relation to the entire world. The Mongol empire was not just another state, it was *the* supreme universal monarchy, and all the lands not within its borders were automatically regarded as subordinate and therefore potential vassals.

As to the Pope's request that the Mongols accept baptism, Guyuk replied: 'Thou, who art the Great Pope, together with all the princes, come in person to serve us. . . . If you do not observe God's command, and if you ignore my command, I shall know you as my enemy. Likewise I shall make you understand. If you do otherwise, God knows what I know.' The Great Khans saw themselves as God's representatives on earth, charged by God with the task of world conquest. Every nation would either have to submit or be destroyed. Cosmas, who had made the Great Seal used to stamp Guyuk's letter, explained the legend he had been asked to work into the design: 'By the strength of Eternal Heaven, Order of the Universal Ruler of the Empire of the Great Mongols. When it reaches the subject and rebel people, let them respect it, let them fear it.'

Before his departure, Carpini was approached by one of the soldiers detailed to escort him. He was told that Guyuk was keen to send his own ambassadors to the Pope and wanted another audience with the clerics to arrange this. It was the convention that the invitation to send Mongol ambassadors should come from the visiting envoys, but Carpini decided against it. He felt it would have been a mistake for Mongol ambassadors to travel on official business through Europe as 'they would see dissensions and wars among us and that it would encourage them to march against us'. On 13 November 1246, Carpini and his party finally departed Guyuk's tent city to begin the long journey home. They travelled through the depth of winter, arriving at Batu's camp in early May the following year. Batu granted them safe passage to Kiev, where they were greeted 'as if we had come back from the dead', sixteen months after they had departed.

While Carpini and his party had been struggling through another Russian winter, a Dominican named Ascelinus of Lombardy was making his way through the Levant, retracing the journey taken by Andrew of Longjumeau in search of Baiju's camp. Unlike Andrew, Friar Ascelinus managed to obtain good directions and arrived at the military governor's camp at Sisian in the Karabagh Highlands in May 1247.

Whatever qualified Ascelinus for this mission it was not any gift for diplomacy. Requested to make the obligatory genuflection, descending three times on the left knee, Ascelinus obstinately refused; nor did he bring with him the customary tributes so that he might be recognized as a serious envoy. Then Ascelinus made things even worse by referring to the Pope as 'the greatest of all men', and went on by demanding that Baiju and his followers should all become Christians.

Having first delivered Ascelinus a stinging rebuke – 'You ask us to become Christians and so [become] dogs like you?' – Baiju sentenced the monks to death, planning to flay them alive and then deliver their straw-stuffed hides to Rome. The monks escaped only through the intervention of Baiju's wife, who insisted that her husband show the customary Mongol respect for clerics – no matter how insolent. Despite his reprieve, the Dominican's obstinate nature was barely tempered and he might yet have come to grief had not an official from Qaraqorum arrived with orders to relieve Baiju of his command. The new governor, Eljigidei, wily tactician, was another of Guyuk's sweeping changes to his administration. Ascelinus departed soon afterwards, bearing letters that reiterated Guyuk's message to the Pope and with very little good to say of the Mongols.

OPTIMISM IN EUROPE

One year after leaving Sira-ordu, Carpini's epic journey was finally over; he arrived at Lyons on 18 November 1247, nearly two and a half years after having left that city. Innocent IV greeted him warmly and was delighted by the encouraging reports that the eastern Christians or Nestorians were prepared to recognize him as their 'particular lord and father and the Holy Roman Church as lady and mistress'. However, the report from the Mongol court, coupled with Guyuk's letter, made him feel less optimistic. Europe had little option, in Carpini's opinion, but to prepare for the worst. The only chance of a reprieve, he suggested, was the growing rift he had observed between Batu and Guyuk, which he thought might possibly delay or distract the Mongols from renewing their advance in the West.

The papal court accepted this news grimly, and then listened hopefully for information on Prester John. The Franciscan confessed he could find no actual evidence of the man, nor of any large and powerful Christian king in the neighbourhood. However, the best piece of news, the one seized upon and broadcast throughout Christendom, was Carpini's description of the powerful influence that the eastern Christians enjoyed at the Mongol court. Clutching at this straw, Carpini even went so far as to predict that Guyuk would some day convert to Christianity. In what was, on the whole, a somewhat depressing – though fascinating – account, this singular fact was enough to generate widespread optimism, especially as it seemed to corroborate the report of Andrew of Longjumeau who had returned from Persia just a few months before.

The heady confidence that soon filled the papal court could not disguise some harsh realities: the Europe to which Carpini had returned was in no position to form a united front against a renewed Mongol attack – the 'dissensions and wars' had got worse during his absence. Three years before, at the Thirteenth Ecumenical Conference, Innocent had resolved to deal with the Mongols, not as the 'Hammer of God' but as a foreign invading power. It had also been decided to conduct yet another Crusade for the Holy Land, which the young and devout King Louis IX of France would lead. Innocent's strategy towards the Mongols was to try to draw the eastern Churches into a pan-Christian alliance – and first reports were encouraging.

However, these plans were put aside when the long-running conflict with Frederick II flared up again, spreading the fighting from Italy up into Germany and threatening to ignite central Europe. Within months of his return Carpini was despatched once again, this time to the court of Louis IX, to plead for assistance in the war against Frederick. But Louis would not abandon the Crusade, and by August he and his wife, Queen Margaret, had set sail for Cyprus. He had spent three years preparing, and had the foresight to take with him many followers with experience of the Middle East, including Andrew of Longjumeau.

MONGOL DECEIT, EUROPEAN NAÏVETY

The French King left behind a Europe even more torn by internal strife, and praying for continued respite from the Tartars. He was unaware, however, that the hemisphere to which he sailed now contained a new and powerful military presence. Louis made his first base at Limassol, but before he had even begun to deploy his army he received two envoys from General Eljigidei, the new Mongol military governor of northern Persia. Eljigidei's ambassadors were two wily Nestorians named David and Mark, one of whom was recognized by Andrew from his earlier travels through Georgia. They bore a letter from Eljigidei which claimed he had been charged by the Great Khan to protect all Christians in western Asia, rebuild their churches and pray for the success of Louis's Crusade. The letters went on to claim that the Great Khan had recently been baptized and that Eljigidei had followed his Khan's example. The ambassadors also delivered a secret message to Louis which they claimed Eljigidei had dared not commit to paper. It was a proposal for a military alliance.

According to David and Mark, Eljigidei was preparing his armies for a winter assault on Baghdad. If the King of France would co-ordinate his plans for an attack upon Egypt at the same time, then the two great Islamic powers, the Sultanate of Egypt and the Caliphate of Baghdad, would be unable to come to each other's assistance – and so the separate ambitions of the Great Khan and the great Pope would doubtless succeed. Eljigidei went further, and in a wonderfully bold stroke suggested that their respective armies should then converge and between them liberate the Holy Land.

To the young French King this was marvellous news. Eljigidei's message had confirmed Carpini's optimistic prediction, as well as more recent reports claiming that the entire Mongol court might soon be converted to Christianity. Soon Louis's court was wild with enthusiasm. He swiftly sent word to the Pope and then set about composing a suitable reply to the Mongol commander. He sent separate letters to both Guyuk Khan and Eljigidei, commending their decision to turn to Christianity and their offer of assistance in the war against Islam. Then, as a tribute to the Great Khan, he had a marvellous portable chapel constructed complete with decorations – all the paraphernalia necessary to celebrate Mass plus a few fragments from the True Cross. When it was finished, Louis sent Andrew of Longjumeau to Eljigidei's camp with the letters, gifts and secret messages regarding the forthcoming campaign.

The naïvety with which Louis responded to David and Mark's message only demonstrates how desperately Europe had come to believe in the Mongols' conversion – in the ancient legend of the powerful Christian kingdom of the East made manifest. While Christian influence at the court was well known, and Guyuk's baptism even possible, it is absolutely certain that neither he nor his court ever seriously embraced Christianity. Eljigidei's ambassadors were a most cunning ruse, executed with great aplomb.

There was one aspect of Mongol military endeavours that remained essential to all their successes, and that was the gathering and exploitation of first-rate intelligence. It might be recalled that, while Ascelinus and his party were held captive in Baiju's camp, Eljigidei had arrived to take command. According to an account of one of the monks in that party, before they were released Ascelinus had been closely questioned about rumours that the Europeans were preparing to launch a fresh campaign to reconquer Jerusalem. It would have been obvious to a man of Eljigidei's calibre what advantages might be gained from a Mongol–European alliance. The scheme was simple, but ingenious. The Caliphate of Baghdad was the last significant power that stood in the way of Mongol ambitions in Persia, but to launch an attack would probably have invited a united Islamic response. If he could be certain that the Egyptian Sultan's armies would be pinned down at the same time, then he stood a better chance of success. The Mongols had no plans to march on the Holy Land, as yet.

Andrew and six other friars set sail with the portable chapel in late January 1249. By the time they arrived at Eljigidei's camp in the spring, Louis and his army were landing in Egypt as agreed. Eljigidei had not attacked Baghdad, nor had he even mobilized, for in the past six months the balance of power had shifted again in Qaraqorum.

A NEW POWER STRUGGLE IN THE MONGOL CAPITAL

In 1248 there had been an attempt to resolve the differences between Guyuk and Batu through a meeting between the two cousins in the Ili valley, about midway between their respective domains. But before Batu reached the rendezvous he received word that the planned reconciliation was in fact a trap; Guyuk intended to arrest him and have him executed. However, all Guyuk's plans came to nothing. His addiction to alcohol coupled with the rigours of the journey were finally too much for him, and he died somewhere along the road to the Ili valley. He was forty-two. His widow, Oghul-Ghaimish, assumed the regency until the next *quriltai* and, as was the custom, had begun conspiring to have her son Shiremun elected as the next Great Khan. This time, however, the house of Ogedei did not have the numbers. Tolui's widow Sorghaghtani Beki, with the support of Batu and most of the other princes, was gathering support for her son Mongke, whom Guyuk had defeated two years before.

Under the present circumstances Eljigidei, who owed his promotion to Guyuk, decided it would be unwise to launch a new campaign until the result of the election was known. So, in order to waste time, he sent Andrew and the portable chapel to Oghul-Ghaimish's camp in Tarbagatai. Nearly nine months later they arrived at the regent's camp, where the gifts intended for her late husband were taken as tribute from the Christian West and proof of their submission to the Mongol court. Poor Andrew was then entrusted with a letter for King Louis which simply enjoined him to return each year with further tribute of gold and silver; if he did not, he would be destroyed. Andrew and his companions had naïvely expected to be welcomed into a Christian realm and treated as allies. Instead, Louis's envoys were hastened away as though they were messengers of a vassal lord.

In all respects the venture had proved a catastrophe. While the Dominicans had been fruitlessly trekking across Asia to the seat of the Mongol court, Louis had been in prison. Having landed in Egypt in June 1249, Louis's army quickly took Damietta unopposed and then marched on towards Cairo, firmly believing that at that moment Eljigidei's armies were laying siege to Baghdad. But Louis's progress was halted long before he reached Cairo by a unit of the Sultan's army led by a young Mamluk commander named Baybars. The Mamluks were Turkic slave soldiers who had entered the Sultan's service back in 1238. In fact they had originally been captured by Batu's son Berke during the raids that preceded the Mongol invasion of eastern Europe, and then sold to the Egyptian Sultan to help finance Batu's war. In the ten years since, the Mamluks had become not only an indispensable element of the Egyptian army but also a significant force at court.

The confrontation between the armour-clad French knights and these once nomadic horsemen was as one-sided as the battles between the Poles and the Mongols. Louis's vanguard was utterly destroyed, forcing the army to fall back. It fought an effective rearguard action, but eventually was cut off from its supply lines and brought close to starvation. Louis had no option but to surrender and he was carried away in chains, stricken with dysentery and near death. He languished in prison until May 1250, when finally a massive ransom of one million gold bezants was paid and he and the remnants of his army were released. Out of 60 000 men only 12 000 sailed with him to Acre, where he made his base for the next four years.

The irony of Louis's situation couldn't have been more poignant. As he and his meagre army sailed from Egypt the Mamluks were in revolt, having murdered the Sultan's heir. The Sultan himself had died the year before, and following the revolt his widow, Shajar al-Durr, had married the Mamluks' commander-in-chief, Aybak. This created a new Islamic regime, but more importantly splintered the rest of the Islamic world and led to years of intrigue and civil war. There could have been no better time in which to launch a decisive campaign against Islam – but Louis did not have the means. He must have writhed with frustration.

In April 1251, Andrew of Longjumeau returned from Mongolia to be received by his King at Caesarea near Acre. According to Louis's biographer, Joinville, the King was appalled at Oghul-Ghaimish's letter and at the Mongols' mendacity. Nevertheless, Andrew's mission was not entirely fruitless; it did plant the seed of the possibility of Christian–Mongol *entente* – even if that response had probably been motivated by a lingering faith in an Eastern saviour. However, as things were, Europe would doubtless think twice before responding to any such suggestion again. In the meantime, as Andrew had been making his way back to Palestine, the question of the succession to the Great Khan was resolved. Oghul-Ghaimish's efforts on behalf of her son had become desperate and at one point she had even attempted to assassinate the other candidate, Mongke; however, the plot was discovered, Oghul-Ghaimish was discredited and on 1 July 1251 Mongke was duly elected. There followed the usual purge of opposition supporters, along with seventy advisers who were executed for their complicity; Oghul-Ghaimish suffered the same fate as Fatima; Chaghadai's grandson Buri had been part of the plot and was therefore doomed; and Shiremun was sent away to the wars in China and murdered there on Mongke's orders. Even Eljigidei and his sons were swept away in the purge.

Mongke Khan then immediately distinguished his reign by declaring his wish to renew the Genghis mandate of world conquest. There would be two massive imperial expeditions: the first was to take up properly the campaign against the Sung Dynasty in southern China and extend the empire's borders in the east. Mongke decided he would lead this campaign himself with the aid of his younger brother Khubilai. The other great expedition he gave to another of his younger brothers, Hulegu.

This was the expansion of the empire in the west – not into Europe, but through Persia, down into Mesopotamia and Syria and eventually invading Egypt. This strike into the Middle East became the most ferocious and devastating attack that Islam ever encountered.

7

MONGOL CRUSADERS

With the enthronement of Mongke, the empire was once again in the hands of an expansionist. The motivating force behind the empire had lain dormant since Ogedei's reign and during that time it had shown distinct signs of decadence and internal decay. Mongke Khan was set to change all that. As this new sense of purpose moved through the Mongol capital, the Pope and his advisers struggled to decipher the confusing signals their envoys had delivered on the intentions of the 'Tartar hordes'. Louis's experience had been a bitter lesson.

However, though Europe waited to see what the fates delivered, this did not mean the end of European contact with the Mongol court. Among King Louis's entourage was a young Flemish monk by the name of William, who was soon to find himself at the very heart of the great empire just as it was about to make another stride on the world stage. Very little is known of William, except that he was born in the French town of Rubruck around 1217, that he lived for some time at a friary in Paris, that he was passionately devout and that he had been in Louis's service at least since his departure for Egypt in 1248.

SPY AND EVANGELIST IN THE LAND OF THE MONGOLS

William of Rubruck enters the story because of his remarkable account of life and customs at the Mongol court. Far more detailed than previous accounts, it describes the workings of the empire's capital at a critical time for both the empire and the rest of the world.

Friar William turned up at the Mongol court because of his own personal mission to preach the gospel among the pagans. He had been inspired by the stories of Andrew of Longjumeau and the writings of Carpini, amongst others, which described Mongol tolerance towards foreign religions. Rubruck had become concerned in particular about what he presumed was the pernicious influence of the 'Nestorians'. He had also been greatly moved by accounts of German slaves who were apparently labouring for one of the Mongol princes. This passionate friar saw it as his calling to travel the breadth of Asia, bring succour to the European slaves and, during this time of great evangelical fervour, convert the Mongols to the true Christian path.

Naturally Louis was reluctant to offer much encouragement to Rubruck's plan. He insisted that the friar should make quite clear to all Mongol officials the unofficial nature of his mission, in case they mistook his presence as an indication of Louis's submission to the Great Khan. However, in return for an account of Rubruck's observations from within the empire, Louis was prepared to give the monk a letter of introduction to Prince Sartaq, one of Batu Khan's sons and a recent convert, requesting safe conduct for the monk to fulfil his mission.

Rubruck set off from Acre at the beginning of 1253 with a party that included the Italian Franciscan Bartholomew of Cremona, a royal secretary named Gosset who brought with him gifts for the Khan, and a Syrian named Omodeo who was to act as guide and interpreter. They travelled by way of Constantinople, across the Black Sea and into Mongol territory, which Rubruck described as like 'stepping into some other world'. They arrived in July at Sartaq's camp, where the locals immediately presumed they were emissaries from King Louis; they were then sent on to Batu Khan's camp, three days' journey away. Batu also found Rubruck's explanations of a religious mission less than convincing, and he too sent them on – to the seat of the great Mongke Khan himself, at Qaraqorum.

During the three and a half months it took to get there,

Rubruck made careful notes on the landscape and people he observed along the way. His extremely detailed account became one of the most important descriptions of Central Asia ever recorded by a European. Fascinated by the customs and beliefs of all the peoples he encountered, he was forever making enquiries of the whereabouts of the monsters and other strange creatures that were supposed to inhabit these lands. The friar was constantly astonished to find no evidence of such beings anywhere.

By October Rubruck and his party were south of Lake Balkhash where he recorded that large numbers of villages had been destroyed 'so that the Tartars could feed their flocks there, for it is very fine pasturage'. Clearly old habits died hard. As with all journeys across the Asian steppe, the going was hard and gruelling. At times they were close to starvation, forced to eat raw mutton because of the lack of fuel. They kept on, driven by Rubruck's obsession to penetrate deep into this heathen wasteland and transform it into the new Eden. However, this proved more difficult than he had ever imagined – especially as his guide and interpreter, Omodeo, was more of a liability than an asset, having virtually none of the local languages.

Just before Christmas they arrived at Mongke's camp, a few miles west of Qaraqorum, and almost immediately the friars were granted an audience with the Great Khan. Once again the Mongols found it hard to swallow William's declaration that he simply wanted to live at court and preach the gospel. It seems that Mongke was untroubled by the lack of precious tribute and accepted that they were not royal emissaries from Louis. However, given the Mongols' own heavy reliance upon spies and informers, they were naturally suspicious of someone from Europe requesting permission to wander about the countryside. For the next two months William and his party were regularly interrogated by the Great Khan's ministers, who were never entirely satisfied with their explanations. Mongke, on the other hand, treated his guests with great courtesy. He granted them many audiences and listened intently to William's sermons.

Some of the eastern Christians at court even maintained that it was simply a matter of time before the Great Khan was baptized; after all, his mother, Sorghaghtani Beki, a niece of the Kereyid King Ong Khan, had been a Christian all her life. Be that as it may, Sorghaghtani had nevertheless always practised the traditional Mongol policy of religious impartiality, and had instilled these virtues in her son. Although a Christian, she was also remembered for having founded a richly endowed Muslim college in Bukhara.

Rubruck was sufficiently observant to notice that Mongke Khan paid equal attention to all the various foreign religions represented in his realm, making certain to attend all the important ceremonies. In a conversation with Rubruck, he was once reported to have explained his religious impartiality thus: 'We Mongols believe there is but one God, by Whom we live and by Whom we die, and towards Him we have an upright heart. . . . But just as God gave different fingers to the hand so has He given different ways to men.' Despite Mongke's highly sophisticated views on religion, the fact is that he remained fundamentally a shamanist, dependent upon fortune-tellers who burnt the shoulder-blade of a sheep to divine the future.

At the beginning of April the Great Khan moved his court to Qaraqorum and Rubruck and his party followed, thus becoming the first Europeans ever to visit the capital of the largest empire that the world had ever seen. He was not impressed. After spending time in Batu's capital, he wrote: 'I was overcome with fear, for his own houses seemed like a great city stretching out a long way and crowded around on every side by peoples to a distance of three or four leagues.' Qaraqorum, on the other hand, had not flourished to quite the same degree, and Rubruck declared that he found it no bigger than the village of Saint Denis to the north of Paris. Nevertheless, he was impressed by the uniquely international population; there was not another city like it anywhere. According to Rubruck it was divided up into various quarters: one for artisans, one for clerics, another for builders and engineers, and so on. There was a 'European colony', which apparently comprised craftsmen, merchants and scribes from Germany, Poland, France and Hungary, and even an Englishman called Basil, all of whom mingled with artisans, scientists and builders from Persia and China. Within its confines there were no fewer than twelve Buddhist temples, two mosques and a church. Along the many highways that linked the far reaches of the empire with Qaraqorum there flowed an unlikely traffic of priests, ambassadors, mystics and charlatans, come to beg indulgences or to take advantage of the Mongols' legendary superstitious nature. In the midst of this cosmopolitan society Rubruck and his entourage set about preaching the gospel.

Even by his own account Rubruck found his mission something of a struggle. Part of his problem was his own over-zealous approach. His teaching was shackled with academic dogma, and his arguments often reduced to threats of hellfire. Eventually even the local Christian community began to tire of him, especially after he threatened the Great Khan himself with eternal damnation. It is reported that Mongke responded to Rubruck's haranguing with the wisdom of a sage:

> The nurse at first lets some drops of milk into the infant's mouth, so that by tasting its sweetness he may be enticed to suck; only then does she offer him her breast. In the same way you should persuade Us, whom you claim to be so totally unacquainted with this doctrine, in a simple and rational manner. Instead you immediately threaten Us with eternal punishments.

Rubruck succeeded in converting just one Nestorian to the Church of Rome, and baptized six children. He did, however, take part in a debate between all the religions at the court, presented before an amused Great Khan and his courtiers. In a remarkable atmosphere of religious freedom, the representative of each creed was expected to challenge the others while at the same time presenting a rational explanation of the virtues and benefits of his own doctrine. In any other regime it would have been an exercise fraught with dangers; at the Mongol court it was an event of some entertainment. As might be expected, William took up the spirit of the debate and immediately launched into an attack against the Buddhists. In the meantime the eastern Christians took on the Islamic representatives, who were not much interested in a debate and refused to respond; so the eastern Christians rounded on the Uighur Buddhists instead. The Taoists seemed to have escaped unscathed; however, the proceedings soon dissolved into a raucous carouse, leaving a disillusioned Rubruck to record that his arguments had captured not one single convert. With his Christian work a complete failure, Rubruck resigned himself to the secondary aspect of his mission – that of gathering intelligence on behalf of King Louis.

If he was not well suited to the role of evangelist, he was even less well equipped to be a spy. Apart from his valuable observations of Mongol life, which were never properly appreciated until they were rediscovered by scholars in the nineteenth century, Rubruck gleaned little of Mongol policies or plans that they were not willing for him to know. The most obvious development taking place throughout his stay at Qaraqorum was the preparations being made for a massive military undertaking. Rubruck learned that, at a *quriltai* held in 1252, Mongke Khan had set out the objectives of his reign: a campaign against the Sung in China and, at the same time, a separate and even larger expedition into Persia and Syria, 'as far as the borders of Egypt', which was to be led by his younger brother Hulegu.

PLANNING THE MIDDLE EASTERN CAMPAIGN

The decision to extend the empire deep into Persia would have tremendous political ramifications in western Asia. Ever since Genghis Khan had swept through Transoxiana and Khurasan, the Mongols had maintained no more than a partial military presence. Under the first military commander, Chormaghun, the remnants of the Khwarazm Shah's empire had been swept away and with it all civil administration. During Batu's great expansion to the west the land between the Caspian and the Black Seas, Azerbaijan, came solidly under Mongol control; the next military governor of the area, Baiju, pushed Mongol influence into Rum – now Turkey – and crushed the Seljuks. When Baiju was replaced by the devious Eljigidei there was talk of a campaign against Baghdad, but nothing came of it. With the accession of Mongke, Eljigidei was swept away with the old regime and Baiju was reinstated as governor. However, Baiju made no sign of any move upon Baghdad, being fully occupied quelling uprisings in Asia Minor and Georgia. Throughout this period there were no substantial Mongol forces garrisoned further south than Azerbaijan and the Araxes valley, so control remained sporadic and chaos reigned.

From the Mongol perspective, a campaign into Persia and Syria was the logical pursuit of their philosophy of world domination. But the essential point behind Mongke's objectives was that further expansion in the west was going to happen in the Middle East, not in Europe. For centuries the Mongols had been familiar with the great influence that Muslim merchants from Persia and the Gulf area enjoyed throughout Asia. More significant was the reputation of Persian scientists, astronomers, astrologers, mathematicians and technologists, who were without equal anywhere in the world. Apart from the sciences, there were also the arts: painting, carpetmaking, music and poetry. The Islamic Middle East was by any standards a vastly sophisticated, wealthy and advanced civilization, and the Mongols could hardly allow it to flourish outside of their sphere. Mongke's objectives were obvious: by invading both the Sung empire in southern China and Persia, he was attempting to place the two great civilizations of the era under Mongol control. It stands as one of the most grandiose plans for world domination ever conceived.

One obvious conclusion that can be drawn from Mongke's decision was that the Mongols appeared to have lost interest in Europe. Indeed, there is no evidence that after Batu's withdrawal from eastern Europe the Mongols ever saw Europe as a prize worthy of the effort it would have taken to conquer. Although the pronouncements of the Great Khans continued to reiterate the conviction that it was the Mongols' God-given right to rule the world, and that all kings were obliged to offer tribute to the Great Khan, the reality was that in global terms Europe really did not matter that much.

Rubruck never imagined that the proposed expedition to the Middle East would benefit the cause of the crusaders in Palestine; on the other hand the eastern Christian community had become convinced that the Mongols were about to unleash a holy war against their ancient enemies, the Muslims. The Mongols' prime objective was the Caliph of Baghdad, but before confronting him they meant to eliminate the other major power in the region, the Ismailis or Assassins. They had emerged because of a schism in the Shia Muslim sect and established themselves in northern and eastern Persia by taking and controlling a series of mountain fortifications. Behind their walls they lived a contemplative life, producing beautifully wrought paintings and metalwork, but beyond their retreats they terrorized those civilizations they deemed heretical and so earned the enmity not just of the rest of the Islamic world but eventually of Europe. The local Ismaili leader had done little to enhance their reputation. Rather than confront his enemies in open combat he preferred to sponsor a campaign of political murder, usually executed with a dagger in the back, as the means to his end.

The Mongols had their own reasons for launching a campaign against the Assassins. First, they had received a plea of help from an Islamic judge in Qazwin, a town near the Assassins' stronghold at Alamut, who had complained that his fellow citizens were forced to wear armour all the time as protection from the Assassins' daggers. According to Rubruck, another reason that determined Mongol attitudes was the discovery of a plot to send no fewer than 400 dagger-wielding Assassins in disguise to Qaraqorum with instructions to murder the Great Khan. The Assassins had encountered the Mongols once before, during Chormaghun's terror raids through northern Persia in

1237–8, which led them to send an envoy to Europe begging for help.

Gradually the new imperial army took shape. It would be the grandest expedition since Batu's invasion of Europe. Mongke Khan allocated one-fifth of the entire Mongol force to Hulegu's command. One thousand 'teams' of Chinese engineers were recruited to manufacture and operate the siege machines, while fifth-columnists were sent ahead to prepare the way. This meant appropriating vast tracts of grazing land for the herds, stock-piling reserves of flour, grain, wine and other stores, building roads and bridges and then organizing a massive round-up of the thousands of horses that grazed across the steppes of western Asia. In the spring of 1253 the first contingents left Mongolia, and in the autumn Hulegu rode out at the head of an enormous army which then moved gradually across central Asia to the outskirts of Samarqand, where it made ready for the final march.

As preparations continued throughout 1254 and 1255, the Eastern Christian community became ever more enthusiastic for a war they believed would soon return them to their original home, the lands of Mesopotamia, from which they had emi-grated to escape persecution under the Muslims. Soon contin-gents of Eastern Christians arrived from Batu's Golden Horde; there were Georgians, Turks and Alans; all wanted to ride with Hulegu's *tumens*. It also happened that Hulegu's most senior commander, Ked-Buqa, was a Christian Naiman, while Hulegu's chief wife, Doquz-Khatun, was renowned for her Christian convictions. To a community that had suffered under the Mus-lims for centuries, Hulegu's campaign had all the hallmarks of a Christian holy war; however, Rubruck knew better. His observa-tions of the Mongol court told him a religious war was as alien to the Mongol generals as were the concepts of mercy and forgiveness. Although the character of Hulegu's army was, in parts, heavily Christian, the commander himself was a Buddhist.

RUBRUCK'S RETURN

While the great army was encamped near Samarqand, Rubruck finally began his long journey home. Mongke gave the friar a letter for Louis in which the Great Khan repudiated the earlier diplomatic missives sent by Guyuk Khan and his regent Oghul-Ghaimish. He explained to Louis: 'How could that wicked woman, more vile than a dog, know about matters of war and affairs of peace?' Mongke goes on to describe his visions of a united world 'from sunrise to sunset' under Mongol rule, and, although he urged Louis to send peace envoys, he did not make any demands for tribute. It was a far more conciliatory letter than previous communications, and one might speculate that perhaps Mongke could see some advantage in trying to win Europe's trust.

Rubruck delayed his departure as long as possible, in the hope that he might glean a clearer signal of Mongol attitudes towards Europe. He had heard that King Hayton, from Armenia, was travelling secretly to Qaraqorum in order to see the Great Khan in connection with the planned expedition, and Rubruck imagined he might learn more of the expedition's real objectives from a fellow Roman Christian. However, by the beginning of July he had tired of waiting and decided to leave. Friar Bartholomew remained behind. Too ill to travel, he remained in Qaraqorum; it is presumed that he died there, the first Italian to die in the Far East.

A few months after Rubruck's departure, King Hayton finally arrived at Qaraqorum. Having heard of the planned campaign, Hayton had immediately realized that an all-out war against the main Islamic powers would have tremendous advantages for Christian Asia. He was received by Mongke and eventually spent fifty days at the capital, during which time he convinced the Great Khan that the entire expedition would be assured of allies in Palestine if it was made clear that Hulegu's expedition was nothing less than a Christian Crusade. Hayton then returned with a *yarligh*, an edict that, in effect, enfranchised the Christian

Churches throughout the empire – and in those areas not yet conquered. He returned to Armenia, and made preparations to join Hulegu's force.

Had Rubruck managed to encounter King Hayton, he might have delivered a completely different report to Louis. In the event, his was yet another depressing account of Mongol intransigence. His mission both as an evangelist and as a spy had been a failure. He brought no accounts of fabled monsters, nor of Prester John. He bitterly regretted not having managed very many conversions and railed against the 'pernicious influence' that the Church of the East, in preference to Rome, enjoyed at the Mongol court. He did, however, confirm that a massive army was currently advancing upon Persia and Syria, but he made no recommendation of an alliance – quite the opposite. He had become so disenchanted with the Mongols that he saw only one policy for Europe. 'Were it allowed me,' he wrote, 'I would to the utmost of my power preach war against them throughout the whole world.' Rubruck's report had a tremendous influence, not just on the French King, but on the rest of the courts of Europe. It dealt another blow to the Prester John legend; but, perhaps more significantly, it was a great discouragement to those who still imagined the possibility of an alliance with a great Eastern Christian king against the Muslim nations.

ACROSS THE OXUS INTO PERSIA

On 1 January 1256 Hulegu's army crossed the Oxus River and brought into Persia the most formidable war machine ever seen. It possessed the very latest in siege engineering, gunpowder from China, catapults that would send balls of flaming naphtha into their enemy's cities, and divisions of rigorously trained mounted archers led by generals who had learnt their skills at the feet of Genghis Khan and Subedei. As news of Hulegu's army spread he was soon presented with a succession of sultans, emirs and atabaks from as far apart as Asia Minor and Herat, all come to pay homage. Its sheer presence brought to an end nearly forty years of rebellion and unrest in the old lands of Khwarazmia, but to the inhabitants of Persia and Syria it was the dawn of a new world order.

The Mongols made first for the Elburz Mountains, where the Assassins lay in wait behind what they believed to be their impregnable fortresses. With extraordinary ingenuity the Mongol generals and their Chinese engineers manoeuvred their artillery up the mountain slopes and set them up around the walls of the fortress of Alamut. But before the order was given to commence firing, the Assassins' Grand Master, Rukn ad-Din, signalled that he wanted to negotiate. Hulegu countered that he must immediately order the destruction of his own fortifications; when Rukn ad-Din prevaricated, the bombardment commenced. Under the most devastatingly accurate artillery fire, the walls quickly tumbled and Rukn ad-Din surrendered. Hulegu took him prisoner, transported him to every Assassin castle they confronted, and paraded him before each garrison with the demand for an immediate surrender. Some obliged, as at Alamut; while others, like Gerdkuh, had to be taken by force. Today the spherical stone missiles fired by the artillery teams at the walls still litter the perimeter of the ruins. Whether each 'eagle's nest' surrendered or was taken, the Mongols put all the inhabitants to the sword – even the women in their homes and the babies in their cradles.

As this slaughter continued, Rukn ad-Din begged Hulegu to allow him to go to Qaraqorum where he would pay homage to the Great Khan and plead for clemency. Hulegu agreed, but when he got to Qaraqorum Mongke Khan refused to see him. It was effectively a sentence of death. On the journey back his Mongol escort turned on the Grand Master and his attendants, who were 'kicked to a pulp'. The Persian historian Juvaini commented that 'the world has been cleansed'. Five hundred years later Edward Gibbon echoed those sentiments, claiming that the Mongols' campaign 'may be considered as a service to mankind'. It took two years for the Mongols to dislodge over

200 'eagles' nests', but in the process they virtually expunged the Assassins from Persia.

THE DESTRUCTION OF BAGHDAD

In 1258, the first objective accomplished, Hulegu turned his army to the west into Mesopotamia and began the march on Baghdad. Since Hulegu had received the submission of all the petty warlords in Baiju's territory, the military governor was free to lead his *tumens* overland and link up with the main army. With further reinforcements from Christian Georgia, keen to be part of an attack upon Baghdad, Hulegu's force was virtually doubled. Demands for surrender were sent to the Caliph and refused.

The young man who currently reigned as the thirty-seventh commander of the faith was unfortunately an incompetent and cowardly individual by the name of Mustasim. His weaknesses were exploited by ruthless officials who had got used to running the city while Caliph Mustasim concentrated on spiritual affairs. As leader of the entire Sunni community he could have tried summoning Muslim armies from as far away as Morocco to defend Baghdad; instead he preferred the advice of his chief minister, Ibn al-Alkami, who assured him that the danger was not great and that the Baghdad defences were adequate. Ibn al-Alkami was at the same time sending secret messages to the approaching army, urging them to attack and describing the pitiful state of the Baghdad defences. Persian accounts of this treachery explain that the chief minister, a Shia Muslim, had been motivated by his resentment of the Caliph's persecution of his Shia brethren. In the meantime ambassadors rode back and forth, offering to pay tribute to Hulegu but refusing to surrender, while behind the city walls there was growing fear and confusion.

When Mustasim finally gave the order that the city should be defended properly, the Mongols were just a day's march away.

A contingent of some 20 000 of the city's garrison rode out to confront the enemy, but as they camped in the fields in sight of the city walls the Mongols surprised them by smashing the dams and dykes nearby and flooding the encampment. Those who did not drown were cut to pieces by the Mongol heavy cavalry.

Meanwhile Baiju's *tumens* had occupied the western suburbs which, once filled with vast warehouses, had been the great commercial heart of the city. On the opposite side, in the eastern Shia suburbs, Hulegu's engineers were constructing a ditch and a rampart that eventually surrounded the city. On 30 January the bombardment of Baghdad began. Events had moved so swiftly that the bullock carts bringing up ammunition, hewn from the Jebel Hamrin Mountains, were still three days away. So the artillery units improvised with stumps of palm trees and foundations from the occupied suburbs. Seven days later the Mongols stormed and took the east wall. There they remained, as gradually the city surrendered. As the garrison filed out, laying down their weapons, they were led away and slaughtered one by one. The Caliph eventually emerged with his family and 3000 courtiers. On 13 February, the sack of Baghdad began.

Though the city had lost its commercial importance, it remained an important cultural, spiritual and intellectual centre. Within the city's walls were magnificent mosques, vast libraries of Persian and Arabian literature, the greatest university in the world, plus numerous palaces belonging to the Caliph and his family and perhaps one of the greatest personal treasures to be found anywhere. It was the greatest city the Mongols conquered in the Middle East, and into this oasis of civilization they brought sword and torch. None of the invaders set about their task with more relish than the Christian contingent from Georgia. The Eastern Christian community hiding inside their churches were spared, but the Muslim population, Shia or Sunni, were ruthlessly dispatched. Most of the women and children were herded together and transported to Qaraqorum, as was the wealth of the Caliph's treasure house.

As the mosques and palaces burned and the cries from the

street echoed into the night, the Caliph and his family were treated to a banquet with Hulegu. Afterwards they were sewn up in the customary Mongol carpet and then trampled to death under the hooves of Mongol horses, and so ended the dynasty of the Abbasid caliphs that had survived for 500 years. The treacherous chief minister, Ibn al-Alkami, was rewarded by being allowed to retain his position under the Mongol rule. Persian accounts claim between 800 000 and 2 million killed within the city walls. At any rate, the stench from rotting corpses was so great that, not for the first time, the Mongols had to evacuate their camp sites. Nevertheless, Persian historians tend to exaggerate the slaughter of Baghdad, for commercial evidence shows a thriving economy just two years later.

EXPEDITION TO SYRIA

Hulegu marched his army north-east towards Tabriz, where he planned to make his base in Persia. He paused briefly by the shores of Lake Urmiyeh and was impressed by the rugged beauty of a rocky island crag that loomed out of its waters. On Shai Island, a largely barren monolith heavily pock-marked with ancient rock tombs, Hulegu built a treasure house where he stored his portion of the spoils. He set up his encampment near Tabriz and waited as news of the fall of Baghdad swept through Syria and Palestine. It was one of the greatest catastrophes that had ever befallen the Islamic world. But the impact was felt far beyond Islam, for the virtual obliteration of one of the greatest cities of the world sent shock waves right across all civilization. The Mongols were again on the march.

Soon the eastern Christians who had lived under the Muslim yoke for five centuries were hailing Hulegu as a latter-day saviour, for the enemies of Christ were about to be thrown into the sea. An Armenian chronicler declared: 'During the time of Baghdad's supremacy like an insatiable bloodsucker she had swallowed up the whole world. Now she has been punished for all the blood she has spilled and the evil she has wrought, the measure of her iniquity being filled.'

As Hulegu marched into Syria, there appeared a long procession of princes come to offer rich tribute and their submission to their new lord. The Prince of Mosul presented Hulegu with a set of gold ear-rings, amongst other treasures, which he placed in the Mongol's ears himself. It was by way of a private joke between his ministers and himself, for he had once boasted that the Mongols would be no threat and that one day he would take the upstart Hulegu by the ears. Another who came with gifts, Prince Kai-Kawus, presented Hulegu with a pair of slippers painted with the prince's own portrait on the soles, so that the Mongol might walk on his face.

In return the princes were being offered the privilege of becoming vassal lords to Hulegu and providing him with soldiers to augment his already massive host, and soon there was barely a single Muslim prince east of the Tigris who ruled without Mongol approval. There were exceptions, of course; the Prince

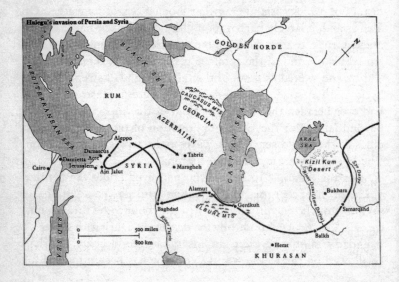

of Mayyafarakin, Kamil Muhammad, had sworn allegiance to the Great Khan in Qaraqorum but had also provided soldiers to help defend the Caliph. When Hulegu learned of Kamil Muhammad's treachery, and that he had recently crucified a Christian priest travelling through his city on a Mongol passport, he commanded that the prince and all the inhabitants of Mayyafarakin be made an example of, a task he gave to some of the Christian contingents. King Hayton's 16 000 Armenians plus a large number of Georgians were despatched to take Mayyafarakin, which they did with some efficiency. The Christian commanders then dealt with Prince Kamil Muhammad with particular relish, first trussing the unfortunate victim like a chicken and then slicing off pieces of his flesh and feeding them to him until he was dead.

Before Hulegu set out to invade Syria the Sultan of that country, al-Nasir, sent his son to negotiate with the Mongol commander. He came claiming that his father wanted to make peace and to offer tribute to the Great Khan in Qaraqorum. Hulegu's reply, written in the most eloquent and flowing Persian prose, simply informed Sultan al-Nasir that he was 'doomed to fall'. Submission would not be enough; Hulegu meant to rule Syria. The Sultan's resources were in a terrible state since he had recently fought and lost a war with the Mamluks of Egypt, causing him to cede territory in Gaza and Jerusalem. Now the Mongols, with an army fast approaching a staggering 300 000, were demanding his immediate surrender – an act he knew would result in his execution. In desperation the Sultan turned to his erstwhile enemies in Cairo, thinking that as fellow Muslims they would come to his aid. In the meantime he had sent a suicidal letter, rejecting Hulegu's terms and defiantly demanding that the Mongols depart from his kingdom. But it all went terribly wrong when the Mamluks, who were just as intimidated by the Mongol presence, showed no interest in coming to the Sultan's defence.

Meanwhile, the mighty citadel at Aleppo had digested the news from Baghdad and defiantly prepared for the coming onslaught. On 12 September 1259, Hulegu swept across the Tigris, marching through Harran, Nasibin and Edessa. As news spread that they had crossed the Euphrates on a pontoon bridge at Manbij, the Church of the East hailed its imminent return to Jerusalem. Sultan al-Nasir had long since fled to Damascus, leaving the Aleppo garrison in the hands of his elderly uncle, Turan Shah. The old man had reasoned that the best form of defence was attack and despatched a large contingent of his force to confront the Mongols in the open. As had happened at Baghdad, the defenders were ambushed and destroyed.

Outside Aleppo, the Mongols drew up a score of artillery teams to demolish the city walls. The bombardment lasted seven days, and on 20 January 1260 they occupied the city. Inside the great citadel the elderly Turan Shah and what remained of the garrison held out for another four weeks, while in the streets below Muslim men were being put to the sword and the women and children were herded out to be transported to Qaraqorum as slaves. Eventually the citadel surrendered. As a mark of respect for the way the old man had defended his post, the Mongols spared Turan Shah's life. When news reached Damascus that Aleppo had fallen, the Sultan abandoned that city too.

As al-Nasir made his way towards Egypt, the only sanctuary left to him, the great city of Damascus surrendered itself to the forces led by Ked-Buqa. His triumphant entry was made into an all-Christian affair, as Muslims were made to bow before the cross which was carried in procession through the streets. Behind it marched a unique Christian alliance: Ked-Buqa, a true Eastern Christian; King Hayton of Armenia; and his father-in-law Count Bohemund, the veteran crusader from Antioch. To add insult to injury, a mosque was converted into a church in which was held a celebratory Mass.

In the meantime Hulegu's patrols had been despatched to hunt down their quarry, the Sultan al-Nasir. He was pursued through Samaria and as far south as Gaza, where he was finally captured. As al-Nasir was being transported to Hulegu's camp, the Mongol had already sent a final threat to the last remaining

Islamic force of any consequence – the Mamluks:

> You have heard how we have conquered a vast empire and
> have purified the earth of disorders which tainted it. It is
> for you to fly and for us to pursue, and whither will you
> fly, and by what road will you escape us? Our horses are
> swift, our arrows sharp, our swords like thunderbolts, our
> hearts as hard as the mountains, our soldiers as numerous
> as the sand. Fortresses will not detain us, nor arms stop us:
> your prayers to heaven will not avail against us.

Then he reminded them (as if they needed it): 'At present you
are the only enemy against whom we have to march.'

The rapidly changing situation was giving some pause to the
remaining crusader forces still entrenched behind their vast
fortifications along the Mediterranean coast. Count Bohemund's
loyalty during the campaign in Syria was rewarded when Hulegu
bequeathed to him the lands between Aleppo and the narrow
strip of coast he already occupied. It seemed as though Christendom's prayers were being answered. But even as this news
reached Rome, it was followed by the report that Bohemund,
under Hulegu's direction, had installed a Greek Orthodox bishop
as patriarch of Antioch in place of a Catholic. To Rome this
was a heresy; to Hulegu it was simply traditional Mongol
impartiality towards all religions. Nevertheless it sent a confusing signal to the western Christian community, especially that
small band of crusader states along the Palestinian coast who
had become locked in a fierce debate about the Mongol invasion
and what it meant to their future.

To everyone in the Middle East it was obvious that Islamic
power stood at the precipice: one more significant Mongol
victory, and Islam as a political power would be finished. The
eastern Christian forces that had campaigned with the Mongols
were convinced that the entire expedition was nothing less than
a Christian Crusade to rid the Holy Land of Islam – or so they
had believed since King Hayton's secret visit to Qaraqorum. So
far the campaign had every appearance of having been

Christian-inspired: Christians had been spared in Baghdad, Aleppo and Damascus; Christian churches were being repaired and the Mongols were giving every indication that they wanted an alliance with the crusader states in the next phase of their campaign. Hulegu, King Hayton and Count Bohemund were at that very moment planning the march on to Jerusalem and its long-awaited return to Christendom.

MONGOL RETRIBUTION IN POLAND

However, behind their crusader castle walls, from Krak des Chevaliers to Acre, the argument raged: should western Christendom throw its lot in with this new superpower, or stand back and remain impartial? Those crusaders like Anno von Sangherhausen, the Grand Master of the Teutonic Knights, who were more familiar with the eastern Christian community, were inclined to encourage an alliance. However, the signals from Rome itself were unequivocal: the Mongols were pagans and were not to be trusted. Whatever the views of the eastern Christians, they were of no consequence when the crusaders took their orders from Rome.

There was good reason for Rome's intransigence, for there had been a fresh Mongol incursion into Europe, rekindling old fears of another invasion. Four years after Mongke had come to the throne in Qaraqorum, Batu Khan of the Golden Horde had died. Over the next three years the khanate passed from Batu's son to his grandson in quick succession, until in 1257 it finally rested with Batu's younger brother Berke. During this period of instability, and especially while much of the army was abroad with Hulegu in Syria, a number of Russian princes saw an opportunity to overthrow the Mongol yoke. Prince Daniel of Galicia, supported by Prince Mendovg of Lithuania, had driven out the Mongol outposts in Volhynia but failed to gain any further territory and retired their forces to the fortified cities of Galicia.

When Berke Khan finally came to power, he wasted no time in gathering together a force large enough to mete out the appropriate punishment. Burundai, the Mongol commander in charge of the exercise, swept through Volhynia and Galicia, forcing all the cities there to destroy their fortifications. In pursuit of the errant princes, and perhaps also to warn off any neighbouring state still harbouring similar ambitions, Burundai took his army into Poland. The destruction he left behind was far greater than that caused during the invasion of 1241. All the towns and villages of northern Poland were destroyed, as were the cities of Lublin, Sandomir and the hapless Cracow – which had hardly recovered from the last encounter. Thousands were slaughtered before Burundai rode back into Russia, having encountered virtually no opposition.

The new Pope, Alexander IV, had implored the neighbouring states to come to Poland's aid, but once again there was no response. In desperation he proclaimed yet another Crusade against the Mongols, which would have meant in effect an invasion of Russia; but there were no volunteers. The only significant act he could accomplish was to excommunicate Count Bohemund for having fought beside the pagan Easterners in Syria, and it was this which had the greatest influence upon the crusader states in Palestine. The news arrived just as the crusader lords were debating an alliance and virtually sealed the issue. At any rate, all the evidence suggested that the Mongol forces were about to deal the death blow, so crusader neutrality would be of no consequence.

AN UNLIKELY ALLIANCE LEADS TO VICTORY

Then, around February 1260, just as Hulegu and his generals were calculating the next stage of their campaign, the march on Jerusalem, a rider entered the Khan's camp with news from China. Since autumn the year before messengers had been making their way along the great Mongol *Yam*, the system of highways and staging posts that embraced the breadth of Asia, to bring the news to the farthest outposts of the empire. While engaged in the campaign against the Sung, Mongke Khan had contracted dysentery and died. In an uncanny repetition of history, Mongke Khan's death saved Islam from certain extinction just as Ogedei Khan's demise had saved Europe from Batu's hordes, for upon hearing the news Hulegu immediately withdrew the bulk of his forces from Syria and regrouped around Maragheh, where he sat and pondered the situation.

With Hulegu's withdrawal the military landscape was transformed. He had left his redoubtable commander, Ked-Buqa, in Damascus with a small fragment of the once great army to stand at the frontier of his empire. The first to test the Mongols' strength were two crusader lords, Julian of Sidon and John of Beirut, who led raids into Mongol territory. Ked-Buqa's retaliation led to the sack of Sidon and the total destruction of an army of Templars led by John of Beirut. The crusaders reeled in fright. But the Mongol action had fully revealed their strength — or, more to the point, their weakness — and news soon spread. As the Mamluks were pondering Hulegu's demand for surrender, sent before his withdrawal from Syria, they learned that a much-depleted contingent was all that held the Mongol frontier. Having assumed they would soon have to defend their capital, the Mamluks now decided to throw caution to the wind and march out to meet the Mongols on their own territory. There would never be a better opportunity to repel the invader, and they signalled their intentions by executing the Mongol envoys and impaling their heads on the spikes of one of Cairo's gates.

The Mamluk commander, Qutuz, had become fired with what he saw as his mission to save Islam and civilization. In an audacious move he sent emissaries to the crusaders, asking for an alliance against the Mongols. Barely able to believe this token from Islam, the crusaders struggled to produce a response. Despite the recent Mongol raids, there were still Christian voices arguing that an alliance with the Mongols was the best chance of ridding the Holy Land of Islam. Whether they realized it or not, as they debated the merits of an alliance with either the Mongols or the Muslims the crusaders were in fact weighing up the future of Christianity and Islam in the Middle East. In the event, the memories of Sidon were too fresh for the pro-Mongolists to have prevailed, and while the crusaders found it impossible actually to fight with the Mamluks, they did eventually send word to Qutuz that they would at least not impede his army's journey north into Syria. It was an absolutely crucial decision.

Qutuz led his army north through Gaza, where they encountered and destroyed a small Mongol force out on a long-range patrol. Encouraged, the Mamluks moved further north, passing through Christian-held territory where they received supplies and fresh horses. While Qutuz and his generals were enjoying crusader hospitality at Acre, Ked-Buqa led his two *tumens*, perhaps 15 000 men, out of Damascus and headed south-west. Amongst his army was a large contingent of native Syrian conscripts. On 3 September 1260 Ked-Buqa crossed the River Jordan and began his final march towards the Mamluk army.

Qutuz in the meantime had also advanced, and the two forces drew up in the valley where legend held that David had slain Goliath. At Ayn Jalut, Goliath's spring, the Mongols finally encountered the Mamluk vanguard. Ked-Buqa ordered a charge, and the Mamluk vanguard turned and fled. But the Mongols had fallen for one of their own tactics, for they were led straight into the main Mamluk force spread thinly across the 6-km (4-mile)-wide valley. Accounts vary about the sizes of the two forces, but what is known is that at some point in the proceedings, possibly as the Mongols discovered they had charged into a trap, the Syrian contingent broke ranks and fled the field. From that moment the Mongols were at a great disadvantage.

Realizing that he was now committed to engaging the entire Mamluk force, Ked-Buqa ordered his ranks to charge the Mamluk flank. This they did, turning it and eventually destroying the Mamluk wing. Qutuz despaired at the lost advantage as the battle swung first one way, then the other. For either side it was a fight to the death, and for most of the day the result might have gone either way. But then two events occurred that decisively turned the tide. As the Mamluk ranks appeared in danger of being routed, Qutúz is reported to have thrown his helmet to the ground and implored his troops to regroup and renew the fight. He reminded them that they were fighting not simply for their lives, but for the very future of Islam. Fired by his call, the Mamluks regrouped and charged the Mongols' ranks. At the same time, fortune struck against the Mongols as their commander Ked-Buqa fell in combat. There is a conflicting report that he was actually captured by the Mamluks and executed on the battlefield; but whatever the case, the result was the same. Against overwhelming odds the Mongol generals finally lost their nerve, turned the army and retreated. They were pursued for 12 km (8 miles) to the town of Beisan, where they drew up to face the Mamluk cavalry. But they had already lost the momentum, and the resulting clash decimated the Mongol ranks. Within days a Mamluk messenger, bearing Ked-Buqa's head on the end of a staff, returned to Cairo to spread the news. Qutuz was about to enter Damascus in triumph.

What had happened in the valley of Ayn Jalut was one of the most significant battles in world history. Although the battle itself was not conclusive – it did not sweep the Mongols from the Middle East – it nevertheless utterly smashed the myth of Mongol invincibility. They were just as fallible as any other army, and subject to the same twists of good and bad fortune. Ayn Jalut also marked the end of any concerted campaign by the Mongols to conquer that part of the world. After Damascus was taken by the Mamluks, and soon afterwards Aleppo, the Mongols sent contingents back into Syria to conduct revenge raids – but there was no sign of a co-ordinated reconquest. All this was not, however, due to Mamluk hegemony alone. The Mamluks had not encountered the full weight of the Mongol force, and never would. There were other reasons for Hulegu's reticence – reasons related to events that were unfolding on the other side of Asia.

8

KHUBILAI KHAN
AND CHINA

At the death of each Khan it was Mongol custom for the widow to rule as regent until the question of his succession had been settled; this policy provided women with a brief opportunity to exercise some influence over the direction of the empire. Unfortunately, during the regencies of Toregene and Oghul-Ghaimish their energies were largely devoted to securing the succession of their favourite sons. However, by far the most influential woman at the Mongol court never actually reigned as regent.

Sorghaghtani Beki, Tolui's widow, bore him four sons before he died, probably of alcoholic poisoning, around 1233. Soon afterwards, Ogedei tried to get Sorghaghtani to marry his son Guyuk – a union between aunt and nephew – in the hope of uniting the two houses of Tolui and Ogedei; but the good widow declined. Her commitment to her children, she explained, prevented her from accepting the responsibility of marriage. One suspects it was more political than maternal instincts that obliged her to turn down the proposition.

As time passed, it became obvious that the qualities that distinguished the sons of Tolui were entirely the result of Sorghaghtani's influence. Throughout the reigns of Ogedei and Guyuk she emerged as easily the most accomplished, learned and certainly the wisest woman in the Mongol court, and as she aged so her importance grew. Rashid al-Din, the Persian historian, described her as 'extremely intelligent and able and towered above all the women in the world'. A poet of the age waxed even more lyrical: 'If I were to see among the race of women

167

another woman like this, I should say that the race of women was far superior to that of men!' One can only speculate how she might have directed the course of the empire had she, a lifelong Christian, managed to rule as regent. How differently might she have received the various papal envoys. But it was not to be.

Instead, Sorghaghtani devoted herself to the education and development of her four sons: Mongke, Khubilai, Hulegu and Ariq Boke. It was her shrewd and careful manoeuvring that forged an alliance with Batu Khan after Guyuk's death and ensured the election of her eldest son, Mongke, as Khan in 1251. Unfortunately the great woman died a year later, surviving only just long enough to share in her son's triumph and to see the empire once again striving to expand. Nevertheless, her influence was felt long afterwards through the actions of her children: a Great Khan who was to revitalize the empire; Hulegu, who conquered Persia, Mesopotamia and Syria; Ariq Boke, another great commander steeped in Mongol lore and tradition; and of course Khubilai, also a gifted warrior, arguably the most learned and most cultured, and easily the most sophisticated of the four.

CHINESE INFLUENCES

Sorghaghtani gave birth to her second son in 1215 at Chung-tu, while her husband and father-in-law were on campaign in northern China. Khubilai was brought up to ride and shoot, as every Mongol was, but Sorghaghtani was also at pains to ensure that he was literate and so from childhood he was attended by tutors who were either Uighurs or Chinese. His early life was spent on his mother's appanage in northern China, and when he was old enough he moved to his own large tract of territory in the Hopei region. Under his mother's tutelage Khubilai became deeply concerned with the administration of his lands, and in particular with the wellbeing of his peasants, who at that time were abandoning their farms and migrating elsewhere. Sorghaghtani taught him to appreciate that the peasantry were leaving because Mongol taxes were far too high, and that, unless something was done quickly, soon there would be no one left to tax. Khubilai dismissed the Mongol tax merchants and installed Chinese officials, who brought in a more affordable and productive tax regime. Soon the young Khubilai drew the attention of his contemporaries because both his attendants and advisers were mostly Chinese. It was not long before other Mongols complained that not only did he spend most of his time in China, hardly ever visiting Qaraqorum, but that he actually seemed to identify with his Chinese subjects.

Despite these complaints, when Mongke Khan set in motion the long-overdue campaign against the Sung he gave his brother Khubilai command of an important part of the campaign: the capture of the kingdom of Ta-li, south of Szechwan Province at the eastern end of the Tibetan Plateau. It was a daunting objective. The kingdom of the Ta-li was strategically vital, coveted by both the Mongols and the Sung as it provided access from the khanate of the Great Khan to the western territories of the Sung empire, and to Burma and Thailand. Populated by a mixture of Tibetans, Central Asians and a heavy suffusion of Chinese, it remained vigorously independent. Khubilai's first obstacle was to march his army all the way from the northern plateau, down through Szechwan and into the mountains of the Tibetan Plateau. Having accomplished this, he and his generals successfully, and somewhat uncharacteristically, subdued the Ta-li with the minimum of bloodshed. It was a huge military success, placing Khubilai amongst the already long list of great Mongol commanders. Mongke Khan rewarded him with even more land to add to his already considerable *ulus* in northern China, to which he returned with his Chinese advisers to begin long-term plans.

The most significant decision he made after his return was to demonstrate his growing commitment to the lands he governed by ordering the construction of a capital. To the Chinese it seemed a perfectly reasonable act, but to the Mongols in

Qaraqorum it was an extremely provocative decision. To avoid provoking too much outrage, Khubilai went to some trouble finding an appropriate location – roughly on the frontier between the steppe and the western edge of Chinese agrarian territory, north of the Luan River and about ten days' ride from the city of Chung-tu. However, his concern for Mongol sensibilities eluded him when it came to its construction, for what emerged was a classic Chinese imperial city in all but name.

He had turned to his most important Chinese adviser, Liu Ping-chung, to supervise the design of what was to be known as K'ai-p'ing. Liu created a walled city based on the Chinese principles of geomancy: a near-perfect square with each side facing one of the four points of the compass. There were in fact three separate walled compounds, one inside the other, containing the Outer City, the Imperial City and, in the very heart of the complex, the Palace City. However, it was in the design of the buildings, halls and temples that made up the Palace City that Liu's influence was most strongly felt. He had called for the construction of eight large Buddhist monasteries in the 'eight corners' of the city, that is at the four cardinal points of the compass and the midpoints in between. These eight points corresponded with the eight fundamental trigrams of the *Yi jing* (*Book of Changes*), the Confucian book of divinations. It could not have been more Chinese. Against the northern wall stood the largest building, the Da'an Ge, a large central hall for audiences and banquets. It was built by Chinese craftsmen and painters, including the famous artist Wang Zhenpeng who had joined Khubilai's employ.

Ten years after construction began Khubilai renamed the city, giving it the Chinese title Shang-tu (Upper Capital), and it was this that was described by Marco Polo as containing rivers and forests running with game, which the Great Khan hunted for sport. In his account Polo mistranslated Shang-tu, calling it Ciandu – which, of course, the poet Coleridge eventually transformed into Xanadu. The groves and fields, 'where Alph the sacred river ran', were laid out in the 6½ hectares (16 acres) that made up the Outer City. It was the Khan's hunting park, an artificial steppe environment that was Khubilai's token affirmation of his Mongol origins.

But long before Khubilai had renamed the city Shang-tu its mere existence aroused opposition at Qaraqorum. To the traditionalists Khubilai had gone native – he had more than identified with his subjects, and seemed utterly infatuated with the attractions of Chinese civilization. To have a prince of the empire building a city in China was bad enough, but when reports arrived that it rivalled Qaraqorum with its marbled halls and magnificent temples it was seen by Mongke Khan's advisers as a challenge to the traditional Mongol way of life. Soon the Khan was hearing that his brother had dispensed with fundamental Mongol taxation policies and was exercising Chinese laws. Inevitably there were charges of treason, and soon a rift developed between the two brothers that threatened to break out into open conflict. At one point plots were even laid to have the young upstart assassinated, but in the event the sibling bonds proved too strong and eventually there was a reconciliation.

It appeared, for a time, as though the conservatives in Qaraqorum had been silenced. Khubilai relinquished some of his tax-gathering powers, and in 1257 the two brothers resumed the campaign against the Sung; Khubilai was once again entrusted with a large contingent of the army. The campaign was an ingenious one, involving the co-ordination of two separate attacks: one from the north and the other, by Khubilai, from the west. Everything progressed well, with Khubilai having the best of the military encounters. But then, with the Mongols on the path to victory, on 11 August 1259 Mongke Khan died of dysentery in the hills at Tiao-yu Shan.

CIVIL WAR OVER THE SUCCESSION TO THE KHANATE

As has been seen, the news brought Hulegu's breathtaking campaign in the Middle East to a juddering halt, with terrible consequences for the Mongol presence there. But Mongke Khan's untimely death had even more dire consequences: it exposed once again the chaotic and unwieldy process of succession and presented an opportunity for the disaffected elements in Qaraqorum to challenge Khubilai openly. Although none of the other great houses of Genghis – Ogedei, Chaghadai or Jochi – presented a serious challenge, the absence of Sorghaghtani's influence over her children meant that the question of succession degenerated into a violent dispute amongst siblings that eventually heaved the empire into civil war.

When news reached Khubilai of his brother's death, he had been leading his army southward in preparation for the co-ordinated attack and had just reached the northern banks of the Yangtze River. But instead of returning north to be present at a *quriltai*, Khubilai decided to press on with his part of the campaign. He was keenly aware of the opposition in Qaraqorum, and probably reasoned that if he secured a spectacular new victory against the Sung it would ensure his success. It was a crucial decision – and a bad one.

For the next two months he campaigned deeper into Sung territory, crossing the Yangtze and eventually laying siege to the heavily fortified town of O'chou. As the Mongols settled in for what looked like being a long siege, the Sung sent forth emissaries in the vain hope that a bribe might send the Mongols away – but times had changed. Khubilai spurned the offers and, thinking time was on his side, decided to sit and wait.

Unfortunately, in those precious months when he was camped outside the walls of O'chou, dramatic moves were taking place back in Mongolia. During all the years that Khubilai and Hulegu had been abroad in China and Persia their youngest brother, Ariq Boke, had remained in the Mongol heartland. His had been a far more parochial upbringing surrounded by a far more conservative nobility – and he had emerged as the representative of traditional Mongol values. To those at court who felt isolated from the new power centres and who despised Hulegu and Khubilai as having betrayed the Mongol ethic and succumbed to the soft life in the towns and cities, Ariq Boke became the champion to drag the empire back to its origins – by force if necessary. Powerful figures in Qaraqorum had flocked to Ariq Boke's side: the late Mongke Khan's sons; one of his widows; the grandchildren of Ogedei, Chaghadai and Jochi; plus many important officials and advisers. They had secretly begun to raise an army, and by November were already marching on K'ai-p'ing and Chung-tu.

When word reached Khubilai he must have cursed the fates, for just as the first major Sung city was about to fall he had to abandon his campaign, and most of the lands he had conquered, to return to his own backyard. Having garrisoned K'ai-p'ing he cloistered himself with his advisers to plan the next move. They unanimously agreed that Khubilai must establish his authority as quickly as possible; so he called a *quriltai* and had himself elected Great Khan on 5 May 1260.

It was another wrong move. Instead of riding to Qaraqorum with his army, confronting his detractors and demanding a *quriltai*, he immediately laid himself open to charges of having usurped the position of Great Khan. His *quriltai* contained none of the major Mongol nobility, and moreover it had been convened on foreign soil. Everything about it was illegitimate. With Qaraqorum now in open revolt Khubilai's response was to appear even more Chinese than before, exhorting his Chinese subjects to come to his aid. In return he offered a reduction in taxes, food for the hungry and a promise to reunite the country. They were the words of a typical Chinese emperor; he could hardly have done a better job of inciting Qaraqorum, and what followed was four years of civil war.

In confronting the forces in Mongolia, Khubilai's strategy was to expose their fundamental weaknesses: their lack of indigenous supplies, especially of grain and manufactures. Qaraqorum had always been a city with little inherent reason for existence save the Great Khan's wish it be so. It survived only because of a massive and regular flow of food and other supplies from northern China and elsewhere. With that source cut off and

Qaraqorum totally isolated, Ariq Boke became desperate. He turned to Central Asia, to the great fertile lands in the south-west that lay in the control of the Chaghadai khans. An opportunity to concoct an alliance arose when the incumbent khan suddenly died. Ariq Boke urged one of his entourage, Alghu – as it happens a grandson of Chaghadai – to lay claim to the khanate. Once Alghu had been duly elected, Ariq Boke would effectively extend his command over nearly a quarter of Asia.

On the other side of Asia, near the shores of Lake Urmiyeh, Hulegu watched with growing anxiety as the war between his brothers developed. Having declared his support for Khubilai, he had become somewhat anxious about his own position. Technically his entire campaign in Persia had been to extend Mongke Khan's lands in the West. Nevertheless, he clearly had ambitions to become a khan himself and to rule the lands he had just conquered. But if Ariq Boke and the forces from the capital prevailed, he must expect to lose everything. The news that Ariq Boke had apparently extended his rule to the Chaghadai khanate, through his vassal Alghu, did not augur well.

An added complication was Berke, Khan of the Golden Horde. As a Muslim, Berke had been deeply pained by the destruction his cousin had wrought on Islamic civilization. The Mamluks, aware of Berke's sentiments, had sought to build an alliance with the Mongol Khan. By 1260 the Mamluks had a new leader in the form of Baybars, who had come to power after a coup d'état. It was he who had secretly sent ambassadors to Berke, urging him to join them in a holy war against Hulegu. Berke agreed, and set about putting together an army large enough to move on Hulegu.

Within two years the internal strains, petty jealousies, cultural divisions and craven greed of the various power groups were wrenching the empire apart. Not only were Mongols fighting Mongols in the very heartland of the empire, but now an alliance had been made by one Mongol ruler with non-Mongols against a fellow Mongol ruler. In the midst of this maelstrom Hulegu put aside his ambitions to reach the Mediterranean, concentrated on defending his territory from Berke's forces and sought allies wherever he could find them.

In 1262 Hulegu wrote to Louis IX, proposing that the King of the Franks join forces with him against the Mamluks. Unfortunately, there is no record of the King's response. These years proved to be Christendom's last gasp in Palestine. With solid Christian help Hulegu might have been able to sweep the Mamluks out of Syria and Palestine. But instead, having shattered two great myths about the Mongols – their invincibility, which lay buried in the sand at Ayn Jalut, and their solidarity, destroyed by the alliance with Berke Khan – the Mamluks now felt omnipotent and were determined to rid the whole of the Middle East of infidels. The first to go would be the last remaining crusader strongholds along the Mediterranean coast.

When Hulegu died in 1265, followed soon afterwards by his Christian wife Doquz-Khatun, the eastern Christian community mourned the death of a latter-day Constantine and Helena – their last hope of regaining Jerusalem. Nevertheless Hulegu's son, Abaqa, continued his father's policies with equal enthusiasm. He carried the war up to Berke and at the same time sent ambassadors to the Vatican, still hoping to enlist the Pope's support for an alliance against the Mamluks. Abaqa believed absolutely, and perhaps naïvely, that Christendom would eventually realize that they shared the same objectives. But the Pope was not easily persuaded. The Christian community in both Palestine and Europe still nursed memories of innumerable Mongol attacks and were convinced that, if they assisted the Mongols in dealing with the Mamluks, it would only be a matter of time before the Mongols turned again upon Christendom. So Abaqa received no help from Europe, and the Mamluks were unimpeded in extending their influence up and down the Mediterranean coast.

Abaqa had no choice but to concentrate on the threat from Berke, which was precisely what the Mamluks had intended when they sought the alliance with the Golden Horde. Both khanates had amassed such enormous armies that at times it looked as though the empire was doomed to disappear in an almighty conflagration. At one point Berke led an army of more than 200 000 while Abaqa stood before another army almost as large. However, the holocaust failed to ignite because of the sudden death of Berke in 1267. His successor, Mongke-Temur, though also a Muslim, had no will to prosecute the war and he withdrew. By now the war in the Mongolian homeland had also been concluded.

Ariq Boke had begun the war with great optimism, but as it unfolded it became apparent that he had neither the wit nor the resources to defeat Khubilai. His great scheme to provide himself with supplies from the Chaghadai khanate failed because his erstwhile client, now Alghu Khan, proved a less than reliable ally. Having been promoted from retainer to khan almost overnight, the young man's ambition suddenly knew no bounds: taking advantage of Ariq Boke's vulnerability, Alghu Khan launched an attack against his former patron. Ariq Boke was soon waging a desperate and ever more hopeless campaign, bereft of supplies and with limited manpower. As the tide turned against him even his staunchest supporters melted away. So as Ariq Boke was trying to cope with this treacherous upstart on his western frontier, Khubilai advanced steadily from the east. By 1264 the young pretender was forced to accept defeat and make peace.

With hostilities at an end Khubilai had effectively become the most powerful man in Asia; but if he imagined he would soon be joined by the rest of the khans at a *quriltai* to be publicly and finally proclaimed Great Khan, he was mistaken. Although no one of any significance challenged his right to be elected, nor was anyone sufficiently moved to be present at his enthronement. The joints of the great empire had been more than stressed during nearly five years of war, and to the far-flung khanate courts the long journey across Asia to witness the making of a Great Khan no longer seemed as imperative as it had for Ogedei or Mongke. In consequence, Khubilai was surrounded by a faint whiff of illegitimacy that remained for the rest of his reign.

REFORMS AND INNOVATIONS

The empire that emerged from these wars was greatly transformed from the one that had been led by Mongke Khan during
the 1250s. There was no longer, in any practical sense, a real
union of khanates all subordinate under the Great Khan. Each
vast khanate was now set upon its own separate path and,
although they all paid nodding tribute to Khubilai, there was
never again any chance of the empire uniting behind the policies
of one man. The great campaign led by Hulegu into Persia was
the last imperial military expedition ever undertaken in the
name of a Great Khan.

Nevertheless, Khubilai was slow to appreciate the change and
for some years still expected his commands to reach to the far
corners of the empire. He always managed to maintain strong
links with the Ilkhan in Persia; but, whether he realized it or
not, the Golden Horde and the Chaghadai khanate were now
beyond his reach. But this situation rarely impinged upon the
life at his court, for without question his enduring preoccupation
was the governance of China.

Although Khubilai was surrounded by a vast entourage of
extremely skilful Chinese administrators, perhaps the most influential figure in Khubilai's court was a Mongol, his senior wife
Chabi. She was a woman blessed with many of the qualities that
had graced her late mother-in-law, Sorghaghtani Beki. Like her,
Chabi took a great interest in the way the land was governed,
often over-ruling Mongol advisers when their policies threatened
to destroy the traditional Chinese agrarian economy. Chabi had
long understood how enormous wealth could be generated from
agriculture – something many Mongols never came to appreciate.
Her influence was felt everywhere, from the day-to-day running
of the court to redesigning Mongol uniforms so that they were
more practical. But what set her above most of Khubilai's
advisers was the vision she shared with her husband of building
a new and lasting dynasty that would rank with all the great
periods in Chinese history. To this end she actively encouraged

her husband to emulate the great Chinese emperor T'ang T'ai-tsung.

Even though Khubilai went to great efforts to emulate past Chinese emperors, to govern the country with the best interests of the Chinese in mind and to identify closely with his Chinese subjects, he always remembered that he was a Mongol and that he reigned as Khan of Khans. His approach towards the governance of China seemed to many of his compatriots anti-Mongol, yet although he broke with many traditional Mongol precedents and made his ambition to be Emperor of China quite clear, he did not lose sight of his responsibilities to his Mongol inheritance.

In organizing his government of China Khubilai appreciated that the old Mongol habit of carving up a conquered nation into appanages for the élite, as had been done after the fall of the Chin, was hopelessly impractical. A new centralized structure had to be created, but it had to be one that ensured the Mongols retained a firm grip on the reins of power. The Mongol population in China was probably a few hundred thousand, whereas the Chinese numbered tens of millions – a daunting prospect. Khubilai adopted a great many suggestions made by his Chinese advisers about the structure of his government, but he made sure that the key positions were invariably held by Mongols or other non-Chinese. He did this by introducing a blatantly racial system of classification for his subjects. He devised three, and later four, separate social strata, the most important being Mongols. These were followed by Central Asians – those who were not Mongols but who were in the Mongol service; then came the northern Chinese; and finally the southern Chinese.

Superimposed on this was a new government structure made up of three large bureaux: the Secretariat, which was responsible for all civil matters; the Privy Council, responsible for military matters; and the Censorate, the most important of the three, which supervised and reported on all government officials throughout the land. All these government departments had representatives in every province, where they executed the major policy decisions made at court. Khubilai's primary objectives, which permeated down through all government departments, were to prevent the risk of local rebellions amongst his Chinese subjects, to ensure that government officials remained loyal and incorruptible, and to encourage the economy.

The China that Khubilai inherited, that is the northern part of it, was in a desperate condition, having still not fully recovered from the ravages of Genghis Khan's campaign during the 1220s and the wars of conquest that followed under Ogedei. It is impossible to produce a precise picture of the tragedy, but statistics help to create an outline. The discrepancy of 30 million between the population before Genghis's campaigns began and that left afterwards suggests that the Mongol campaigns were virtually genocidal in character, and, perhaps in response to that, the early records of Khubilai's reign suggest that he was much distressed by the state of his realm. It might be too much to claim that Khubilai had been motivated by regret for the way in which his grandfather had prosecuted his wars; nevertheless the records show that Khubilai devoted large resources to the relief of that beleaguered population. He granted tax exemptions to areas reported to be on the verge of collapse, reduced the taxes of peasants who produced silk because of the damage their industry had suffered during the wars, delivered grain to widows and orphans, and ordered his Mongol officers not to place excessive demands on those peasants engaged in turning land back to agriculture.

To encourage farmers to return to their lands he even established an Office for the Stimulation of Agriculture – quite an extraordinary concept for a Mongol. At the same time he ordered the building of hundreds of granaries, especially in the north where famine was a constant threat, and eventually managed to organize the peasant farmers into collectives called *she*. Each *she* would be responsible for reclaiming land, planting crops, stocking lakes and rivers with fish, irrigation and flood control. The *she* had an appointed leader who had authority to reward success and punish failure. The key element here was that these were tiny self-governing groups, structures which effectively gave ordinary Chinese peasants responsibility over their own lives. The *she* also became a useful structure for maintaining control, conducting censuses, educating the masses and passing information. Khubilai even passed laws that prevented his fellow countrymen from grazing their herds on land that was controlled by a local *she*.

The Khan also developed policies for the benefit of groups with whom the Mongols traditionally had good relations – artisans and merchants. By fostering a great number of vast civil projects, he ensured there was always work for artisans and craftsmen; at the same time he created laws that restricted the chance of corruption amongst the officials who supervised their work. But even more important to the economy was his encouragement of trade with the rest of Asia.

China had always been an insular nation, self-sufficient in most raw materials and deeply uninterested in the outside world. Those merchants that did wash up on China's shores were regarded with great disdain by most Confucian officials: they were either charlatans or parasites, while trade itself was thought to be a somewhat disreputable profession.

Khubilai, being a Mongol, saw merchants in a completely different light and elevated them to a very high status. There already existed a very solid relationship between the Mongol aristocracy and merchant associations, known as *ortaghs*, which were usually set up with what might be described as Mongol 'venture capital' and which operated large trading expeditions across Asia, bringing back exotic goods and a profit for the original investors. The *ortagh* also operated in reverse, lending to the Mongol courts, especially when new conquests were being planned. In China, Khubilai eventually established an office to formalize the relationship between the government and the *ortaghs*. He actively encouraged these associations to flourish within China, where he could control both the exchange of goods and money at the border. This relationship formed part of a grander scheme to manage and formalize the entire Chinese economy.

Upon entering Chinese territory all merchants were obliged to exchange their gold and silver for paper money, which was carefully issued and controlled by Khubilai's exchequer. In fact, throughout the domain the population was encouraged to exchange precious metals for paper currency, which became the foundation of Khubilai's remarkably sophisticated economic programme. The merchants accepted these terms for the new system allowed them access to the whole of the Chinese market and facilitated internal trade; in return the exchequer maintained a tight control on inflation and was therefore a ready source of capital for future military expeditions.

The Mongol court also elevated other social groups to a new and higher status, against Confucian traditions. Along with merchants and artisans, physicians were greatly valued: Khubilai's court invited learned practitioners from both India and Muslim lands to travel to China and practise their skills. Hospitals were built and eventually a medical academy was established to regulate the training of physicians. Scientists too flourished under Khubilai, especially astronomers and mathematicians.

It was in Persia that the greatest advancements in astronomy and the calculation of calendars were being realized. Under Hulegu's direction a large observatory was built at Maragheh in 1263, and by the 1260s important new discoveries were pouring forth, news of which had travelled to China. In 1267 Khubilai brought the Persian astronomer Jamal al-Din to his capital and invited him to help Chinese astronomers build the same kind of instruments that had been developed in Persia. Out of this exchange between the Great Khan's domain and the Ilkhanate, Khubilai established the Institute of Muslim Astronomy where the Chinese astronomer Kuo Shou-ching produced his famous Calendar Delivering the Seasons – which survived as the fundamental Chinese calendar for nearly 400 years.

Khubilai Khan and China

Long before Kuo Shou-ching's great work was complete, Khubilai set his seal upon Chinese life in a way that would endure even longer: the construction of what would become the great national capital. The grandson of the great destroyer would be remembered as the great builder. The new city was situated near the old Chin capital of Chung-tu, in the most prosperous and populous part of northern China. Work on Ta-tu (Great Capital) was begun in 1266, and it was to be constructed on traditional Confucian lines, for it was Khubilai's wish that the city would eventually win the hearts and minds of the Chinese intelligentsia.

It was surrounded by a vast rammed earth wall nearly 30 km (some 20 miles) in circumference. As with K'ai-p'ing, his city at the edge of the steppe, inside the outer wall were two compounds that housed separate sections of the city. The innermost of these enclosed the Imperial City where Khubilai and his entourage lived, while beyond that wall were the various ranks of civil servants and other government officials. Beyond the outer wall, outside the city proper, lived ordinary Chinese and Central Asians.

In those respects the city was a model Chinese capital, yet it was not wholly Chinese. The chief architect, Yeh-hei-tieh-erh, was a Muslim from Central Asia and the craftsmen who worked on the site came from the four corners of the empire. Khubilai's sleeping quarters inside the palace were hung with carpets, silk screens and rugs like the inside of a typical Mongol *ger*. Although the city was laid out with traditional lakes, bridges and gardens, those gardens were dotted with Mongol *gers* where members of the royal family were expected to live. It differed from a traditional Chinese city in other aspects too. For a start the site was chosen so that it could be well defended and would enjoy good communications with the outside world. Look-out towers were constructed at the major gates, and provision was made for a good water supply and sufficient store houses for grain.

With a workforce of nearly 30 000 men the city took shape remarkably quickly. By 1271 work had already begun on the palaces and temples of the Imperial City, where Khubilai took up residence in 1274. As Ta-tu took shape, K'ai-p'ing was renamed Shang-tu (Upper Capital) and was relegated to the status of an extensive hunting residence to which the Khan would retreat during the oppressive humidity of Ta-tu's summer.

A little time after work on the city was completed Khubilai instigated the extension of **the** Grand Canal, an even larger project that was designed to allow the shipment of grain from the prosperous south up to the new capital. Using a staggering 3 million labourers, 218 km (136 miles) of canal were dug from Ch'ing-ning to Lin-ch'ing, allowing continuous water transportation from the Yangtze River to Ta-tu. There, by all accounts, the magnificent new city grew richer and more glorious as Khubilai's reign proceeded. It became not only the heart of Khubilai's own personal domain, but with time the capital of all China – for as work on Ta-tu progressed apace, Khubilai was putting into motion his greatest legacy.

A MIGHTY NAVAL POWER CONQUERS THE SUNG

Although Khubilai was deeply influenced by Chinese civilization, as were a Iarge proportion of the Mongol élite who had gravitated to the new capital, he remained fundamentally a Mongol. Nowhere was that more telling than in his attitude towards expanding the empire. Since his withdrawal from Sung territory at the start of the civil war, he had attempted to induce the Sung into accepting him as their universal ruler in return for a certain degree of self-government. Although this non-belligerent approach was supported with a long list of concessions, like the release of Sung prisoners, there was no mistaking that behind Khubilai's entreaties lay the tacit threat of the Mongol's awesome military power. But the Sung could never conceive of relinquishing their sovereignty and eventually hostilities broke out again, finally exploding in 1265 when a Sung army was defeated at the coastal town of Tiao-yu shan. At that battle, Khubilai's forces captured more than 140 of the enemy's ships and in the process transformed the Mongol empire itself into a major naval power.

However uncharacteristic it may seem for a cavalry-led war-machine to fight on the sea, the Mongols nevertheless took to naval warfare just as they had taken up other foreign fighting techniques like artillery, siege machines and gunpowder. The influence of a prominent Sung defector, Liu Cheng, was strong: he had convinced Khubilai and his generals that they would never defeat the Sung without a navy. So even before the great victory in 1265 Khubilai had been gathering together an armada, either by confiscating Sung vessels or having the Koreans build them for him. By 1268 he had put together a navy made up of four separate fleets. With this he set about the longest and, thanks to Marco Polo's account, the most famous campaign of the war.

The cities of Hsiang-yang and Fan-ch'eng lay on opposite banks of the Han River, and were effectively the final defensive positions guarding access to the Yangtze River basin – and in turn the heart of the Sung empire. Hsiang-yang was massively fortified; Rashid al-Din claimed it had a 'strong castle, a stout wall and a deep moat'. The Mongols began their campaign by laying siege to the fortress, but this proved a waste of time as the Sung were readily getting supplies by boat up the Yangtze. Khubilai's generals called for the construction of 500 boats with which to patrol the waters of the Han River, while troops moved on neighbouring Fan-ch'eng.

As the Mongol forces grew in size the Sung defenders panicked and tried to break out. Those that managed to get beyond the gates were captured and executed. The Sung then attempted to run the blockade, and sent a fleet of no fewer than 3000 ships up the Han; however, these were met and defeated by Khubilai's Korean sailors and fifty Sung vessels were captured.

Gradually the military situation developed into a stalemate. Hsiang-yang was utterly impregnable and the Sung could not be induced to surrender. They had sufficient essential supplies for a prolonged siege, and occasionally supplies managed to get through the blockade as well. The Mongols gradually succeeded in isolating the two cities from the rest of the Sung empire, but they could not actually take them. The siege rolled on, year after year, and Khubilai became more and more impatient.

Desperate for some means of breaking through, he sought help from Hulegu's son Abaqa, for it was known that the Persians had great siege engineers. In 1272, two such experts arrived at Khubilai's court and were sent on to the battle zone. These two engineers, Isma'il and Ala al-Din, surveyed the Sung fortifications and then set about designing and building a number of very large machines, a mangonel and catapult, that would hurl the most enormous missiles at the walls. According to an account of Marco Polo's visit to China, 'When the machinery went off the noise shook heaven and earth; everything that it hit was smashed and destroyed.' In December Fan-ch'eng fell after only a few days of shelling. New machines were constructed for Hsiang-yang, and that city fell in March the following year.

Led by General Bayan, a veteran of Hulegu's campaign in Persia, the Mongol forces moved irresistibly forward towards the Sung capital of Hangchow. He crossed the Yangtze at the beginning of 1275, encountering on the far bank a huge Sung force that was routed. Tens of thousands were killed, and the main force retreated. In March 1276 Bayan encountered the Sung commander at Ting-chia chou, and again the Mongols proved unstoppable. The superior artillery and cohesiveness of their army was too much for the terrified Sung, who soon broke ranks and fled the field. In the Sung court at Hangchow there was growing consternation. Two years earlier the young emperor Tu-tsung had suddenly died, leaving heirs who were still children. His successor, Hsien, was just four years old. Actual power resided with the late emperor's mother, the Empress Dowager Hsieh. She was by now an ill old woman, growing

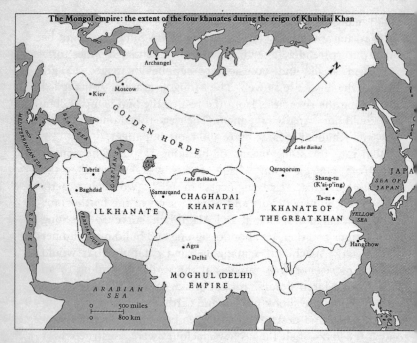

The Mongol empire: the extent of the four khanates during the reign of Khubilai Khan

more anxious with each piece of bad news. When Bayan's army was on the approach road to Hangchow, the Empress Dowager refused to desert the city and sent a messenger to the Mongol camp offering tribute if they would abandon the war. But Bayan dismissed the offer and continued down the road.

As the pressure mounted the Empress Dowager continued to procrastinate, but eventually it all became too much for her and she conceded defeat. When the Mongol armies entered her city, instead of putting the place to the torch and slaughtering the inhabitants they behaved, for once, like a typical conquering army and set about making a survey of the city's wealth and facilities. Bayan returned to Shang-tu with the Sung royal court, where they were presented to Khubilai. Still conscious that he needed to win the support of the most highly populated country on earth, Khubilai, under very pertinent advice from his wife

186

Chabi, treated the Sung royalty with great respect, providing them with most of their accustomed luxuries.

However, not all the Sung royal family had been transported to Shang-tu. Before Bayan's arrival at Hangchow, two half-brothers of the child emperor had escaped. En route to sanctuary the elder of the two had been crowned emperor, and he immediately became the focus of renewed Sung resistance. But in every practical sense the Sung had already been crushed, and the skirmishes that continued for the next three years were an irritating delay to the extension of Khubilai's rule over all of China. That came finally in 1279, when in a sea battle off the coast of Yai-shan the last Sung emperor was lost overboard while the Mongol fleet was inflicting another crushing defeat.

CULTURAL FLOWERING UNDER THE NEW YUAN DYNASTY

As has already been seen, long before the conquest of the Sung was complete Khubilai had already put in place a political structure that would eventually govern the whole of China. However the crowning glory of this plan, enthusiastically encouraged by Chabi, was to establish a new dynasty which would survive long after his own death. In selecting a name, Khubilai was keen that it be seen by his Chinese subjects as belonging to the long tradition of Confucian emperors – so something Chinese was essential. The choice of the word Yuan, which meant 'origin', also recalled the famous Confucian *Book of Changes*, where the term refers to the 'primal force' or the very 'origins of the universe'. In declaring his Yuan Dynasty, Khubilai was consciously employing references from classical Chinese literature to allude not only to his own pre-eminence, but to the fact that his dynasty marked the beginning of a new and politically unified China. It would remain so right up to the present.

The reign of Khubilai Khan was probably the most productive and beneficial of all the reigns of the Great Khans. Its over-riding contribution was to unite the nation and to lay the foundations for an unprecedented era of peace and prosperity. Under Khubilai, trading links were forged with Persia and eventually Europe. Trade flourished across the great continent as it had never done in the past, not just by land but also by sea. Khubilai constructed a large merchant fleet that plied all the major ports of south-east Asia, India and the Persian Gulf. European merchants, Genoese and Venetian in particular, began to visit China – the Polos being the obvious name that springs to mind. They loom large in our image of Khubilai Khan because of Marco's account of his time in Cathay and the somewhat exaggerated claims he made about the official functions he is supposed to have carried out there. Yuan records, however, fail to register one jot of information about any of the Polos, and it would appear they were no more significant than any of the hundreds of other merchant travellers who made the arduous journey across Asia to the Great Khan's court. No one really knows how many Europeans did make that journey, but whatever the number it was nothing compared with the thousands of merchants from the Middle East and south-east Asia.

Few commodities required by the Chinese could not be provided from within their own borders. But on the other hand they produced a great deal of merchandise that found a ready market abroad. Chief amongst these, of course, was silk – an industry which the Mongols soon monopolized. No Mongol needed to be told the value of Chinese manufactures in foreign markets, and Khubilai took many measures to encourage the export of indigenous crafts. Next to silk, the most valuable commodity was ceramics. Khubilai decreed that all kilns within the country had to be licensed, regulated and taxed. At the same time his envoys promoted a thriving trade with the countries of south-east Asia and the Persian Gulf. The industry boomed, and Yuan ceramics were exported in prodigious quantities.

Khubilai also contributed to the ceramics industry in a creative way. The somewhat tedious artistic restrictions that had been imposed by previous regimes were abolished and potters were free to use their imaginations. Some breathtaking creations appeared as a result, including the famous blue-and-white porcelains which later characterized Ming work.

What happened in the potting kilns up and down the country was mirrored in many other spheres of the arts and crafts, for Khubilai's very business-minded court was also deeply devoted to the arts. Khubilai took on the patronage of a number of artists, adding greatly to the large Imperial Painting Collection that he had captured from the Sung. This had been transported to Ta-tu, where Khubilai built a special gallery to house it. As his own collection grew it soon became apparent to him and the scholars he employed that a distinctive Yuan school of painting had developed, and that examples of this style had to be preserved. Some recent scholars have even referred to a 'revolution' in Chinese painting. Again it was a question of Mongol sensibilities not having been schooled in the Chinese classics and being prepared to allow greater freedom and innovation.

When these policies were applied to the theatre, again they produced new and original works – especially as money was available to build theatres in the growing cities and to sponsor new companies. More than 160 Yuan plays have survived, plus the titles of another 500. What emerged from this canon was a range of subjects that had never been tackled on the stage before; unfettered by imperial censors, Chinese drama shed the stiff, formalized style of an earlier era and became more relaxed and accessible.

Khubilai's patronage of the arts was not simply an attempt to banish his 'barbarian' heritage; it had a political aspect to it as well. The construction of galleries, the collection of art and the production of drama all fostered a cultural atmosphere in Ta-tu which was attractive to the wealthy Sung families whom Khubilai needed to attract to his court if his reign was to have real credibility throughout the country. Having removed the barrier of the frontier, Khubilai made it not only possible but attractive for southerners to mix once again with their northern cousins. By encouraging this migration of Sung gentry up to his court, he strengthened the ties with the south and with it the legitimacy of his reign.

ILL-FATED INCURSIONS INTO JAPAN

Had Khubilai concentrated on nothing else but governing his realm, his glory and that of his dynasty might have shone longer and more brightly than it did. But as the man aged he became distracted by a need to reaffirm his Mongol origins, and so he launched a number of ill-fated military campaigns which both tarnished his reputation and almost bankrupted the country. The most famous of these were the two invasions of Japan: the first in 1274 in the midst of the Sung campaign, and the second in 1281. These expeditions were motivated by the urge to expand the empire in the great Mongol tradition. Apart from India there was precious little land in Asia that was not under Mongol rule, so the Japanese islands were the obvious solution.

Following the 'insolent' reply that the Japanese sent to his demand that they submit, Khubilai prepared for war. The recalcitrant Koreans were pressganged into providing the fleet and sailors that would carry some 20 000 troops – more than sufficient to deal with the disorganized and poorly equipped Japanese. On 19 November 1274, the Mongols landed and made easy progress against the Japanese forces. But as night fell a great storm blew up; the Korean sailors insisted that the fleet put to the open sea – otherwise it would be dashed against the rocks and their only means of retreat lost. The Mongols reluctantly withdrew from their positions and climbed back on board their vessels. What happened next is history. The ships were scattered, hundreds foundered and more than 13 000 lives were lost. The invasion had to be abandoned.

In 1280, after the Sung had been defeated, Khubilai set about his revenge. Over 900 ships were gathered to carry 40 000 troops from northern China, while a further 100 000 Chinese would depart from the south. When they landed at Nokonshima Bay on the island of Kyushu, the Mongols found that the Japanese had built a defensive wall along the coast. For two months they battled away against the Japanese defences, when suddenly the fates intervened once again. Another typhoon blew up, and the Koreans again tried to get their fleet back out to sea. In the ensuing panic more than 60 000 of Khubilai's army drowned or were slaughtered trying to get off the shore. To the Japanese this second storm served as proof that they inhabited a land that was precious to the Gods and that the storms had been 'divine winds' (*kamikaze*) sent to sweep away the invader.

Further military expeditions were despatched in the years to come, into Burma and by sea down to the island of Java, but met with little success. The triumphs that had crowned Khubilai's youth eluded him in later years, and more and more his expeditions to far-off island kingdoms seemed to lack the logic that had driven previous Mongol campaigns. As his life became filled with disappointments, especially after the deaths of Chabi in 1281 and his son Chen-chin in 1285, the great man became a recluse and withdrew from the world. He gave up hunting, became devoted to food and drink and soon became extremely overweight. He eventually died, a sad and miserable figure, in February 1294. His body was carried across to Mongolia where it was buried in what is now Hentiy province. As with his grandfather before him, no tomb was constructed above ground. The site of his burial is lost to eternity.

9

DECLINE AND FALL

Despite all the civil wars, military setbacks and other digressions that plagued the various khanates, the reign of Khubilai Khan was nevertheless the apogee of the empire's history. He exercised nominal supremacy over the greatest land-based empire in history, and while his writ may not have extended over all the empire's subjects in central and western Asia, his supremacy was at least acknowledged by the Khans of the Golden Horde – and of course by the Mongols in Persia who remained his loyal and obedient servants. There the descendants of Hulegu had adopted the title of Ilkhans, meaning amicable or subordinate khans to the Great Khan, and at their capital in Maragheh and later in Tabriz Khubilai's viceroy maintained an imperial presence, applying Khubilai's seal to all state documents. In the words of Marco Polo, he was 'the greatest lord that ever was born in the world or that now is'.

A VAST TRADE NETWORK

Though the end of Khubilai's reign was clouded by military and personal disappointments, his singular success in reuniting China would alone have guaranteed his position as one of the great figures in world history. However, it might also be argued that by continuing the policies of his grandfather to their logical conclusion – by internationalizing the empire – Khubilai made an even greater contribution to world history. The Mongols' conviction that they had been granted a divine mandate to rule the world presupposed that the world extended far beyond the physical reach of the Mongol armies, and Khubilai did everything he could to extend contact to the limits of the civilized world – to south-east Asia and Europe. Chinese insularity was swept aside by a flood of foreign visitors come to the seat of the Great Khan. Khubilai's merchant fleet developed important markets in India, Sri Lanka, Malaysia and Java; and, because of the close links with the Ilkhanate, it also ventured as far west as the Persian Gulf, contributing to the growth of the new port of Ormuz.

Arab dhows also sailed east and became regular visitors at the ports of Hangchow, Quinsay and Zaiton, and with the construction of the Grand Canal ocean-going vessels regularly called at Ta-tu, making it one of the busiest inland ports anywhere. More than 200 000 ships navigated up and down the Yangtze each year. Silk, rice, sugar, ceramics, pearls and other precious stones were exported in return for exotic medicines, herbs, ivory and other luxuries. Chinese manufactures reached everywhere under the custody of Mongol world dominance, and for the first time in human history Europe had direct contact with Cathay, through trade. Merchants travelled the vast Mongol highways from the Crimea, through the land of the Golden Horde to Sarai and Utrar, across the Altai Mountains and into the empire of the Great Khan, to Ta-tu. Others travelled from the cities along the Yangtze across the empty steppes to Besh-balik, through the Chaghadai Khanate to Samarqand and Bukhara, and down to the cities of Persia.

APPEALS TO EUROPE

There was also an increase in diplomatic traffic between the empire and Europe, particularly to and from the Ilkhanate. This took on a more urgent character after 1260, a year in which many historians claim the serious fracturing of Mongol unity began. Before that date, most contacts had been instigated by the Pope and were devised to appease the Mongols and perhaps even effect a conversion. However, after the humiliation at Ayn Jalut the traffic was reversed; the Mongols began making serious appeals for an alliance with the Christian forces in Palestine, if that would mean the swift elimination of Muslim resistance. Following Hulegu's now famous letter to Louis IX, written in 1262, many attempts were made by both sides to establish good relations. Letters passed back and forth between the respective courts as first Abaqa, Hulegu's successor, and then in turn his successors, tried to nail down an alliance with Christendom. Europe's response was always favourable (especially if there was a prospect of some large-scale conversions), though ineffectual. No European power actually ever despatched an army, but the Mongols were nothing if not persistent and by the time of the fourth Ilkhan, Arghun, their appeals to Europe had reached a new pitch.

In 1287 Arghun sent an emissary to Rome, an Eastern Christian monk by the name of Rabban Sauma who had travelled to the Middle East on pilgrimage from Ta-tu. Unable to reach the Holy Land because of the conflicts in Syria, Rabban Sauma was commissioned by Arghun to impress the crowned heads of Europe with how well Christianity had flourished under the empire. The envoy did just that: in Rome he took part in long theological discussions with cardinals, in Paris he was received by Philip IV 'the Fair' in the glorious Ste-Chapelle, and in Gascony he so impressed Edward I of England that he was allowed to conduct a Mass and give holy communion to the King. On his return through Rome he conducted further Masses during Holy Week and Easter, this time in the presence of the Pope himself, after which the cardinals rejoiced, declaring: 'the language is different but the use is the same.'

Rabban Sauma returned with an extremely positive response from Philip IV, who proposed: 'If the armies of the Ilkhan go to war against Egypt [the Mamluks], we too shall set out to go to war and to attack in common operation.' To which Arghun replied:

... we decided, after consulting heaven, to mount our
horses in the last month of winter in the Year of the Tiger
[1290] and to dismount outside of Damascus on the 15th
of the first month of spring [1291]. Now, We make it
known to you that in accordance with Our honest word,
we shall send Our armies [to arrive] at the [time and place]
and, if by the authority of heaven, We conquer these people,
We shall give you Jerusalem.

It was a time when Christianity enjoyed unprecedented accept-
ance right across the empire – not just in Persia, but in Mongolia
and China, where Khubilai encouraged its spread as a way of
improving his contacts with Europeans and so proving to his
Chinese subjects that he was indeed the Great Khan of the
world. Following Rabban Sauma's visit to Rome, during which
he had reaffirmed the willingness of the Church of the East to
accept the Pope's supremacy, a bishopric was eventually established at Sultaniyya, a new city being constructed by the Ilkhans
in Persia, and another in Ta-tu itself.

During Arghun's reign, relations with the Pope were so strong
that it must have seemed possible that the Ilkhanate might
convert to Christianity. How that might have affected the course
of Middle Eastern history is open to speculation, but needless to
say it did not come about. The Mamluks had by March 1291
already stormed the crusader fortress at Acre, the last Christian
outpost in Palestine, and within a few days Arghun had died of
a long illness. His successor, Geikhatu, devoted his short life to
drink and the pursuit of young boys, and never once showed the
slightest interest in either war or alliances.

THE PERSIAN ILKHANATE

So for the first forty years of Mongol rule, Persia was forced to
accept the demotion of Islam as the pre-eminent religion of the
area. To the locals' great distress, in all the great towns and

cities Buddhist temples were constructed in even greater abundance than the new Christian churches. Although some of the Ilkhans showed distinct leanings towards either Buddhism or Christianity, in the main they were fairly impartial – that is until the reign of Ghazan the 'Reformer', who became Ilkhan in 1295.

The year before, in faraway China, the great Khubilai Khan had died. Although all the other khans accepted his successor, Temur Oljeitu, as Great Khan in name, he did not enjoy anything like the same authority as his father. There would never be another universal khan at the head of the empire, and the next generation of Ilkhans never felt they had to demonstrate the same deference as had their forefathers. By the 1290s the Ilkhanate was going through a period of great internal unrest: the economy had virtually collapsed, foreign debts were not being met, and the cities were torn by riots and the threat of insurrection. This had largely been brought about by a combination of Geikhatu's heady excesses, a haphazard and somewhat ruthless form of tax collection and an ill-judged attempt to cure these ills through the forced introduction of Chinese-like paper currency to an economy that had been based upon gold and silver for more than 2000 years.

When the throne became vacant in 1295, the new pretender, Ghazan the 'Reformer', was advised that if he wanted to be khan he had better find some way of forging a link with the already restive populace, who were by now tired of being ruled by pagans. As there was no longer any need to seek Ta-tu's approval for the election of a local khan, Ghazan split with Mongol tradition and embraced Islam, as did most of his Mongol generals.

Ghazan had other changes in mind too. According to the Persian historian Rashid al-Din, who was also his chief minister, when the new Ilkhan argued with the Mongol élite about reforming the Ilkhanate administration, he explained himself in the following words: 'If you insult the peasant, take his oxen and seed, and trample his crops into the ground – what will you do in the future?' Just like Khubilai, thirty years before, the

Mongol khan had begun to identify with his subjects. Their wellbeing was equated with the wellbeing of the state. He went on: 'You must think, too, when you beat and torture their wives and children, that just as our wives and children are dear to our hearts, so are theirs to them. They are human beings, just as we are.' The influence of civilization had again prevailed over the instincts of the nomad.

Under Ghazan's firm and pragmatic government, the economy gradually improved. The system of taxation was reformed, as was the judiciary, and incentives were offered to the peasantry to return to the land. Most importantly, Mesopotamia and Persia were returned to the bosom of Islam, where they have remained ever since.

Ghazan's brother, Oljeitu, was the next Ilkhan, and he too adopted the Muslim faith and continued the process of reform. However his greatest monument was built in stone: the lavish embellishment of the new city of Sultaniyya with its domed and octagonal buildings, many of which were architectural master-pieces – none more so than his own tomb, constructed in 1313. Just as Khubilai had wanted to prove himself a great builder as well as conqueror, so the Ilkhans were keen to demonstrate their wealth with lavish constructions.

The Mausoleum of Oljeitu is one of the great Islamic land-marks; its cupola stands over 75 m (nearly 250 feet) above the ground and is decorated with the most dazzling blue ceramic tiles. The windows are made of intricate cast iron, while the interior walls are decorated with typically ornate stonework. When it was built it was the largest domed cupola anywhere in the world – a breathtaking engineering breakthrough, and a milestone in Islamic architecture. It was a resoundingly pro-Islamic statement and underscores how the Mongol aristocracy in this part of the world had absorbed the Islamic culture.

This was also an era of great artistic expression in general, fostered by the Ilkhan's patronage. Poetry, painting and ceram-ics, but above all architecture, all flourished under the Mongols. Oljeitu's son, Abu Sa'id, who in 1316 became the first Ilkhan with an Islamic name, ruled during what was described as the 'best period of the domination of the Mongols'. The economy boomed, a treaty was negotiated with the Mamluks and Persia looked forward to peace and prosperity.

The only thing that Abu Sa'id failed to produce was an heir, and when he died in 1335 so did the house of Hulegu. There was no one to take up the reins of power, and the line of the Ilkhans abruptly ceased. The majority of the Mongol élite who had not embraced Islam had emigrated, while those who had assimilated were simply absorbed into the population. Mongol control over Persia ceased and the Ilkhanate itself disappeared. Meanwhile, Persia drifted without a unified government until another Turko-Mongol warrior, Timur the Lame, rode out of Samarqand thirty years later.

NATURAL CATASTROPHE AND REBELLION

The Ilkhanate was the first Mongol nation to collapse. The next was China. Under Khubilai's successors China, and the empire as a whole, enjoyed thirty years of stability and peace. However, following the assassination of the fifth Yuan emperor in 1323 there erupted more than ten years of factional fighting between various branches of the Mongol aristocracy. Altogether five separate descendants of Khubilai were made emperor by different warring factions. In 1333 Toghon Temur, the eleventh Yuan emperor, was crowned; and although he ruled uninterrupted for the next thirty-five years, he did so over a dynasty that was already in terminal decline.

Before his enthronement, while the Yuan factions were still squabbling amongst themselves, southern China had been racked by a series of peasant rebellions. These were not proto-nationalist movements, but uprisings born out of simple poverty. In earlier times they would have been promptly crushed, but the Mongol garrisons were no longer led by seasoned campaigners and many of the officers in charge had never actually been to war. Gradually the rebellions turned into a contagious infection of guerrilla movements that spread north until by the 1330s open civil war had become established in central China. As the Yuan authorities seemed helpless against the rebels, the local Chinese gentry raised their own private militia, thus increasing the numbers of armed soldiery in the country.

In the midst of this rising sea of troubles, a number of natural disasters struck which would have tried the strengths of even the most resilient administration. First there was an earthquake, followed by the great flood of 1352 when the Yellow River burst its banks and inundated vast tracts of countryside, bringing with it both disease and famine. To cope with the great damage the Yuan authorities set about conscripting a vast army of labourers to repair the dykes and dams. This was frustrated by yet another disaster in the following year, when a terrible pestilence swept through the country and killed enormous numbers. According to traditional Chinese superstitions, nature was no longer in harmony with the ruling dynasty, and this did not augur well for its future. Because of labour shortages work on the flood control became haphazard. Conditions were harsh and the pay low, which led to further rebellions. Out of these new insurrections emerged a number of bandit leaders who began to attract to their cause people from different classes. Soon landowners, master artisans and even the clergy began flocking to what became a massive, yet wholly disorganized national rebellion. It had become a great popular movement against the Emperor's utterly ineffectual attempts at dealing with the various natural disasters.

By 1356 a single leader had emerged from amongst the rebel forces: Chu Yuan-chang. Under his charismatic leadership the rebellion became more focused, and soon the gentry were also flocking to his banner, now they could sense a real opportunity to be rid of the foreign dynasty once and for all. Chu Yuan-chang's forces, augmented by the numerous militia armies, marched north and eventually captured Nanking, thus cutting off supplies to the north and creating a rallying-centre for other rebel groups. With the support of the gentry his cause had acquired a degree of legitimacy, but before he confronted Yuan authority head-on he was urged to form an alternative government – and for the third time in history a peasant became the founder of a Chinese dynasty.

He chose the name Ming Hung-wu, and the motif for the new Ming Dynasty would be 'Rule Like the T'ang and the Sung'; a return to traditional Chinese values. As the Ming forces grew in strength, the Mongols lost sight of the danger they were in and became embroiled in another brief civil war, once again between the houses of Ogedei and Tolui. While the Mongols were at each other's throats, the Ming forces consolidated their hold on the south and effectively eliminated Yuan authority anywhere south of the Yangtze River. By 1368, Chu Yuan-chang was ready to march on Ta-tu, which he did virtually unopposed. By the time the Ming army had breached the city walls the last Yuan Emperor, Toghon Temur, had fled to Qaraqorum where he died in 1370.

It is no coincidence that the first khanates to collapse, the Persian and Chinese, also happened to be the most urbanized and sophisticated. In both cases the Mongol rulers were effectively overwhelmed by the difficulties of governing large sedentary societies. Though China had indeed become too much for the Mongols to cope with, their brief reign brought that society closer to the rest of the world than it had ever been in its entire history. Persian merchants plied their wares in its markets, designed its irrigation systems and sometimes even governed its cities. Nevertheless, most Chinese chroniclers saw the Mongol dynasty as a most disagreeable period of their history and dismissed the benefits of contact with the rest of the world as an unfortunate infection that was eventually cauterized.

The physical manifestation of their determination to keep the Mongols out was of course the construction of the Great Wall, which the new Ming Dynasty undertook in the sixteenth century. Though the Mongol empire had brought Europe into contact with China, the influences flowed almost exclusively in one direction: despite the foreign religions, merchant houses and even architecture, China remained the most culturally self-sufficient of civilizations. Most Christian and Islamic presence withered after the death of Khubilai, the last emperor with truly international ambitions. The Chinese took very little notice of Persian culture, though the Persians were influenced especially in the areas of painting and ceramics. But it was Europe that benefited and learned the most. Its knowledge of Asia expanded enormously and led directly to the great Age of Discovery. When Christopher Columbus set sail in 1492 he did so in search of the sea route to Cathay, the land of the Great Khan.

THE GOLDEN HORDE

In contrast with Persia and China, the Mongols in central Asia and Russia put down very deep roots. After the great campaign through Poland and Hungary in 1242, Batu made his base in the lower Volga region and eventually laid the foundations of the city of Sarai, situated on the banks of the Akhtuba River. From here he maintained control over the Russian princes and watched the traffic of merchants and envoys that proceeded from Europe across the steppe to Qaraqorum and China. With the rich tribute he exacted from the Russian states, the Golden Horde – as the Russians came to call Batu's khanate – grew fabulously rich.

However it was Batu's younger brother, Berke Khan, elected in 1257, who finally determined the territory of the Golden Horde. Its heart lay in the lower Volga and extended to the steppes around the rivers Don and Dnieper, the Crimean peninsula, the northern slopes of the Caucasus Mountains and even into Bulgaria and Thrace. If anything Berke strengthened Mongol control, ruthlessly crushing the slightest hint of a rebellion amongst the Russians. He might also have launched another invasion of Europe had he not been diverted by Hulegu's savage campaign against Islam.

Being a Muslim himself, Berke had been appalled by the destruction that had been wrought upon Baghdad and the eventual quarrel that erupted between the Ilkhanate and the Golden Horde not only shelved his ambitions towards Europe, it also guaranteed the survival of the new Mamluk kingdom that had emerged from Cairo.

The next Khan, Mongke-Temur, who was a son of Batu's, led the Golden Horde into an era of great prosperity from which it emerged a real world power. Peace was agreed with the Ilkhanate, after Khubilai's insistence, while relations were maintained with the Mamluks in Egypt. Trade flourished between Egypt and Russia, and north of Batu's capital a new city was eventually constructed called Berke Sarai (New Sarai), where many of the mosques and palaces were built by Egyptian architects. But under Mongke-Temur's successors the Golden Horde never shone quite as brightly. New campaigns were launched into Poland and Hungary, but this time the Mongols were defeated and turned back; there was no Subedei to lead the armies.

In the early fourteenth century, under Ozbeg Khan, the Golden Horde officially adopted Islam as the state religion and throughout the Middle East the Muslim states rejoiced. Nevertheless, good relations were maintained with the Christian West and the Genoese strengthened their foothold at Kaffa on the Black Sea. After Ozbeg the Golden Horde seemed to wither somewhat, especially when the line of Jochi-Batu finally came to an end in 1359. Other Mongol pretenders from the Chaghadai khanate attempted to place puppet khans on the throne at Sarai, but none of these enjoyed proper power or distinction. In 1371, with the khanate appearing to disintegrate, the Russian princes refused to make their annual journey to Sarai to pay tribute, and when a Mongol army was sent to persuade them it was defeated by the Grand Duke of Moscow at Kulikovo Pole. However Russian freedom was still just a dream, for there had emerged a new power out of Transoxiana that would wreak havoc throughout Central Asia.

Timur the Lame, or Tamerlane in Western literature, had been born around 1330 near Samarqand. He progressed from banditry to international conqueror in much the same way as Genghis Khan. Although he was descended from the Mongols he was in fact a Turkic Muslim, and his youth had been spent in the cities of Transoxiana, not the empty steppe. He had developed a massive army, modelled along Mongol lines, and with it set out on a campaign of destruction that, by all accounts, was even worse than Genghis's excesses.

Timur's campaigns were really more like plundering raids which extended throughout Khwarazmia, Transoxiana and eventually, through one of his protégés, up into Russia. Toktamish, a nephew of an earlier khan, was granted by Timur the lordships of a number of Transoxianan cities and, through Timur's patronage, was eventually made Khan of the Golden Horde in 1377. In 1381, Toktamish led an army furnished by Timur up into Russia as a punishment for the defeat at Kulikovo Pole. He left countless cities and towns in absolute ruin, pillaged Moscow and put thousands of its inhabitants to the sword. The Russian states were back to where they had been under Batu.

Later a war developed between Toktamish and his patron, which shattered the Golden Horde and left Toktamish a penniless refugee wandering the Central Asian steppe. Timur sacked Sarai, but never bothered to annex the lands of the Golden Horde. He made one determined plunge north towards Moscow, but turned back and instead set his sights on conquering China. He was on his way there in 1405 when he died. Timur had left neither government nor successors and the Golden Horde, mortally wounded, staggered on until 1419. By this time it had fragmented into a number of separate power centres, at Astrakhan, Kazan and notably in the Crimea, which survived until it was annexed by Catherine the Great. Russian independence only finally emerged under Ivan II 'The Terrible', who refused to kiss the stirrup of the Khan in 1502. No Mongol army appeared strong enough to force the Muscovites into submission, and 265 years after Batu's campaign into the West the Golden Horde finally disappeared.

THE BLACK DEATH: A GIFT FROM CENTRAL ASIA

One final legacy that the Mongols bequeathed to Europe, albeit unwittingly, sailed from the city of Kaffa, on the Black Sea, in 1346. The year before, an army of Kipchaks in the service of Janibeg Khan, the penultimate Khan of the Golden Horde, were besieging the city when a dreadful pestilence swept through their ranks. As the disease took so many casualties, the Mongol commander decided to bring the siege to a quick end before his army was itself decimated. In what must be the first recorded instance of biological warfare, the Mongol commander had the diseased corpses catapulted over the city walls and then waited for the pestilence to do the rest. From Kaffa it travelled, via Genoese merchants, along the sea routes to the Mediterranean ports of southern Europe. Then it swept up through Spain and France, east into Germany, and across the English Channel to the British Isles. Even in the depth of winter it continued relentlessly into Scandinavia and even reached as far as Greenland. The Black Death, as it came to be known, was the most devastating catastrophe in European history – killing one in three of the population. Nothing ever perpetrated by Genghis, or any of his offspring, compared with the death toll caused by the arrival of this disease. It is assumed that the opening up of the trade routes from Central Asia allowed the Black Death to be transmitted to both western and eastern Asia; for just five years later, it is assumed that the same pestilence struck China during the last years of the Yuan Dynasty.

Decline and Fall

THE MOGHULS

The Chaghadai Khanate survived well into the sixteenth century, though the house of Chaghadai kept its influence far longer. The name of Genghis Khan retained an enormous reputation throughout Central Asia and helped perpetuate Mongol control in the absence of any other power. In fact, the prestige attached to the name was so great that when Timur set about his career he concocted a number of ways of either marrying into the house of Genghis, or at the very least maintaining members of the family as puppets. A hundred years after Timur's death, the name Genghis still carried significance throughout Asia. In the early sixteenth century a prince of Transoxiana named Babur, who was a descendant both of Timur and Genghis Khan himself, fled south to Afghanistan and eventually to India to escape the Ozbeg Turks.

Babur took up his Mongol heritage by carving out an empire for himself in northern India, where he established the great Moghul Dynasty (Moghul being the Persian pronunciation of Mongol). He conducted a campaign against the ruling Lodi Dynasty, and captured their capital, Agra, in 1526. Following the defeat of Sikandar Lodi, Babur sent his son to Agra to secure the Lodi treasury. There the son is said to have discovered the Maharani of Gwalior cowering with her family. According to legend, she apparently offered him a huge diamond if he would spare her and her family; it was the famous Koh-i-noor, now among the British crown jewels.

Babur spent the last years of his life at Agra, where he constructed a wonderful garden, one of four famous Moghul *char baghs*, in Agra. The Moghuls went on to construct some of the most magnificent palaces and fortresses in India, but their crowning glory was the mausoleum built for the Mumtaz Mahal, wife of the fifth emperor, Shah Jahan. The great Taj Mahal, the jewel of India, is a most unlikely legacy of the Mongols, those great destroyers who first swept out of the eastern steppe. Yet there it stands on the banks of the Yamuna River, the very antithesis of its barbaric heritage.

Decline and Fall

CHINA AND MONGOLIA IN THE WAKE OF GENGHIS KHAN

Following the establishment of the Ming Dynasty in China the Mongols made a series of attempts, under various tribal leaders, to return to China and reclaim their lost power. However, they had only sporadic success; they lacked both military and political leadership, though their armies had lost none of their fighting skills. Their most serious problem was their lack of unity, for Mongolia itself had become split between two major tribal groups, the Oirats in the west and the Khalkhas in the east, and these became the rivals for the remains of the old empire. Nevertheless Mongol raids continued into China, and in the mid-fifteenth century the Oirats succeeded in capturing the Ming Emperor. However, they lacked the leadership to take up any kind of campaign of conquest and settled for ransom.

In the seventeenth century the new Manchu Dynasty came to an accommodation with the Khalkha people in eastern Mongolia, who agreed to a loose Chinese rule in preference to accepting the supremacy of the Oirats. The western tribe had turned its attention to Central Asia, which they dominated for more than a hundred years until they were finally defeated by a Manchu army in 1758. This led to the Mongol nation undergoing an even greater division, for the rise of the Manchus coincided with the expansion of the Russian empire from out of the west. Those people in the north around Lake Baikal came under Russian control, while those south of the Gobi Desert were dominated by China. This situation continued right into the twentieth century. In 1924 Sukhe Bator led the Communist take-over of northern Mongolia and created, with Soviet agreement, the People's Republic of Mongolia; and following the creation of the People's Republic of China in 1949, an Inner Mongolian Autonomous Region was created out of the other half of the old nation.

Chinese control over Inner Mongolia remains as strong today as it was under the Manchus, and although there is a certain degree of tolerance for the observance of traditional Mongol rituals, there is at present no sign that the population will be allowed to unite with their brethren across the border. To the north-west, Mongolia, until recently a vassal state of the Soviet empire, is at present trying to find its feet now that it is free of Communist dogma. For the moment, the only sheet anchor that binds together the entire population is the ever-powerful figure of their once-great Genghis Khan. On the labels of vodka bottles, on coins, on carpets, at rock concerts and at political rallies – in almost every facet of contemporary Mongol life – the face of Genghis has become the most potent national symbol. It is a shibboleth for a people whose ancestors once ruled an empire that stretched from the Korean peninsula to the River Danube.

BIBLIOGRAPHY

Barfield, Thomas J., *The Perilous Frontier: Nomadic Empires and China*, Basil Blackwell Inc., Cambridge, Mass., and Oxford, 1989

Bryer, Anthony, 'Edward I and the Mongols', in *History Today* XIV/10, October 1964

Chambers, James, *The Devil's Horsemen: The Mongol Invasion of Europe*, Weidenfeld & Nicolson, London, 1979, and Cassell, London, 1988

Cleaves, Francis Woodman, *The Secret History of the Mongols*, Vols. 1 & 2, Harvard University Press, Cambridge, Mass., 1982

Cross, F. L. and Livingstone, E. A., (eds), *The Oxford Dictionary of the Christian Church*, Oxford University Press, London, 1974

Edwards, E. H., *Horses: Their Role in the History of Man*, Willow Books, London, 1987

Fuller, J. F. C., *Decisive Battles of the Western World*, Eyre and Spottiswoode, London, 1954

Giles, J. A., *Matthew Paris's English History*, Henry G. Bohn, London, 1852

Griffiths, John C., *Afghanistan: Key to a Continent*, André Deutsch, London, 1981

Hartog, Leo de, *Genghis Khan, Conqueror of the World*, I. B. Tauris & Co. Ltd, London, 1989. Originally published as *Djenghis Khan's Werelds Grootste Veroveraar*, by Elsevier, Amsterdam, 1971

Jackson, Peter, (trans.) and Morgan, David, *The Mission of Friar William of Rubruck: His Journey to the Court of the Great Khan Mongke, 1253–1255*, Hakluyt Society, London, 1990

Jankovich, Miklos, *They Rode into Europe* (trans. Dent, A.), George G. Harrap, London, 1971

Bibliography

Juvaini, Ala-ad-Din Ata Malik, *The History of the World Conqueror* (trans. Boyle, John Andrew), Manchester University Press, Manchester, 1958

Lamb, Harold, *Genghis Khan: The Emperor of All Men*, Robert McBride, New York, 1928

Liddell Hart, B. H., *Great Captains Unveiled*, Cedric Chivers Ltd, Bath, 1971

McNiell, William H., *Plagues and People*, Doubleday and Anchor, New York, 1977

Martin, H. Desmond, *The Rise of Chingis Khan and his Conquest of North China*, The Johns Hopkins Press, Baltimore, 1950

Matheson, Sylvia A., *Persia: An Archaeological Guide*, Faber & Faber, London, 1972

Mitchell, Robert and Forbes, Neville (trans.), *The Chronicle of Novgorod*, 1017–1471, Camden Society, London, 1914

Morgan, David, *The Mongols*, Basil Blackwell, Oxford, 1986

Ratchewiltz, I. de, *Papal Envoys to the Great Khans*, Faber & Faber, London, 1971

Ratchnevsky, Paul, *Genghis Khan, His Life and Legacy* (trans. Haining, Thomas Nivison), Basil Blackwell Inc., Cambridge, Mass., and Oxford, 1991. Originally published as *Cinggis-Khan: Sein Leben und Wirken*, Franz Steiner Verlag, GMBH, 1983

Rossabi, Morris, *Khubilai Khan, His Life and Times*, University of California Press, Berkeley, 1988

Saunders, J. J., *The History of the Mongol Conquests*, Routledge & Kegan Paul Ltd, London, 1971

Severin, Tim, *In Search of Genghis Khan*, Hutchinson, London, 1991

Shatzman Steinhardt, Nancy, *Chinese Imperial City Planning*, University of Hawaii Press, Honolulu, 1990

Sheppard, Capt. E. W., 'Military Methods of the Mongols', *The Army Quarterly*, Vol. 18, 1929, pp. 305–15

Spuler, Bernhard, *History of the Mongols Based on Eastern and Western Accounts of the Thirteenth and Fourteenth Century* (trans. H. and S. Drummond), Routledge & Kegan Paul Ltd, London, 1972

Wilber, Donald N., *The Architecture of Islamic Iran*, Princeton University Press, New Jersey, 1955

Young, John M. L., *By Foot to China: Missions of the Church of the East, to 1400*, Young, Japan, 1984

Bibliography

Yule, Henry (trans.), *The Book of Ser Marco Polo, the Venetian, Concerning the Kingdoms and Marvels of the East by Henri Cordier*, John Murray, London, 1903

INDEX

213

Index

Index